IOWA

The Middle Land

OTHER BOOKS BY DOROTHY SCHWIEDER

Patterns and Perspectives in Iowa History (editor)

*Black Diamonds: Life and Work in Iowa's Coal Mining Communities,
1895-1925*

A Peculiar People: Iowa's Old Order Amish
(with Elmer Schwieder)

Buxton: Work and Racial Equality in a Coal Mining Community
(with Joseph Hraba and Elmer Schwieder)

Iowa Past to Present: The People and the Prairie
(with Thomas Morain and Lynn Nielsen)

75 Years of Service: Cooperative Extension in Iowa

IOWA

The Middle Land

DOROTHY SCHWIEDER

Iowa State University Press / Ames

Dorothy Schwieder is professor of history at Iowa State University. A native of South Dakota, she received her Ph.D. from the University of Iowa and has served several terms as trustee of the State Historical Society of Iowa. In 1993 she received the Lifetime Achievement Award from the Iowa Humanities Board. Author of six books, Schwieder is interested in Iowa history, midwestern women, and communitarian societies, particularly the Old Order Amish. She is currently researching her grandparents' and parents' experiences in South Dakota.

© 1996 Iowa State University Press, Ames, Iowa 50014

Authorization to photocopy items for internal or personal use, or the internal or personal use of specific clients, is granted by Iowa State University Press, provided that the base fee of $.10 per copy is paid directly to the Copyright Clearance Center, 27 Congress Street, Salem, MA 01970. For those organizations that have been granted a photocopy license by CCC, a separate system of payments has been arranged. The fee code for users of the Transactional Reporting Service is 0-8138-2307-2/96 (hardcover); 0-8138-2306-4/96 (paperback) $.10.

∞ Printed on acid-free paper in the United States of America

First edition, 1996

Library of Congress Cataloging-in-Publication Data

Schwieder, Dorothy
   Iowa : the middle land / Dorothy Schwieder.—1st ed.
     p.   cm.
   Includes bibliographical references and index.
   ISBN 0-8138-2307-2 (acid-free paper).—ISBN 0-8138-2306-4 (pbk. : acid-free paper)
   1. Iowa—History. I. Title.
   F621.S38   1996
   977.7—dc20   95-45200

To my granddaughters, Mary Ann and Elizabeth Ann Risius

May they never forget their Iowa roots

CONTENTS

PREFACE

In 1996 Iowans celebrate 150 years of statehood. This book tells the story of the settlement and development of the twenty-ninth state admitted to the Union on December 29, 1846. The state's sesquicentennial seems an appropriate time to examine once again the major events and developments of the past 150 years, as well as to recognize the accomplishments of both ordinary and not so ordinary Iowans.

Many labels and descriptions have been applied to Iowa throughout its 150 years of statehood—terms such as "land where the tall corn grows," "land between two rivers," and "beautiful land" are encountered frequently. At the same time, some people have described Iowa as dull and provincial, whereas others perceive it as "a perfect gem" of a place.

The late Laurence Lafore, professor of history at the University of Iowa, described his view of Iowa in *Harpers Magazine* in 1971. Although he discussed many traits of Iowans themselves, his succinct description of the land best captures the essence of the state: "It is the country—and its accessibility—that most beguiles the new arrival from the [East]. The land is very beautiful, and the special quality of its beauty is coherence and order." Lafore explained that Iowa "has its own unmistakable aspect, whose most conspicuous trait is geometry. The roads run sternly to compass points, as they do throughout the Midwest." In his description of the land, Lafore captured the sense of stability, beauty, and by implication, the air of industry that pervades the state.[1]

As historian Joseph Wall observed in his bicentennial history, in Iowa the land dominates. It does so in a particularly tidy fashion. Anyone driving through the Iowa countryside in late July will see the sense of "coherence and order" displayed by tasseling rows of tall corn and low, bushy clumps of soybeans. The countryside imposes a sense of order through the regular placement of township roads, most clearly viewed from the air. Iowa farmsteads, although declining in number, add to the sense of order, as most farms have neat, landscaped yards, often with rows of trees placed around the farms' perimeters. Recently a relative visiting from Denver announced almost incredulously on a drive through the countryside, "Why, the grass goes right up to the barn door!"

The size and shape of the state also contribute to the sense of coherence and order. Iowa is—with the exception of some irregularities along the western and eastern borders—more squarely shaped than any other midwestern state. Where else can one describe the location of a county by stating it is five tiers up from the bottom or five tiers down from the top? When compared to midwestern states to the east such as Ohio, Indiana, or Illinois, or states to the west such as the Dakotas, Iowa has less diversity in its terrain and climatic features. The state, therefore, has greater uniformity in land appearance and resources than other midwestern states, thus allowing agriculture to be a dominant industry everywhere.

This commonality through the years of agricultural interests (whether or not one lives on a farm) has produced a sense of like-mindedness among Iowans. This is demonstrated by the fact that people here describe themselves as Iowans. As Professor Lafore has written: "Habits of speech are indicative of a reality: people rarely refer to themselves as Pennsylvanians; New Yorkers are the residents of a city; and there is no word by which a citizen of Massachusetts or Connecticut can call himself. But Iowans always speak of themselves as Iowans."[2]

Given the state's location, its time of initial settlement and its general social and demographic characteristics, another apt description might be "middle land." Perhaps this description is best supported by Iowa's geographical location, as the state is tucked almost midpoint between the east and west coasts. If one narrows the perspective and examines only the Midwest, Iowa is situated close to the middle of that region.

The physical characteristics of the state also support the term "middle land." As discussed in Chapter 3, Iowa served as a transitional or middle zone between woodland regions to the east and the Great Plains to the west. When settlers from the northeastern United States arrived here, they discovered a region with limited trees but millions of acres of tall grass or prairie. The new environment required some adjustment and, in turn, helped those moving on prepare for the Great Plains, an area almost totally devoid of trees.

Iowa's first inhabitants, some seventeen different American-Indian tribes, can also be viewed in the context of the middle land. Whereas tribes in the northeast possessed a woodland culture, Native Americans living in the central part of North America in the seventeenth and eighteenth centuries belonged to the prairie-plains tradition, whereby they combined the practices of hunting and farming. The Sauk and Meskwaki, two tribes closely associated with Iowa, survived by hunting both large and small animals as well as by raising corn, beans, and other vegetables. Following Iowa's initial Euro-American settlement in the nineteenth century, communities and industries quickly developed. Even Iowa's nineteenth-century towns bore the stamp of the middle land in terms of physical layout. Some communities in southern and eastern Iowa (and a few in northern Iowa) were organized with squares located in the center of town and local businesses scattered around the squares' perimeters. As railroads reached central Iowa and continued building on to the Missouri River, the road companies platted towns, often with a single thoroughfare serving as main street. Developers built the depot, and typically a hotel, elevator, and lumberyard, near the tracks, while businesses lined both sides of the main street that ran perpendicular to the tracks. The so-called railroad town would be even more evident in the plains state.

By the late twentieth century, although urban life was very much a part of Iowa, in a regional context Iowa still remained a land in the middle. To the east, states such as Ohio and Indiana had become more industrial; to the west, states like North and South Dakota had remained more agricultural. Certainly industries had developed in Iowa, but these would be smaller and less numerous than in most states to the east. Iowa would, therefore, demonstrate a greater balance between industry and agriculture than most other midwestern states.

The middle-land context also tells us much about the people who have called Iowa home. Certainly there is a sense of moderation in the way people have lived. Iowa has never been known as a state of excess: People here traditionally have not known great wealth, nor have they known great poverty. Iowans place considerable value on family and family activities; they are proud of their communities, both large and small. There is a sense of rootedness in the state that implies stability, permanence, and continuity; there is also a sense of centeredness that connotes balance in both perspective and behavior. At the same time, Iowans are not known for showiness, glitz, or hype. In a state where people tend to be moderate to conservative in their political views, accepting of the status quo, and not given to wide swings of emotions or erratic behavior, it is perhaps no accident that in recent times Iowa has had two of the longest-serving governors in the nation: Robert D. Ray and Terry E. Branstad.

At the same time, it should be noted that Iowa does contain diversity in its geography, economic base, and social structure. River towns along the Mississippi not only have a distinct architecture, but historically have had a separate economic rhythm from the rest of the state. Along the Missouri River, Sioux City seems more western than Midwest, with its strong economic orientation to South Dakota and Nebraska. Northeastern Iowa, known as "Little Switzerland" is in sharp contrast to much of central Iowa, with its flatter topography; and politically, Iowa has long since stopped being the preserve of one political party. Even in a cultural sense, Iowa has variety. Although the state has only a small number of racial minorities, within the wider population cultural differences abound among those who trace their ancestry back to a multitude of European countries. And there is the matter of speech: Traveling into southern Iowa (in the first tier up from the bottom!), one hears speech patterns that seem more akin to Missouri than to Iowa.

In order to best treat different aspects of Iowa's development, this book is divided into three parts. Part I deals with Iowa's early years and begins by examining the history of Native Americans, including the eventual conflict between the tribes and white settlers. Other chapters cover the initial exploration of the region and the creation of the institutions that would play crucial roles throughout the state's history. Also included is the story of pioneering and a description of Iowa's early white settlers, as well as a treatment of early economic development, particularly the impact of the railroads. Part I includes a chapter on the Civil War, a shattering experience for Iowans, even though the state experienced no military battles. Although some areas of northwestern Iowa were still unsettled when the Civil War began, in effect, that event brought the settlement period to an end. Part I ends with a chapter on the experiences of nineteenth-century immigrants and African Americans.

Part II deals with the middle years of the state's development, 1870–1930, and presents the material in topical fashion. Admittedly, there is no perfect way to organize the many social, economic, and political issues needing to be covered in the period. The initial economic and political foundations had been constructed earlier, and after 1870 the state continued to expand in every way: Major industries developed; town and city life became more organized and more culturally diverse; urban centers became more visible; and agricultural interests quickly dominated the state, both economically and politically. The period from 1870 to 1930, moreover, brought confrontation over the important social and political issues of Prohibition and women's suffrage. Although there was great change in the middle period, Iowa remained a state of small towns, and small-town values seemed not only to permeate the state, but also to dominate the image projected to the nation.

Part III begins with the Great Depression and covers the history of the state until the most recent years. Part III reflects the fact that every research project rests on the sources available. Because little scholarly work has been done on topics in Iowa history since the 1930s, chapters 15, 16, and 17 are, of necessity, less developed than earlier ones. During the years from 1940 to the present, World War II marked a period of terrible sacrifice for Iowa families but, at the same time, served as a watershed in Iowa's history. Before the war the state could be described as predominately rural; soon after, urbanization accelerated. The 1950s would be a time of economic difficulty for farm families, but by the sixties and seventies good times had returned. The agricultural depression of the 1980s, along with hard times for Iowa's smaller communities serving as farm service centers, is still felt today. By the mid-1990s, however, Iowans find their basic social and cultural institutions intact and their pride in communities ongoing. At the same time, as the state's farmers have always done, Iowans everywhere seem to display a "congenital optimism" about the future.

Given limitations on length, it has not been possible to include all aspects of Iowa history; or, to put it another way, one book cannot be all things to all people. I have chosen to emphasize social and economic issues while giving limited attention to political events and personalities. I have done this because heretofore Iowa's social history has been badly neglected, whereas political history has been amply treated, particularly by Leland Sage in *A History of Iowa*. Moreover, given the difficulty of covering all major topics in one volume, I have opted not to include material on prehistory or on a technical discussion of early landforms. Rather,

I have chosen to develop important social and economic topics previously slighted.

In his introduction to *A History of Iowa,* Sage wrote that it was time for Iowa historians to move beyond "the mugbook and the children's book," and begin writing histories based on recent scholarship. Sage suggested a three-step process to "give Iowa a storehouse of information worthy of the stamp of History": First, several single-volume Iowa histories should be written; second, a multiauthor dictionary of Iowa history should be published; and third, the "crowning work" should ideally be a multivolume history.[3] I concur completely with Professor Sage's observations and hope that the present volume will contribute to the process.

This project has extended over many years, and in the process of completing it I have become indebted to many people and numerous institutions. First and foremost, I wish to thank Iowa State University for release time from several courses in 1987 and for a Faculty Improvement Leave in 1993-94. Moreover, I wish to thank three department chairs— Richard Lowitt, Andrejs Plakans, and George McJimsey—for their strong support for the project. My thanks also go to Audrey Burton, former manuscript typist in the history department, for typing a portion of the manuscript. To Jane Zaring, Iowa State University Press, a special thank-you for carefully guiding the manuscript through the editing process.

During the research phase of the project, I did work at the Parks Library at ISU (including Special Collections) and in the State Historical Society libraries in Des Moines and Iowa City. The staff in all these facilities provided prompt and courteous service, often calling my attention to material I might otherwise have overlooked. Other staff members at the State Historical Society, particularly Marvin Bergman, Christie Dailey, and former Division Director David Crosson, have given enthusiastic support for the project.

I am also indebted to good friends who share a professional interest in the field. Anthropologist Deborah Fink has listened endlessly to my "interpretations," always offering good, sound advice. Tom Morain, formerly of Living History Farms and now administrator of the State Historical Society of Iowa, through his many years of working as an Iowa historian, has given me innumerable insights into Iowa topics. And to the late Leland Sage, a thank-you for his fine political history of Iowa; it provided an excellent guide to the state's political history and helped me immeasurably.

There are two additional debts that go back some twenty-five years. I'm indebted to the late Walter Rundell, former chair of the ISU History Department, for seeing merit in the teaching of a course in Iowa history; and I am indebted to George C. Christensen, former ISU vice president for academic affairs, for giving me the opportunity to do so. Without that support, I would not have become involved in the field of Iowa history and this book would not have been written.

Finally, I wish to say thank-you to my family for their total support of and assistance for this project, including my husband, Elmer; my two children, David Schwieder and Diane Risius; my son-in-law, Lyle Risius; and my two granddaughters, Mary and Elizabeth Risius, to whom this book is dedicated.

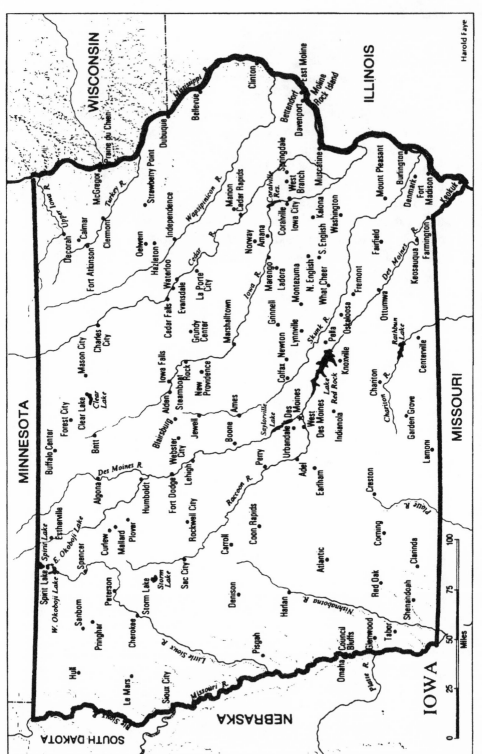

Iowa's major towns and rivers. From Joseph Wall, Iowa: A Bicentennial History, *reprinted with permission.*

Harold Faye

I

The Early Years

Early Populations, Explorations, and Government

1

Native Americans in Iowa

On July 4, 1838, an elderly Sauk chief addressed a group of white settlers in the small frontier community of Fort Madison. Chief Black Hawk, seventy-one years old and long venerated by his own people, told his audience: "It [the land] is now yours. Keep it as we did. It will produce good crops." During his lifetime Black Hawk had witnessed catastrophic change among his people. As a boy, the chief belonged to a tribe that, along with their close allies, the Meskwaki, had dominated the Upper Mississippi River Valley. White settlement began to dislodge the two tribes in the late 1820s, and by 1845, seven years after Black Hawk's death, both tribes had been removed from Iowa. For over two hundred years, however, the Sauk and Meskwaki had dominated a region including western Illinois and eastern Iowa, along with parts of Missouri and Wisconsin and Minnesota.

Other tribes also inhabited the region of Iowa during the seventeenth,

Chief Black Hawk, longtime leader of the Sauk tribe, shown in his later years. Photo courtesy of the State Historical Society of Iowa, Iowa City.

eighteenth, and early nineteenth centuries. At various times the Ioway, the Santee Sioux, the Winnebago, the Potawatomi, the Missouri, and the Oto all resided here. These tribes were part of the prairie-plains Indian culture located in the central portion of what would later be the continental United States. Within Iowa, tribes hunted, fished, gathered food, and pursued agriculture, thus combining both a sedentary and a migratory lifestyle. The federal government began their removal in 1830; the last tribe to relinquish its Iowa lands, the Santee Sioux, left in 1851. Native Americans experienced in the 1600s and 1700s what whites would discover in the 1800s: Iowa was indeed a bountiful and prosperous land.

The experience of Native Americans in Iowa approximated in several major ways their experience in the northeastern section of the present-day United States. Beginning in the early 1600s, tribes in New England felt pressure from a gradually expanding white population. For some, like the Pequot Indians, that contact would bring almost complete destruction. But for most tribes, colonization by Europeans would mean relocating farther west. The coming of Europeans also meant the beginning of the fur trade. In exchange for trapped furs, particularly beaver pelts, whites gave Indians manufactured goods, including knives, muskets, pots, blankets, and cloth. Over time the Indians became more reliant on the white man's goods than on their handmade items.

Pressure from two sources would result in the eventual relocation of northeastern tribes to areas in the central and western regions of the country. In the 1600s the Iroquois in the colony of New York worked to increase their trading activities with various European powers. As they did so, they expanded their influence over a larger territory, thus displacing other tribes and forcing them west. Later, in 1830, the federal government responded to growing demands for land from white settlers by passing the Indian Removal Act. The act determined that tribes east of the Mississippi would be moved west of the river. A few years later officials amended the act, whereby the Missouri River rather than the Mississippi served as the demarcation line between Indians and whites.

Tribes residing in Iowa would be affected by many of the same influences as those operating on eastern tribes. The Ioway would be forced to give up some land in the Iowa region as a result of pressure from the Sauk and Meskwaki. All tribes, including the Ioway, would eventually be affected by the government's removal policy, being resettled elsewhere. Tribes in the Iowa region would also deal extensively with Indian traders, thus incorporating more and more of the Europeans' manufactured goods into their lives.

The Ioway, the tribe for which our state is named, would reside here for several hundred years. Like other tribes in the prairie-plains region, the Ioway combined hunting and agriculture to support themselves. The Ioway were a part of the Siouan language family, which meant they had language similarities with the Dakota, Oto, Winnebago, and other tribes located in the central United States. According to Ioway tradition, the tribe had earlier lived in the Northeast, possibly around the Great Lakes. The same tradition relates that the Ioway and Winnebago were once united in one tribe. Sometime during the 1600s the Ioway moved westward, relocating near the Mississippi River, while the Winnebago remained behind. Some tribes called the Ioway the Pa-ho-ja, meaning "dusty noses." Apparently they had settled near streams with sandbars, and this accounted for the fine dust that blew onto their faces.[1]

The first contact between the Ioway and Europeans came in 1676 when a band of Ioway journeyed to Green Bay in search of metal kettles, beads, knives, and cloth. The next recorded contact, in 1685, took place when Frenchmen visited Ioway villages along the Upper Iowa River. Frenchman Nicolas Perrot had been commissioned to bring about peaceful relations between Indian tribes in that vicinity.[2] Throughout various European accounts of the Ioway, the name was spelled in countless ways, including Ayoes and Aiaouez.

The Ioway were regarded as good farmers and hunters who utilized all different parts of their Iowa environment, including the rivers, prairies, forests, and plains. For their dwellings the Ioways used material at hand, including saplings, reeds, bark, thatch grasses, and earth. One authority estimated that the size of settlements varied from only a few acres to approximately 100 acres. Corn was a major food, and agricultural experts believe it took one-half acre of land planted in corn to feed one person. In 1700 officials estimated the population of the Ioway at fifteen hundred, so collectively they needed 750 acres cultivated in corn to feed all members.[3]

One of the tribe's earliest locations in the Iowa region was along the Upper Iowa River in what is now Allamakee and Winneshiek counties. Because steep bluffs rise several hundred feet from both sides of the river, the Ioways probably located their villages a short distance back from the edge of the bluffs, thus allowing some camouflage for their settlements. Location along the bluffs also provided a good vantage point for the Ioway to observe the prairie below. The area contained the resources needed for a good life. The fertile floodplains allowed for cultivation of corn, beans, and other vegetables; the river provided fish, clams, and turtles. The nearby hills were covered with many different types of trees, which provided building materials for shelter. Wild fruits were also abundant in the area, including plums, blackberries, raspberries, wild cherries, and crab apples. Nearby woods contained both large and small fur-bearing animals which provided meat for the tribe and furs for trading. On the open prairie the Ioway hunted elk and prairie chickens. It is also possible that early Ioway members traveled to western Iowa and southern Minnesota to hunt bison, staying away for two or three months at a time to conduct the hunt and prepare the hides and meat.[4]

Traditionally in Native-American societies, women had distinct agricultural roles that included planting, cultivating, and harvesting food. The Ioway were no exception to that practice. When planting corn, women used a pointed stick to dig a hole; later they cultivated the individual plants with a hoe. After harvest women were responsible for placing food in the storage caches, which were holes dug in the ground, often in the shape of bowls two to five feet deep and two to seven feet wide. Women also accompanied the males on the hunt, being responsible for raising and lowering the tepees.

Seasonal mobility characterized the Ioway lifestyle. In summer the villages were probably deserted except for the oldest and youngest members; most tribal members typically left the village to hunt, fish, and collect rushes and other building materials. In the fall villagers reassembled, dividing their summer's collection and harvesting the corn. Some corn was dried and stored in the caches. At fire pits unearthed at village sites along the Upper Iowa River, archaeologists have discovered the remains of roasting ears probably left to cook many centuries ago. Several of the pits were located close together, indicating, perhaps, that women did this work communally.[5]

Native Americans had many ways to prepare corn, an excellent food, as it was filling, nutritious, and would keep for a long time. Corn could be parched or dried for storage; it could be cooked along with beans, a dish known as succotash. Sometimes Indian women added bear meat and honey as well as pounded-up chokecherries. Corn could be cooked in a kettle over a fire or, as the fire pits indicated, wrapped and cooked in the ground. Boiling was done in clay pottery vessels made by tribal women.

The Ioway demonstrated considerable geographic mobility, relocating in many parts of Iowa as well as nearby areas. For a time the tribe lived in southern Minnesota, close to Iowa's great lakes; later they relocated in western Iowa (near the mouth of the Platte River), and later still in south central Iowa near the Chariton River. By 1700 it is believed that the Ioway lived near Spirit Lake. In the early 1700s Frenchman Pierre Le Seur built Fort Vert at the mouth of the Blue Earth River, at which time he came in contact with the Ioway and recorded: "These Indians are industrious and accustomed to cultivating the ground, and it is hoped to obtain from them some food supplies." But before an arrangement could be made, the Ioway had moved again, this time to the Missouri-Big Sioux rivers area. Although the Ioway probably moved south for several reasons, the increased aggressiveness of the Dakota or Sioux who resided to the north might have influenced them. By the 1720s the Ioway had settled at the site of present-day Council Bluffs, and by 1764 they had moved to the area near the present-day Quad Cities.[6]

During the 1700s the Ioway enjoyed preeminence in the Iowa region. They possessed horses, which aided their mobility, their hunting, and probably their ability to defend themselves. By 1700 the Ioway had acquired European goods, including metal kettles and hatchets. There is evidence they traded with both the French and Spanish, and to maintain this trade, they trapped small fur-bearing animals in Iowa, Minnesota, and the Dakotas. As they continued to rely more and more heavily on European manufactured goods, they gradually ceased pursuing their own crafts, like flint making and pottery. Later they traded with the British.[7]

By the early 1800s the Ioway were located in southeastern Iowa, which placed them in close proximity to the Sauk and Meskwaki, located to the east along the Mississippi and Rock rivers. Although there is evidence that the Ioway sometimes cooperated with these two tribes, there is also evidence that conflict developed between them. The Sauk and Meskwaki, seeking more hunting ground in what is now eastern Iowa, gradually began taking aggressive action against the Ioway. In 1821 a major battle occurred, with the Sauk and Meskwaki decisively defeating the Ioway.

After a short sojourn in Missouri, the Ioway returned to the Iowa region, where they claimed land from the Des Moines River to the Missouri River, roughly the western third of the present state. In 1835, at a council meeting in Prairie du Chien, the Ioway, along with the Missouri, Omaha, and Oto tribes, ceded their land in western Iowa. For the Ioway this marked the end of their land ownership in Iowa. Seven years later the federal government removed them to northeastern Kansas, to the Great Nemaha Reservation. This was not a happy time for the tribe. In the process of preparing for removal, the tribal structure came apart with quarreling among tribal members and heavy drinking.[8]

While the Ioway were a highly visible tribe in Iowa and commanded much respect during the 1700s, the Sauk and Meskwaki proved to be the dominant tribes in the Upper Mississippi Valley from the mid-1700s to their removal from Iowa in 1845. The Sauk and Meskwaki belonged to the Algonquin family, whose tribes earlier had dominated the northeastern United States. A part of the woodland culture, the Algonquin tribes lived more sedentary lives than the prairie-plains Indians, relying heavily on the products of the forest and on river travel in birch-bark canoes.

Early-European records locate the Sauk and Meskwaki tribes in what is now Michigan. By the mid-1600s, however, the two tribes had responded to pressure by the Iroquois, who were expanding and struggling for control of the fur trade to the east. Forced out of Michigan by the Iroquois, the Sauk and Meskwaki moved into present-day Wisconsin. The Sauk settled near Lake Michigan at Green Bay, while the Meskwaki relocated farther inland near the great portage between the Fox and Wisconsin rivers. The Meskwaki soon discovered that their settlement in the portage area created conflicts with the French. Periodically Frenchmen traveled across the area on their way to the Wisconsin River and, in turn, the Mississippi. The Indians believed that the French could cross the portage only with their permission. After unsuccessful diplomatic efforts, war erupted in 1712 between the two groups, continuing until 1730. As a result of this struggle, the Meskwaki left the area, accompanied by the Sauk. Gradually both tribes moved southward into present-day western Illinois.

Throughout their settlement in Wisconsin, and possibly even in Michigan, the Sauk and Meskwaki lived fairly close together and shared some cooperative activities. Members of the two tribes intermarried, and each tribe came to the defense of the other in time of attack. While the two tribes were confederated, combining for purposes of both peace and war, they never merged into a single tribe. Both retained distinct, internal tribal organizations, complete with separate clans, chiefs, and other leaders.[9]

Located in Illinois by 1765, the Sauk built their communities along the Rock River, close to the confluence of the Rock and Mississippi rivers, and in what would later be eastern Iowa, while the Meskwaki built villages along the west bank of the Mississippi, north of the confluence of the two rivers. Saukenuk was the largest Sauk village, whereas Musquekenuk was the largest village of the Meskwaki. Within the large area dominated by the two tribes, they carried on their longtime practices of trapping small fur-bearing animals for trade, first with the British and later with American companies. At the same time, the two tribes pursued agriculture and hunting. Indian women planted corn, beans, squash, pumpkins, and probably other vegetables. One account stated that the tribes had "reached an unusual degree of agricultural prosperity, utilizing several hundred acres of land for their cornfields." In late spring tribal members traveled north to Minnesota to tap maple trees, using the syrup as their main condiment.[10]

According to William Hagan, the Sauk and the Meskwaki lived migratory lives, even though they remained in the same villages for many years. The permanent villages, where the Indians carried on their agricultural work, served as summer residences. Summer dwellings were called longhouses and varied in length from seventy-five to one hundred feet and from twenty to thirty feet in width. They divided the longhouses into compartments so that each longhouse accommodated several families. The winter dwellings, known as wickiups, were smaller and more quickly constructed. These dwellings were built much like the huts of the Ioway and provided the Indians with winter accommodations.[11]

The Sauk and the Meskwaki were each divided into twelve patrilineal clans, each clan represented by a totemic name such as elk, bear, or eagle. All of the clans provided representatives to the tribal councils. The clans, moreover, provided the tribes with a form of political organization, as two clans from each tribe had the right to nominate the civil chief and the war chief, the tribes' main leaders. In effect, the civil chief handled mainly internal matters, deciding when the tribes should leave on their winter hunts and when they should return in the spring. This individual also helped settle disputes between members. If the prevailing civil chief was well liked and considered capable, the mantle of leadership usually passed to one of his sons, thus making the position hereditary.[12]

By contrast, the position of war chief was usually not hereditary. The

war chief dealt with external matters, being responsible for providing protection for his people and leading them into battle. Black Hawk, believed
to have been a Sauk war chief, was chosen on the basis of bravery in battle and leadership qualities. Some war chiefs served only short periods of
time before they were replaced by other warriors who had shown even
greater bravery while fighting the enemy.[13]

Although there is limited historical material on Sauk and Meskwaki
leaders, Black Hawk was clearly a visible and respected chief. Born in a
Sauk village along the Rock River in 1767, Black Hawk would live much
of his life in Saukenuk. Donald Jackson, who edited Black Hawk's own
story, *Black Hawk: An Autobiography,* writes that the Indian was not a
"principal chief, but there are indications that he was a war chief during a
part of his lifetime." In a more recent assessment John Hallwas concludes
that Black Hawk, though perhaps not in the tradition of Tecumseh, was
nevertheless a highly able and respected leader who took his responsibilities seriously. Black Hawk had a strong personal attachment to Saukenuk,
believing the spirits of his ancestors inhabited the area. Thus, leaving the
area as he was forced to do in 1831 proved extremely painful.[14]

Even if Black Hawk's position within his tribe is not clearly established, there is little doubt about the warrior's reputation among whites.
As early as 1809 Black Hawk led an unsuccessful Indian attack against
Fort Madison, located at the present site of the city of Fort Madison. In his
later years Black Hawk would be viewed as a controversial figure and
would serve as the main symbol of Native American resistance to white
settlement. Keokuk, on the other hand, also a Sauk chief, apparently believed there was little the Indians could do to resist the whites' movement
onto Indian lands and advocated cooperating with the federal government.
After the removal to Iowa in 1831 and the Black Hawk War in 1832,
Keokuk became the main leader for the Sauk and the Meskwaki in Iowa.

Among the two tribes, work was gender specific. Indian women
planted and harvested crops, cooked food, cared for children, and made
domestic articles such as woven mats, pottery vessels, and articles of
clothing. Indian men hunted food, protected tribal members, and served in
positions of leadership. Europeans, confronted with the view of Indian females carrying heavy loads of wood and performing agricultural work, assumed they were little more than beasts of burden. At the same time, Europeans often concluded that the male activities of hunting, fishing, and

horseback riding were pursuits of pleasure. These views tended to rein-
force the European view that Indian women did the meaningful work
while Indian men were lazy and led lives of leisure. From the tribal members' perspective, however, females worked in a far safer environment,
close to the village and close to protection. Indian males, meanwhile, were
more vulnerable to attack or the possibility of injury, as they often traveled far from the main villages and had the responsibility of fending off
attackers. At the same time, Sauk and Meskwaki women typically ruled
the lodge. Women owned the blankets, robes, and cooking utensils that
they used in their domestic work. If an Indian woman decided to leave her
husband, she could take her possessions along.[15]

Along with their trapping and trading, the Meskwaki also mined lead
in the vicinity of present-day Dubuque. The location of their villages,
north of the Rock River and along the west side of the Mississippi, placed
them near the Driftless Area, a region rich in lead ore. It is not known how
long the Meskwaki pursued lead mining nor how they first developed the
process of melting the ore. It is possible that early contacts with the French
led to the mining activity. Historical records indicate the French were in
this vicinity in the early 1600s and that they noticed the outcropping of
lead deposits.[16]

Even though the Sauk and the Meskwaki were solidly entrenched in
the Upper Mississippi Valley in the first decade of the nineteenth century,
changes were under way in other parts of the nation that eventually led to
their removal. In 1803 President Thomas Jefferson purchased Louisiana
from France, thus adding an area of 827,987 square miles to the United
States. The new area lay between the Mississippi River and the Rocky
Mountains and stretched from the Canadian border to the Gulf of Mexico.
Jefferson regarded the acquisition as new area that would allow for the
continued expansion of white settlers into the west.

At the same time, President Jefferson gave orders to William Henry
Harrison, governor of the newly organized Indiana Territory (which provided supervision for the district that included the Iowa region), to conduct treaties with Native Americans in the territory in anticipation of eventual white settlement. Although the federal government had determined in
1791 that land would be acquired from Indians through the treaty-making
process, conditions surrounding the Treaty of 1804 were highly suspect.
Governor Harrison did not negotiate with duly elected representatives

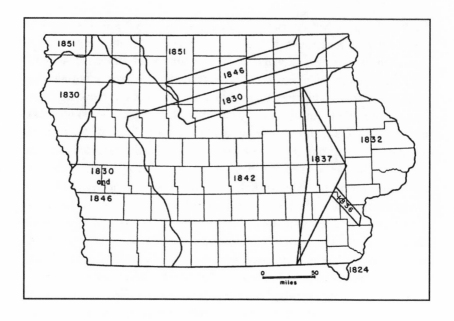

Indian cessions by treaties of 1824, 1830, 1832, 1836,
1837, 1842, 1846, and 1851. From Leland Sage,
A History of Iowa.

from the Sauk and Meskwaki tribes at a specifically convened council meeting. Rather, he conducted the treaty when he happened to be in St. Louis on unrelated business. Arriving there, Harrison heard that five chiefs from the Sauk and Meskwaki tribes were also in town. He used the occasion to arrange for a meeting and then induced the Indians to sign a treaty that sold away 51 million acres of land. Whatever the original intent of the federal government in regard to treaty making, the meeting in St. Louis was a sham. In effect, the five Indians, without any authorization from their tribes, had signed away most of their homeland (much of it in present-day Illinois). In return Harrison agreed on behalf of the federal government to pay the Indians two thousand dollars' worth of gifts and annuities; four hundred dollars went to the Meskwaki and six hundred dollars to the Sauk.[17]

The Treaty of 1804 started a long procession of events that culminated in the Black Hawk War. From 1804 on Black Hawk insisted that the treaty was fraudulent and therefore should not be enforced. Because of the treaty negotiations and other events, Black Hawk believed that the American government was untrustworthy. In turn Black Hawk shifted his allegiance to the British. He fought on the side of the British in the War of 1812 and would continually indicate his loyalty to that government. Although there were many reasons for dissension between Black Hawk and the American government, it seems likely that Black Hawk's mistrust of Americans began with the Treaty of 1804, eventually taking the form of attacks against American military forts.

One location that would soon draw Black Hawk's ire was Fort Madison. Constructed in 1809, Fort Madison would have little to recommend it as a successful military outpost. In 1808, when commanding officer First Lieutenant Alpha Kingsley arrived at the selected site, the mouth of the Des Moines River, he determined that it was a poor location and moved farther north. He then selected a site where the present city of Fort Madison is located. Soldiers built the fort, surrounding it with a high stockade, and in typical military fashion located the trading post outside the stockade. Within a short time Kingsley and his men realized that the site had several disadvantages. Indians could move undetected through a ravine located alongside the fort and then position themselves beyond a ridge that lay behind the fort.[18]

Black Hawk and his followers indicated their dissatisfaction with the fort almost from the beginning. On April 10, 1809, Black Hawk and another chief, Pas-he-pa-ho, led a party of Indians to the fort. After concluding business at the trading post, Black Hawk announced that the Indians wished to come inside the fort to dance for the soldiers. Kingsley had previously been alerted that the Indians might be planning an attack, so he turned down their invitation. The Indians started to push against the gate, but once it was opened, they faced a loaded cannon surrounded with soldiers, all with their flintlock muskets loaded and primed. The Indians decided that was not the time to demand entry. They would return again and again, however, to harass the soldiers, and on at least one occasion fatally shot several of them.[19]

By 1813 Fort Madison had undergone several administrative changes. The second commanding officer, a Lieutenant Hamilton, decided the fort was indefensible and that it was not fulfilling its original mission. He ordered his men to begin digging a trench (at night, so that their action would not be detected by nearby Indians) to the river; once the trench was completed, the soldiers crawled to the river and then floated silently down-stream. The last man set fire to the buildings. When the Indians realized what had happened, it was too late to stop the soldiers or to salvage anything from the fort.[20]

Fort Madison would be only the first of many forts in the region. In the midteens the government constructed Fort Armstrong on Rock Island; soon after soldiers built Fort Crawford at Prairie du Chien. In 1823 the government built Fort Snelling at the present site of St. Paul. In Iowa alone, the federal government constructed twenty-two forts. Many, such as Fort Atkinson, would be operational for only a few years, but all would serve notice on the local tribes that the American government controlled the Upper Mississippi Valley and would expect the tribes to trade with American rather than with British companies.

By 1829 the federal government decided to remove the Sauk and the Meskwaki from their land in western Illinois, as white settlers were moving into nearby areas. At this point the Treaty of 1804 would again prove to be controversial. In Article 7 of the document, General Harrison agreed to allow the tribes to remain on treaty land until the lands were sold to private individuals. In 1829 some white settlement had taken place in western Illinois, but not all the treaty land was in private hands. Following the military's order to leave Illinois, Keokuk quickly agreed and led his followers across the river. But Black Hawk refused, insisting that his band be allowed to stay in their villages until all land had been sold. Black Hawk continued to stall, but in 1831 soldiers informed him and his followers that they must leave Saukenuk voluntarily or be forcibly removed to the Iowa side.[21]

Once in Iowa, Black Hawk and his people faced great hardship. They suffered from hunger while remembering the cornfields and other food left at Saukenuk. Brooding through the winter of 1831–32, Black Hawk apparently decided that he would lead his faithful band back to their old home. The following spring, encouraged by apparently false—and unrealistic—reports that both Winnebago Indians and the British in Canada would assist him, the sixty-five-year-old leader led some four hundred Sauk braves, with their wives and children, back to Saukenuk. Black Hawk's plans then called for the group to travel north along the Rock River, first to join with the Winnebago and later with the British. Soon after the Indians arrived in Illinois, however, General Henry Atkinson, commander of troops in the Western District, called out the militia to pursue Black Hawk. Meanwhile, Black Hawk slowly came to the realization that no help was coming from the north. What followed in the next three months is what historians have called the Black Hawk War. As Joseph Wall has written: "It was not a war; it was a pathetic final act of defiance against reality."[22]

The three-month campaign would see the military pursue the small Indian band northward through Illinois and finally into Wisconsin Territory. At several points along the way, soldiers caught up with the Indians, but always they managed to slip away. Finally at the point where the Bad Axe River flows into the Mississippi, the military managed to set a successful snare.

Some Indians drowned while trying to swim the Mississippi River, and some who did make it across were slain by the Sioux waiting on the west bank. Within a short time the military had rounded up the survivors, taking some Indians, including Black Hawk and two of his sons, into custody. Soldiers soon transported Black Hawk to a St. Louis prison.

The following April, Black Hawk, along with several other Indians, was taken back East. Their itinerary included a visit with President Andrew Jackson and a tour of several major American cities. Both visits were directed toward the same end: to impress upon the Indians that it was futile to oppose the all-powerful federal government. Black Hawk was then imprisoned for a time and lived out the remainder of his days in southeastern Iowa. He died in October 1838.[23]

The Black Hawk War would have major repercussions for many future generations of both Indians and whites. As punishment for carrying out an uprising against the United States government, the Sauk and the Meskwaki were instructed to cede to the government a part of their Iowa land. This tract would be known as the Black Hawk Purchase and would extend about 195 miles from the Missouri border to the southern boundary of the Neutral Ground (about the middle of both Fayette and Clayton counties); it would extend approximately fifty miles west from the Mississippi River. In return the federal government promised the Indians twenty thousand dollars annually for thirty years. The Indians agreed to move west out of the Black Hawk Purchase by June 1, 1833. A small strip of land known as the Keokuk Reserve was retained in the area for Chief Keokuk.[24]

The movement of the Sauk and the Meskwaki out of the Black Hawk Purchase was only the beginning of several moves that would eventually culminate in the tribes' complete removal from Iowa. By the 1830s the two tribes were deeply in debt to Indian traders and were being pressured to sell more land. In 1836 Chief Keokuk and his followers ceded the Keokuk Reserve. A year later the chiefs met again with government officials. This time the Indians sold a million and a quarter acres. By 1838 the Sauk and the Meskwaki, once firmly in control of a vast part of the Upper Mississippi Valley, found themselves pushed into an area less than one-fifth the size of their original holdings.[25]

The steady march of whites into the nation's midsection would not end in eastern Iowa. Accordingly, the Indians would be approached again, only three years later, to sell away all their remaining land. Meeting at an Indian agency in southeastern Iowa in 1841, territorial governor John Chambers led the three-man delegation, along with interpreters. James Grimes, a twenty-four-year-old lawyer from Burlington, acted as secretary. A large delegation described as "chiefs, braves, warriors, and headmen" represented the Sauk and Meskwaki.

Governor Chambers quickly presented the government's offer: In exchange for their remaining land, the Indians would receive $1 million in annuities and the government would assume the tribes' debts to traders of $350,000. The Indians would then be removed to the headwaters of the Des Moines River, an area west of the Blue Earth River. To insure their safety from Sioux attacks, the government proposed to build three military forts.[26]

The Indian response was deliberate and firm: They must decline the offer. Chief Keokuk spoke first: "It is impossible for us to accept your proposals. We can't subsist in the country where you wish us to go. It is impossible for us to live there." Wapello, also a Sauk chief, eloquently stated the reasons why the Indians could not accept the offer:

We were once a powerful, but now a small nation. ... I remember when Wiskonsin [sic] was ours. ... We sold it to you. Rock River and Rock Island was once ours. We sold them to you. Dubuque was once ours. We sold that to you. ... Rock River was the only place where we lived happily and we sold that to you. This is all the country we have left, and we are so few now, we cannot conquer other countries. You now see me and all my nation. Have pity on us. We are but few and are fast melting away.[27]

Undoubtedly angered by the chiefs' refusal, Governor Chambers ended the deliberations with a final admonishment. He reminded the Indians they had large trading debts and the traders would not be patient. He predicted that the traders would extend no more credit, and within a year the chiefs would realize they must sell their remaining land.[28]

Governor Chambers's reference to trading debts touched on another problem faced by the Sauk and the Meskwaki as well as by other tribes in the region. When the federal government began paying annuities to tribes for purchase of their land, the government paid the annuities in goods. But by 1820 the government had begun paying annuities in cash. The result was an infiltration into Indian territories of trading firms who offered the Indians a wide assortment of both essential and nonessential goods. Robert Trennert believes that the traders often charged the Indians exorbitant prices, with the margin of profit sometimes 900 percent. Moreover, he notes, the Indians appeared to buy anything.[29]

As the Indians continued to buy from traders, they soon discovered their annuities would not cover all their purchases. The traders then advanced the tribes credit against their next year's annuities. By the time the cash annuities arrived for the following year, the entire amount might already be owed to the trading companies. Trennert writes that by 1840 the annuity money went directly from the hands of the Indian agents to the hands of the trading firms' officials, bypassing the Indians altogether. Trennert further observes that, since the government got land and the traders got money, only the Indians, left with poverty, fared badly.[30]

The trader-Indian relationship also affected land sales. As Indian debts mounted, and as the amount of credit extended to Indians increased correspondingly, the traders joined the list of individuals urging the Indians to sell more land. By 1841 the House of Ewing was not only pressuring the Sauk and the Meskwaki to pay their debts but was also pressuring the federal government to conclude yet another treaty with the two tribes.[31]

Given the pressure exerted by traders, and the fact that the Sauk and Meskwaki's only salable possession was land, it is not surprising that Governor Chambers's prophecy came true. One year later a similar council reconvened at the Indian Agency, this time at the request of the Indians. In 1842, however, the government took a harder line: They would pay $1 million for the land but would not cover the Indians' debts due the traders. After some negotiations the government relented somewhat and assumed $250,000 out of the $350,000 debt. Further, the treaty stipulated that the Indians could remain in the area for three years; they would then be moved south in 1845 to the Osage River Reservation in east central Kansas. The government, meanwhile, would construct Fort Des Moines to aid in the removal process.[32]

Government officials arranged for both Sauk and Meskwaki members to leave Fort Des Moines on October 11, 1845. They soon discovered, however, that while the Sauk—organized by Chief Keokuk—headed toward the Kansas reservation, the Meskwaki were heading in the opposite direction. The Meskwaki had stated earlier that they did not want to leave Iowa. Soldiers pursued the Meskwaki, approximately two hundred in number, and brought them back to Fort Des Moines. Time after time for the next eight months, the military repeatedly tracked down Meskwaki only to have them quickly disappear. In the summer of 1846 Indian agent John Beach reported that of the total 1,271 Meskwaki, only 250 were at the Osage River Reservation.[33]

The Meskwaki who remained in Iowa continued to provide for themselves much as they had before 1843; they also attempted to separate themselves from the Sauk. Beginning in 1804, the federal government had regarded the two tribes as one and the same, using the term, "united Sac and Fox tribe" in the treaty of that year. In 1846 Chief Poweshiek and fifteen other Meskwaki went to Fort Leavenworth to confer with military authorities, explaining that they wished to remain in Iowa and desired recognition as a separate tribe; they hoped this recognition would lead to separate annuities. They further requested that the annuities be paid at a site other than the Osage River Reservation. For some years the Meskwaki had been unhappy with what they viewed as domination by the larger Sauk tribe.[34]

In July 1856 the Iowa legislature responded to one of the Meskwaki's requests by authorizing them to purchase land in the state. State officials also requested that the federal government pay the Meskwaki annuity in Iowa, a request that was not granted for ten years. The Meskwaki did, however, immediately buy land in Tama County. Ultimately they purchased over 3,000 acres, and the land purchases led to the creation of the Meskwaki Settlement where tribal members still reside today.

While the Meskwaki would eventually find a way to remain in Iowa, that would not be the case with another tribe, the Santee Sioux. These Native Americans had earlier inhabited land in northwestern and north central Iowa. Although the Santee Sioux had been present in the Iowa region since at least the early 1600s, their situation was quite different from the Ioway or the Sauk and the Meskwaki. For the latter three tribes, the Iowa region served as home for many years. The Santee, on the other hand, were actually the southern-fringe settlement of a tribe located in southern Minnesota. In 1851 the Sioux ceded their land to the federal government and were relocated in the Dakotas. Like the Meskwaki, some Sioux would later come back to their former homeland, hunting and fishing to sustain themselves. On one foray a small band of Sioux, led by Inkpaduta, attacked settlers in the Iowa great-lakes region, killing thirty-two. The white families, including the Rowland Gardners and Henry Luces, and Dr. Isaac H. Heriott, had moved into an area knowing they could expect no protection from the United States military. In fact, Fort Dodge, the fort nearest the lakes area, had been abandoned in 1853.[35]

Inkpaduta's motivation for the attacks (and the capture of four white women) has long been a subject of debate. Some scholars point out that several years earlier a white man, Henry Lott, had killed a Sioux chief, Sidominadota, and his family; Inkpaduta might have been seeking revenge for these murders. Perhaps more convincing is that the winter of 1856-57 was exceedingly harsh and created suffering among both Indians and whites. The winter's snowfall was heavy, and temperatures were exceptionally low for much of the season. The Indians found it difficult to hunt and trap and frequently begged food from white settlers. By spring the harsh conditions might simply have made life too difficult for Inkpaduta and his small band. In early March they began attacking whites in the great-lakes vicinity. Among the captives was the fourteen-year-old daughter of Rowland and Mary Gardner. Abigail Gardner would survive the hostage ordeal and, along with another woman, be ransomed back from her captors. The perpetrator of the attack, Inkpaduta, was never captured. It is believed he escaped into Minnesota and from there moved into the Dakotas. Today the reconstructed Gardner cabin serves as a small museum, marking the area where members of the Gardner family died.[36]

Although the Ioway, Sauk, and Meskwaki were the most visible and influential Native Americans in Iowa, several other tribes resided here only for a short time. In 1832 the Winnebago signed a treaty with the federal government giving up their lands in Wisconsin and Illinois. The treaty called for the tribe to be relocated in the Neutral Ground, a strip of land located in northeastern Iowa and formerly owned by the Santee Sioux, and by the Sauk and Meskwaki. The Winnebago's actual stay in Iowa would be short, as they were moved to the Neutral Ground in 1840 and moved again eight years later to a reservation in eastern Nebraska. To provide protection and supervision for the Winnebago while in Iowa, the federal government constructed Fort Atkinson in extreme northeastern Iowa.

The Potawatomi would also reside in Iowa for a short time. In 1833 the federal government signed a treaty with this tribe, taking over its lands in Illinois and moving them to western Iowa. The Iowa area contained 5 million acres located in the southwestern portion of the present state. The treaty stipulated that the government would build mills for the Indians to operate and would send agents to "train them in the pursuits of settled agriculture." But before these plans could be implemented, the government once again considered resettlement for the tribe. Ten years after the Potawatomi had arrived in western Iowa, their Indian agent reported: "The tide of emigration has rolled onwards to the far West, until the whites are now crowded closely on the southern side of these lands." With this refrain the results were predictable: The Indians would be removed one more time.[37]

By 1851 all lands in Iowa had passed from the hands of Native Americans to those of the federal government. Reminders of the Indians' presence here would be limited mostly to the naming of some Iowa counties after Indian tribes and chiefs. The exception would be the presence of the Meskwaki Indian Settlement in Tama County. Life would be difficult for many Meskwaki, with poverty and hardship a way of life. Today travelers can visit the settlement in August when the tribe celebrates its heritage during an annual powwow. In 1985 tribal members constructed a gambling casino there.

Because of the pressure of white settlement and the passage of the Indian Removal Act in 1830, Iowa contains no Indian reservations, as do neighboring states to the north and to the west. In effect, Indians in Iowa were relocated southward or westward during the mid-1800s. The name Iowa would remain, but little else to give visible evidence of the long, long habitation of Native Americans in the middle land.

2

Exploration, Early Settlement, and Political Development

I n June 1673 a small party of French explorers slipped quietly out of the mouth of the Wisconsin River onto the broad expanse known as the Mississippi. The Frenchmen were the first Europeans to gaze upon a vast new land that lay far beyond English settlement on the eastern seacoast or French settlement in New France. The excursion party, headed by Louis Jolliet and accompanied by Jesuit priest Jacques Marquette, had orders to explore the Mississippi River to its end. On June 25 Jolliet and Marquette would come ashore on the west bank of the Mississippi, the first Europeans to set foot on Iowa soil. Following this expedition, the region later known as Iowa would attract increasing attention

---

Sketch of Fort Madison showing irregular shape of stockade. Note the buildings outside the fort, which housed the fur-trading operation and personnel. Photo courtesy of the State Historical Society of Iowa, Iowa City.

from other Europeans. Both France and Spain controlled the Upper Mississippi Valley for a time, though French settlement predominated. Other explorers like La Salle would visit the area, but it would not be until 1803—through the purchase of Louisiana—that it would become part of the United States. The Jolliet and Marquette expedition marked the first step in major explorations and subsequent settlement of the Iowa country.

At the time of the 1673 expedition, the future state of Iowa was unclaimed by any European power. English, French, and Spanish settlements lay far to the north, east, and south of the Upper Mississippi Valley, and all powers had imperial designs. Jolliet and Marquette's expedition, generally acknowledged to be searching for the mouth of the Mississippi River and seeking ways to increase the fur trade, also reflected French expansionary ambitions. By 1673 French settlements along the St. Lawrence River in New France were bordered by English outposts to the north and permanent colonies to the south. The French had relied primarily on the fur trade as the basis for their New France settlements; this policy had shortchanged industries, such as agriculture, that would have attracted more settlers. One option for French officials eager to enlarge their domain was to expand to the west and south of the Great Lakes, thus bracketing the English settlements along the Atlantic seaboard.

In 1673 Governor Louis Frontenac of New France ordered an expedition to explore the Mississippi River and to locate its mouth. Frontenac selected Louis Jolliet, known locally as a woodsman and mapmaker, to head the expedition. A Catholic priest, Father Marquette, was to accompany Jolliet, a practice typically followed by the French government in its efforts to convert the natives to Catholicism.

On June 25, after eight days on the river, the explorers observed footsteps in the sand along the west bank. Jolliet and Marquette went ashore and some six miles inland encountered a group of Native Americans known as Peorias. The Indians were probably part of the Illini tribe centered in present-day Illinois who were temporarily hunting on the Iowa side of the river. The Indians greeted the Frenchmen in friendly fashion, sharing food and information about the area to the south. Father Marquette's account, the only surviving record of the encounter, described a feast given by the Peorias that included "Indian corn boiled in water and seasoned with fat; a platter of fish ... ; dog meat; and wild ox."[1] After several days the Frenchmen continued downriver.

During the next one hundred years, the Mississippi Valley was visited by numerous European explorers. In 1682 René-Robert Cavelier de La Salle traveled the Mississippi to its mouth, claiming the entire river and its valley in the name of King Louis XIV of France. La Salle named the area Louisiana, after Louis XIV, who had provided the money and resources for the expedition. La Salle's exploration meant that France now had its "vastly expanded empire" and presumably a way to prevent England's expansion into the interior of North America.

In 1763 the British defeated the French in the French and Indian War (sometimes called the Seven Years War), a major war for control of North America. As a result of their victory, the British took control of New France and much of the area between the original thirteen colonies and the Mississippi River. They did not gain Louisiana, however. In 1762 Napoleon had secretly transferred the area to Spain, to keep it from the British should they win the war. Although the transfer prevented the British from claiming Louisiana in 1763, given their dominance in the region, it seemed only a matter of time before they moved into the area.

Through their possession of Louisiana, the French had the basis for an expanded empire in North America, but involvement in four wars—lasting some twenty-seven years—prevented them from carrying out their plan. Although the French did reclaim Louisiana briefly before 1803, France's presence in the Iowa region essentially came to an end with the French and Indian War. Towns with French names like Decorah would remain, but French influence would be far more evident in communities on the Lower Mississippi—including St. Louis and New Orleans—than on the upper half of the river.

The second European power to have a presence in the Iowa region would leave even less of an imprint. Although Spain ceded Louisiana back to France in 1801, technically Spain retained control of the region until 1804. Until that date Spain's holdings in North America were vast, including the entire Southwest of what is now the continental United States. Historians have typically viewed Spanish influence in the Iowa region in terms of three land grants made along the Mississippi River. As Leland Sage has pointed out, although the Spanish government made the grants, none were to Spaniards nor "were associated with Spanish culture."[2]

The first and most significant grant involved French-Canadian Julien Dubuque, who came to the area around present-day Dubuque in the 1780s. Dubuque quickly made contact with the Meskwaki in a village on Catfish

Creek. Apparently winning the Meskwaki's trust, Dubuque received permission to work the local lead mines, a right not previously granted to a white person. No doubt, good relations were enhanced by Dubuque's marriage to a young Indian woman, Potosa. Even so, Dubuque was not above using trickery to win concessions from his hosts. On one occasion Dubuque threatened to set fire to Catfish Creek if the Meskwaki did not grant a request. Dubuque then had an aide travel upstream and pour oil onto the water. As the oil slick floated by, he threw a firebrand into the water, igniting the oil. The terrified Indians immediately agreed to Dubuque's request, fearing he would burn their villages.[3]

Dubuque soon hired ten white laborers and began both to mine lead and to develop a farming operation. The men worked as teamsters, smelters, storekeepers, woodsmen, boatmen, and overseers of the mines. The actual mining, presumably the most difficult work, was done by Indian women and men. The workers constructed drift mines and extracted the lead ore with shovels, hoes, pickaxes, and crowbars. Dubuque also reportedly developed mining operations on the east side of the Mississippi around Fever River. Each spring and fall he transported the lead to St. Louis in exchange for goods used in the Indian trade.[4]

Dubuque prospered for a number of years but eventually became heavily indebted to a wealthy St. Louis merchant, Auguste Chouteau. At one point Dubuque sold Chouteau a part of his grant for $10,848, but Dubuque was to retain control of this area during his lifetime. Although he continued trading operations during the last decade of his life, Dubuque was unable to recover financially. When he died in 1810 at age forty-five, the man the Indians called Little Night was bankrupt. During his time along the Mississippi, Dubuque's camp would be the only white settlement in what later would be the state of Iowa.[5]

During Spain's tenure in Louisiana, the future of the region was permanently altered by the outcome of the American Revolution. Even though Spain then controlled Louisiana, given the area's location and resources, there was probably little doubt it would eventually become part of the new American nation. With the signing of the Treaty of Paris in 1783, the United States government took control of the area between the original thirteen colonies and the Mississippi River.

Ten years later attention would again be centered on Louisiana. As long as Spain, viewed as weak and nonthreatening, controlled Louisiana,

American officials felt little concern. But in 1802 France regained control of the area, with plans to incorporate it into a New World empire. Napoleon's plans called for the Caribbean island of Santo Domingo to be the center of development; Louisiana would then serve as the breadbasket for this new French undertaking.[6] Not only were Napoleon's plans threatening to the new nation, but a more immediate concern was Napoleon's closing of the port of New Orleans to American trade. In response President Jefferson sent American negotiators to Paris to purchase the port city of New Orleans, thus preventing potential shipping problems. Once there, the Americans were astonished when Napoleon offered to sell the entire territory of Louisiana for $15 million. With the purchase, the size of the American nation more than doubled, and the region later to become Iowa officially became part of the United States.

The acquisition of Louisiana led to additional exploration, the most famous being the Meriwether Lewis and William Clark expedition to the Pacific Ocean. In 1804 Lewis and Clark, along with their crew of twenty-seven, poled and pulled their boats up the Missouri River, passing what would later be Iowa's western border. The only crew member to lose his life on the trip, Sergeant Charles Floyd, died of a ruptured appendix while in the Iowa area. His friends buried him near the juncture of two rivers, the Missouri and a smaller stream later named the Floyd River in his honor. A monument in Sioux City is dedicated to Floyd's memory.

In 1805 a second major expedition left St. Louis with instructions to explore the Upper Mississippi River to its source. Led by Lieutenant Zebulon Pike, the twenty-man crew traveled up the river in a seventy-foot keel boat. Pike's orders included observing the weather and the area's natural resources, collecting information on local Indians, and selecting sites for military forts. Pike encountered many American and French traders on the river and visited the camp of Julien Dubuque, still the only white settlement on the western side of the Upper Mississippi.[7]

Pike also encountered many Indians on the river, and although they offered to trade small items, Pike observed that they were generally fearful of the Americans: "It is surprizing what a dread the Indians ... have of the Americans. I have often seen them go around islands, to avoid meeting my boat. It appears ... the traders have taken great pains, to impress upon the minds of the savages, the idea of our being a very vindictive, ferocious, and warlike people."[8]

Pike continued upriver, not reaching what he viewed as the headwaters of the Mississippi until January 1806. The group returned to St. Louis in April with valuable information about the Upper Mississippi Valley, including the troublesome "De Moine Rapids" near present-day Keokuk, and with recommendations for military forts.[9]

Although Louisiana officially belonged to the United States as of March 10, 1804, before legal settlement could begin, Congress needed to create a territorial government or governments to supervise the area. Congress responded quickly with legislation that divided Louisiana into two parts: the Territory of Orleans, which extended northward to the 33-degree parallel, and the District of Louisiana that extended from that point north to the Canadian border. Because white settlement was almost nonexistent in the district, officials assigned supervision to officials in the Indiana Territory. As Leland Sage has observed, "Except for an occasional piece of business at the office of the superintendent of Indian affairs at St. Louis, it is doubtful if the Indiana officials took much notice of its ward."[10]

During the next thirty-four years, until Iowa became an independent territory, the Iowa region would go through numerous political changes:

Iowa in the District of Louisiana: 1804–5
Iowa in the Territory of Louisiana: 1805–12
Iowa in the Territory of Missouri: 1812–21
Iowa with no governmental jurisdiction: 1821–34
Iowa in the Territory of Michigan: 1834–36
Iowa in the Territory of Wisconsin: 1836–38
Iowa as the Territory of Iowa: 1838–46

As this outline indicates, federal officials simply assigned Iowa to the nearest political entity for most of the period from 1804 to 1838.

In 1821, however, Iowa had become an orphan, with no governmental jurisdiction, a condition that would continue for thirteen years. During that time several significant events took place that demanded governmental action. In 1832 the Black Hawk War resulted in the acquisition of the Black Hawk Purchase. In June of the following year white settlers began to move into this area. As Leland Sage has observed so often, the area was not officially opened for settlement, but land-hungry settlers arrived anyway. Whites had been moving into the Dubuque region even earlier, attracted by the deposits of lead.

In 1834 an event in the Dubuque area demanded action by the federal government. In the spring of that year an Irish immigrant miner, Patrick O'Connor, shot and killed his cabin mate and mining partner, George O'Keaf. It is not clear why O'Connor committed the murder, although he was believed drunk at the time. Angry Dubuque residents hurriedly set up a committee to administer justice; in turn the committee assembled a jury of twenty-four, directing O'Connor to select twelve of the men to try him for the crime. The accused did not deny killing O'Keaf but defiantly declared that he could not be tried because "Ye have no laws in this country."[11] The jury disregarded the accused's defense and convicted him of murder. By June 20, 1834, O'Connor's appeals had failed and he was hanged.[12]

The Dubuque incident brought quick action by the federal government, which placed Iowa under the jurisdiction of the Michigan Territory. At the same time, the government divided Iowa into two counties, Du Buque and De Moine. Courthouses in the two counties were to handle legal matters and enforce the territorial laws of Michigan. Although the Iowa district finally had a government, as Joseph Wall has observed, it was "at best a tenuous and inchoate affair." Officials in the territorial capital, some six hundred miles away, probably had little interest in Iowa under any conditions, but even less in 1834 as they were preoccupied with efforts to achieve statehood.[13] Michigan officials achieved their goal in 1837, and for two years Iowa became a part of the Territory of Wisconsin.

In 1836 local authorities carried out the first census in Iowa. Dubuque County (originally Du Buque) contained 4,274 residents—2,825 males and 1,449 females. That number reflected frontier conditions in general, with males typically outnumbering females. Of the female population, 610 were over twenty-one and 839 were under that age; with males, those over twenty-one, 1,964, outnumbered those under age, 861. Dubuque officials listed 862 heads of household, which meant, in light of the total population, that households averaged just under five persons.[14]

In Des Moines County (originally De Moine), authorities reported a total of 6,290 residents, again with more males than females: 3,531 to 2,759. Also, with both sexes, residents under twenty-one outnumbered those over twenty-one. In Des Moines County, the female age differences were particularly striking, with 1,067 over and 1,692 under twenty-one. The preponderance in both counties of underage females possibly reflected several different frontier conditions. Typically, frontier populations were younger than in more settled areas, which would put many women in their childbearing years. In turn the children would likely be underage and therefore listed in the census as offspring. With older couples, offspring were often out of the home and therefore not counted as part of the family by census takers. Although the average size of families in Iowa in 1836 is unknown, nationally, women who married between 1800 and 1849 had 4.9 children. Rural women, including frontier women in newly settled areas like eastern Iowa in 1836, typically had larger families than did urban women.[15] Although Dubuque and Des Moines counties contained substantial numbers of females, beginning in 1850 and taking the state's total population, males outnumbered females in every federal census through 1950. The lower number of males under twenty-one probably reflected the typically higher out-migration rate for males than for females.

In 1838 Iowans finally acquired independent territorial status. Although some southern politicians opposed the move, fearing more northern than southern votes in Congress, that body approved the Organic Law of the Territory of Iowa, effective as of July 4, 1838. The boundaries included much of the present state plus a part of Minnesota and both Dakotas, making the Territory of Iowa roughly twice the size of the present state.

For Iowans territorial status brought increased political power. While a part of the Wisconsin Territory, Iowa's two counties sent a total of six members to the Wisconsin Territorial Council and twelve representatives to the territorial legislature. With the territorial capital over three hundred miles away in Belmont, it is doubtful if Iowa delegates attended regularly. The creation of the Iowa Territory meant a governor residing in Iowa, the creation of a territorial legislature with power to handle limited political affairs, and the creation of a territorial supreme court. Officials selected Burlington as the temporary territorial capital, which greatly decreased travel for Iowa delegates.

The creation of the Iowa Territory was the first real step in obtaining statehood. In 1787 Congress had passed the Northwest Ordinance, which determined that the Old Northwest—which eventually included five states—would go through several stages resulting in statehood for residents there. The law then became the model for territories that later became states. The Northwest Ordinance was monumental in its intent, as it determined that anyone who settled outside the original thirteen states would not be relegated to permanent colonial status. Rather, territorial areas like Iowa would go through an apprenticeship period whereby residents would be gradually introduced to self-government.

The Northwest Ordinance mandated three stages leading toward statehood. The creation of the territory represented the first stage, whereby the President appointed all major officials: governor, secretary, chief justice and associate justices of the Iowa Territorial Supreme Court, territorial attorney, and marshal. The second stage was achieved when the territory's population reached five thousand males. The territory could then create a legislature—with delegates elected by local residents—and elect one delegate to serve in Congress who could speak but not vote. The third step came when the territorial population reached sixty thousand; officials could then apply for statehood. In Iowa, since the male population totaled over five thousand when territorial status was conferred, officials immediately proceeded to set up a legislature.

July 4, 1838, marked the first day of Iowa's territorial status. Iowa's population had reached 22,859 that year, with most people residing in communities along the Mississippi River. Iowans raised their glasses to toast the new territory, although rain fell much of the day, keeping potentially boisterous citizens in check. In Burlington, the territorial capital, citizens drank forty-six toasts, eight of them "praising Iowa." At the celebration in Fort Madison, a most unlikely guest, Chief Black Hawk, was in attendance. According to Richard, Lord Acton, Black Hawk made his last public appearance that day. The chief, an old man in 1838 and living out his final days near Fort Madison, spoke to the assemblage. Declaring his love for the river and the land, the chief spoke in a sad but conciliatory tone: "I shake hands with you, and as it is my wish, I hope you are my friends."[16]

Although Iowans might drink numerous toasts to their new political status, they would not be joined in "raising a glass" by the newly appointed governor. Robert Lucas, Iowa's first territorial governor, was a teetotaler, true to his Methodist upbringing. The promotion of temperance at a time when Americans drank heavily no doubt helps to explain Lucas's reputation as a moral reformer. Lucas also objected strenuously to gambling. The newly appointed governor vowed that in appointing judicial officers, he "would refuse to nominate 'any individual of bad moral character, or, [who] may be addicted to intemperance or gambling.'"[17]

Lucas came to the new territory following a distinguished political career in Ohio. There he had served in the legislature, being elected speaker of the upper house. Beginning in 1832 Ohio voters elected him to two consecutive terms as governor. He also had the honor of presiding over the first Democratic National Convention in Baltimore in 1832. Lucas's political views, experience, and visibility made him a logical choice for the Iowa governorship. President Martin Van Buren appointed Lucas both to a three-year term as territorial governor and as Superintendent of Indian Affairs in the territory.[18]

Lucas had little time to enjoy the prestige of his appointment, as many issues demanded attention. Land surveys had got under way in Iowa in 1836, with land sales beginning in 1838. Large numbers of settlers were arriving daily, and interior county governments had to be organized. Lucas also had to deal with the creation of the new legislative assembly composed of two houses, a council, and a house of representatives. Before those bodies became realities, however, the governor had to authorize a census and, on the basis of that count, apportion the assembly.[19]

The governor also faced other pressing issues. He had the task of immediately selecting the temporary capital of the territory and then the permanent capital, to be named Iowa City. The location chosen for the latter lay along the Iowa River in Johnson County. John Francis Rague, designer and builder of the Illinois capitol, was selected as architect for what would later be known as the "Old Capitol." The next year the governor handled a boundary dispute with Missouri. Although there was great excitement when a Missouri sheriff attempted to collect taxes from Iowans living in the disputed area, the matter was eventually settled in Iowa's favor in 1849.[20]

Historians traditionally have not studied the wives of territorial or early state officials, but recent scholarship provides us with a view of Iowa's first "first lady," Friendly Lucas. Born in Vermont in 1796, she later moved with her parents and five siblings to Ohio. Described as "barely five feet tall, with dark hair and regular features in an oval face," Friendly married Robert Lucas in 1816. Friendly, twenty years old at the time, was marrying a man fifteen years her senior and a widower with one daughter.[21]

At a time when wives were expected to be dutiful and to cheerfully accept their husband's decisions in all matters, Friendly Lucas exhibited considerable independence. Governor Lucas arrived in Iowa in 1838, but Friendly, along with their two youngest children, remained behind until 1840. The Lucases retained their home near Piketon, Ohio, and Friendly stayed to supervise the farmstead, apparently reluctant to leave Ohio. Three of her children preceded her to Iowa, the oldest, twenty-one-year-old Abigail, serving as hostess for her father in Burlington. When his term as governor ended, Robert and Friendly built a modest brick home on a farm outside Iowa City (then the territorial capital) known as Plum Grove. Lucas continued to be active in Iowa politics until his death in 1853; Friendly remained at Plum Grove and died in 1873.[22]

Iowa had barely attained territorial status when officials began to call for a discussion of statehood. During his second year as territorial governor, Lucas urged Iowans to work immediately for statehood. The governor was so confident of support for his proposal, that in his initial statement he even suggested state boundaries. The legislative assembly voted down Lucas's statehood proposal, but the governor did not give up easily. The following year he persuaded the assembly to offer a referendum at the August election: Iowans favoring statehood were to write "Convention" on their ballots; those opposed were to write "No Convention." When officials tallied the votes, fewer than 25 percent of eligible voters had supported statehood. Iowa's second territorial governor, John Chambers, also supported seeking statehood quickly. In his first message to the citizens of Iowa, Chambers stressed the financial benefits that statehood would confer, such as a five-hundred-thousand-dollar grant of land to pay for internal improvements. But again Iowans rejected the proposal.[23]

Although Lucas and Chambers advocated statehood, most Iowans rejected it for several reasons. Opponents pointed out that, first, they already had ample self-government, and second, they did not believe that statehood would increase their well-being. But most important, those opposed feared increased taxation if statehood was conferred. Under the territorial system, they argued, the federal government paid most territorial expenses, and therefore adults typically paid low taxes. As William Petersen has commented, many residents had incurred debt in purchasing land and they did not want any additional expense.[24]

Inevitably, the debate for statehood involved political-party spoils. In the early 1840s Democrats were in the majority in Iowa, but with the election of President William Henry Harrison, the Whig party dominated at the national level. The Iowa Whigs, with the notable exception of Chambers, opposed statehood because with territorial status they maintained the right to appoint territorial officers. If statehood was conferred, with more Democrats than Whigs in the state, the Democrats would elect state officers. If statehood was delayed, however, the Whigs might be able to build a majority.

By 1844 Iowa's population had increased to more than seventy-five thousand, and the question of statehood could no longer be ignored. Governor Chambers again requested an election to decide the issue. By 1844 fears of increased taxation were offset by the Distribution Act of 1841, whereby states received funds from the sale of public lands. Although the political parties split again on the issue of statehood—Democrats for and Whigs against—many Iowans had changed their minds and in April voted in favor of the referendum, 6,719 to 3,974. Voters then elected delegates to a constitutional convention to be held in Iowa City on October 7. Delegates included former governor Robert Lucas as well as James Clarke, Stephen Hempstead, and Ralph P. Lowe, all of whom would later become either territorial or state governors.[25]

The state constitutional convention lasted almost a month. The completed document called for a governor with a two-year term; a two-house legislature consisting of a House of Representatives and a Senate, with two- and four-year terms, respectively; a state supreme court selected by the General Assembly; and district court judges elected by the voters. Delegates proposed that the future state's northern and western boundaries follow former governor Lucas's suggestion, which included a part of southern Minnesota but not the present northwestern corner of Iowa. The constitution provided for religious freedom for all Iowans, and as good Jacksonian Democrats, the delegates placed major restrictions on the creation of banks, mandating that the founding of each corporation (or bank) required not only a separate state law, but also approval by the voters.[26] In effect, Iowans' actions reflected Southerners' views, including those of Andrew Jackson, that banks were suspect and unnecessary institutions.

Delegates debated various issues, including whether or not convention sessions should begin with prayer. Iowa City ministers offered their services free, but one delegate then objected to the time taken up by prayer. In the end delegates voted against having daily prayer, 44 to 26. A major discussion involved state officials' salaries. Former governor Lucas hoped delegates would not make salaries too low, explaining that his annual compensation as territorial governor had been $2,500 and that he had also received almost the same amount for handling Indian affairs, plus expenses. In the end delegates ignored Lucas's suggestion, setting the governor's salary at $800 annually. Throughout the debate on salaries, delegates continually voiced the need for economy and the fear that state officials would not earn their money. Delegate Chapman asserted that "he would 'pay a fair price for services rendered but not a dollar for dignity.'" He did not want men paid to live as "gentlemen, with no services to perform."[27] The delegates' views harked back fifty-some years to the debates over the United States Constitution, when Americans feared that the new government would allow elected officials to seek special privilege and personal gain.

Once the proposed constitution was completed, officials forwarded it to Washington for final approval by Congress. That body looked favorably upon Iowa's application, as Florida, a slave territory, had been waiting since 1838 for statehood. Since the early 1800s the nation had experienced increasing sectional antagonisms whereby both Northern and Southern states—equally balanced in 1800—worked zealously to maintain the balance of power. Since the early 1800s Southern and Northern states had been paired when coming into the Union, thus maintaining a balance.

Although Iowa's application came along at the right time in regard to maintaining sectional equalibrium, there was one difficulty: Some Northerners hoped to increase the number of northern states by creating at least five states out of the Wisconsin and Iowa territories. Since that was not possible if Congress accepted Lucas's boundaries, an Ohio congressman successfully amended the statehood bill, using the western and northern boundaries earlier suggested by a French-American explorer, Joseph Nicollet (leaving Iowa's eastern and southern borders unchanged). If accepted, Nicollet's boundary would have excluded approximately thirty counties in western Iowa and added some area in northern and northeastern Iowa. Iowans quickly rejected the statehood bill in April 1844, but only by 996 votes. At issue was acceptance of the Nicollet boundary as well as the Whigs' hope that if they could delay the vote, they might secure a majority of voters and thus liberalize the constitution in regard to chartering banks.[28]

But the statehood question was not to be delayed. Eight months later

Iowa's third territorial governor, Democrat James Clarke, urged the territorial assembly to try again. Iowa's territorial delegate to Congress, Augustus Caesar Dodge, introduced a statehood bill proposing a return to the earlier Lucas boundary. In March 1846 Representative Stephen Douglas, the House authority on territorial matters, proposed a compromise: recognize the Missouri-Big Sioux rivers as Iowa's western border and 43° 30' as the northern border. Once again Iowans held a constitutional convention, and on September 9, 1846, Governor Clarke declared the constitution of 1846 ratified and adopted. State elections were set for October. Approximately three months later, on December 28, President James K. Polk took the final step when he signed the bill of admission making Iowa the twenty-ninth state of the Union.[29] In the ensuing election the Democrats would triumph again, electing a little-known figure, Ansel Briggs, as the state's first governor. In a timing glitch Briggs, a stagecoach driver from Jackson County, was inaugurated as governor of Iowa on December 3, although the state technically did not exist until December 28.

Iowans' efforts to achieve statehood again reflected the state's position as the "middle land." The twenty-ninth state to enter the Union, Iowa was not among the first group of territories, nor among the last, to achieve statehood. Rather, the Hawkeye State came roughly in the middle. Iowa's territorial and state constitutions drew heavily on the constitutions of territories and states to the east. Moreover, as Leland Sage has pointed out, Representative Stephen Douglas used Iowa's territorial charter as a model in drawing up a bill for the Territory of Oregon, "changing only a few details to fit the needs of that distant region."[30] Iowa's first territorial officials had gained their political experience in states to the east, such as Ohio. And, no doubt, some individuals who continued westward drew on their Iowa experience to aid in the development of later governments. Iowa's final borders produced an area wherein counties were fairly standard in size and shape. Given its early political history and the subsequent political boundaries, Iowa again qualifies for the description "the middle land."

3

Pioneers on the Prairie

On June 1, 1833, hundreds of eager settlers crossed the Mississippi River to take up land in eastern Iowa. Their arrival marked the beginning of permanent white settlement here, and for the next forty years Iowa would become home to hundreds of thousands of people from all over the nation and from Europe. Most would be attracted by glowing accounts of Iowa's many physical resources. By the early 1870s farms and small towns covered most parts of the state, and settlement in the northwestern counties signaled the end of the frontier era. Providing evidence of Iowa's rapid settlement, population rose from 10,531 in 1836 to 1,194,020 in 1870. By the latter date, not only was the state mostly settled, but it had clearly demonstrated its potential as a major agricultural region.

Throughout the settlement period, five frontier zones would materi-

Extent of prairie region in the central United States. From
Schwieder, Morain, and Nielsen, Iowa Past to Present.

alize, the first developing in the 1830s in southeastern Iowa, and the last in northwest Iowa in the 1860s and 1870s. In the process of settling, newcomers would first encounter woodland areas in extreme southeastern Iowa, then move into a prairie or tall-grass region that dominated most of the state, and finally move into northwestern Iowa. The latter region, while still a prairie environment, had conditions approximating those in the Great Plains. Iowa thus served as the transition zone between timbered regions to the east and the vast plains area that lay to the west.

The first people arriving in Iowa tended to move inland along major rivers and streams. Settlers established farms along the Mississippi, as well as along the Des Moines, the Cedar, and the Iowa rivers. Most newcomers took up timberland, knowing, as had earlier pioneers, that wood and water were essential for successful settlement. The earliest settlers in extreme eastern and southeastern Iowa had little difficulty finding timbered land.

Most of the first arrivals migrated from areas in the eastern half of the country, where timber had been plentiful. For several centuries residents of New England and the Middle Atlantic region had found sufficient timber to supply their basic needs. They had built furniture, homes, and outbuildings from wood as well as used it for fuel and fencing. The stake-and-rider fence, sometimes called the worm fence because of its zigzag shape, dominated the New England countryside. For some settlers wood also provided material for farm implements. Easterners' heavy reliance on wood prompted American historians to describe the lifestyle as one of woodcraft. Naturalist John Madson provided a more vivid perspective on the early abundance of eastern timber when he wrote: "It is said that a grey squirrel could travel inland from the Atlantic coast for nearly a thousand miles and never touch the ground."[1]

As settlers moved into eastern and southeastern Iowa, the woodland experience would be repeated only temporarily. Although the first wave of newcomers to cross the Mississippi River settled in timbered areas, those who came a few years later found it necessary to move farther into the interior, thus encountering the prairie. The prairie, or the tall-grass region, was not entirely new to Iowa's pioneers. Some families had settled for a time in small prairie clearings in Ohio and Indiana, whereas many more people had experienced the Grand Prairie in northern Illinois. Settlement there had helped people adjust to the physical features of a larger tall-grass area. Once in Iowa, however, settlers would perceive the prairie in all its glory. Described by John Madson as the "purest of the prairie states," Iowa was three-fourths to four-fifths prairie land, with hardwoods, particularly oak and hickory, covering the remaining area.

Early explorers, like Lieutenant Colonel Stephen Kearney, provided vivid descriptions of the prairie. In 1835 Officer Kearney received orders from the War Department to travel across Iowa, seeking possible sites for military forts. Kearney and a small band of Dragoons—soldiers trained for frontier duty—left Keokuk in June 1835, traveling in northwesterly fashion along the Des Moines River. As the men moved farther into Iowa's interior, the prairie grass grew taller. Kearney recorded that initially the grass reached the men's stirrups, but as they moved into central Iowa, the grass measured six to ten feet tall. It grew so tall, in fact, the soldiers could pull it up around their horses and knot it on top. The Dragoons soon dis-

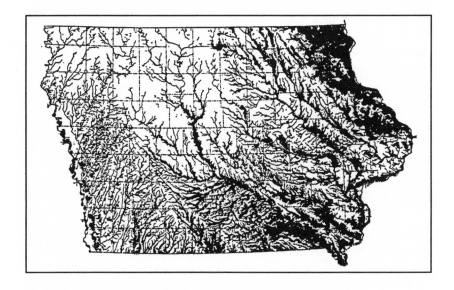

Native vegetation in Iowa, showing forested areas (shaded black) located along rivers. From Leland Sage, A History of Iowa.

covered that if a horse or cow wandered away from camp, someone had to stand on his saddle or ride to a nearby ridge to detect the animal in the waving grass. The soldiers found the prairie alive with color, as many different flowers bloomed between late spring and early fall.[2]

For the soldiers, who were all too familiar with typical army rations, the prairie contained an unexpected pleasure. Soon into the trip Kearney noted an abundance of wild strawberries, so numerous, they stained the horses' hooves and fetlocks, making "the whole track red for miles." And, he noted, the expedition had brought along several cows, so the men were enjoying strawberries and cream![3]

In contrast to Kearney's almost exuberant description of the prairie, the first settlers responded somewhat negatively. One newcomer reacted with considerable gloom when he gazed over the undulating land: "When the eye of the experienced farmer, roves for the first time over the prairies of the west, he is struck with the dreariness of the prospect. ... The absence of timber, seems to him an evil without remedy, and in his judgement millions of acres appear destined to bloom in eternal wilderness." Women also reacted negatively to the seemingly endless expanse of waving grass. Orpah and Ryal Strang moved from New York State to Marshall County in the mid-1850s, where Ryal was quite taken with the gently rolling countryside. But his wife was not. As she viewed the treeless prairie, she tearfully whispered to her husband, "There are no trees, Ryal. I shall die of it."[4]

But the settlers' view of the prairie would soon change. By the 1840s Iowa's newcomers were writing relatives back east, proclaiming the wonders of prairie land. In 1843 David Olmstead wrote his parents in Vermont that they should join him in Iowa: "You said in your last letter that hard work was wearing on you. [If you would come to Iowa] instead of wearing yourself out [on] an ungrateful soil, you might have abundance with one fourth the labor which you bestow on your cold and stony ground."[5]

By the 1850s the view was even more favorable. In 1856 an Iowa resident wrote to eastern relatives: "it does not cost near as much to improve and make a farm here as it does in a wooden country. It does not require one-half the fencing." He added that farming was easy once the land had been broken and "it is not very hard to break."[6]

Novelists have also described the early prairie. In *Vandemark's Folly*, Herbert Quick wrote what has become a widely quoted description of the

Iowa prairie. When the novel's central character, Cow Vandemark, travels west of Dubuque and catches his first glimpse of the prairie, he is moved to tears by its beauty:

> I shall never forget the sight. It was like a great green sea. ... The hillsides were thick with the [plants] in their furry spring coats protecting them against the frost and chill ... [and] on the warmer southern slopes a few of the splendid bird's foot violets of the prairie were showing the azure color which would soon make some of the hillsides as blue as the sky. ... The keen northwest wind swept before it a flock of white clouds; and under the clouds went their shadows, walking over the lovely hills like dark ships over an emerald sea.[7]

For all observers, the prairie produced strong emotional reactions.

In the first thirty years of settlement, most white Iowa residents were native-born, moving from the Northeast or from the South. The federal census of 1860 shows most native-born Iowans had been born in Ohio, Indiana, Pennsylvania, New York, and Illinois. A smaller number had migrated from the southern states of Kentucky, Missouri, Virginia, Tennessee, and North Carolina. A small percentage had immigrated from foreign countries, particularly Germany, Ireland, and England.[8]

People arriving in the mid-1800s came mostly in family units. Allan Bogue's research of a select number of Iowa counties indicates that generally the male head of household was between the ages of twenty-five and forty-five; pioneer women tended to be a few years younger. A long-held view that pioneer families were typically headed by young males and females, often in their teens, is not supported by census data. Rather, the typical pioneer couple were older and had started a family by the time they'd arrived. Most pioneers, moreover, had experience with farming; in effect, they'd brought along the basic knowledge of clearing and planting ground, harvesting crops, and building log cabins and other structures.[9]

Luther and Betsy Rist provide an example of older Iowa migrants. In the 1850s the Rist family left Uxbridge, Massachusetts, intending to settle somewhere in the Midwest. They visited briefly with relatives in Anoka, Minnesota, and in the spring of 1856 settled permanently near Algona. Along with Luther and Betsy, the family included sixteen-year-old Abbie and an older son, Sylvester. Another son, Frank, his wife, Eugenia, and their two children also made the move from Massachusetts. Luther and Sylvester farmed and Frank drove a stagecoach; Abbie soon married a local store owner who had also migrated from Massachusetts. The Rist experience was typical in that married children and their spouses often relocated with parents or siblings.[10]

Historical sources show that many people moving into Iowa "stopped over" at places along the way. Not everyone, in other words, traveled directly from their state of birth to Iowa, and some had lived a year or two in each stopping-over location. The experience of Susan and Jabe Wyatt illustrates that point. On their wedding day in 1838, the Wyatts left Virginia and headed for Ohio, where they believed an improved farm awaited them. The young couple arrived to find no house, so they hurriedly put up a log cabin. Jabe soon became unhappy with the Ohio farmstead, however, and decided they should head farther west. During the next five years the Wyatts moved four more times, living briefly in Indiana, Illinois, and Missouri; they finally settled permanently in Jasper County, Iowa, close to Baxter.[11]

The Wyatts' experience underscores the hardship and tragedy that pioneer families sometimes encountered. In Missouri a tornado struck the family's log cabin, carrying away the Wyatts' three-month-old daughter. While searching for the baby, the two older children became badly chilled; two weeks later they were both dead from pneumonia. The baby, meanwhile, had been found safe on a pile of leaves. Susan and Jabe silently buried their two children in what must have seemed like a hostile, forsaken land. They agreed they must leave Missouri immediately because of its sad memories.[12]

The Wyatts' experience also touches on another aspect of pioneer living—that of severing ties with family back home. During their many moves Susan Wyatt had written to her parents but had received no reply. Many years later a granddaughter would discover that none of Susan's letters had reached relatives in Virginia; they presumed that Susan had not survived the trip west. Whereas for some pioneers like the Rists moving west meant sharing the experience with family, for others not only did it bring a future of separation and loneliness, but also uncertainty about family members left behind.[13]

The Wyatts and other newcomers would soon learn that Iowa's environment could be severe, unpredictable, and even life threatening. A major concern initially was prairie fires, common in areas where land remained uncultivated. Early settlers quickly learned several techniques to protect themselves against rapidly moving grass fires, such as starting backfires or plowing fire lanes or breaks around farmsteads. Prairie fires produced great fear, awe, and helplessness; some of the most vivid descriptions of pioneer living, such as that left by May Lacey Crowder, a pioneer youngster, relate to prairie fires:

> Soon the flames became visible. The fire was coming with racehorse speed, for the grass was long and heavy and a prairie fire always creates a strong wind. Great sheets of flame seemed to break off and go sailing through the air directly over the house and stables, but nothing inside the firebreaks was ignited and soon the danger was past. The burned over prairie, however, was drearier than before.[14]

Winter also brought special concerns. On bitterly cold days with snow and strong winds, pioneers discovered it was only too easy to lose their sense of direction and get lost. William McCormick, who pioneered in Wright County in the mid-1800s, almost lost his life in a storm when he ventured out to check his animal traps. As McCormick returned to his farmstead in a raging blizzard, he came near the farmhouse, calling the family dog, which alerted the family that he was nearby. Anxious family members, however, were unable to see him through the blinding snowstorm. As McCormick continued to call out, it became apparent that he was moving farther away and had simply walked right by the farmhouse. A short time later he responded to the shouts of his wife and found his way back to the house.[15] For settlers living through a blinding snowstorm, it was clear the elements could be deadly for all living creatures.

A major interest regarding the westward movement is how families like the Wyatts, Rists, and McCormicks learned about prospective homes in the West. As early as the 1830s published materials, including guidebooks, maps, and accounts of early expeditions such as those of Stephen Long and Zachary Pike, were available to potential travelers.

Also important was the fact that the first settlers wrote glowing accounts of their experiences to friends and family back home, both in this country and abroad. In 1847 a group of about eight hundred Hollanders settled in Marion County. The following year one member, Sjoerd Sipma, wrote a long letter to family and friends in Holland, informing them of conditions in the newly founded Dutch settlement. Sipma's letter mostly conveyed a positive tone; he encouraged other Hollanders to immigrate here, provided they were willing to work hard. The letters of Swedish immigrant Peter Cassel also informed relatives and friends back home about life in eastern Iowa. Cassel was among the first group of Swedes to settle in Jefferson County, and he played a major role in encouraging other Swedes to emigrate.[16]

Railroads also published materials to attract people to the state. In 1858 the Dubuque and Pacific Railroad (later to be part of the Illinois Central) published a thirty-nine-page pamphlet containing a myriad of information on Iowa's physical characteristics and population. Among the many glowing observations, the author wrote that Iowa was an extremely healthy state in which to live, evidenced by the fact that the state's death rate was among the lowest in the nation. One could also expect to find fewer paupers or criminals in Iowa than elsewhere, he argued. The author explained that "a small amount of labor will produce a larger amount of the necessities of life in the West than in the East. A man who can make more by honest labor in the daytime than he can by stealing at night, will not be a thief."[17]

Although people moved west for a multitude of reasons, the dominant motivation was economic, or a general desire to improve one's lot in life. In Iowa in the nineteenth century, that economic motivation generally manifested itself in the desire to acquire land. Throughout the century newcomers to Iowa could obtain land in a variety of ways. As in most regions the time at which individuals arrived determined where land was available and which land laws were in effect, thereby determining price and method of securing land.

Although the first settlers in the Black Hawk Purchase could quickly locate a piece of ground and begin to create a farmstead, they could not immediately purchase the land. Federal legislation enacted in 1785 determined that all public lands must be surveyed before being sold. Land surveys did not begin in Iowa until 1836, and the first land sales did not take place until two years later. Early settlers, however, eventually had protection provided by the Preemption Act of 1841, which allowed them the first right to purchase their land at $1.25 per acre. The first settlers were, in effect, squatters, and the Preemption Act recognized squatters' rights.

A second option involved purchasing land outright from the federal goverment. By 1833 the price of public land had fallen to $1.25 an acre and would remain there throughout the century. A family purchasing 80 acres, therefore, the size of many Iowa pioneer farmsteads, would pay one hundred dollars for their land. Cash sales accounted for 33.7 percent of all Iowa land sales.[18]

Although we know that about one-third of Iowa's total land area—almost 36 million acres—was purchased for cash, we do not know how long it took settlers to accumulate the money. Pioneers typically had little cash, relying heavily on bartering to obtain needed supplies. Family and community histories indicate that after arriving in Iowa, many males worked for several years to save money for land purchases. Czech-American males in the Clutier area worked at a local stone quarry. Sometimes newcomers carried on dual occupations. The Savage family settled on a farm in Henry County in the 1850s, where the father worked as a tailor, and a son, John, taught at a neighborhood school. Both Savages earned a small amount from doing road work in their neighborhood. Some families, perhaps a majority, did trapping to bring in extra money. William McCormick, who migrated to Iowa in the 1860s, trapped both mink and muskrat.[19]

George and Elizabeth Ogg also provide an example of how people acquired and financed land. The Oggs and their five children left Pennsylvania in 1855, headed for the Midwest. Along the way Ogg served as a traveling blacksmith to support his family. At one point, when Ogg became ill, the family almost starved, having only bran flour left in the wagon. The Oggs settled in Allamakee County, where Ogg continued his blacksmithing. Presumably the family saved some money, as ten years later they relocated in Jasper County, purchasing 160 acres for seven dollars per acre. The Oggs had paid off their land debt by 1866, one year after moving to their new home.[20]

Military land warrants provided yet another way mid-nineteenth-century Iowa settlers acquired land. Beginning some seventy-five years earlier the federal government rewarded soldiers who had served in the American Revolution with land warrants or scrip, which they could redeem for public land. Soldiers who fought in the Mexican War, the Civil War, and various Indian campaigns often received such warrants. Abraham Lincoln, for example, received a total of 160 acres of land in Iowa as

a result of service in the Black Hawk War. A large number of eastern re-
cipients never traveled west to claim land but rather sold warrants to others, sometimes to speculators. Two individuals acquiring land through
military warrants were Simeon and Chloe Dow. Simeon, born in New
Hampshire in 1821, later moved with his parents to Michigan, where he
met and married Chloe Smith. In the early 1850s the couple headed west,
carrying along enough soldiers' warrants to entitle them to almost 2,600
acres of land in western Iowa. They used the warrants in Crawford County
in 1855. Military warrants accounted for 39.7 percent of all Iowa land ac-
quisitions.[21]

Iowans also purchased railroad land, although this method accounted
for only 11.7 percent of Iowa's total land area. In 1856 Congress passed the
Iowa Land Bill, which gave 4 million acres to the state to aid in railroad
construction. Those railroads receiving land grants were the ones eventually known as the Illinois Central, Chicago and North Western, Rock Island, and Burlington. The price charged for land by various railroads varied. The Rock Island sold much of its land for an average of $8.60, while
the Burlington Railroad sold 350,000 acres at $12.17 per acre. In general,
the longer the railroads held their land, the higher the price they could
eventually charge.[22]

The most widely heralded land law nationally, the Homestead Act,
had little effect on land seekers in Iowa. By 1862, when Congress passed
the legislation, only extreme northwestern Iowa contained sizable
amounts of unclaimed land; much of the land there had already been
claimed by Iowa State College (under the Morrill Act) or turned over to
the Illinois Central under the 1856 land bill. Only 2.5 percent of all Iowa
land was claimed under the Homestead Act.

Although Iowans would acquire land in a variety of ways, it is not so
clear what constituted an average land holding in the mid-1800s. Some
families purchased 80 acres on their arrival and gradually added to that
amount. The George Ogg family purchased an additional 80 acres from
another settler a few years after their arrival in Jasper County. John and
William Savage, a father-and-son partnership in Henry County, originally
obtained 70 acres in the mid-1850s; during the next fifteen years the father
purchased an additional 195 acres, 5 acres in timber. In addition, John
Savage rented land almost every year during the 1860s and 1870s. No
doubt, since John and William Savage had a partnership, it was easier for

them than for most settlers to expand their operation. On the other hand, the average size of farm acreages sometimes decreased. Allan Bogue discovered that in Hamilton County in 1860, farm units averaged 205 acres; by 1880, the average size had decreased to 112 acres.[23]

Once land was acquired, the process of building a homestead began. The first concern was shelter, which often had to be hurriedly built. According to Glenda Riley, many families lived in their wagons for several weeks while they constructed cabins.[24] Families settling in eastern Iowa usually found sufficient timber to build log cabins. Typically these were seven logs high with wooden shakes covering the roof. Most had only one room, often measuring sixteen by eighteen feet. Families settling in western Iowa often did not find adequate timber, thus having to use other material. Like later settlers on the Great Plains, many people in northwestern Iowa turned to another abundant resource—the earth itself. Using the rich black soil, newcomers constructed sod houses. These were cheap to build, as families needed only to buy a small amount of wood and tar paper. Sod-house dwellers described their abodes as warm in the winter and cool in the summer. They did have problems, however, as heavy rains produced leaky roofs, and insects, snakes, and rodents were sometimes unwelcome visitors.

Furnishings in pioneer homes were sparse. Most migrating families, whether traveling by covered wagon, steamboat, or railroad, could bring along only a few household items. Some families found it necessary to build tables, benches, and beds once they arrived. For the first year or two many newcomers had to tolerate dirt floors, and later, when time allowed, they put down puncheon or wood floors. Most cabins had only one bed, reserved for parents and perhaps the youngest child. Older children slept in the garret or loft during warm weather, and in front of the fireplace during cold weather. By modern standards pioneer homes were crowded, noisy, and unclean.

Although people may now look back nostalgically to the 1800s, believing that time to be a simpler one, upon closer scrutiny life in a log cabin or sod house was filled with hardships and inconveniences. In cold weather all members had to huddle in the small dwelling, a condition that probably led to the term "cabin fever." In bitterly cold weather people stayed in bed as much as possible, simply to stay warm. Even while sleeping, pioneers could experience problems: One man had his big toe freeze when it poked out from under the covers during the night. The fireplace, a log cabin's only heating source and a main source of light, often spewed smoke into the dwelling and gave off limited heat. Given their small size, pioneer homes had little space for amenities such as houseplants; as one pioneer account explained, if placed back in the corner, houseplants froze. Moreover, in a single-room log cabin or sod house, neither adults nor children had any privacy.[25]

Outside the log cabin or sod house, the farmstead also reflected the simplicity of pioneer living. The first outbuildings were typically only pole-and-straw lean-tos for cattle. Often these structures had three sides, with each side constructed of widely spaced poles and a straw-covered roof. In effect, the structures provided cattle with limited shelter from wind and snow. Many Iowa pioneers would not build barns for a decade or more after their arrival.

Each pioneer farmstead contained a garden, often one-half acre in size, and raised both wheat and corn. Gardens had to be carefully fenced to keep out rabbits, chickens, and other small animals. Before the Civil War farmers mostly concerned themselves with fencing in cultivated areas, which, in effect, fenced cattle out. Since most livestock roamed free, farmers often notched animals' ears in a particular way to show ownership. Fencing laws would not be passed in the Hawkeye State until after the Civil War.

The pioneer farmer's tools were simple and few. Earle Ross has written that "a chopping axe, a broadaxe, a frow, an augur, and a plane" constituted the essential tools. The farmer also had a rudimentary breaking plow used to turn the virgin prairie. Ross writes that this tool was "simply and cheaply made from the wheels of the settler's wagon, a handmade axle, and a long beam which could be raised or lowered to regulate the depth of the furrow." A drag, also homemade, was needed to prepare fields for planting. Then, along with his hoe, rake, sickle, scythe, cradle, and flail, the pioneer farmer was prepared to carry out his work.[26]

Newcomers soon discovered that breaking sod, or plowing the prairie for the first time, was strenuous work. Oxen provided the pulling power, and farmers sometimes used three or four yoke of oxen at one time. For those who did not or could not do their own plowing, sodbusters could often be hired for $2.50 an acre. One pioneer explained that when the prairie ground was turned for the first time, given the profusion of the prairie plants' long roots, it sounded like someone ripping cloth. Another pioneer described it as sounding like a volley of pistol shots.[27] Eventually the introduction of the John Deere steel breaking plow made prairie plowing easier.

Crops raised by early Iowans included wheat, corn, buckwheat, and rye. Corn provided the main food for both humans and animals. It could be planted easily and left in the field during the winter. On the other hand, farmers viewed wheat as a cash crop. In the 1850s cattle raising would also become a major industry for Iowans. Other crops included wool, and some fruit, particularly apples. Iowans raised considerably more wool during the Civil War because of a huge wartime demand, and also greatly increased their production of wheat.

Records of the William and Mary Savage family, who came to Henry County from New York in the 1850s, provide detailed information on the farming operation of an Iowa pioneer family. Between 1860 and 1880 Savage kept careful records of his agricultural operation, indicating that the family carried on a diverse agricultural program. In 1861 Savage listed income from hogs, apples (the family maintained an eight-acre apple orchard), pork and lard, beef, wool, chickens, eggs, hides, and butter. The sale of hogs brought in $214.93, and apples $52.23. For the next nineteen years the Savages would continue to sell a variety of agricultural products, but the hogs typically brought in the most cash. In 1880 hog receipts totaled $767.12. During the Civil War, when the price of wool rose, the Savages responded by increasing the size of their flock.[28]

The Savage-family records not only provide information about agricultural production and income, but also shed light on the matter of subsistence farming. It has long been assumed that pioneer families lived in a state of subsistence or self-sufficiency for the first five or ten years of settlement. If a family was isolated from commercial centers, they had little choice but to concentrate on food production for themselves and their livestock, along with possible bartering with neighbors. Because transportation facilities were limited or nonexistent, newcomers had no way to market their products. The subsistence period varied in Iowa: No doubt settlers in eastern Iowa experienced a longer subsistence period than settlers in northwestern Iowa, where railroads actually preceded some settlement. Although the Savages were not among the first settlers in Henry County, they did settle there within the pioneer era. Four years after their arrival, the Savages were marketing at least ten different products. The typical view that pioneer families routinely remained in the subsistence category for even five years is not supported by the Savage-family experience.

The image of the rugged, self-reliant pioneer family, struggling in near isolation on the fringe of settlement, is inconsistent with the Iowa experience. Though there were always a few people who ventured far ahead of settlement, for the most part individual townships and counties in Iowa filled up fairly rapidly, as the following population figures indicate:

TABLE 3.1.   Population of Iowa, 1836-46

Year	Population	Year	Population
1836	10,531	1850	192,214
1838	22,859	1860	674,913
1840	43,116	1870	1,194,020
1846*	96,088	1880	1,624,615

* Year of statehood

Once settled on the land, men, women, and older children faced heavy work schedules. Men built and maintained farm buildings and fences, planted and harvested crops, and cared for livestock; pioneer women found their days filled with tasks related to food, clothing, child, and medical care. Production, preservation, and preparation of food occupied most of the women's time. They raised large gardens, drying much of the produce for the winter's food supply. Families butchered their own meat, and this required cooking, drying, smoking, or salting. Women also made soap and candles for everyday use, as well as sewed linens, bedding, and clothing.

For women, wash day proved especially difficult. Because of the strenuous task of hauling water, some women regarded washing as a two-day affair: one day to haul water and the next to wash clothes. Sometimes women carried their clothes to a nearby stream to be washed, thus eliminating the need to carry water. All clothes, linens, bedding, and other household items had to be rubbed vigorously on a scrub board resting in a tub of hot water.

Rarely could women's attention be focused solely on their laundry, as other domestic chores and small children required constant attention. Pioneer woman Matilda Paul wrote: "I did all the washing by hand, rubbing every garment, and often stood on one foot while rubbing and rocking the baby's cradle with the other foot to keep her from waking up." Emily Hawley Gillespie also commented about the need to combine different tasks. Emily expressed some satisfaction that she was able to get her regular housework done by nine A.M. so she could begin the family wash. Finishing at three or four o'clock in the afternoon, she then mopped all the floors and sometimes baked a pie or cake for her family's supper.[29]

Both men and women had to contend with sickness and disease, constant concerns on the Iowa frontier. Pioneers settling in Iowa and other parts of the Upper Mississippi Valley experienced three cholera epidemics, in 1832, 1848, and 1862. A more constant affliction was fever and ague, whereby victims alternated between chills and fever. Pioneers speculated that when the prairie soil was first plowed, it released a gas that brought on the chills and fever. In reality, pools of stagnant water served as breeding grounds for mosquitoes, which spread the disease, later recognized as a form of malaria. Fever and ague rarely led to death, but they could severely weaken individuals who might then fall victim to infection or a communicable disease. Women often served as both nurses and doctors, having learned from their mothers how to make salves, poultices, and herbal teas. Women also served as midwives.

Although pioneers of all ages died as a result of disease and accidents, the death of young children, understandably, brought the greatest sorrow. The diary of pioneer woman Kitturah Belknap poignantly expressed that emotion. Kitturah Belknap came to Iowa with her husband, George, in 1839 and remained for nine years before moving on to Oregon. During their Iowa sojourn Kitturah bore four children, three of whom died. In November 1843 Kitturah wrote: "I have experienced the first real trial of my life. After a few days of suffering our little Hannah died of lung fever so we are left with one baby." In June 1845 Kitturah wrote again about death: "I have had to pass thru another season of sorrow. Death has again entered our house. This time it claimed our dear little John for its victim. It was hard for me to give him up but dropsy on the brain ended its work in four short days."[30]

Even with heavy domestic responsibilities, pioneer women frequently managed to be income producers, a fact long obscured for several reasons. During the nineteenth century men and women were primarily defined in quite separate ways, a distinction encapsulated in the term "doctrine of separate spheres." Men were viewed as breadwinners and individuals who spent much of their time in the outside world working, taking part in politics or other activities. Women were viewed as domestic creatures, submerged in their activities as wives and mothers, with no involvement in outside affairs. Accordingly, only men were expected to be wage earners. A second reason women's earnings have been obscured is that for many years census takers did not list women's work roles unless they were formal wage earners. While at home carrying out domestic tasks, women might earn money for doing sewing, laundry, or taking in boarders. These work roles, however, were not recorded by census takers and hence remained hidden from public view.[31]

Regardless of census reports, other historical records indicate that women often performed a variety of tasks that brought money into the home. Most commonly recognized has been the farm woman's production of poultry, eggs, butter, cheese, and cream. The fact that women typically bartered these products for grocery staples and clothing at the local store probably helped obscure their financial significance. Some women, however, did even more in regard to generating income. Emily Hawley Gillespie proved especially enterprising in earning money. At one point she made bonnets, which she sold to neighbor women, realizing a profit of $1.70 each; Emily also did sewing for neighbor women. Early in her marriage Emily and her mother-in-law provided travelers with overnight lodging and meals. In October 1862 Emily noted in her diary that eight travelers had stayed the night, and the next day she lamented: "It is about all Ma and me can do to cook and wait on them." They received $9.00 for their efforts. Between October 14 and November 3, 1862, the Gillespie family put up over twenty-one people at the rate of $1.00 per person. They also charged $.50 for the noon meal and $.15 for tea.[32]

Gillespie's diary touches on yet another aspect of pioneer living in Iowa—the matter of physical isolation. Highly acclaimed novels of pioneer life such as Ole Rölvaag's *Giants in the Earth* and Hamlin Garland's *Main Travelled Roads* portray midwestern pioneer living as not only filled with great physical hardship, but also with extreme isolation and loneliness. Although Iowa pioneers certainly experienced some isolation, because Iowa was settled fairly rapidly and because farmsteads were often within less than a mile of one another, physical isolation was not as severe as that experienced in the Great Plains. At the same time, it should be emphasized that farm life per se implies isolation, and to varying degrees physical isolation remained a fact of life on Iowa farms well into the twentieth century.

Gillespie's diary allows for an important distinction between two terms sometimes used interchangeably in regard to pioneer living: isolation and loneliness. Gillespie came to Iowa as a single twenty-two-year-old woman and immediately began keeping house for a relative; fifteen months later she married a local farmer. Both before and after her marriage, Gillespie found herself caught up in the social and economic life of the rural neighborhood. Her diary indicates she visited with neighbor women, exchanged work with them, boarded hired hands and threshers, and on Christmas day in 1861 entertained seventy-five people at a fundraising supper for the Soldiers' Relief Society.[33]

Throughout this period, however, Gillespie continually confided to her diary she was homesick, lonely, and sometimes despondent. She wrote frequently to her family back in Michigan expressing her desire to see them and her friends, telling them of her depressed feelings. No doubt the image conveyed to her Michigan family was one of intense isolation and loneliness. It is instructive to observe the distinction between the two terms: No doubt Gillespie was lonely for her family and friends back east, but her diary indicates that she rarely spent a single day in Iowa without the companionship of relatives, neighbors, friends, or passersby. Gillespie might have experienced loneliness, but she was not isolated.[34]

By the early 1870s the pioneer era had come to an end in the Hawkeye State; all parts of Iowa then had some settlement, although certain areas remained sparsely inhabited. A half-dozen small cities lay along the Mississippi River, with small towns scattered throughout the rest of the state. The settlement period had been relatively short, as Iowa's rich prairie soil proved a great attraction for prospective land seekers. The subsistence period of settlement had been shorter than for states to the east, given the rapid influx of settlers, Iowa's excellent soil, adequate rainfall, and the availability of river transportation. By the end of the 1850s, moreover, railroad service existed in parts of eastern Iowa.

Iowa's location within the continental United States would give the state a particular distinction as a transition zone between the east and west,

a matter of importance in regard to physical adjustments required for settlement. Predominantly a prairie or tall-grass area, Iowa (as well as
smaller prairie areas of Illinois and Indiana) lay between a woodland region to the east and the Great Plains to the west. As people moved from
east to west, they encountered their first major adjustment problems in
prairie regions that lacked sufficient timber to continue the type of settlement pursued in the northeast. The adjustments made on the Iowa prairie
softened the more extreme adjustments needed to survive on the Great
Plains. Whereas Iowa pioneers had been required to make limited adjustments or modifications, plains settlers had to make major adjustments to a
region with limited rainfall and therefore less potential for agriculture.

Iowa's settlement experience, in comparison with areas to both the
east and west, was relatively predictable and uniform. No landforms such
as mountains or badlands slowed migration, and no Indian tribes impeded
settlement. Although the quality of land varied throughout the state—as
land valuations would later indicate—all land was suitable for agriculture
and livestock raising. In keeping with the Land Ordinance of 1785, once
land had been surveyed in Iowa, it was soon sold at public auctions, accompanied by deeds that included legal definitions of purchase. This action precluded later disputes over boundaries.

Although, it would be unfair and misleading to suggest that Iowa pioneers worked less hard or required less commitment than did pioneers
elsewhere, it should be noted that people arriving here between the early
1830s and the 1870s often found optimal conditions for settlement. Iowa's
land was relatively level and required little clearing of timber or removal
of rocks and stones before cultivation could begin. Most newcomers had
previously been involved in agriculture and stock raising, and therefore
did not have to learn a new occupation. Land could be acquired in a variety of ways, thus making it possible for a large number of people to do so.
The great majority of settlers, moreover, had come from the northeast
quadrant of the United States, thus sharing a common heritage that
reached back to western Europe and the British Isles. Commonalities of
background, interests, and experiences not only served Iowa pioneers well
in their efforts to settle a new frontier, but also provided a foreshadowing
of the state's social and economic composition and interests well into the
next century.[35]

4

Economic Development in the Nineteenth Century

Throughout the nineteenth century Iowa witnessed rapid economic growth. Although railroad building was of paramount importance, economic expansion proceeded on many levels. Soon after initial settlement in any area, towns appeared and quickly became centers of economic activity for surrounding areas. Within communities, craftsmen and professionals set up shop, ready to serve both town and countryside. Although disrupted by the Civil War, settlement and economic development quickly resumed in 1865. Five years later, with four railroad lines spanning the state and more lines under construction, other industrial operations would soon appear. In effect, during the period from 1833 to 1870, Iowans laid the economic foundation for

*A scene in the 1890s near Clinton showing the steamboat
W. J. Young, Jr., alongside a towboat moving a log raft
downriver. Photo courtesy of the State Historical Society
of Iowa, Iowa City.*

their state, perhaps best described as the first economic phase, both to serve themselves and to allow for future growth. After completion of extensive railroad lines, the state witnessed the beginning of innumerable industries, as described in Chapter 13. This chapter, however, deals with the first economic phase, consisting of initial community settlements along the Mississippi, development of the steamboat industry, and construction of major railroads. Because of activities in the first phase, by 1880 Iowa contained an excellent system of transportation, of which officials could boast that no one in the state was ever more than eight miles from a railroad.

In 1849 Sjoerd Sipma, a recent immigrant to Pella, wrote to friends in Holland about his new life in America. An astute observer of the local scene, Sipma related to prospective immigrants what they might expect in Iowa. He explained that transportation was a problem, as it was too expensive to ship goods from his home in Marion County to the Mississippi River: "If all merchandise had to be transported to the Mississippi from here, farmers would go bankrupt because it takes forty hours for the goods to be driven down to the river. If the wagoners take the goods, the cost is seventy-five cents per hundred pounds." But with typical frontier optimism, Sipma dismissed the transportation problem, convinced that within three years the Des Moines River, which flowed only a few miles south of Pella, would be capable of carrying river traffic, much like the Mississippi.[1]

Sipma's letter underscores the extreme importance of transportation, even in a newly settled area. Studies such as those of the Savage family in Henry County show that often within the second year of settlement, farmers produced surpluses that could be disposed of only if shipping facilities existed. As Sipma indicated, the first major effort to provide such facilities came with river travel. Steamboats had begun operating on the Upper Mississippi in 1823, and following that, river travel became common.

Even before agricultural products such as grain and pork became major commodities, steamboats were carrying a wide assortment of passengers and cargo. With St. Louis as a major collection point for military personnel and provisions, the army had used steamboats as early as 1823 for sending soldiers and provisions to military forts on the Upper Mississippi. On the return trip, boats carried cargo produced in the area, such as lead products and fur pelts, down to the ports of St. Louis and New Orleans. While the fur trade gradually dwindled because of the increasing scarcity of beaver and other small fur-bearing animals, lead mining continued in the Upper Mississippi Valley into the 1860s. Workmen had developed lead mines in the 1820s near Galena, Illinois, located along the Galena River, a tributary of the Mississippi. Before the appearance of steamboats, lead had been floated downriver to St. Louis in canoes or on flatboats. The development of steamboating on the Upper Mississippi, however, allowed for expansion of the lead industry. As deposits began to play out in the Galena area, the industry moved northwestward to the area around present-day Dubuque; by the 1850s that community boasted it was the nation's major producer of lead. In the following decade the center of lead mining moved northward to yet another site, southwestern Wisconsin.

Because steamboating had begun on the Upper Mississippi in the 1820s, a transportation system was already in place when permanent settlement began in Iowa in 1833. By the 1850s agricultural commodities such as grain made up a major part of riverboat trade; also by that date, steamboat companies had come to rely on an additional type of cargo—the immigrant. Before completion of railroads across the state, thousands of immigrants traveled from western Europe and the British Isles to the port of New Orleans. There they boarded boats for the remainder of the trip to cities such as Burlington, Davenport, or Dubuque. The trip took approximately three weeks and cost about $3.50 per person.

Deck passage, so called because people taking this form of travel were located on the lowest or main deck of the boat, appealed to immigrants because the cost was only one-fourth of cabin passage. Although cheap, deck passage had few other advantages. Deckers, as they became known, simply slept on the deck itself without the comfort of beds or bunks. As Louis Hunter has pointed out in his study of steamboating on western rivers, deck passengers had only what was left over after the needs of the regular passengers were met. Deckers also had to compete for space with cargo placed on the main deck. Deck passengers, therefore, sat or slept close to "the noise, heat and hazards involved in operating the boat." One decker wrote the following description of his travels: "There was nowhere a more secure place than ... upon a pile of wood. There I lay for 3 nights upon the hard cordwood and was as a result so shaken by the vibrating power of the paddle wheels that for many days afterward I suffered severe pain in my spine and limbs." Deck passengers were largely responsible for their own food. Many purchased sausage, dried herring, crackers, and cheese in New Orleans to carry them through the three-week trip to Iowa.[2]

The worst aspect of deck passage came in the form of disease. With crowded conditions, poor food, and often lack of shelter from winds and rains, many fell ill. The most dreaded affliction was cholera. During the nineteenth century cholera epidemics broke out in the Upper Mississippi Valley on three occasions: 1832, 1848, and in the 1860s. Louis Hunter recorded that the years between 1848 and 1851 were the worst for cholera fatalities: "Steamboat after steamboat arrived at the upper river ports with burdens of the sick and dying and tales of many dead along the way. ... Sometimes entire crews deserted on learning that cholera was on board."[3]

For people traveling cabin passage, however, life on a Mississippi River steamboat could be almost luxurious. By the 1850s steamboats had become "great floating hotels" that contained theaters, bars, large dining rooms, and fancy staterooms or cabins. Also by that decade, competition was ever present for the riverboat companies, and some responded by creating even more opulent conditions. Companies sometimes imported chefs from Europe so they could boast of the fanciest food on the river.

For all passengers nineteenth-century steamboat travel contained some danger. Boats frequently hit snags or floating logs, which tore holes in the boats' hulls. Boilers might explode, spraying scalding water on nearby passengers and crew. If a boat caught fire, the only way to unload passengers safely was to ground the boat, hoping the passengers could scramble up a nearby riverbank. Before 1870 steamboats carried no lifeboats or fire-fighting equipment because companies insisted these items weighted boats down, making them uncompetitive. After 1870, however, the federal and some state governments passed regulations regarding contagious-disease quarantines, limits on the number of each boat's passengers, sufficient space allotments for passengers, and food requirements. By that date steamboats still carried passengers, but most immigrants had begun to travel by railroad.

While most historical interest has focused on the economic activities of steamboating, little attention has been given to the workers who kept the boats moving up and down the river. Most accounts of these steamboatmen paint them in decidedly negative tones. Timothy Mahoney writes that "Travelers and townsmen regularly remarked on the rough, anti-social behavior of the poorly paid, undereducated foreign or black riverboat laborers." A riverboat traveler in the early 1850s, while expressing little sympathy for the workers' general demeanor, observed that life on the river was hard, as the men's "sleeping bunks [were] miserably furnished, and their whole physical condition [was] exceedingly uncomfortable."[4]

The work schedule for steamboatmen called for two sets of workers, with each set working in four-hour shifts. Therefore, one set of men was always off duty, and though the men worked hard, they apparently also played hard. Mahoney points out that the number of workers in any town was in direct proportion to the "amount of steamboat traffic on the wharf." On a typical spring day some 160 to 240 men would arrive in a town like Galena to "patronize saloons, gaming halls, eating establishments, and places of entertainment, creating brief but often tense confrontations between locals and these transient outsiders near the wharf."[5]

Violence on steamboats themselves was not uncommon. In April 1846, after a captain had reportedly "whipped and beaten" an Irish deckhand, the captain forced the Irishman to leave the boat at Bellevue. Upriver at Galena, friends of the deckhand confronted the captain and left him "beaten and 'dangerously wounded.'" In 1858 in Davenport a confrontation between deck workers and local police left two policemen wounded.[6]

Beginning in 1833, ten years after the first steamboat traversed the Upper Mississippi, communities began to form along Iowa's eastern border. Dubuque has the distinction of being the first settlement in Iowa, followed in the same decade by Clinton, Davenport, Muscatine, Burlington, and Fort Madison. Each community initially developed local economic enterprises. Dubuque, for example, became noted for lead mining in the 1850s and also developed the Dubuque Boat and Boiler Company, which manufactured steamboats. Clinton became known primarily for its lumber industry. Logs that were floated down from Wisconsin and Minnesota provided wood for lumber, laths, and shingles, followed later by the manufacture of window frames, sash, doors, stairwork, and other wood finishings. Burlington became a major slaughtering center for cattle and hogs and also manufactured buggies and carriages. The city, like most of the other major Iowa river communities, developed breweries. In the first two decades of development in each community, the initial generation of river-town settlers believed they could independently "specialize and generate external and transport economies [that would] broaden the reach of [their town's] trade, draw other towns into dependent economic relationships with it, and emerge as a significant regional entrepôt."[7]

Davenport perhaps had the best location, being situated on the part of the Mississippi that flows east and west. Two other features proved positive for Davenport's development: first, the tributary of Rock River coming in from the east and the presence of Rock Island, located in the middle of the Mississippi; and second, a set of rapids located just north of the island. The presence of the rapids meant that boats had to lighten their load at this point by unloading cargo, transporting it a short distance, and then reloading it, all of which called for the hiring of workers. Davenport developed rapidly with lumber and flour mills. In the 1850s farmers in the area began to produce more wheat, with merchants shipping substantial amounts of grain to St. Louis. By the mid-1850s, according to Mahoney, Davenport was considered the "boom town" of eastern Iowa.[8]

As Iowa's river communities entered their third decade of existence, another form of transportation would command attention. In the 1850s railroad fever would invade the Hawkeye State, and soon every community was caught up in the excitement of planning a railroad. As with the development of steamboating, regional considerations would be paramount.

During the 1850s Chicago would become a major railroad center in the upper Midwest, a development of vital importance for Iowa's railroad promoters. By the beginning of the Civil War, at least eleven eastern railroads had expanded their lines to Chicago. Even before that date, in the 1850s, four railroads had proceeded west from Chicago, building their lines to the Mississippi River and each terminating opposite (or nearly opposite) a major Iowa city. With the development of the four lines—eventually known as the Illinois Central, the Chicago and North Western, the Rock Island, and the Burlington Northern—economic opportunities appeared unlimited. If the four river cities organized railroads that could tie up with the Illinois lines, then transportation would be assured to Chicago and, in turn, to eastern and foreign markets beyond. Railroads would operate all year, whereas steamboats usually faced several inactive months because of frozen rivers.

With the continued construction of Illinois routes, railroad excitement in Iowa reached an even higher pitch. Residents of the four Iowa cities across from the projected terminuses of the Illinois lines began organizing railroad companies. As William Petersen has pointed out, people believed "railroads were literally magic wands which had but to touch a community to create prosperity, luxury, and unlimited opportunity for development." If one's community could secure a railroad, residents believed, it "assured the fortunes of land-owners and citizens alike."[9]

The first route to be planned and built in the state was the Mississippi and Missouri Railroad; Antoine Le Claire, a founder and prominent citizen of Davenport, organized the company there in 1853. Work began the following year, and plans called for the route to be finished from Davenport to Iowa City by the end of 1855. Even though the company hired extra workers in the fall of that year, it appeared doubtful that the railroad would reach Iowa City in time. In a dramatic effort, and indicative of Iowans' enthusiasm and support for railroads, local citizens turned out on the last day to help assure that each rail was in place by the stroke of midnight on December 31.

At the same time, citizens in Dubuque, Clinton, and Burlington also proceeded with railroad plans. In Burlington local boosters had earlier been involved in promoting a variety of transportation systems even before railroad fever hit. Burlingtonians had long been frustrated over the problems they faced with river traffic. Thirty miles south, the river contained the Lower Rapids, which made it impossible for large boats to travel that stretch during low water. Downstream a few more miles, Keokuk, also a bustling river community, served as a major rival for commerce. Burlington residents believed the presence of the Lower Rapids, which made shipping from their port considerably more expensive, gave Keokuk businessmen an unfair advantage. Burlington residents had pushed for federal funds to have the Lower Rapids cleared, but without success.[10]

Burlington promoters then turned their attention to plank roads to solve their transportation problems. The roads, first developed in Russia and Canada in the 1840s, were constructed of "long heavy planks which were laid on top of wooden 'stringers' which were in turn set into a graded roadbed." In the 1850s eastern states like New York had constructed plank roads, and about the same time Burlingtonians expressed interest in the process. Burlington residents were particularly interested in finding a way to develop trade with area farmers by constructing a route to Mount Pleasant. By 1851 the route had been finished, but as George Boeck has pointed out, it was really anticlimactic. By then Burlingtonians, like residents of other river cities, had already switched their interest to railroads.[11]

Accordingly, Burlington citizens waited for an opportunity to become part of an Illinois line. That opportunity presented itself when local officials heard that the Chicago and Aurora Railroad (later to become the Burlington) would reach the Mississippi at Oquawka, Illinois, a small community about ten miles upstream. Burlington promoters then began to push their own interests by proposing that the railroad reroute itself to reach the Mississippi opposite their city. Once this change had been made, Burlington boosters went to work to raise money for the extension of the route into Iowa.

Like Burlington's boosters, the promoters of all major routes in Iowa felt the need for local contributions because state aid was not a possibility. In the 1840s numerous state governments, particularly Indiana, had accumulated excessive debt in efforts to build canals for transportation purposes. State legislators decided that Iowa would not fall victim to the process; accordingly, they set Iowa's state debt limit at one hundred thousand dollars. Given this constitutional restraint on state aid, contributions from counties, towns, and townships became crucial for the development of the four major east-west lines.[12]

The first major effort to raise local funds came in the form of bond issues floated in eastern counties. Dubuque, Clinton, Scott, and Des Moines counties all voted bond issues averaging between seventy-five thousand and one hundred thousand dollars in the early 1850s. As local railroad companies organized in each vicinity, the money raised was given to the railroads in turn for stock in these corporations. Between 1853 and 1857 many other eastern counties followed suit. Action by county governments was sometimes followed by similar action within the larger communities. Citizens of Burlington voted a loan of seventy-five thousand dollars in 1855, and local individuals also contributed eighty thousand dollars. In total, Iowans would raise about $50 million through local aid.[13]

While local governments continued their fund-raising, Iowans also received substantial federal aid. For several years Iowa's congressional delegation had pushed hard to secure federal land grants to assist railroad building in the state; a precedent for such action had been established in 1852 when the Illinois Central received such a grant. Finally, in 1856, Congress made a grant of 4 million acres to the state, stipulating the land be divided between four railroads selected by the General Assembly. That body, in turn, made the logical selection of railroad companies located in Dubuque, Clinton, Davenport, and Burlington. Of these four prospective routes, the legislation specified that three must end in Council Bluffs, and all four routes must be completed within a certain time period. Each railroad would receive alternate sections of land for a distance of six miles from either side of the right-of-way. If land had already been claimed in these areas, then comparable land would be granted elsewhere. In effect, each railroad received through the land grant 3,840 acres for each mile of track constructed. The financial return for the 3,840 acres varied from company to company. The Illinois Central needed to sell much of its land quickly, whereas the Burlington managed to retain land for a longer time. Overall, railroad companies averaged about ten dollars per acre from land received in 1856. The land grants accounted for about one-ninth of the total state of Iowa.[14]

Although the land grants gave the four railroads the potential of large amounts of land—and, in the view of many Iowans, a solution to their financial problems—the railroads did not receive all the land at one time. The state legislature actually used a "carrot and stick" approach: For each twenty miles of track built by a railroad, the railroad company would be eligible for 120 sections of land. Because of this stipulation, railroads continued to seek other types of local aid. Each community, anxious to encourage a railroad to build through its town, responded with additional forms of local aid. One practice used widely by towns in central and western Iowa was to grant free town lots to railroads. Some towns donated ten to twenty lots; others were even more generous. The lots provided land on which the railroad could build its depot and freight facilities. Some communities also offered a tax-exempt status to the railroads, exempting the company from local property taxes for ninety-nine years. At the same time, a few communities began to make demands of their own. The town of Pacific Junction in southwestern Iowa hoped not only to get a railroad but to keep any other town in the county from doing so. The town fathers offered the Burlington one hundred town lots if they would build only one station within the county.[15]

The last measure of local aid came in the form of outright gifts. In 1868 the Iowa General Assembly authorized townships, towns, or incorporated cities to "vote taxes, not to exceed 5 per cent of the value of taxable property" and to turn the tax over to the railroads as a gift. A number of towns and townships in Worth, Mills, Fayette, Hamilton, Jackson, and Madison counties quickly took advantage of the new law.[16]

As railroad building proceeded across the state, one basic purpose of the roads changed. In the eastern half of Iowa, the railroads had linked up existing communities. By the time construction reached central Iowa, in effect the railroads "ran out of" towns, or generally outdistanced settlement. In an effort to ensure a sufficient population to use their services, the four major routes turned their attention to town building. The experience of the Illinois Central provides a good example of the town-building operation.

Beginning in Dubuque in 1853, the Illinois Central (then known as the Dubuque and Pacific Railroad) built through existing communities until it reached Iowa Falls. From there to the railroad's destination of Sioux City, however, only a few communities existed. John I. Blair, who had formerly been involved in the Chicago and North Western, directed the establishment of town sites and the sale of town lots along the projected Illinois Central route. Blair's company laid out some twenty town sites, including Manson, Fonda, Storm Lake, Alta, Marcus, Remsen, and Le Mars. The town company determined the sites, then platted the blocks and lots within each site. As soon as the line opened to that point, officials auctioned off lots and, in effect, created a town almost overnight.[17]

By 1867 the first railroad, the Chicago and North Western, completed its route from the Mississippi to the Missouri. In doing so, the railroad was the first line to tie up with the Union Pacific, which earlier had become a part of the first transcontinental route across the west. As early as 1864 Iowa railroad promoters had known that Council Bluffs was to be the eastern terminus for the Union Pacific, and all four routes had pushed hard to be the first to reach that community. The Burlington and Rock Island would reach the Missouri in 1869, and the Illinois Central would reach Sioux City the following year.

Even with completion of the four original east-west lines, Iowa railroad building did not cease. A fifth line, the Chicago, Milwaukee, St. Paul and Pacific, eventually completed its route across northern Iowa in the late

1870s and then built a second route from Sabula to Council Bluffs. Promoters also constructed north-south railroad lines as well as numerous commuter lines. The Fort Dodge, Des Moines and Southern was an important commuter line in central Iowa that operated into the mid-twentieth century. The line traveled from Des Moines through Ames and Boone into Fort Dodge. At one time the line also served passengers in Lehigh, Rockwell City, and Webster City. Officials discontinued some service in 1926, but one passenger train a day made the trip until the 1960s. Des Moines businessmen could take the train to various small communities along the way and then return the following day to the capital city.[18]

Even though construction of the major east-west lines has dominated the study of Iowa railroading, the greatest growth actually took place between 1880 and 1890, when an additional 3,435 miles of track were built, thus creating many branch lines in the state. In effect, the branch lines incorporated many additional communities into the state's railroad network, thus binding together all sections of the state. By 1900 Iowa contained 9,185 miles of railroad trackage, placing it seventh or eighth in the nation in total railroad mileage.[19]

While railroads were obviously of great economic importance, the social implications of expanded transportation was also significant. With passenger service available everywhere in the state, families could travel to nearby towns for shopping, medical care, or simply for pleasure. Towns like Jefferson had six passenger trains a day, three going east and three going west. Mail deliveries were often twice a day, and goods could be ordered from nearby cities or from mail-order companies hundreds of miles away. For people who wished to travel greater distances, boarding the train at Jefferson meant one could travel not only to nearby Ames, but to Chicago or New York. With the railroads, dependable year-round transportation had finally been assured.

Railroads also had significant impact on communities in other ways. Depots became hubs of activity as traveling men arrived to do business in the community. Dray companies greeted trains to deliver freight to local businesses, while, before the time of automobiles, a local hack and driver awaited the train's arrival to transport passengers around town. Hotels often built close to the depot to provide convenience for travelers and to accommodate traveling men, providing them with tables on which to display their merchandise. The depot itself often became one of the most attractive sites in town, as frequently the grounds were landscaped and well maintained. Local officials believed that the depot served as the entry point into the community, and that passengers formed their impression of the town from the appearance of the depot. Given the vast importance of railroads to Iowa, their extensive routes, and their companies' growing political power in the state legislature, it is not surprising that by the 1870s the companies themselves proclaimed, "The railroad is king."

As the foregoing accounts indicate, railroad development brought major positive change to the entire state. At the same time, there were unforeseen consequences for river cities. In Burlington, as Philip Jordan has noted, the social and economic tone of the town changed with the decline of steamboating and the rise of railroads. Jordan has observed that as long as Iowans relied on river travel, most lines of trade and communication went north and south. Burlington families vacationed in Southern cities, where they socialized and went shopping; local businessmen often obtained credit from Southern bankers. Moreover, Southerners traveled north to vacation and thus to escape "hot weather and summer sickness." Jordan observes that Burlington from 1833 to 1860 had a particular social and cultural tone because of the North-South tie.[20] After 1860, however, those ties with the South dissolved and in their place economic and social links developed with Chicago and cities in the Northeast. In effect, before the Civil War, St. Louis and New Orleans played key roles in regard to trade and commerce in the Upper Mississippi Valley, whereas after the war Chicago became the major economic hub for Iowa.

Other river communities also experienced unexpected change with the shift in mercantile connections from St. Louis to Chicago. As communities began to develop, each worked diligently to develop local economic enterprises that would attract additional population and, in turn, produce greater economic development. But after railroads expanded into Iowa, local businessmen and manufacturers experienced an unexpected fate: In effect, these businesses often found themselves bypassed or forced out of business as "one by one local economic actions were drawn into the regional economic dynamics centered at the metropolis [Chicago]."[21] In Davenport, which had enjoyed considerable prosperity in the mid-1850s, the Rock Island Railroad reached the community in 1856. The economic orientation of the town then quickly shifted from St. Louis to Chicago, thereby bringing "entrepreneurs, agents, and capitalists from the East and

Chicago interested in opening branches of wholesaling houses or in founding processing plants and manufacturing establishments to supply the newly acquired markets." Local industries found they could not meet the new competition. As Timothy Mahoney has shown, Davenport then seemed "strangely disoriented." Local officials had anticipated that the arrival of the railroad would enhance local economic enterprises; instead, the railroad with its entourage of outside business interests was causing Davenport to become "an outpost of the metropolis."[22]

From the 1830s to the 1880s, transportation development was a major part of Iowa's economic expansion. Early town boosters, perhaps with too much conviction, fervently believed every community must have a railroad to flourish. Without question railroad development proved vital to the development of many communities and the continual growth of agriculture. After 1870, with railroad lines in place, Iowans could move into a second phase of economic development whereby industries appeared, most of which were agriculturally related. Steamboat travel on the Mississippi remained important but went through adjustments as river traffic began to carry more grain and fewer people and to handle more leisure-time excursions. The economic ties forged with Chicago and points east continued, while Iowa's ties with Southern cities remained limited.

5

Iowans and the Civil War Era

On April 12, 1861, the shelling of Fort Sumter marked the beginning of the Civil War. Although Union and Confederate troops would fight no battles in Iowa, sparing the state any physical devastation, like all Americans, Iowans were profoundly affected by the conflict. Though the war itself deserves considerable attention, the preceding thirty years must also be considered, as these decades were replete with political and social issues that, by 1860, had significantly affected Iowans' thinking and behavior. Even though Iowa was a free territory (and later a free state), its citizens were concerned with slavery-related issues such as western expansion and the political rights of free African Americans. Like most Northerners, Iowans often had contradictory attitudes toward blacks and their status within society. Events preceding the war also influenced Iowans in their political thinking, and in the 1850s the state experienced political realignment. Once the war began,

Union soldiers at Bellevue embarking for a southern
destination. Photo courtesy of the State Historical Society
of Iowa, Iowa City.

however, most Iowans supported the Union cause. After four terrible years of war, during which some seventy thousand Iowans fought for the Union, Iowans witnessed rapid change in the areas of economic development and political rights for citizens of African descent.

Although the war itself would not start until fifteen years after Iowa achieved statehood, important questions about black slavery extended back into the territorial period. Iowa's free status, however, did not mean that Iowans believed in equality between the races. Most Iowans favored the abolition of slavery, believing the "peculiar institution" to be morally and religiously wrong; these same people, however, viewed African Americans as inferior to whites and believed that the two races should be kept apart. These seemingly contradictory views, shared with many other Northerners, led to legislation intended to keep free blacks out of Iowa. The first, passed in 1839, required all blacks coming into Iowa Territory to possess a certificate of freedom and the ability to post a five-hundred-dollar bond. Territorial officials required the first provision as proof of free status and the second to prevent the individual from becoming a public charge. These laws were later referred to as Iowa's Black Code, reminiscent of the Black Codes passed in the post–Civil War South that governed the movements and behavior of blacks there.[1]

While Iowa was still a territory (1838–46), an event took place that symbolized Iowans' contradictory attitude toward blacks' political status. In 1839 the territorial supreme court in its first case issued an opinion known as "In the matter of Ralph (a colored man) on Habeas Corpus." The case concerned a black slave, known only as Ralph, who came to Dubuque from Marion County, Missouri, in 1834 to work as a lead miner. Ralph had persuaded his master, Jordan Montgomery, to allow him to come to Dubuque with the intent of buying his freedom. Montgomery had determined that Ralph's value was $550.[2]

But once in Dubuque, Ralph discovered living costs were high, and it was difficult to do more than pay for board and room. By 1839, after Ralph had been in Dubuque for five years, Montgomery experienced financial difficulties and sent two agents to reclaim the black man. The agents appeared before a Dubuque justice of the peace to swear an affidavit that Ralph was the property of Jordan Montgomery and that they, the agents, represented Montgomery. The two then headed back to Missouri with Ralph in custody. Fortunately for Ralph, Alexander Butterworth, who worked a lead claim next to the black man's, heard about the arrest and moved to counteract it. He obtained a writ of habeas corpus on Ralph's behalf, which secured Ralph's release.[3]

Ralph's case was soon before the supreme court of the Territory of Iowa. In Burlington on July 4, 1839, lawyers made their arguments, and Chief Justice Charles Mason issued the decision later that day; the unanimous opinion went in Ralph's favor. The two justices (a third was absent) decided that since Montgomery had given his permission for Ralph to come to Iowa, Ralph could not be regarded as a runaway slave, and, therefore, Montgomery had no right to reclaim him. The justices added that although Ralph did owe Montgomery $550, Montgomery could not recover that money by reducing Ralph to the status of a slave. Ralph remained in the Dubuque area for a time and later moved to the Muscatine area.[4]

The case of Ralph, while interesting in its own right, did not bring about a more favorable view toward free blacks in Iowa. During the next few years the Iowa territorial legislature would pass several more discriminatory laws. These included preventing black males from joining the territorial militia or serving in the legislature. Moreover, blacks could not serve as witnesses against whites in any court cases, were not eligible for statutory relief, and could not attend public schools. An additional law declared marriages between blacks and whites illegal. The Black Code legislation also remained in effect.

Even while denying blacks legal rights and passing legislation intended to keep them out of the state, many Iowans took an active part in helping Southern black slaves escape into Canada. One more time Iowans were demonstrating their consistently inconsistent behavior toward African Americans. Although Underground Railroad activity had appeared before 1850, after that date more people became involved, especially Congregationalists and Quakers. In 1850, with the passage of the strengthened Fugitive Slave Act (a part of the Compromise of 1850), people found guilty of aiding and abetting runaway slaves could be fined up to one thousand dollars and sentenced to six months in jail. The stronger law, however, rather than discouraging Northerners from involvement in slave escapes, actually encouraged them.[5]

In Iowa a general underground route ran from Tabor, in the southwestern corner of the state, through Lewis, Fontanelle, Winterset, and

Lynnville to Grinnell. From there travelers moved on to Iowa City and then Clinton, where they crossed the Mississippi River into Illinois. Because of penalties if one was apprehended for assisting runaway slaves, participants were naturally reluctant to talk or write about their activities. The Reverend John Todd was one Iowan who did so, writing some thirty years after his involvement in the Underground Railroad. Reverend Todd, a Congregationalist minister, came to Tabor in the late 1840s, bringing along his congregation from Clarksfield, Ohio. Once in Iowa, Todd and his parishioners started a Congregational church and a Congregational school known as Tabor College.[6]

Like many of his parishioners, Reverend Todd had strong antislavery views and was soon involved in helping escaped slaves reach Iowa's eastern border. Not only did Todd and fellow Taborites assist slaves to move through their area, they also worked for the release of free blacks who had been mistakenly arrested. Reverend Todd recorded that on one occasion several white men took three free blacks captive in the vicinity of Council Bluffs. One black man managed to escape, but the remaining two captives were taken to St. Louis, where they "were lodged in a slave pen ... awaiting the day of sale in the slave market of that city."[7]

Convinced that the African Americans were not runaways, Reverend Todd and a companion, a Dr. Blanchard, followed the party to St. Louis only to be denied the right to speak to Missouri authorities about the case. When Reverend Todd persisted in his charge that two innocent blacks had been arrested, the Missouri authorities finally agreed to a rather unusual arrangement: Dr. Blanchard would walk through the compound where the blacks were held. If either black person in question appeared to recognize the doctor, the authorities would accept that as evidence of an improper arrest. As Dr. Blanchard started through the area, it seemed that he would not be noticed. But as he neared the end of the compound, the black woman, Maria, rushed to embrace him. The authorities then freed the blacks to return to Iowa.[8]

The matter of slavery would also affect Iowans through the passage of the Kansas-Nebraska Act. In 1854 Illinois senator Stephen Douglas introduced a bill into Congress calling for the organization of the Kansas and Nebraska territories. The bill called for the repeal of the Missouri Compromise, which had guaranteed that in the Louisiana Purchase all area north of 36° 30′ would be free from slavery. In place of the Missouri

Compromise, Douglas advocated the principle of popular sovereignty. In other words, the people who settled the Kansas and Nebraska territories would eventually determine whether the areas would be slave or free. Douglas, like many Northerners, was intent on constructing a northern transcontinental railroad, and a necessary first step was to organize the territory through which the railroad would be built.

The passage of the Kansas-Nebraska Act resulted in many proslavery people from Missouri and antislavery people from New England traveling to Kansas, determined to create communities that reflected their particular points of view. Some New Englanders traveled across Iowa, stopping to solicit aid from sympathetic citizens. Iowans gave assistance in the form of free lodging, food, and sometimes even money for rifles. On one trip New Englanders stopped to seek help from Governor James Grimes, a known abolitionist. Grimes told the visitors the state could not officially aid their cause, but he did indicate that unofficially they might receive help. The state had just received a shipment of 1,500 rifles, Grimes announced, and then added that he would be out of his office for about an hour. He then conveniently left the key to the arsenal on his desk. The visitors quickly got the governor's message, and when the New Englanders left town a short time later, the state was minus its latest shipment of guns.[9]

The Kansas-Nebraska situation also brought a well-known New England abolitionist to Iowa. John Brown made at least four trips to the state between 1855 and 1859, visiting Tabor, Des Moines, Grinnell, and Springdale. Brown received a warm welcome here, particularly among the state's Quakers. In Springdale in 1857, Brown made preparations for his attack on Harpers Ferry, the government arsenal in Virginia. In his entourage were ten men, including his own son and a fugitive slave. Brown returned to Springdale in 1859 to finalize plans for the Harpers Ferry raid. When that ill-fated event finally took place, it included six Iowans, among them Edwin and Barclay Coppoc, two young Quakers.[10]

For Iowans the most immediate consequence of the Kansas-Nebraska Act was political realignment. From the beginning of territorial days most Iowans had belonged to the party of Andrew Jackson. The repeal of the Missouri Compromise (as part of the Kansas-Nebraska Act) greatly angered Iowans, causing many to rethink their political allegiance. By the end of that decade the state had become more Republican than Democrat.

James Grimes played an important role in that political transition. Born in New Hampshire in 1816, Grimes attended Dartmouth College and later began practicing law. In 1836, when he was not yet twenty years old, Grimes arrived in Burlington, ready to hang out his shingle. Voters elected Grimes to the first territorial legislative assembly, where he played an important role in Iowa's Whig party. In 1854 he was nominated for governor on the Whig ticket and energetically set about uniting all antislavery groups, including the Free Soil–Free Democracy party. The emotional climate of the times was reflected in the type of campaign waged by Grimes, in which he appealed blatantly to local prejudices. Grimes asserted that if the concept of popular sovereignty (as proposed by the Kansas-Nebraska Act) became law, the first thousand settlers in a territory could create a state religion, Catholic or Mormon perhaps, which would exclude all other creeds from the rights of citizenship. Grimes also stressed the possibility of slave states on Iowa's western border. In the election Grimes defeated Democratic candidate Curtis Bates by approximately 2,000 votes out of 44,527 votes cast.[11]

The following year Grimes and the Free Soilers began forming the Republican party in Iowa; in January 1856 they issued a call for the first Republican state convention. Again Grimes faced a monumental task. By the end of 1855 Iowa contained numerous political parties, including the Know Nothings, Free Soilers, old-line conservative Whigs, Anti-Nebraska Democrats, and a few mainline Democrats. In February the convention took place in Iowa City with a wide range of political groups represented. The delegates agreed on a platform condemning the extension of slavery into western territories but remained vague on other issues. Once the new party was organized, Iowans' vote in the 1856 presidential election was never in doubt. The Republican candidate, John Fremont, received forty-five thousand votes to the Democratic candidate James Buchanan's thirty-seven thousand. Most Democratic votes came from the two southern tiers of counties, a few western counties, and Dubuque. At the state level Grimes was reelected governor, only this time as a Republican rather than as a Whig. The Republicans also carried the General Assembly.[12]

The election of state Republican officials in 1856 foreshadowed a lengthy dominance by the Republican party in Iowa. For the next seventy-five years Iowans would go to the polls and, in election after election, vote in their favorite Republican candidates. The only exception to a clean sweep by the Republicans between 1856 and the 1930s would be the election of Horace Boies in 1889, and again in 1891. Boies's victories, according to one Iowa scholar, probably were due more to Iowans' rebelling against the issue of Prohibition than voting for candidate Boies.[13]

Once the Civil War started, most Iowans strongly supported the Union. Iowa provided a large number of men for the Union army, particularly in light of the fact that a part of the state was still unsettled. The first call for soldiers, for ninety-day service only, was quickly oversubscribed. Following this three-month stint, three-year enlistments were typical. Unlike today, when Americans are accustomed to a federal selective-service process, the government in the 1860s relied on a state-by-state quota to be carried out by state governments. Iowans had no difficulty filling their quotas during most of the war. An often-told story about Governor Samuel J. Kirkwood reflects that fact. When Governor Kirkwood was doing his spring planting in 1861, he received word that President Lincoln wanted Iowa to furnish a regiment of militia. Kirkwood excitedly announced: "Why! The President wanted a whole regiment of men! Do you suppose I can raise as many as that?" Kirkwood's concern proved groundless as within two weeks he had the necessary thousand volunteers; he then wired Washington: "For God's sake send us arms! We have the men."[14]

Motivation for enlisting in the army obviously varied among individuals. Letters and diaries indicate that some men joined the military because they sensed a great adventure. Most men had never traveled far from home, and serving in the army would provide an opportunity to see more of the country. Certainly some men, perhaps the majority, possessed a sense of patriotism and a feeling of support for President Lincoln and his resolve to keep the Union together. The experience of nine young men from Spring Grove in Buchanan County gives convincing evidence of their patriotism; their letters and diaries support the view that they, at least, became soldiers to help preserve the Union. At the same time, there seemed to be little evidence that these young men felt strongly about freeing black slaves.[15]

The nine young men from Spring Grove—Isaac Arwine, John Cartwright, Isaac N. Holman, Stephen Holman, Vinson Holman, Pierce Walton, William Whisennand, John Leatherman, and Eli Holland—left Independence together on August 28 with some two thousand onlookers wishing them well. As part of the Ninth Iowa Infantry Regiment, crowds cheered them at every station along the way to Dubuque. Like other enlistees from Iowa, after being transported to an Iowa camp such as

Dubuque's Camp Franklin, the men were transferred to St. Louis, where they were "processed, assigned to training centers, and ultimately dispatched to their battlefield units or other duties." In St. Louis the men were given instruction in military drill and assigned weapons. For the next three months the nine Spring Grove men found themselves guarding a railroad between Pacific City and Rolla, Missouri. Like soldiers elsewhere, the Ninth Iowa Infantry experienced considerable ill health before members saw action. One soldier wrote on December 21 that 175 of the regiment had been hospitalized "mostly suffering from measles, mumps, pneumonia and typhoid." The nine young men also experienced the monotony and boredom of war. Vinson Holman wrote on January 8, "One of the offalist meanist days I ever saw. ... there was an inspection of our things but it did not amount to nothing."[16]

During the remainder of their tour, most of the Spring Grove men would see duty in several areas. At Pea Ridge, Arkansas, the Ninth Iowa took heavy losses, suffering a casualty rate of approximately 40 percent. In March 1862 one of the men, Isaac Arwine, died. His brother-in-law, Vinson Holman, graphically recorded Arwine's death:

> We put a couple of blankets around him in a big grave and covered him up. It looks hard but cant be helped. We have no boards to make any kind of a box. there wasnt no Man that suffered any more while he lived—his pain was so great that it gave him the lock Jaw—he was in his rite mind all the while— half of his breath came out of a wound on his back—he smelt awfal—it was enough to make any body sick to be around. ... he said he was very sorry that he could not get home once more but he said it was the fate of war and his time has come and he must go. ... I dont believe he would have suffered any more if he had been burnt up.[17]

Only six months after enlisting, three of the nine Spring Grove men were dead and three disabled. Of the latter, Stephen Holman recovered from his wounds and rejoined the regiment in July. Vinson Holman and Eli Holland also remained in the army. Vinson Holman died in December 1863 in Memphis from jaundice. When the war ended, only one of the Spring Grove men, Eli Holland, was still a part of the Ninth Iowa Infantry Regiment.[18]

Like Isaac Arwine, John Cartwright, William Whisennand, and Vinson Holman, thousands of other Iowans lost their lives in the war. Out of the approximately 70,000 Iowans who served, 3,540 were killed or mortally wounded. Another 8,498 died of disease, while 515 died in prison camps of disease or starvation. A total of 8,500 were seriously wounded but survived. Many men fought in the Lower Mississippi Valley and in Georgia, where they were unaccustomed to the environment and had little immunity to local disease.[19]

Some Iowans, like George Tod of Fort Dodge, served as mere youths. As a sixteen-year-old, Tod persuaded military officials to accept him into the army as a drummer boy, since he had not reached the minimum-age limit for regular soldiering. Accompanying troops into battle, Tod was captured two years later and sent to Andersonville, the Confederate's most notorious prison. Once there, young Tod survived mostly on resourcefulness. He located a tree stump, which he used for fuel, preparing meals for other men for pay. Escaping from the prison, he was soon recaptured. Tod escaped again, this time evading Confederate authorities for six months until he finally managed to link up with Union troops.[20]

While thousands of Iowa men enlisted in the army, several hundred received commissions and served as officers. Grenville Dodge is perhaps the best-known Civil War officer from Iowa. Born in Massachusetts in 1831, Dodge was trained in civil and military engineering before coming west to survey for railroad routes. Immediately following the outbreak of war, Dodge raised a company of volunteers from his home area of Council Bluffs. Governor Kirkwood then sent Dodge to Washington to secure arms and ammunition for Iowa's newly enlisted soldiers. Dodge succeeded admirably, returning with six thousand muskets. Following Dodge's commission as colonel of the Fourth Iowa Infantry, he and his men fought in southern Missouri and in the Battle of Pea Ridge in northern Arkansas. Dodge suffered wounds in both battles. Following Pea Ridge, however, Dodge was transferred to the Army of Tennessee, where he came to the attention of General U. S. Grant. Dodge had proved particularly adept at directing the rebuilding of Southern railroads and made his greatest contribution to the war effort through directing the construction of bridges and the rebuilding of Southern railroads for use by the Union army.[21]

Although seldom recognized by historians, Dodge was also innovative in the gathering of military intelligence in the South. In recruiting both men and women to be agents, Dodge exercised great caution. His most trusted spy, Philip Henson, was a Southern Unionist and was perceived by Dodge to be very good at his work. Dodge typically paid an agent $250 per mission, but in some cases, particularly where Henson was involved, Dodge tried to compensate the person in extra ways. After Henson's first mission Dodge gave the agent a fine horse and later paid him $1,000 for one assignment. Some spies, like Mary Malone, were used over and over by Dodge, though others were employed only for a short time. If agents were captured, they could count on no help from Dodge or any Union official. Henson was captured twice, the first time by General Robert E. Lee; both times, however, Henson managed to convince his captors that he was a loyal Southerner.[22]

Although many Iowans enlisted and some were commissioned, those drafted could hire substitutes. If the draftee did not wish to serve, he had two options. He could pay three hundred dollars for commutation, or he could pay for a substitute. According to Leland Sage, many men simply evaded the law by being absent when the draft notice arrived.[23] While serving in the army himself, Cyrus Carpenter, later governor of Iowa, wrote his fiancée in Fort Dodge that he did not want his younger brother going into the army, as he feared for the younger man's health. Carpenter was willing to pay up to one thousand dollars for a substitute, to keep his brother at home. Matilda Peitzke Paul, an Iowa farm woman, had a seventeen-year-old brother who served as a substitute soldier for a year. She remembered his homecoming:

> One afternoon ... the stage driver stopped at our door bringing a pale and sick-looking passenger. It was my oldest brother who was returning from the Civil War. He was sick most of the time while in the south ... and finally was dismissed and brought home sick and unable to sit up. ... He was very weak and slept most of the time. ... He was too young to be drafted to go to war but was hired as a substitute by a man who had been drafted.[24]

Though most Iowans supported the war, a sizable and vocal minority did not. Sometimes referred to as Copperheads and sometimes—in a kinder vein—as Peace Democrats, antiwar Iowans often experienced

ridicule, physical intimidation, and even possible lynching. Although critics might charge that Copperheads were the riffraff of Iowa society, that
was not usually the case. One prominent Iowan who opposed the war was
Charles Mason, the first chief justice of the Iowa Territorial Supreme
Court. Born on a farm in New York State, Mason had attended West Point,
where he had excelled academically: He graduated in 1829, ranking first
in his class. While there, he became friends with numerous Southerners,
including Robert E. Lee, Jefferson Davis, and Joseph E. Johnston. Later,
in the 1850s, Mason served as an official in the United States Patent Office.

Dennis Mahony of Dubuque was also a Peace Democrat. Born in Ireland, Mahony immigrated with his parents to the United States. Settling in
Dubuque with its large Catholic population seemed a logical move for
Mahony, where he eventually became editor of the Dubuque *Herald.* With
his own newspaper to express his views, Mahony became an outspoken
critic of President Lincoln and his policies. Mahony did not approve of
slavery, but he did believe the Southern states had a right to decide their
own position on the issue. Mahony charged the President with fighting an
illegal war because Congress had not issued a declaration of war against
the seceded states.[25]

Mahony, along with several other Iowans, would pay a price for dis-
sent. He was arrested in 1862, along with other dissenters, sent to Washington, D.C., and kept in jail with no charges being filed against him. In
effect, Mahony's constitutional rights had been violated because, when ar-
resting him, federal officials had suspended the writ of habeas corpus. Mahony's arrest brought cries of outrage from many Iowans, including Governor Kirkwood, who wrote federal officials requesting Mahony's release.
Three months later Mahony was released but not told the reason for his
imprisonment. Hubert Wubben described Mahony as a "bitter man" after
his release from Old Capital Prison. Mahony continued his protests
against the war.[26]

A third Peace Democrat or Copperhead, George Wallace Jones, was
also highly visible in the state, serving as a United States senator. Jones
had been a former classmate of Jefferson Davis at Transylvania University
and continued to correspond with Davis after the start of the war. Federal
authorities intercepted Jones's letters and, as a result, regarded him with
suspicion. Even though Jones protested his innocence and reiterated his

support for the Union, he served two months in prison and soon after disappeared from public life.[27]

As the examples of Mason, Mahony, and Jones show, there were few common characteristics shared by Iowans labeled Copperheads. Some had been born in the North and some in the South. Some, like the Quakers, opposed the war on religious grounds, believing that all wars were wrong. By 1860 many Friends resided in Iowa towns clearly considered Quaker communities, including New Providence, West Branch, Springdale, and Salem.

Economic reasons also influenced some Iowans to oppose the war and therefore lay themselves open to the charge that they were Copperheads. By 1860 the state contained numerous immigrant groups, many of whom lived in river cities like Dubuque. As David Lendt has pointed out in his study of the Copperhead Press in Iowa, some first-generation Irish Americans feared that if black slaves were freed, they might come north and compete for jobs. Believing blacks might work for cheaper wages than whites, some immigrants therefore opposed the war on economic grounds. Farmers and businessmen in eastern Iowa also opposed the war. By 1860 some farmers shipped their agricultural products by railroad, but many continued to rely on river transportation. As long as the Mississippi River remained open, goods could be shipped to Southern markets, particularly New Orleans. Farmers and eastern-Iowa businessmen feared a war might close off river traffic and opposed the war on those grounds.[28]

Given the strong patriotic sentiment of most Iowans and the unpopularity of the antiwar element, it is not surprising that confrontations occurred. The most serious incident was the Tally War, also known as the Skunk River War. On August 1, 1863, Peace Democrats held a rally outside of South English, after which they rode through the town. Residents of South English, known for their pro-Republican feelings, did not take kindly to the presence of antiwar people. The two groups exchanged words, and as the confrontation grew more heated, there was an exchange of gunfire. The Reverend Cyphert Tally, the main speaker at the antiwar rally, was killed instantly. Outraged by his death, Tally's friends vowed revenge and reassembled some sixteen miles south, at the Skunk River. Town residents requested that Governor Kirkwood send troops to provide protection against the Skunk River army—estimated unrealistically all the way from five hundred to four thousand men. Kirkwood did dispatch troops, but before they arrived, Tally's supporters had largely disbanded. Officials later arrested twelve suspects in Tally's murder, but a grand jury failed to indict anyone. Local residents apparently knew the guilty party but managed to keep the person's identity secret for many years.[29]

College campuses were also not immune from emotional outbursts regarding antiwar sentiment. The 1863 commencement at Cornell College bordered on a near riot when several young men and women appeared wearing Copperhead badges cut from one-cent pieces: "One girl about 18 years of age who had a Copperhead pin was assaulted by the loyal women present, and a severe scuffle ensued, during which the girl aforesaid had her wearing apparel [sic] badly used up. The young men gave up their badges and shouted three cheers for the nation."[30] At the University of Iowa, officials expelled a student for "wearing his Copperhead badge in defiance of rules of the University."[31]

While the war dominated Iowans' thoughts and activities, life on the home front often proceeded much as before. For many families life was obviously disrupted with fathers, husbands, and brothers marching off to war; yet Iowans still had to contend with the usual array of domestic issues related to day-to-day living. Behavior of young people was a constant concern of parents, and the war years were no exception. The Burlington *Hawk-Eye* noted in April 1862, "It is a generally admitted fact ... that many good citizens of Burlington are raising up idle and worthless children, more particularly boys." A Des Moines resident exclaimed that "young America" needed some supervision. He lamented that "Lads scarcely out of the pantelets can smoke, chew tobacco and swear equal to the most accomplished rowdies in the larger cities." Other newspapers around the state expressed similar views. Some citizens sounded the alarm in regard to a long-standing moral problem—houses of prostitution. Davenport citizens expressed concern that naive, newly recruited soldiers would be seduced by local prostitutes, some of whom were also described as thieves. Apparently at least a few Davenport citizens lost patience with the situation, as they burned down "a house of doubtful purity."[32]

Prohibition also concerned Iowans both before and during the war. The issue had surfaced as early as 1855, when the newly formed Republican legislature passed the state's first Prohibition law. Even though the law was repealed a few years later, the issue did not disappear. Some cities, like Davenport, experienced strong temperance revivals. A

Dubuque resident believed that the state needed a state inebriate asylum to deal with problem drinkers. He theorized if they were forced to go without liquor for a sufficient period of time, "they might acquire strength to resist temptation."[33]

As fathers, husbands, and other male relatives went into the military, women took over farms and businesses and generally became both mothers and fathers to their children. With a farm-labor shortage in 1862, some newspaper editors urged women to take on field work. The Dubuque *Herald* noted that it would be good for women "to leave behind corsets, belts and cosmetics" and, in turn, "strengthen their frames ... grow robust instead of slender, rosy instead of pallid, brown rather than delicate" as they became field hands.[34] Regardless of motivation, many women did assume farm work and management responsibilities. One woman decided that by buying nine cows and thus making and selling butter, she could support her family. Women also took over family businesses during the war.[35]

Hundreds of Iowa women contributed to the war effort through relief work. Early in the conflict, women formed soldiers'-relief societies through which they raised money for clothing, supplies, and food for men on the front lines. Much of the relief effort was directed to Keokuk, Iowa's southeasternmost city, which served as the hub of Civil War activities for the state. Keokuk served as a collection point for relief supplies, which were then shipped south on the Mississippi River.

Of all the women involved in relief work, the most prominent was Annie Wittenmyer. A young widow at the time, Wittenmyer watched three brothers go off to war. Wittenmyer helped organize Keokuk's Soldiers' Aid Society, serving as its corresponding secretary. She also traveled into the field to observe conditions firsthand. On a trip to Missouri, Wittenmyer visited her youngest brother, who was recuperating in an army hospital. Appalled that he had only strong black coffee, fried fat bacon, and a slice of bread to eat, Wittenmyer suggested to army officials that diet kitchens be established. She reasoned that only with adequate food could patients like her brother recover. Wittenmyer's concerns about inadequate food produced results, as the U.S. Christian Commission eventually funded diet kitchens. Before the end of the war, Wittenmyer urged the creation of yet another new facility: homes for soldiers' orphans. This request had originated with soldiers themselves, fearful that if they did not return from the war, their children might be homeless. Eventually two such homes were established.[36]

The spring of 1865 would bring an end to the bloody conflict that had brought untold suffering to Iowans and Americans everywhere. On April 9, 1865, at Appomattox Court House in Virginia, Generals Robert E. Lee and Ulysses S. Grant agreed on terms to end the fighting between the Union and the Confederacy. Almost four years to the day after the war began, Iowa soldiers could finally think of returning home to resume their disrupted lives. Back in Iowa, however, they would soon witness considerable change. Railroad building had resumed in 1865, and two years later Iowans could boast of a railroad running from the Mississippi to the Missouri River. More economic expansion soon followed, as in the 1870s, Iowans witnessed the development of numerous farm-related industries.

Iowans also experienced major political realignment that foreshadowed many years of Republican dominance. By the mid-1850s most Iowans had indicated a preference for the Republican party, and that view would waver only slightly for the next one hundred years. Iowa governors, with one exception, would be Republicans from the mid-1850s to the 1930s; the General Assembly would also be controlled by Republicans. Herbert Hoover, born in the Quaker community of West Branch, remembered his home community as solidly Republican and, in turn, as a community that regarded Democrats in a rather dubious light:

> There was only one Democrat in the village. He occasionally fell under the influence of liquor; therefore in the opinion of our village he represented all the forces of evil. At times he relapsed to goodness in the form of a ration of a single gumdrop to the small boys who did errands at his store. He also bought the old iron [which paid] for firecrackers on the Fourth of July. He was, therefore, tolerated and he served well and efficiently for a moral and political example.[37]

Although the Civil War obviously had a major impact on the state, many changes that followed stemmed not from the conflict itself but from events and conditions that preceded it. Iowans appeared to be well ensconced within the Republican party by 1860. Republicans' ability to wave the "bloody shirt" strengthened their position, but it did not produce the original allegiance to the party.

The issue of economic expansion might be viewed in this same context, as it can be argued that, at best, the war only slowed Iowa's settlement and economic expansion. Iowa's population continued to grow after the war, particularly with thousands of foreigners settling here. It is difficult to imagine any aspect of major economic development that might have been significantly different had the war not occurred.

Finally, the Civil War can be viewed as marking the end of the frontier period in Iowa. It serves as a convenient demarcation after which railroads were completed, initial settlement ended, and major industrial expansion begun. Given these changes, for most Iowans contemplating their future in the period immediately after the war, that future must have looked bright indeed.

6

Cultural Diversity: Immigrants and African Americans in the Hawkeye State, 1833–80

During its first fifty years of settlement, Iowa attracted a small but growing number of African Americans from the South, and emigrants from numerous European countries. Although many of the latter group located in cities in the Northeast, a sizable number traveled into the nation's heartland, settling in large numbers on the rolling prairies of the Midwest. African Americans also began arriving in Iowa even before statehood. The first blacks settled in Mississippi River towns—having migrated upriver from the South—and in communities along Iowa's southern border. Although Iowa would not contain large numbers of any racial minority or European-born population in the nineteenth century (or even in the twentieth), African Americans and European emigrants who did settle here brought considerable cultural diver-

---

A Turner Hall at Davenport provided facilities for
German Americans. Photo courtesy of the State
Historical Society of Iowa, Iowa City.

sity to the state. Observers have often tended to group all European-born together, dismissing them as culturally homogeneous; however, though western Europeans shared some traits, there were countless cultural, religious, and economic differences between English, Irish, Swedish, and German emigrees.

The experiences of African Americans and most European emigrants in Iowa stood in sharp contrast. State officials openly recruited white Europeans in the 1870s, feeling that Iowa needed more settlers to help spur economic growth.[1] For Iowa's black residents, however, the experience would be decidedly mixed. In the early 1840s Iowa was described as one of the most racist territories in the country, but after the Civil War, Iowans would rapidly alter that view by extending numerous legal rights to blacks. At the same time, African Americans here as elsewhere would face barriers to employment, housing, and equal access to local services. As Iowa's experience makes so abundantly clear, the securing of legal rights did not automatically lead to an open, integrated society with equal access to all. The history of Iowa's major racial and immigrant groups will be treated in two parts in this book. This chapter deals with the groups' early history—from the 1830s through the post–Civil War period—whereas Chapter 11 covers the years from 1880 to 1930.

The migration of African Americans from the South into Iowa can be classified into three general categories: those who came in the 1840s and 1850s by way of the Mississippi River; those who came in the same period but traveled up the Missouri River; and those who came in the post–Civil War era, mainly to work as coal miners. In the first two categories, the migrants usually sought work in river towns such as Davenport or Sioux City. Often the migrants were either attracted to or recruited for work where white labor was scarce. The number of blacks in Iowa increased between 1840 and 1860—from 188 to 1,069—but the total number still remained low.[2]

Once in Iowa, black males worked as laborers in river communities, loading and unloading cargo from riverboats, chopping and stacking wood used as fuel; they also worked as lead miners in the Dubuque area, and in every river community as porters and waiters. Steamboat traffic was lighter on the Missouri than on the Mississippi, which probably meant fewer jobs for black males in Sioux City and Council Bluffs. Black women worked as domestics, laundresses, cooks, and housekeepers. In general, both African-American males and females had little choice but to take menial, lower-paying jobs, since higher-paying jobs were usually open only to whites.[3]

Not all blacks who settled in river towns were laborers, however. Alexander Clark, called the "most prominent Negro in Iowa from Civil War days almost to the close of the century," arrived here in 1842. Clark was born in Pennsylvania in 1826, lived in Cincinnati for a time, where he learned the barbering trade, and then opened a shop in Muscatine. Described as "shrewd in business matters," Clark later purchased timberland and contracted to provide wood for steamboats. He retired from barbering at the age of forty-two, apparently enjoying a prosperous retirement.[4]

African Americans settled in all major river communities before the Civil War. Lead mining was already an important industry in the Dubuque region when that community came into existence in 1833, and a small number of blacks were present there from its inception. When Methodists set out to raise funds for the town's first church in 1834, at least six local African Americans—some of whom may have been slaves—had their names listed as subscribers, pledging amounts from 12.5 to 50 cents. One black woman, Charlotte Morgan, was a charter member of the congregation. By 1840 Dubuque's blacks numbered seventy-two, about 5 percent of the town's population, and 42 percent of all blacks living in Iowa. Later in the decade that population would decline by half.[5]

As Robert Dykstra has observed, little is known about individual blacks who came to Dubuque before the Civil War. A Missouri slave known only as Ralph arrived in 1834. As discussed in Chapter 5, Ralph became a free man as a result of living on free soil. One year earlier, Nathaniel and Charlotte Morgan came to Dubuque from the mining community of Galena, Illinois. Both husband and wife went to work in a local boardinghouse; later Nathaniel worked as a hotel cook and waiter while Charlotte worked as a laundress. Unlike Ralph, Nat Morgan did not fare well in Dubuque. After Nat and Charlotte had lived there for seven years, local men accused Nat of stealing a trunk full of clothes. Although he denied the theft, the white men whipped and beat him almost to death before hanging him. Officials never recovered the trunk and later acquitted Morgan's killers.[6]

Other areas settled by African Americans before the Civil War included Muscatine, known by 1850 as the "new capital of Afro-American Iowa." In 1840 the town had twenty-five black residents, with some working for a local sawmill owner and the others apparently employed as house servants. Within the next ten years black residents were able to establish independent households. As Dykstra has written, unlike Dubuque blacks, blacks in Muscatine were able to develop "a true black community, possessing its own institutions and structure of leadership." The organization of an African Methodist Episcopal church in 1849 provided evidence of that community. Muscatine's early black citizens included, in addition to Alexander Clark, Thomas C. Motts, the town's wealthiest black citizen. Motts owned a barbershop as well as a coal-delivery business and, by age forty-six, owned real estate worth six thousand dollars. By 1850 Muscatine's black workforce included a laborer, a painter, a blacksmith, three cooks, four barbers, and two teamsters.[7] Because census takers did not typically single out women who took boarders into their homes, it is possible that women earned money from that practice, thus serving as unacknowledged but important wage earners.

Even though small numbers of blacks had been present in Iowa since territorial days, the political and social climate was usually inhospitable, if not hostile. Robert Dykstra has called Iowa "one of the most racist territories in the North in the 1840s."[8] As discussed in Chapter 5, Iowans had enacted territorial laws known as the Black Code, which erected barriers against blacks locating here. Both the territorial and state constitutions frequently used the word "white" when dealing with privileges such as voting and serving in the legislatures, thus excluding African Americans. Statutes also excluded black children from attending public schools.[9]

In 1851 Iowans again revealed their hostile attitude toward blacks. In that year the General Assembly passed an "exclusionary law" that prohibited African Americans from coming into Iowa, the first Northern state to do so. The law stated that blacks already living here could remain and own property, but officials were required to notify newcomers within three days that they had to leave. If they did not, they could be arrested and fined two dollars for each day they remained.[10]

Once the exclusionary law passed, however, it did not become effective, due to a rather unlikely circumstance. At the time, all laws passed by the General Assembly were to be listed in the Mount Pleasant *True Democrat,* a necessary prerequisite before legislation could go into effect.

The *True Democrat* editor held antislavery views and, not wishing to promote the discriminatory policy, failed to publish the exclusionary law. As a result, the law never went into effect. That outcome, however, does not alter the fact that Iowans, like most Northerners at the time, believed the presence of blacks in their state was undesirable.[11]

Following the Civil War, the legal status of Iowa's African Americans would undergo rapid and startling change. In 1868 Iowans extended suffrage to black males. This was a highly unusual move, as before 1868 only five New England states did so, and in the decade of the sixties only two states, Minnesota and Iowa, took such action. During the next fifteen years African Americans would witness even more positive changes in legal and educational areas.

The reasons for granting black male suffrage have been debated through the pages of Iowa's history journals. Robert Dykstra has argued that Republicans, by 1865 Iowa's dominant political party, included a provision in their 1865 platform to enfranchise black males simply because it was the right moral position. Once the provision became a party objective, many Republicans (including state legislators) continued to support the amendment until it appeared before the general electorate in 1868. In other words, enfranchising black males was the right action taken for the right reasons. Voters approved the referendum in effect, calling for removal of the word "white" in the voting clause of the state constitution. Dykstra believes that this action turned Iowa into "one of the most egalitarian states in the Union."[12]

At the same time, Hubert H. Wubben has argued that, essentially, Iowans continued to be racist in their views in 1865. Wubben questions the depth of Iowa Republicans' convictions regarding black male suffrage and believes other factors were involved. These included certain parliamentary maneuverings that brought support of the plank and, subsequently, Republican support for the issue. Wubben writes that the Republicans thought they could not "lose on any issue which they had introduced and which [the Democrats opposed]." Once the convention voted to include the suffrage plank, Wubben believes, the party felt committed to continue supporting it, regardless of public antipathy. Wubben argues that "positive evidence to support the idea that by the summer of 1865 Iowa Republicans were disposed toward black suffrage ... is hard to find," even though he acknowledges that many Republicans believed enfranchising black males was the proper moral position.[13] As Wubben indicates, however, holding that view was quite different from taking decisive, direct action in light of strong opposition.

The same year that black male suffrage was granted, education for black children became a public issue, particularly their right to attend the public schools. Before the Civil War black children were legally barred from attending public schools. An early educational law passed in 1847 stated: "Schools would be 'open and free alike to all white persons in the school district between the ages of five and twenty-one years.'" An even earlier law called for county assessors to list only "the white inhabitants of all ages" in each county.[14]

In 1850, although still legally barred from doing so, 17 black youngsters apparently attended public schools. The census of 1850 listed 12 males and 5 females—out of a total of 122 blacks of legal school age—attending school (as reported by their families).[15] Apparently this situation continued, with black children attending school in some counties but not in others. In 1858 the General Assembly passed legislation calling for school boards to provide separate facilities for black youths, except where white persons already attending gave unanimous consent for black attendance. Although state school reports made no mention of separate school buildings for blacks, according to Leola Bergmann, separate schools existed in at least three communities, Muscatine, Keokuk, and Dubuque. With the exception of only a few communities, however, following the passage of the 1858 law, black children apparently continued to attend some white public schools rather than segregated ones.[16]

Educational barriers against black children, however, would soon be eliminated. In 1868 Alexander Clark brought suit against the Muscatine school because his daughter, Susan, was not allowed to attend the public school maintained for white children. Clark won the case when the Iowa Supreme Court ruled that the school board could not require children to attend a separate school because of "race, religion, or economic status." A second case in 1874 and a third case in 1875 supported the previous decision. In 1875 the court also ruled that segregation of passengers on Mississippi steamboats was illegal, a rule that extended to common carriers throughout the state. These actions, as Joseph Wall has pointed out, preceded by twenty years the establishment by the United States Supreme Court of the "separate but equal" doctrine. Moreover, Iowa had taken this action before most other Northern states did so.[17]

In 1884 the last enactment of major nineteenth-century legislation took place regarding African Americans when the General Assembly passed the Civil Rights Act, patterned after the federal Civil Rights Act of 1875. The law stated that "all persons within this state shall be entitled to the full and equal enjoyment of the accommodations, advantages, facilities and privileges of inns, public conveyances, barber shops, theaters and other places of amusement." Eight years later the General Assembly added more categories to the law, including restaurants, lunch counters, bathhouses, and "other places where refreshments are served." With this legislation Iowans within sixteen years had moved to grant full legal rights to black males, extend public education to black children, and guarantee access to many public facilities. Though Iowans had earlier displayed intense hostility toward African Americans, within an amazingly brief period they had reversed positions, thus making their state one of the most progressive in civil equality for blacks.[18]

The moral conscience that motivated Iowans to extend various legal rights to blacks did not carry over into the economic sphere. Black citizens' rights to vote or attend public schools often had little, if any, effect in helping them find decent jobs or adequate housing. Employment patterns remained much the same as before the Civil War, with both black males and females typically relegated to menial-work positions.

After the Civil War river cities continued to provide blacks with limited employment opportunities. At Keokuk, where steamboat cargo required special handling because of rapids in the river, black workers by 1870 were hauling the cargo that earlier had been transported by Irish laborers. River traffic remained high through the 1870s, providing work for both white and black laborers. Railroad building, which started in the 1850s, provided employment for some blacks, and by the 1870s provided African Americans with work as porters, waiters, and cooks.

Sioux City attracted an increasing number of African Americans after the Civil War. Initially blacks worked as steamboat deckhands and later helped build sidewalks and put down cedar-block pavement in the city. According to Leola Bergmann, blacks started many businesses in Sioux City, including "barber shops, laundries, dance halls, gambling houses, and restaurants." In some cases, such as a rug-cleaning establishment, blacks started the first businesses. As in other communities, Sioux City blacks worked as waiters and doormen, but also as mailmen and policemen. After 1900, when many black-owned businesses closed, blacks went to work in local packing plants.[19]

Throughout the nineteenth century a limited number of African Americans also settled on the land. In the 1850s a small group left Illinois and resettled in Westfield Township in Fayette County. Within three years the group contained fifty-nine people, and all but one of the males were farmers. Leola Bergmann writes that before or during the Civil War, blacks coming into Iowa "often settled on the first suitable piece of land or in the first little village they came to after crossing the border." Adam and Martha Johnson provide an example of that migration. In the late 1880s the Johnsons left Tennessee and settled in Taylor County, where they purchased 160 acres of land.[20]

After the Civil War, African Americans became involved in coal mining, an industry that would play a major part in their lives for the next fifty years. In 1880 Henry Miller, an Albia coal operator, imported black men from Missouri to break a strike. Miller would be the first in a long line of Iowa operators to resort to this practice. Typically, after the strike was settled, some black workers continued as miners. After 1880 coal operators also recruited Southern blacks, particularly from Virginia, as regular miners.[21]

Although the number of blacks remained small in most coal camps, the community of Muchakinock proved an exception. In 1880 the Consolidation Coal Company (a subsidiary of the Chicago and North Western Railroad) took over Muchakinock and, faced with a strike, sent African American Hobe Armstrong south to recruit workers. Armstrong recruited heavily in the areas of Charlottesville and Staunton, Virginia. Later Consolidation recruited blacks as regular mine workers with the result that Muchakinock soon became identified as a black community.[22]

By the 1880s the number of Iowa African Americans had reached 9,516 with the largest numbers located in Lee, Polk, Pottawattamie, Mahaska, Wapello, Henry, Des Moines, Page, Scott, and Boone counties. Counties bordering either the Mississippi or Missouri rivers, including Lee, Pottawattamie, Des Moines, and Scott, presumably had retained their black populations from before the 1860s; moreover, these counties contained urban areas, such as Sioux City, Council Bluffs, Davenport, and Burlington. Page County apparently attracted numerous black families both before and after the Civil War. Leola Bergmann explains, "The town of Amity, Page County, was the first Underground Railroad station north of the Missouri line in the southwestern corner of the State and many fugitives found refuge there and in other villages of the county." After the Civil War started, additional blacks crossed into Iowa and settled in Page County. Bergmann also notes that after the war blacks began to move from rural areas to urban areas, a tendency that would become more pronounced in later decades.[23]

At a slightly earlier time than African Americans started settling in Iowa, the first foreign-born arrived. Beginning in the 1820s, even before Iowa became a territory, English, Irish, and German immigrants came to work in the lead mines around present-day Dubuque; by the mid-1800s the number of immigrants was gradually increasing as more people emigrated from the British Isles and the German provinces, as well as from Scandinavia, Bohemia, and Holland. In the early years of settlement Iowa attracted only a small number of foreign-born, with that number gradually increasing before the Civil War and then expanding more rapidly after the war. Iowa contained 20,969 persons of foreign birth in 1850; the number increased to 204,692 by 1870, and 261,650 by 1880.[24]

Although each nationality group would differ in background and in expectations, some generalizations can be made about the Iowa immigrant experience. Europeans would emigrate here in two distinct groups: those coming between 1820 and 1900, and those arriving between 1900 and 1920. The first phase involved emigrants from western Europe and the British Isles and took place at a time when the country was expanding rapidly both territorially and industrially; therefore, additional factory workers and farmers were not only welcomed, but sometimes recruited. After 1900 the numbers arriving from western Europe and the British Isles lessened while the number of emigrants from southern and eastern Europe increased.

During the first phase of immigration, Germans, Irish, English, and Scandinavians predominated, immigrating primarily in family units. Sometimes one or two family members arrived first, as in the case of Victor and Maria Petersson, and then assisted additional relatives, thus creating a chain of successive migration. The Peterssons, twenty-year-old Victor and his twelve-year-old sister, Maria, left Sweden in 1879 bound for Muchakinock. It appears the emigration of Victor and Maria was the first step in a well-planned venture, as within two years their remaining five siblings, except for the oldest brother, had also arrived in Muchakinock, including one sister's husband and three children. Several years later Victor and Maria's mother, uncle, and three cousins joined the family. Subsequently, the uncle convinced his brother and two sisters to come to America. In total, within roughly a decade, twenty-six people bound together by family ties left the village of Karlskoga for a new life in a coal-mining community in southeastern Iowa.[25] Although the Petersson males initially went to work as coal miners, most immigrants from western Europe would become farmers.

Regardless of origins, the decision to emigrate rested generally on a variety of conditions, some present in the homeland and some in the host country. This motivational duality has been described as push-pull factors. Europe in the nineteenth century contained millions of people who labored long and hard, with few prospects of improving their economic lot. In country after country, poor and middling families viewed emigration as a way out of a life with either dismal or limited rewards, particularly for their offspring. One second-generation Swedish American, Myron Anderson, explained why his family left Sweden for American in 1866: "Times were hard in Sweden. ... The famine of 1860 was particularly severe and led to much immigration. ... Conditions were due in part to overpopulation. The clergy and governmental agencies were conscious of this difficulty and tried to restrain men from marrying until they were well past 30 years of age."[26]

Poverty provided a push factor for Europeans in both earlier and later phases of immigration. While hardship existed in all countries, the Irish experienced the most extreme conditions. In the 1840s the potato crop, the nation's main—and in some cases, almost total—food source simply vanished. The result was that millions of Irish either starved or were forced to leave Ireland. In general, land hunger would provide a major motivation or push factor for all European groups.

Although positive economic conditions in America served as the greatest attraction—or pull factor—to those considering emigration, other considerations were also present. Some groups, unhappy with threats to religious freedom in their homeland, knew they could worship freely in the United States. Religious considerations served as the primary attraction for a group of seven hundred Hollanders who settled in Marion

County in 1847. Swedes who settled near Dayton left their homeland partially for religious reasons. Sweden contained a state church in which members had little control over church politics or even over the selection of a pastor. The church appointed ministers for life, so if parishioners did not approve of a pastor, they had little choice but to tolerate him. Many Swedes resented the fact that the minister lived better than the parishioners.

Some Europeans departed their homelands for political reasons, political freedom in America being a great lure. In 1848 a group of Germans known as Forty-eighters arrived in the United States. These immigrants had taken part in a revolution in Europe, and because they were on the losing side, they feared for their safety. Some Forty-eighters settled in Davenport. In contrast to most nineteenth-century immigrants who had limited education and financial resources, most Forty-eighters were professionals who soon became involved in Davenport's professional and business community.[27] Other Germans would leave Europe because they feared military conscription for themselves or for their sons.

Once Europeans had made the decision to emigrate, they faced a long, arduous, and often dangerous journey across the Atlantic. During the days of the sailing ships (before 1850) emigrants could expect to spend six weeks or longer at sea. Because it was cheapest, most emigrants traveled steerage class, which meant they occupied the lowest decks in the boat, and ones with little ventilation. The only way to get fresh air into the steerage area was to open the hatches along the main deck. In bad weather, however, these were quickly closed to prevent the boat from taking on water.[28]

In the 1840s steamships became involved in transatlantic travel, producing a far faster way to travel from Europe to America. At first steamships carried only mail and a few passengers, but by the 1850s companies began to see the advantage of carrying more passengers. By 1852 regular steamship service operated between Liverpool and New York, with each boat carrying approximately four hundred passengers.

Some emigrants continued to use sailing ships for economic reasons. When August Anderson left Sweden in 1864 as a nine-year-old boy, he and his family traveled on a sailing ship because the cost was about half that of steamship travel. The company required that passengers provide most of their own food, enough to last three months. Accordingly, August's mother baked a three-month supply of hard, flat rye bread known as *Knäckerbröd,* while August's father caught and prepared a large supply of herring. The family probably also brought along a supply of potatoes and turnips.[29]

The Andersons and their six children experienced severe hardships on the crossing: The boat was crowded and dysentery was common; there was no water for washing, and toilet facilities were primitive; medical help was unavailable. During stormy weather the quarters were closed, which kept out both light and fresh air, causing passengers to fear they might suffocate. Worst of all, the Andersons' two-year-old son died on the voyage. Arriving in North America, the family went first to Quebec, then to Galesburg, Illinois, and later settled in Iowa.[30]

Among the many immigrant groups coming to Iowa, the Germans would be by far the most numerous. Emigrants arriving from German provinces settled in the Mississippi River communities, particularly Dubuque, Davenport, and Burlington. A few years later, as a result of the revolutions of 1848, 1.5 million Germans immigrated to the United States; of that number, about thirty thousand settled in Iowa.[31]

Germans in Davenport quickly reestablished the *Turnverein,* an organization created in their homeland with the motto "A sound mind in a sound body." The Turners, as the group came to be called in America, helped German Americans improve their physical and mental abilities, as well as provided a place to gather with fellow immigrants. The founding members of Davenport's first Turner group believed they should not only promote traditional goals as stated in the group's motto but also play an activist role in politics both in Germany and in the United States. The group soon shifted their interest from German concerns to domestic political issues, however. Topics discussed and debated by members included "Bureaucracy and Democracy," "Status of Women," "Lecture on the Natural Sciences," and "How Can We Counteract the Temperance Movement?" At the same time, the organization continued to emphasize physical activity for members. From soon after its founding in 1852, until well into the twentieth century, the Davenport club was recognized as one of the nation's largest and most financially sound Turner organizations.[32]

German Americans in other river communities also began forming Turner organizations, and at one time thirty-seven such groups existed in

Iowa. Like the original Davenport Turners, other members gradually shifted from emphasizing political discussions and intellectual endeavors to becoming more involved in social activities and gymnastic events. Members attended Turnfests organized at the local, regional, and national levels, where members socialized and competed in various physical activities. Females competed in some events, but always in smaller numbers than their male counterparts.[33]

One such event took place in 1873, when three thousand people attended a Turnfest in Dubuque. There members competed in gymnastic competition, with special events held for juvenile males. The Dubuque event reflected the diversity of activities and interests within the organization: In addition to gymnastic competition, the Turnfest agenda included performances by choral clubs and bands, organized marches, a declamation contest, and speech making by visiting dignitaries. Over time the type of physical activities offered by the Turners expanded to include fencing, boxing, marching, track-and-field events, rope climbing, and participation in drill teams.[34]

While most immigrant groups created organizations to perpetuate their Old World culture, help ease members into a new society, and maintain solidarity, the Germans through their Turner organizations clearly had the greatest success in accomplishing these goals. Most important, Turner organizations spoke to the needs of the immigrants themselves, providing them with a "sort of haven and anchor place." Turner clubs also served as mutual-aid societies whereby sick or unemployed members could receive weekly compensation. The Turners worked hard to promote both good physical health and intellectual development. And, through their political discussions and debates, they helped introduce members to American politics, informing them of important issues and urging members to acquire American citizenship. The Turners also affected wider society, as they worked hard, especially in Davenport, to have physical education taught in the public schools. As Janice Beran has pointed out, "The Turners are acknowledged as the first public school physical educators in Iowa."[35]

Though Germans expressed interest in a wide variety of political issues, they focused their greatest attention on Prohibition. As a group, German Americans strongly opposed Prohibition, an issue that dominated Iowa politics for over a century. A main point of concern for German Americans was how they might spend their Sundays. In Europe, Germans typically regarded the Sabbath as a day of rest and recreation during which people might go bowling, attend a trap shoot, or go to a beer garden to listen to music and drink beer. Spending the Sabbath in such manner was characterized by the term "Continental Sunday." Arriving in the United States, Germans quickly encountered the "Puritan Sunday," whereby people were expected to spend the day quietly, at home or at church. To many Germans beer was a staple of life that could not easily be done away with.

An incident that underscores the German Americans' view toward beer drinking took place in Davenport. Marx and Anna Goettsch, first-generation German Americans, had a son attending Cornell University; after being away for two years, the son returned home for a visit. A family historian described the reunion: "When [Julius] did return to Davenport, the first thing his mother asked him was not about school but rather 'How is the beer in Ithaca?' Julius replied that he really could not say since he did not have enough money to buy much of it. At this Anna turned white and exclaimed, 'My boy! My boy! Look what they've done to my boy! He's sick and hungry and doesn't get enough to drink!' "[36] Arriving home, Anna "ran into the kitchen and brought out a bucket of beer and a steaming dinner of sausage and sauerkraut." She was "horrified" that any of her sons would live in a place so "strange and alien" they could not get a basic staple like beer.[37]

While the river cities, particularly Davenport, would include many German-American professionals, business owners, and artisans, the greatest number of German immigrants in Iowa would become farmers. By the end of the century, every county in the state would have some German families settled on the land. Outside of Scott County, Carroll County would have the highest number of German Americans. Germans would continue immigrating after the turn of the century into areas such as Kossuth County, where German families would settle even into the teens.

German Americans not only displayed great diversity in occupations, but also in religious preference. While the two main groups were Catholic and Lutheran (some Evangelical, but a larger number Missouri Synod), Germans also embraced other denominations. Ethnic denominations such as German Baptist, German Methodist, German Presbyterian, and German Evangelical and Reform churches were scattered throughout the state.

While Germans had the greatest number of foreign-born in Iowa, the

Swedes also constituted a major immigrant group. Like the Germans, the Swedes demonstrated considerable diversity in settlement locations, occupations, and religious affiliations. Although most Swedes came to Iowa to purchase land and pursue agriculture, thousands took up crafts, business, and coal mining. In general, immigrants tended to come directly from their country of origin to Iowa, but substantial numbers of Swedes "stopped over" or first settled in Illinois. Galesburg, Victoria, and Bishop Hill were major Illinois communities where Swedish families resided before moving on to Iowa.

Iowa's first Swedish community, New Sweden, was founded in 1846 in Jefferson County. The town also had the distinction of being the first permanent nineteenth-century Swedish settlement in America. Peter Cassel, one of the original settlers from Kisa in Östergötland, not only helped found New Sweden, but also played a significant role in attracting other Swedes to America. New Sweden quickly attracted additional Swedish emigrants and by 1860 had over six hundred residents. Some Swedes, moreover, who settled elsewhere in the United States had originally intended to come to New Sweden. One such group from Östergötland encountered financial difficulties in Pennsylvania and, apparently not able to travel farther, remained in the state at Sugar Grove. As one Swedish scholar noted, the founding of New Sweden "spurred Swedish immigration to the entire country."[38]

After the founding of New Sweden, other Swedish communities appeared in Iowa. In 1846 a group of about thirty people headed by the Dalander family left Sweden, intending to join Peter Cassel at New Sweden. Following instructions sent them by Cassel, the group traveled by steamboat until they reached southeastern Iowa. Cassel apparently instructed the group that once they reached Iowa's southern border, they would immediately come to a tributary that flowed into the Mississippi from the west. This river would lead them to Cassel's settlement. It is not clear if Cassel's instructions were incomplete or if the group proceeded incorrectly, but once off the steamboat, the Dalander party proceeded along the north side of the Des Moines River rather than along the proper river, the Skunk. Some time later the Swedes found themselves at Fort Des Moines, located at the present site of Des Moines, where soldiers assured them there was no Swedish settlement in the area. The Swedes, however, convinced that their instructions must be right, continued upriver. They eventually arrived at the solitary settlement of Thomas Gaston, where they were able to buy sufficient food to survive the winter. By the following spring the group decided they liked the appearance of the area and decided to stay. Originally called Swede Point, their settlement was later renamed Madrid.[39]

While Swedish immigrants would eventually locate in almost every part of the state, one of the largest settlements took place in Montgomery County, eventually extending into Page, Cass, and Fremont counties. Known as the Halland settlement, and centered in the community of Stanton, it was named after B. M. Halland, a Swedish Lutheran minister of the Augustana Synod. Halland played the role of both settler and promoter. In 1869 the Burlington Railroad, building through southwestern Iowa, offered Halland the opportunity to select certain townships along the railroad's right-of-way to be held for the settlement of Swedes. In April 1869 Halland selected three townships in Montgomery County and two townships in Page County. The first settlers arrived from Neoga, Illinois, in the fall of the year, and many spent the winter in dugouts. The following spring they established farmsteads, paying between six dollars and eleven dollars per acre for land.[40]

While many Swedes pursued agriculture, a large number went to work as coal miners. For some early settlers, like those in Webster County, the mines offered an opportunity to supplement their income with winter employment. In Boone County some first- and second-generation Swedish immigrants regarded mining as part-time work, whereas others regarded it as a full-time occupation. In Muchakinock Swedish-born people made up the second-largest ethnic group within the camp.

The Swedes, like all immigrant groups in Iowa, would quickly organize churches and associations through which they could maintain their Old World culture. Although nineteenth-century Sweden had a state religion, the Swedish Lutheran Church, not all Swedish immigrants would remain within that denomination. For example, Swedes who settled in Des Moines in the latter nineteenth century quickly established Swedish Baptist and Swedish Methodist churches. In fact, Swedes there organized the Swedish Baptist Conference of Iowa in 1883. Other churches founded by the group included the Evangelical Free Church and the Swedish Mission Church.[41]

In Des Moines, Swedes also formed many mutual-aid societies. The first, the Swedish Laboring Society (later known as the Society Scandia), was founded in 1873 for the purpose of promoting thrift and savings. Members were to make monthly payments that could later be withdrawn by individuals in financial need. The Des Moines Swedish Americans organized their own insurance company, the Swedish Mutual Fire Insurance Company in 1881. The group also formed fraternal organizations, including the Norden Singing Society in 1896, composed of both Swedish and Norwegian Americans, and the Order of Vikings in 1916.[42]

The second major Scandinavian group, the Norwegians, made their first Iowa settlement in the late 1830s. This group had settled initially in Missouri but, unhappy with land there, headed north into Iowa and settled at Sugar Creek, six miles from Keokuk. Following this original settlement, few other Norwegians came to Iowa until the 1850s, when the number increased substantially, with most coming into the northern Iowa counties of Winnebago and Winneshiek. Most of these newcomers (or their parents) had earlier settled in Wisconsin or Illinois. Many Norwegians settled in and around Decorah, and today the community is home to the Vesterheim, a Norwegian-American museum. Some scholars have written that Norwegians chose northeast Iowa, with its uneven terrain and forested areas, because it reminded them of Norway. Although Norwegians would not be as widely scattered throughout the state as the Germans and, to a lesser degree, the Swedes, there would be sizable settlements in other areas, particularly Story County. Norwegian Americans, especially in the Decorah area, would have a wide range of occupations, but in general, most would pursue farming.

The Norwegians also quickly set about creating ways to preserve Norwegian culture, religion, language, and group solidarity. One of the ways they did this was through the publication of the *Decorah-Posten,* a Norwegian-language newspaper. Started in 1874 by B. Anundsen, a recent immigrant, the publication would eventually become the largest Norwegian-language newspaper in the country. Editor Anundsen immediately proclaimed the newspaper would contain "no politics," but rather local news; literary material, including short stories, poetry, and essays, would be emphasized. Anundsen avoided areas such as politics and religion, sure to embroil subscribers in controversy.[43]

Along with his distinct editorial policy, Anundsen experimented with other tactics. In the 1890s the newspaper began to make special offers available to its subscribers. In an unusual move, the *Decorah-Posten* offered a newspaper subscription for one year— plus a sewing machine— for the incredible price of $22.25. This practice resulted in local women referring to the sewing machine, sold under the name of Husvennen, as the *Decorah-Posten* sewing machine. The newspaper also offered watches, scissors, and even rubber stamps (with individuals' names) as premiums for subscriptions.[44]

The *Decorah-Posten* remained in existence for almost one hundred years, developing a large, loyal following. When readers moved to a new area, they took their subscription along, resulting in the popular slogan "Wherever Norwegians go, *Decorah-Posten* follows." Residents of Norway also subscribed to the newspaper—according to one account, they subscribed to find out what was happening in their own country. In reality, Norwegians read the newspaper to learn about immigrant activities in the United States. The paper's circulation peaked in the mid-1920s, when it totaled about forty-five thousand paying readers.[45]

Decorah would also be home to another distinctive Norwegian institution, Luther College. Founded in 1861, the school was begun as an all-male institution, which trained young men for the Lutheran ministry and stressed a classical curriculum.[46] Given the heavy concentration of Norwegians in the Decorah area and the development of the *Decorah-Posten*, Luther College, and the Vesterheim, the area has clearly served as the center of Norwegian-American activity in Iowa and in the Midwest.

The Danes, the third Scandinavian group, began arriving in Iowa some thirty years after the first Swedish settlement. Like other Europeans, Danes left their homeland because of economic difficulties; many also left because of religious conversion. Beginning in the 1850s religious groups, including the Mormons, Methodists, and Baptists, sought converts in Denmark. Once converted, Danes were encouraged to come to the United States. The Mormons, especially, were successful in recruiting, and between 1850 and 1860 over two thousand Danes came to this country, headed for the Great Salt Lake. Many Danes crossed the state of Iowa with the Mormon Handcart Brigade between 1856 and 1860. The handcart expedition originated when Mormon officials, given a shortage of funds to provide for travel, arranged for new converts to walk from the end of the railroad line in Coralville to Salt Lake City, a distance of some thirteen hundred miles. The converts pulled their supplies and possessions in hand-carts they had built in Coralville.[47]

Although small numbers of Danes settled in Clinton, Iowa City, and Cedar Rapids, the majority settled in southwest Iowa. This was a logical location, as the Danes did not start emigrating in significant numbers until 1870. By then much of the state had been settled and only the southwestern and northwestern parts still contained substantial areas of unsettled land. As railroads expanded into southwestern Iowa, some Danes worked as railroad hands, an activity leading to the first Danish settlement there. While working in Cass County, nine Danes purchased a section of land in Jackson Township. In 1868–69 the first Danish settlers survived the winter by living in a ten-by-fifteen-foot dugout. This group, along with a Baptist settlement at Cuppy's Grove, marked the beginning of the Danish settlement in southwest Iowa, eventually the largest rural settlement of Danes in the United States.[48]

Like other immigrant groups, the Danes wished to preserve their Danish heritage and used the traditional method of organizing a "society." Early in their settlement in Clinton and Davenport, Danes formed the Danish Society of Clinton and Lyons. According to the constitution and by-laws, the purpose was to promote the "interest and welfare" of Danes in the United States "by social entertainments and mutual assistance, by advice and aid in case of sickness." The Danes continued to form many societies, including those that promoted interest in art, literature, and athletics, and at Grand View College, the Danish-American Historical Association. Other groups included singing, temperance, language, school, and sewing societies; many lasted for only a short time. In 1884 the Danes established the Danish Mutual Insurance Association, and seven years later, a building-and-loan association in Des Moines.[49]

For Danes in southwestern Iowa, the town of Elk Horn in southern Shelby County became a major congregating place. Kristian Anker, a local Lutheran minister, described the cohesiveness of the community in the 1880s: "Visitors often say Elk Horn is a little Denmark. ... One may live for months in Elk Horn without needing to use any language other than Danish." Anker added: "If the Danish school and church do their work, I can not conceive of the time when Danish will not be the community language." Anker was referring, no doubt, to the fact that Elk Horn had numerous institutions with which to perpetuate Danish culture and language, including a folk high school and college. Surrounding areas also had large Danish settlements. Kimballton in neighboring Audubon County, Ringsted in Emmet County and Fredsville in Grundy County were also sometimes referred to as "little Denmarks."[50]

In the nineteenth century Iowa would attract significant numbers of emigrants from the British Isles. Between 1850 and 1880 emigrants from Ireland were the most numerous, with the English-born second. Emigrants from Wales and Scotland also settled in Iowa during the same decades, but in far fewer numbers than did either the Irish or English. Many of these newcomers went into farming, but many also went to work in Iowa's coal mines. Unlike the Swedes, emigrants from the British Isles often had experience as miners in their homelands. Many left England after 1847 because of a failure of the Miners' Association, an English trade union, believing that they could do better economically in the American coal industry.

British miners had considerable impact on the American coal industry. Most men were strongly committed to trade unions, and in many ways the British provided both a social and economic model for American miners. The British also brought along their mining technology. The two basic types of coal mining—the room-and-pillar and the long-wall methods—were used in Britain earlier, and later adopted by the American industry.[51] Many Welsh miners settled in and around Hiteman, a major coal-mining community in Monroe County. Located close to the county seat of Albia, Hiteman remained an important mining center well into the twentieth century. The Welsh brought along many cultural practices from their homeland, including the Eisteddfod, a Welsh singing contest. For years Hiteman residents held annual Eisteddfod contests, attracting participants from surrounding communities as well as from northeastern Missouri.[52]

Like the Welsh, emigrants from Scotland often went to work in Iowa's coal industry. Coal mining had been well established in Scotland long before the 1800s, and mining conditions there were viewed as the worst in Britain. Those conditions, no doubt, served as a push factor for some Scots to emigrate. The Scotch Americans were more visible before the turn of the century than later, with the largest group of foreign-born,

7,701, recorded in the census of 1890. While some remained in mining after 1900, others left the mines after a few years to purchase land and take
up farming. Like their English counterparts, Scottish miners played an active role in unions, especially the United Mine Workers of America.[53]

Although some Irish went to work in the coal mines, far more came
into Iowa to work as general laborers. Census reports show that in every
major river city, particularly Dubuque, Irish males frequently listed their
occupation as "laborer," whereby they dug ditches, loaded and unloaded
steamboat cargo, operated drays, and performed other manual labor. A
large number of Irish also came to Iowa to work on the railroads. The initial construction of Iowa's east-west railroad lines came only about a
decade after the Irish began immigrating to the United States because of
the potato famine. Railroads like the Illinois Central advertised in eastern
seaports for workers, and the Irish responded.[54] Some Irishmen later purchased land and became farmers. The Irish were visible in many areas
throughout the state, including Dubuque, Palo Alto, and Dallas counties.
Emmetsburg in northwest Iowa celebrates its Irish heritage with a parade
on St. Patrick's Day while local bars serve green beer.

The fourth group from the British Isles, the English, settled in many
parts of the state, particularly in the southern half. English immigrants, unlike most foreign-born groups who came from the poor and middling
classes, included members of the upper class. The presence of wealthy
Englishmen produced an unusual English settlement, the Close Brothers
Colony in northwest Iowa.

In 1876 William Close, then a Cambridge University student, came
to America to row in the Centennial Regatta at Philadelphia. While on that
trip, Close became interested in the possibility of investing in American
land. Three years later he returned to the United States and began purchasing land in Iowa. Within a short time Close and two of his brothers
bought land near Denison, Le Mars, and in southwestern Minnesota. Once
into the real-estate business, the brothers began advertising their holdings
in English newspapers, hoping to attract English people both to buy and
to rent the Close land. Like other immigrants, the Close brothers were eager to re-create the social institutions and traditions they had known in
England, albeit in their case not lower- or middling-class establishments.
One result was the creation of two pubs in Le Mars, the House of Com-
mons and the House of Lords. The Englishmen also organized polo

matches and horse races. When Queen Victoria celebrated fifty years on the British throne, the English population in and around Le Mars celebrated the event in grand style.[55]

The Close brothers did succeed in attracting people from their homeland to settle on the Iowa prairie, although many remained only a few years before returning to England. The brothers failed, however, to re-create the social hierarchy they had known in England. Northwest Iowa, with a generally level terrain and sparse settlement, did not provide either the physical or social setting that the English settlers desired. Even though the Close brothers failed in some endeavors, they succeeded in others. After leaving Iowa, the two surviving brothers, William and James, lived most comfortably on the profits they had made from their many business ventures in the Hawkeye State.[56]

Hollanders were also a part of the first phase of immigration and, perhaps of all groups, have demonstrated the greatest social and religious cohesion: They have remained closely associated with two areas, Pella and Orange City, and have continued to be closely identified with the Reformed Church of America. Although Hollanders would be among the smaller immigrant groups, their religious and economic cohesion have given them special distinction.[57]

The first Hollanders to settle in Iowa would arrive in 1847. The group of some seven hundred had originally intended to make St. Louis their home, but arriving there in 1847, they quickly decided they did not like the area, considering it to be unhealthy. They then sent a committee to look at land in Iowa, and impressed with the Iowa landscape, they purchased 18,000 acres (later to be expanded to 47,000 acres). The Hollanders purchased government land for $1.25 an acre and also purchased some land from private individuals for $80.00 to $100.00 an acre. They named their first community "Pella" and set to work building sod houses with thatched straw roofs; these were soon replaced with frame houses. The Dutch quickly began their farming operations and before long were sending cheese, hams, and bacon to St. Louis. Hog production was new to the Hollanders, and unlike most native-born farmers, who let their hogs roam at will, the Dutch built fences to keep the hogs confined. The Hollanders benefited from the gold rush in 1849, when travelers on their way to California stopped at Pella to purchase food and supplies.[58]

The leader of the Hollanders, Henry Peter Scholte, served many different roles within the new community, including minister. Scholte and others had come to America seeking economic opportunity as well as an escape from what they viewed as a repressive religious situation. State officials in Holland were attempting to force all residents to join and support the official state church, a move deeply resented by Scholte and his followers. Scholte, viewed as an extremely able businessman and religious leader, supervised the land purchases and settlement process. Later the Hollanders and their descendants would found other communities in northwest Iowa, including Orange City, Sioux Center, Maurice, Hospers, and Remsen. Today descendants of those original seven hundred immigrants hold annual Tulip Festivals in both Pella and Orange City in which they commemorate the sacrifices of their forebears.[59]

Although most immigrants from eastern and central Europe did not arrive until the late nineteenth or early twentieth centuries, immigrants from Bohemia (later a part of Czechoslovakia and today a part of the Czech Republic) would be an exception. Bohemian immigrants would begin arriving in the 1850s, settling first in and around the village of Spillville, where many pursued farming. In contrast to Germans and Scandinavians, many Czechs had learned skilled trades before they arrived in Iowa. Frequently Czech immigrants would "stop over" in an eastern or midwestern city, particularly Chicago, for several years. In the cities they often learned the skills of woodworking. Once in Iowa, they might continue that work in connection with farming. Two Czech brothers, Frank and Joseph Biley, came to the Spillville area to farm, although they had previously learned the art of wood carving. Both bachelors, the brothers spent many winter evenings carving large, ornate clocks, which are displayed in the Biley Brothers Clock Museum in Spillville. Visitors there can also visit the local Catholic cemetery, which contains many iron-cross markers, reminiscent of cemeteries in central Europe. A proud moment in Spillville's history came in the summer of 1893 when the noted Bohemian composer, Antonín Dvořák, spent several weeks there while working on musical compositions.

By the late 1860s Czech immigrants often headed for Cedar Rapids instead of Spillville, going to work as craftsmen or for local industries. Many Czechs traveled directly from their homeland to Iowa, as evidenced by the fact that steamship companies sold tickets from German ports straight through to Cedar Rapids. By 1870 the Cedar Rapids city directory listed Czechs as present in almost all the city's craft occupations. From that decade on, Cedar Rapids would be the Czech center of Iowa.[60] Small communities close to Cedar Rapids, such as Clutier, Vining, Swisher, and Chelsea, would also later become known as Czech communities.

Within Cedar Rapids, Czech Americans would quickly establish social institutions. Residents built a Bohemian dance hall, and local people often enjoyed dawn dances where, as the term implies, they danced until dawn. Czech-American women participated in the "dracky," where they gathered to strip the down from feathers, using the fluffy material for pillows and feather beds. Czech-American children often joined the Sokol, an organization that stressed physical fitness through gymnastics. In 1891 local Czech Americans formed the Bohemian Savings and Loan Association, which made it easier for Czech-American families to borrow money to buy homes.[61] Today Cedar Rapids continues to be strongly identified with the Czech heritage, and visitors there will find a Czech village and museum.

As the history of the foregoing groups indicate, cultural pluralism had become a fact of life in the Hawkeye State by the 1880s. Census figures indicate that not only had thousands of emigrants arrived from different areas of Europe, but emigrants numbering in the hundreds had arrived from countries such as France, Switzerland, and Belgium. Moreover, Iowa contained an increasing number of African Americans, many of whom arrived to work in the coal-mining industry.

In the years that lay ahead, the basic patterns established in the earlier period of the state's history would continue: As expansion in agriculture and industry offered opportunity to many Iowans, including thousands of first-, second-, and even third-generation European Americans, African Americans frequently would find themselves denied a share in the fruits of that growth.

II

The Middle Years

Economic and Social Maturation,
Cultural Conflict, and Political Development

7

Religious and Educational Institutions in Iowa: Establishing the Foundations

From territorial days to the present, Iowans have been particularly proud of their schools and churches. In the nineteenth century newly arrived settlers, many coming from northeastern states with ties stretching back to New England, displayed a zeal for establishing educational and religious institutions; immigrants also moved quickly to establish religious organizations. As William Petersen has observed, "the church was a vital force on the frontier."[1] Newly arrived settlers also moved quickly to build schools, although, in general, these nineteenth- and early-twentieth-century creations were sometimes of dubious quality. The religious and educational institutions that Iowans established reflected the early settlers' cultural and religious backgrounds,

---

Youngsters posing for class pictures at Jackson Township School No. 5, Sac County, ca. 1907–8. Note the wide range of ages. Photo courtesy of the State Historical Society of Iowa, Iowa City.

both here and abroad, and therefore varied in form and purpose. One commonality applied to all groups, however, as most nineteenth-century Iowans worked hard to ensure that their progeny would be both churched and schooled.

Iowa's earliest religious institutions were dominated by the Roman Catholics and the Methodists. Although the Catholic Church was highly centralized through its dioceses, the Methodists would be only one, albeit the largest, of many Protestant denominations. Iowa would clearly be a state of many faiths, given the large number of Protestant groups present here. By the 1930s the federal census would report that Iowa contained more than eighty different Protestant bodies.[2]

Iowa's Protestant groups would be both numerous and diverse. Among the larger denominations, Lutherans would include several groups or synods associated with particular nationalities, such as Norwegian Lutherans, Danish Lutherans, and the German Lutheran or Missouri Synod. Baptists were also present in Iowa from early settlement; in the 1800s Baptist ministers were often called preacher-farmers because they combined the two occupations. Episcopalians would establish their first church, Trinity Church, in Muscatine in 1839. A few years later, in the 1840s, the United Brethren in Christ (later changed to the Evangelical United Brethren Church) organized a church, while a congregation of the Church of the Brethren formed in 1844.[3] The Church of Jesus Christ of Latter-day Saints, has had a special association with Iowa, as in the 1840s Mormons trekked across southern Iowa on their way to the Great Salt Lake Valley; some travelers dropped off along the way and started congregations in southern and southwestern Iowa. Although a sense of cooperation existed, a spirit of rivalry was also present among Protestant groups, and between Protestants and Catholics.

Each major religious group would take a somewhat unique approach in establishing itself in Iowa. All Protestant denominations increased their membership, due in part to the fact that Protestants in the eastern United States viewed Iowa as a mission field with great potential for converts. Congregationalists and Presbyterians would send ministers into Iowa, often under the auspices of the American Home Missionary Society. The Methodists would use a distinct approach, relying on circuit riders to take the Gospel to the people. At the same time, the early Quakers established not only congregations but entire communities, including West Branch and New Providence. Catholics would rely heavily on foreign-born priests and sisters to serve church members already settled here, a practice evidenced throughout the country until the Civil War. After the war most priests and sisters trained in American institutions. American Catholicism would not only recruit Catholic clergy from Europe but also seek money from European sources to build churches and—duplicating the European "parish mentality"—establish schools, orphanages, and hospitals.

Roman Catholics were the first to arrive in the Iowa region. The earliest priests came from New France to serve the white inhabitants in mining communities such as Galena, Illinois. Catholics did not begin building churches in Iowa, however, until permanent settlement began in 1833. Father Samuel Mazzuchelli, an Italian Dominican, played an important role in establishing Catholicism in eastern Iowa. Father Mazzuchelli first supervised the construction of a church in Dubuque and then in 1839 began missionary work along the Mississippi; he was responsible for starting numerous new churches in river communities, designing many of the buildings himself.[4] The major Catholic figure in frontier Iowa, the Most Reverend Mathias Loras, would arrive in Dubuque in 1839, to serve as Iowa's first Catholic bishop. Born in France to a well-to-do family, Father Loras eventually "felt the pull of the foreign missions" and in 1829 immigrated to the United States. After serving the Catholic diocese of Mobile, Alabama, he arrived in Dubuque. The bishop faced severe challenges in his new post as the Dubuque diocese covered a huge area, stretching from the northern boundary of Missouri to Canada, and from the Mississippi to the Missouri River. Bishop Loras, moreover, was fifty years old in 1839, and not accustomed to life in a primitive, sparsely settled region.[5]

Once in Iowa, the bishop determined not only to serve Catholics living here, but to enlarge that number through a colonization project; he would thus fill "the fertile, vacant prairies of Iowa with Catholics." He warned that if Catholics did not do so, Protestants would. Supported by European missionary societies, the bishop purchased land whenever possible and wrote letters to Catholic publications in both America and Europe advertising his mission. Although the bishop attracted fewer Catholics than he had hoped, he did succeed in starting a number of ethnic Catholic communities in eastern Iowa.[6]

During his tenure Bishop Loras greatly expanded the number of priests and churches in the diocese. When he arrived, there were four priests, three churches, and several hundred members; by 1857 the diocese had grown to thirty-seven priests, fifty-two churches, forty-seven mission stations and forty-nine thousand members.[7] With the initial Catholic settlement in Dubuque and its subsequent expansion, the church developed a clearly identifiable center in the state, which exists to the present. As Iowa's population increased, the Catholic hierarchy expanded accordingly. In 1850 church officials divided the Dubuque diocese, creating the diocese of St. Paul in the northern part of the original area; later, officials formed three more dioceses in Iowa: Davenport in 1881; Sioux City in 1902; and Des Moines in 1911.[8]

Bishop Loras faced the constant problem of ethnic rivalries, particularly between Germans and Irish. Each group expected to be served by a priest of the same nationality, and in the early days of the diocese that was difficult, if not impossible, to arrange. Sometimes Irish and German Catholics fought over the name of the church and sat in two different areas of the church. According to Thomas Auge, that separation "extended even to the grave, for [in one congregation] the cemetery was divided into German and Irish sections."[9]

One aspect of the Catholic Church not shared by its Protestant counterparts was the important role assigned to Catholic women. From early in its history in Iowa, the church was assisted by various orders of nuns to help carry out religious work. The two most active orders in Iowa came from Ireland and France. In Dubuque the Sisters of Charity opened St. Mary's Academy in 1843, and in 1901 the academy became Clarke College. Eventually seven sister orders would be located in Dubuque. Sister orders throughout the state opened schools, hospitals, and other institutions. One group, the Sisters of the Holy Humility of Mary, arrived in Ottumwa in 1877, after originating in France some twenty years earlier. The sisters came to Ottumwa because a local priest, Monsignor John Kreckel, had invited them to start a school for parish boys. When they arrived, the group consisted of seven sisters and five novices.[10]

For the next seventy years the Sisters of Humility would be visible in Ottumwa as well as in other Iowa communities. After starting the boys' school designed to "carry through a complete commercial or scientific course," the sisters faced other challenges. In 1878 Wapello County officials discovered that certain mental patients housed at a state facility in

Mount Pleasant would be returned to Wapello County. The board of supervisors appealed to the sisters to staff a facility for the mentally ill persons. The sisters hurriedly set up a temporary facility on the third floor of the convent, caring for the patients for almost four years. In the meantime, the sisters had helped to set up a hospital in the city. They also maintained an orphans' home, first in the convent and then in a separate facility. In 1895 church officials moved the latter facility to Davenport, where it became the St. Vincent's Home.[11]

Of all their interests, however, education was paramount to the Sisters of Humility. After setting up a school in Ottumwa, they also staffed schools in Fort Madison and Mount Pleasant. Later, in the 1890s, the order would open schools in ten additional communities, including Des Moines, where the sisters established St. Anthony's School primarily for local Italian-American children. Higher education would also be a part of their mission when in 1939, at the request of their bishop, they would found and staff Marycrest College in Davenport.[12]

Among Iowa's Protestant denominations, the Methodist Episcopal Church would become the largest, being particularly successful in attracting members during Iowa's settlement period. The Methodists were centralized, with a distinct hierarchy of church officials, and yet sufficiently flexible so the church could meet the needs of an expanding frontier. In the early days of settlement people had little, if any, money to construct churches; therefore, Methodists believed, circuit riders should take the church to the people. The typical circuit rider lived out of his saddlebags as he traveled his circuit, usually on a two-week schedule. He had little education, but he had felt "the call" to preach the gospel. Accordingly, his sermons were usually simple prose delivered "from the heart." Because the vast majority of Iowa's early settlers had limited education, the circuit riders' simple but earnest preachings had great appeal. Moreover, as the frontier continued to move west, the Methodists could adjust quickly by setting up another circuit to serve the most recently settled area.

The Methodist circuit rider would do far more than take religion to the people: He would serve as a moderating and educational influence on western society. In maintaining order at church services, the preacher sometimes had to curb rowdyism, thus helping to maintain law and order; Methodist preachers also stood for "moderation in religious practices," rather than inciting great emotionalism during services. The preacher played a particularly important role in his work for temperance, advocating that church members take an abstinence pledge. Methodist officials were responding to a society, particularly in the first part of the nineteenth century, in which Americans assumed that alcoholic beverages should be a part of all special occasions, whether baptisms, weddings, or funerals. Of all Protestant denominations, the Methodist Church took the strongest stand on the temperance issue, declaring that liquor was evil and urging members to abstain totally. William Sweet has written "the Methodist Church was the original Temperance Society in the West, if not in the nation."[13] The circuit rider also played an educational role as he carried books from settlement to settlement.

In 1833 the Methodists would have the distinction of building the first church in Iowa when they constructed a church in Dubuque. Earlier, the first Methodist service there had been conducted in a tavern. Reverend Barton Randle supervised the construction of the church, which was built of logs and measured twenty by twenty-six feet; the small structure cost $255. When not used by the Methodists, the building was available to other denominations.[14]

As Methodists organized congregations in permanent communities like Dubuque, the bishop assigned ministers to serve there. Methodists, then, had a distinct organization consisting of several layers of leadership, and one that called for a high degree of member participation. Church officials included the bishop, who presided over the conference; the district superintendent, who maintained close contact with churches in his district, visiting them quarterly; and a minister assigned to a particular community. In each church laymen served as class leaders when members came together once a week to discuss religious subjects. The class meeting was the smallest of the Methodist gatherings.

During the nineteenth century the Methodist Church would go through several reorganizations in regard to conferences. Originally Iowa—known as the Iowa District—was a part of the Illinois Conference; later Iowa was divided into three districts. Eventually officials divided the state into four conferences, but by 1949 these had been been merged into two: the Iowa–Des Moines Conference and the North Iowa Conference.[15]

Although the Methodist Church was not influenced by foreign-born clergy as were the Catholics, the church did come to include ethnic congregations. Two groups, German Methodists and Swedish Methodists, briefly had their own conferences, but both eventually transferred back into regular conferences. For a time ministers offered sermons in German and Swedish. In 1849 a Swedish Methodist Episcopal Church was organized at New Sweden, the first Swedish community in Iowa.[16]

A second Protestant group, the Congregationalists, also became active in Iowa at an early date. During the nineteenth century they often worked with the Presbyterians in establishing churches in the West. Early in the century the two denominations jointly set up the Act of Union. This plan called for the two bodies to pool their resources, thus stretching them further than either church could do alone. In effect, the Act of Union determined that no western community would have both a Congregational and a Presbyterian church, since the second denomination to arrive would move on to the next community to establish a church.

The Congregationalists and Presbyterians would also work together in several other ways. Both denominations would be involved with the American Home Missionary Society, an eastern organization that recruited ministers to go into western areas to organize churches. Both denominations promoted the organization of Sunday schools and supported and promoted the American Bible Society, with the goal of placing a Bible in the hands of every literate person in the West. In effect, these two denominations reflected the view of easterners that the West was a great mission field desperately in need of religious officials to organize and staff churches. This idea would guarantee that westerners would be churched, and therefore civilized.[17]

The Congregational Church first became visible in Iowa through the efforts of the Iowa Band. In 1843 eleven theological students at Andover Seminary in Massachusetts agreed to come to Iowa to establish congregations. The men all settled in different communities in eastern Iowa with the resolve to establish churches individually, and to establish a college together. William Salter, the longest-living member of the group, started a church at Maquoketa and then served the Burlington Congregational Church for sixty-some years.

Reverend Salter's time at Maquoketa illustrates the difficulties faced by religious men of all faiths. Typically, Salter found few people "who professed religion." His first church, organized in 1843, met initially in an old blacksmith shop. When Salter traveled the countryside to solicit money for a new church, he had little success, hearing such responses as

"[We] are too poor, have too much else to do, must build a schoolhouse, don't like the proposed location," and so on. Salter frequently wrote about sickness and poverty in the countryside.[18]

William Salter and other members of the Iowa Band—all college graduates—would feel strongly about imparting learning to their congregations. In effect, Congregationalist ministers had a dual purpose in the West: to preach the Gospel and to raise the intellectual level of their parishioners. As the men labored to establish churches in communities such as Eddyville, Cascade, and Farmington, they "took pleasure in sharing their book learning and Yankee culture with their ... parishioners. They quoted poetry and the classics as well as verses from the Old and New Testaments."[19]

Given that Iowa was part of the great western mission field, it was perhaps natural that a sense of rivalry would permeate the thinking of all religious officials. Salter would not be immune from such feelings. In Maquoketa he reacted with sadness and discouragement upon finding "a Methodist emotionalist attracting members from his congregation." He later learned that a Methodist circuit rider had "stirred up the settlers against Congregationalism." In the previous year he had recorded in his diary that a Baptist preacher from Pennsylvania had been in the Maquoketa area seeking converts. Nor would Salter ignore the Catholics, expressing irritation upon hearing that Catholic schools were instructing Protestant youth.[20]

At the same time, smaller religious groups would also be arriving in Iowa. The Quakers would create numerous communities in Iowa before the Civil War. The first Friends had arrived in colonial America in the mid-1600s, shortly after their founding in England, and would gradually establish communities throughout America. A small group arrived in Iowa in the 1830s and laid out the town of Salem. This community served as something of a center for Quakers, who then spread out to start other Iowa communities, such as Springville in Linn County and Springdale in Cedar County. The Friends established a preparatory meeting for a beginning community, then a monthly meeting for a settled community, a quarterly meeting to provide supervision for monthly meetings, and finally a yearly meeting for all members. The first Yearly Meeting of Iowa Friends was held at Spring Creek in 1863.[21]

Although the Friends, like most religious bodies, experienced divisions among members over religious practices and beliefs, all Friends opposed slavery. This belief would lead to involvement in Iowa's Underground Railroad movement before the Civil War. The Friends' pacifist views—their role as a peace church—have been prominent in Iowa. The Friends' total number in Iowa has remained small; in 1936 the federal census listed the total population of Quakers (both Orthodox Conservative Friends and Society of Friends) at 6,430.[22]

Jewish settlers would also begin moving into Iowa soon after permanent settlement began. Like the Quakers, the Jews would remain a small group. A few Jewish settlers would become farmers, but most pursued trade and thus became urban dwellers. Alexander Levi was apparently the first Jewish settler in Iowa, arriving in Dubuque in 1833. Levi, a French Jew, soon started a grocery store there and later opened a dry-goods store. As Michael J. Bell points out in his study of Jews in Iowa, most Jewish communities in the state were founded by a single individual such as Levi. By 1846 the number of Jewish settlers had grown to sixteen. Most of the early Jews were peddlers who lived in either Illinois or Missouri, but who traveled through Iowa.[23]

Jews in early Iowa included Nathan Louis and Solomon Fine, who arrived in Fort Madison in October 1841 and began to sell their goods. The Younker brothers, who eventually started a department store in Des Moines, would work initially as peddlers, traveling from town to town, and from farm to farm, selling dry goods and domestic wares. Many Jewish families then established stores—often clothing stores—in communities like Keokuk, Oskaloosa, and Centerville. According to Bell, more than three-fourths of Jewish-owned stores in Iowa by 1860 had been started by men who had served the areas as peddlers. Since Jews did not proselytize, but rather gathered with others of their faith, their total number was often small.[24]

Michael Bell points out that the earliest successful efforts to create communal life for Jews in Iowa took place in Keokuk, where Jews formed a benevolent society. The first activity of that group, the Benevolent Children of Jerusalem, was to "purchase ground for a burying place, to assist the sick and needy and arrange a meeting place for religious purposes."[25] The Jewish residents in Keokuk next organized a Ladies Benevolent Association, which marked the beginning of Jewish women's control of their charity, a practice that continued in Iowa into the twentieth century. Later that year the first Jewish congregation, Benai Israel, organized; the group originally met in rented rooms in downtown Keokuk. Later B'Nai Israel organized at Davenport in 1861; and a Congregation B'Nai Jeshurun organized in Des Moines in 1872. In 1869 Jews in Sioux City would first organize a Jewish Cemetery Association, and by 1900 the community had attracted an "unusually high" Jewish population. This resulted from Sioux City's location along the Missouri River and its access to trade in several surrounding states as well as with immigrating Russian Jews. The number of Jewish residents would increase in the 1800s, but after 1900 some Jewish communities, like that in Sioux City, would decline, while others, like Des Moines, would expand. By 1936 the federal census reported twenty-six Jewish congregations in Iowa, with 11,888 members.[26]

While religious institutions were central to Iowans' lives, so was the matter of education. Iowans would quickly establish one-room schoolhouses and within a few years would set up academies, the forerunner of high schools. Colleges and universities would quickly follow. Although elementary education was sometimes haphazard, most Iowans had a strong belief in the value of good education and took great pride in the state's high literacy rates. Like Americans elsewhere, Iowans believed that education—at least in limited form—was necessary to provide for good citizenship and, in turn, good government.

The antecedents for Iowans' educational views go back to New England at a much earlier time. The Puritans who arrived there in the 1620s and 1630s brought along a strong commitment to education, believing that education (primarily the ability to read) was essential to the creation of a proper society. More specifically, the Puritans, who viewed themselves as creating a religious state, believed that in order to find religious salvation, one must be able to read the Bible. Originally, in New England, parents were expected to teach their children to read, a practice carried over from England. When parents failed to do so, the Puritan fathers soon passed laws in the Massachusetts colonial legislature requiring communities to provide schooling. Although schools developed unevenly in Massachusetts and other parts of New England, the Massachusetts legislation nevertheless marked the beginning of the idea that education was a public responsibility.

This idea that education was a responsibility of the general public—

would eventually be incorporated into federal legislation. As more and more Americans began to move west after the American Revolution, Congress passed several laws governing the surveying and disposal of the public domain, including the Land Ordinance of 1785. The law stipulated that Section 16 of every township should be set aside for the support of a public school. In effect, wherever Americans might settle in the Old Northwest or beyond, they would have support for public education.

Iowa's first school opened even before permanent settlement was under way. In 1830 a young Kentuckian, Berryman Jennings, taught in a log cabin in Lee County. As settlement increased, parents established other subscription schools whereby parents paid teachers directly for educating their children. Teachers' salaries varied from year to year. In District Number 3 in Iowa City, teachers received twenty-four dollars per month in 1849, thirty-seven dollars in 1850, and thirty dollars in 1851; typically, female teachers received less pay than male teachers. Teachers received little assistance from parents or from the local government. As one historian described it: "teachers in those days 'made their own systems, recommended their own kind of text-books, manufactured their own [teaching materials and equipment], and collected their own bills.' "[27] Early-day curricula usually included reading, writing, arithmetic, spelling, and geography.

In 1858 the state legislature passed the School Act of 1858, sometimes called the Free School Act, which laid the foundation for Iowa's public-school system. A major feature of the act determined that property taxes be assessed to support public education. The act also authorized the establishment of one high school in each county and called for the creation of the office of a state superintendent of public instruction, and superintendents of education, for each county. The act created larger school districts by organizing townships as districts and by reorganizing independent districts (in effect since 1849) as subdistricts of the townships. This move created the district township system. At the same time, cities and towns with a minimum of one thousand inhabitants could organize schools independently of the township. Eventually, in 1866, a town or village of two hundred people could also organize its own school.[28]

Each district township elected officials to serve on the township school board. These boards had considerable power, as they decided how many schools were needed in the township, the length of the school year, whether or not to organize a high school in the district, and courses to be taught. The wide range of responsibilities assumed by local officials underscores the view held by Iowans and other Americans: Local officials should control and regulate public education.

Throughout the nineteenth century 70 to 80 percent of pupils attended school in the open country. From the 1850s to the 1890s many aspects of rural schools remained unchanged and exhibited little standardization; many schools continued to be ungraded. Regardless of deficiencies, Iowans seemed exceptionally proud of their schools, and in 1870, when the federal census revealed Iowa had the nation's highest literacy rate, that pride seemed justified.[29]

A high literacy rate notwithstanding, state officials soon began to upgrade public education. In the 1880s Iowa's legislature initiated teacher-certification requirements. Teachers, if they wished to remain in teaching, had to attend institutes at the county seat for one week each summer. State officials gradually strengthened certification requirements, requiring teachers to take even longer institutes or to obtain college credits. Though many private schools existed in Iowa, in 1876 the state also founded a college specifically to train teachers—the Iowa State Normal School in Cedar Falls.[30]

As officials implemented certification requirements, male teachers—who had often regarded teaching as temporary work—began to turn to other, more lucrative pursuits. Women, who had few occupational choices, more typically fulfilled certification requirements and continued as teachers. The result in Iowa, as elsewhere, was the feminization of teaching. As Keach Johnson points out, by 1905, 86 percent of elementary teachers in Iowa were female.[31]

While grammar schools represented the major educational concern during the mid-1800s, there were always some students who desired further schooling. The result was the establishment of academies, which generally taught courses such as mathematics, history, and philosophy or those courses not considered a part of the three R's. William Petersen writes: "The academy took up where the one-room school left off and was a combination of our present-day average high school, with a touch of the small modern college."[32] Academies were generally privately supported and therefore did not require government support.

Forerunners of high schools sometimes carried the name of seminaries. Mount Pleasant Female Seminary, opened in 1842, provides an example of a separate female institution. Like similar schools throughout the country, the seminary staff believed that women required close supervision, both in regard to social activities and academic work. The staff allowed no callers on Sunday, and on other days, gentlemen, other than brothers and fathers, could call only with special permission. The seminary staff believed "young women were not to be trusted with money for the purchase of books; funds should be deposited with the principal." According to the school catalog, even "confectionaries and such eatables" were undesirable, as they "bred discontent and sickness among the pupils."[33]

In the 1850s a new type of post-grammar-school institution, the high school, was beginning to gain favor. The first high school appeared in Boston in the 1820s, and the institution then began moving westward. Iowa's first high school was organized in Bloomington Township, Muscatine County, in 1851. Tipton followed in 1856 and had the distinction of graduating the first class—with thirteen students—in 1858. Course offerings included algebra, geometry, history, and bookkeeping. With the advent of high schools, academies quickly lost favor, as the former were supported by tax funds while the latter required private support.[34]

Even though Iowans remained proud of their state's educational institutions, educators found cause for concern. In 1889 officials surveyed the state's school-age population, and the results were discouraging. The study disclosed that in towns, only 75 percent of the school-age population was enrolled in school, and of that number only 47 percent actually attended. In open-country schools, the results were even more disappointing. Of the 60 percent enrolled out of the school-age population, only 40 percent actually attended. One reason for poor attendance, no doubt, was lack of a mandatory-attendance policy. Some parents, moreover, perceived the public-school curriculum as confined "too exclusively to intellectual development" to meet the general needs of society.[35]

In his study of education in Iowa, Keach Johnson has carefully detailed the inadequate conditions of rural schools in the 1890s. He points out that the quality of teaching was deemed poor, with many teachers having little training; also, teachers' pay was low, so little incentive existed for more-qualified people to become teachers. In some rural schools the board hired a different teacher for each term, meaning that children had three different teachers in one year. Teachers received some supervision, mainly from county superintendents of schools, who were overworked and sometimes had insufficient qualifications themselves. One educator described the impossible tasks facing these officials: "An Iowa county contains about 550 square miles—employs nearly 200 teachers—has from 100 to 300 school officials—and from 4,000 to 8,000 children of school age. ... The county superintendent who can keep his hand on all of these school interests and direct them properly must have a hand like that of Providence."[36]

School buildings also came in for criticism. Henry Sabin, state superintendent of schools for eight years, observed: "All over the state are [rural] school grounds, bare, dreary and desolate, without a tree to shelter the children from the winter's blast or the summer's sun. ... Outhouses with doors off the hinges, clapboards off the sides, defiled and defaced, a disgrace to a civilized community." Sabin described the schools themselves as poorly ventilated, poorly heated, and poorly maintained, which he related to schoolchildren's ill health.[37]

But not all assessments of country schooling have been negative. In *The Old Country School,* Wayne E. Fuller writes that rural schools in the Midwest exposed children to many positive experiences and provided excellent moral training as well as character building. Fuller notes that many of the lessons in morality often came from the writings of William Holmes McGuffey: "The teaching of such lessons ... and their recollections confirm how effective lessons were in teaching [students] not only to be honest and courageous but to be ambitious, to reach beyond themselves, to overcome obstacles, and not to be discouraged."[38] Fuller believes that rural schools exposed children to good literature, citing Hamlin Garland's experience: "[From the pages of my reader] I learned to know and love the poems of Scott, Byron, Southey, Wordsworth and a long line of English masters."[39]

Fuller cites the supportive roles both teachers and local residents played in their schools. Teachers calmed the fears of beginning students, praised the creativity of the children, and encouraged them to pursue their education. At the same time, he gives countless examples of fathers and mothers who were closely involved with their children's schooling. Fuller believes that schools had "a familylike atmosphere" because people lived close together and knew every other family in the district. Even older residents who no longer had children in school visited frequently, thus indicating their sincere interest in education.[40]

After 1890 events outside the state prompted Iowa educators to look at their schools in a new light. By the 1890s major changes were occurring in American life: The country as a whole was becoming increasingly urban and industralized; and in the 1890s the United States would become the leading manufacturing nation in the world. Although Iowa remained largely rural, state educators believed that external changes necessitated revamping the public schools to prepare Iowa's youth to cope with a rapidly changing world. Educators believed that new courses should be taught that would help young people adjust to and survive in the new environment. Further, educators believed schools must "identify with the democratic, scientific, and technological forces of modern society. They must reach out to all segments of the population." Schools must also work with other social agencies to "educate the whole child."[41]

Some twenty years later two important changes took place regarding the state's high schools. In the first, state officials moved to upgrade teaching instruction and increase the number of teachers. In 1911 given a continuing shortage of rural teachers, a two-year teaching program was made a part of the high-school curriculum. Students took a two-year course, and if they passed the subjects, they graduated from high school, ready to teach country school. Also in that year the General Assembly passed legislation requiring school districts without high schools to pay the tuition of qualified students who wished to attend high school. This move proved to be a great incentive for local boards to establish such schools themselves: In 1910 Iowa had 406 high schools; by 1934 there were 953.[42]

During the 1910s efforts to improve rural education also focused on encouraging consolidation of schools. State educators had long complained that Iowa simply contained too many schools. In 1900, for example, the state had a total of 14,296 self-governing school units. A closer look at just one county illustrates this concern: In 1900 Sioux County contained 172 rural schools and 11 independent school districts with seventy-six teachers. Some schools enrolled fewer than a dozen children. By 1920, since few Iowa schools had moved to consolidate, the legislature added an incentive: Any rural school open for eight months, with ten or more pupils, that provided good maintenance for the school and outhouse, and "hired a teacher with a bit of training," would qualify for a state subsidy.

This incentive had little effect, as by 1925 only 10 percent of schools had accepted the subsidy.[43]

In their study of Iowa's public educational system, Richard Jensen and Mark Friedberger determined that by the 1920s "Iowa operated ... two school systems—a modern one for towns, cities and the most progressive rural areas, and a traditional one [for] the majority of farmers." Examining a select number of Iowa townships (including villages, towns, and cities), the authors conclude that within the modern sector "the business of education was clearly understood as modernization," to equip youths to move beyond local areas and to cope with changes in the wider society. Teachers were well qualified in the modern systems, described as "professionals working in proud new buildings, under the supervision of experts, with access to good libraries and teaching materials, and judged against the best national standards by cosmopolitans."[44]

By contrast, Jensen and Friedberger write, the traditional school system, most clearly represented by one-room schools, had changed little since the latter nineteenth century. Even the buildings themselves remained drab and dull. The quality of teaching in open-country schools "varied enormously." Teachers typically lived at home or with relatives, generally teaching for a few years and then getting married. In one study of 107 Cedar County rural teachers in the 1920s, the county superintendent judged "eleven to be superior, only 30 good," leaving one to infer that the remaining 66 were at least somewhat inferior as teachers. According to a 1920s study of Iowa farm life, even the young people demonstrated "a flat, monotonous life." Farm men and women served on local school boards, but "none were conversant with modern educational ideas." The authors point out that the one way to improve rural schools—through consolidation—was overwhelmingly rejected by rural school boards. They desired, rather, to retain the status quo, to minimize expenditures, and to guarantee continued local control of their schools.[45]

Other historians maintain that by the late 1920s Iowa's rural schools had undergone considerable improvement, although the earlier basic ideology of schools as character builders remained. In the nineteenth century the purpose of the schools was to produce good citizens trained to be good workers who could avoid the temptations of idleness; moreover, schools were meant to instill traditional moral values. By the 1920s, according to one educational historian, "Iowa teachers ... like their predecessors in the

1890s, taught future citizens to view industrial virtue as central to moral life, and to value it for making them useful, productive, and wealthy while it also preserved the social order of state and nation." Positive changes had also taken place in rural schools, as teachers were better trained and a course of study had been developed that provided direction and uniformity to the curriculum.[46]

Even before Iowa's public-school system had taken shape, citizens had begun to think about higher education. During the nineteenth century Iowa colleges, sponsored and supported by different denominations, proliferated. Iowa Wesleyan University would be the first, developing out of Mount Pleasant Collegiate Institute, an early-day academy. The Methodist Church took over the school in 1849 and four years later changed the name to Iowa Wesleyan University. In 1855 the Iowa General Assembly authorized the school to teach courses in medicine, law, and theology. Later the college created a college of law and a college of pharmacy, which survived for only a short time. By 1912 college trustees realized, however, that they could not continue to operate a university—with various colleges—and changed the name to Iowa Wesleyan College.

The Methodist Church approached the matter of higher education in the same methodical fashion as it had earlier pursued evangelizing. Because church officials believed that Methodist young people in every part of the state should have the opportunity to attend a Methodist school—and given the difficulty of traveling in nineteenth-century Iowa—a four-year institution was established in each part of the state. With Iowa Wesleyan already in existence in southeastern Iowa, church officials turned their attention elsewhere.

Between 1855 and 1896 the Iowa Methodist Episcopal Church would establish or take over four more schools. Church officials would first create Cornell College in Mount Vernon in 1855, formerly known as the Iowa Conference Seminary. During the same year the Methodist Church took charge of the Fayette Seminary in Fayette, and in 1857 the school became known as Upper Iowa University. In 1928 Methodist officials attempted to merge the school with Cornell College, but officials at Upper Iowa refused, opting to remain independent. In the meantime the Methodists had established their fourth Iowa college. The Indianola Male and Female Seminary, founded in 1860, would become Simpson College in 1885.

George Washington Carver would be one of the school's most famous students, attending in 1890. Carver later recalled his experience there: "I managed to get to dear old Simpson with ten cents in cash, and every opportunity was given me to pursue my most cherished desire."[47] Morningside College at Sioux City became the fifth Methodist College in Iowa, opening its doors in 1896.

The Catholic Church also moved rapidly to establish institutions of higher learning in the state. Unlike Protestant denominations, however, Catholic schools were not coeducational. The first Catholic school opened in Dubuque in 1839 as St. Raphael's Seminary; the school was to train priests and also included an academy for boys. The school eventually changed both its name and location and finally, in 1939, became Loras College, named after Iowa's first Catholic bishop. From the mid–nineteenth century until the early twentieth, Catholic officials established several more schools. In 1885 officials opened St. Ambrose Seminary for male students in Davenport and in 1939 established a women's college, Marycrest, also in Davenport. The two schools have maintained a close association. Clarke College for women originated in Dubuque in 1843 as St. Mary's Female Academy and in 1928 became Clarke College. In 1930 Catholic officials started Briar Cliff College for women at Sioux City.[48]

Although Methodist and Catholic schools predominated, most other Protestant denominations also created colleges for their young people. The Presbyterians established the University of Dubuque, which had perhaps the most varied history of any Iowa college. It originated as a school to train German pastors for local churches, but by 1911 had evolved into an institution with three separate divisions—preparatory (Dubuque Academy), college (Dubuque German College), and seminary (German Presbyterian Theological Seminary). In 1919 the school changed its name to the University of Dubuque but remained affiliated with the Presbyterian Church. That denomination would establish four other schools in the state, including Coe College at Cedar Rapids, Parson College at Fairfield, Highland Park College at Des Moines, and Buena Vista College at Storm Lake. They would also take over Lenox College at Hopkinton.[49]

Other denominations were also active in higher education. A Congregational school would originate at Davenport in 1848, known as Iowa College, but would later move to Grinnell. The college stood as testimony to the work of the Iowa Band, with their early slogan of "Each to found a church, all to found a college." Known as the Harvard of the West because of its high academic standards, the school was renamed Grinnell College in 1908. Other denominations active in higher education include the Baptists, who established Des Moines College and Central College at Pella (later sold to the Dutch Reformed Church); the Disciples of Christ, with Drake University; and the Lutheran Church, which established Wartburg College and Luther College. During the 1870s Iowa Quakers would also open Penn College in Oskaloosa, later to be renamed William Penn College. Given the rapid expansion of religious schools, by 1900 Iowa abounded with small private institutions; in fact, twenty-two existed by 1870.[50]

Many Iowa colleges originating in the nineteenth century would survive, but some would not. Seminaries and institutes had the highest rate of failure, although some developed into four-year institutions. Lenox College did not survive, nor did Tabor College in western Iowa. Des Moines College purchased Highland Park College and operated as Des Moines University but eventually closed its doors in the early thirties. Amity College, established in College Springs, Page County, in 1857, had as its original mission to serve as a manual-labor institution for both sexes. By 1917, even though the institution had become recognized as a college with the ability to confer degrees, it was forced to close.[51]

As the foregoing indicates, religious institutions dominated Iowa's postprimary education in the nineteenth century. Whereas local communities established and controlled primary schools, private agencies (usually churches) started academies, seminaries, and colleges. Early settlers had experienced this arrangement in the Northeast and had carried it along to their homes in the West. As Stow Persons has pointed out, "Each [of these schools] regarded a particular denominational group as its special clientele, and each cultivated a distinctive moral and social atmosphere to distinguish itself from the others and from the public university."[52]

At the same time, the practice of "establishing state universities at federal expense" was evident by 1846 when Iowa became a state. That "expense" came in the form of some 46,000 acres that had earlier been given to the Territory of Iowa with the understanding that once Iowa became a state, the land could be sold to provide support for the new institution. Accordingly, the General Assembly on February 25, 1847, established a state university at Iowa City. The selection of the site did not take place, however, without considerable agitation by other communities hoping to have the school located in their midst. To placate these communities, the General Assembly determined that branches of the university would be established at Dubuque and Fairfield, while Andrew, Oskaloosa, and Mount Pleasant would have normal schools. None of these plans materialized, thus allowing the state to use its limited resources for the development of the University of Iowa and subsequently for Iowa State College and Iowa's State Teachers College.[53]

The early years of the University of Iowa were anything but promising. Although created by legislative action in 1847, the school did not begin classes until 1855. On paper the university had nine departments and offered several degrees, including the Ph.D. in all nine departments (following six years of work). Officials soon added a Normal Department and a Preparatory Department. In reality the faculty consisted of four people who offered courses in four areas; the 1856–57 catalog listed an enrollment of 124 students. Given a shortage of students, the university closed in 1858 (except for the Normal Department) and reopened two years later. A new president, Silas Totten, reorganized the school with six departments. In 1868 officials moved a law school from Des Moines to Iowa City and the following year established a medical school; in 1882 the Department of Dentistry was established, followed three years later by the creation of the Department of Pharmacy.[54] From the beginning the university admitted both males and females, a practice not widely followed by colleges and universities at the time.

Enrollment at the University of Iowa increased slowly during the latter nineteenth century; by 1900 the total had reached 1,542. The faculty by that time had increased to 102. According to Stow Persons, the recruitment of "scholarly faculty remained for many years a hit-or-miss affair." Funding was also a major problem. President Charles Schaeffer reported to the governing board in 1889 that the state had spent just under $14 million on its public institutions, with only 4.5 percent of that amount going to support the University of Iowa. By comparison, 41 percent went to support the state's three mental hospitals and 14 percent to support the state's two penitentiaries.[55]

From its beginning the university faced the problem of students being inadequately prepared for college work. In establishing Iowa's public educational system, officials had assumed that students would progress from the state's elementary schools into academies or high schools, and then on to the university. In reality students arriving at the university were not adequately prepared for college-level work. Accordingly, in 1855 the state legislature created a University Preparatory Department. As Persons has written, "for over twenty years a two- or three-year program in mathematics, science, and classical languages prepared students for college-level work." The teaching of the preparatory classes caused some critics to nickname the university the Johnson County High School. In 1878 state officials abolished the Preparatory Department, believing the state's high schools were then properly preparing students. Since that was not yet the case, the university created a subfreshman year, again responding to students' educational deficiencies.[56]

Only three years after the University of Iowa initiated its first classes, Iowans began agitating to establish a very different type of college, an institution dedicated to agriculture and the mechanical arts. Some state officials had argued that the university should have a professor of agriculture or perhaps even a separate college of agriculture, but others believed that a separate facility would better serve the interests of the state's farmers. In 1858 the General Assembly responded by founding the Iowa State Agricultural College and Model Farm in Story County. The passage of the Morrill Act in 1862 provided some 203,309 acres of land to underwrite the venture, and in the spring of 1869 classes began. Iowa State Agricultural College, like the University of Iowa, admitted males and females on an equal basis.[57]

A distinguishing feature of the agricultural college was "required manual labor," whereby all students worked several hours each day, for which they were paid about ten cents an hour. For a time the system received enthusiastic support, but gradually doubts began to surface. As Earle Ross has pointed out, some students "were more eager to earn than to learn," and at times their views of their earning capacity were "unbounded." One male student, for example, hoped to work a sufficient amount to meet all of his own expenses as well as to send money home. School officials soon learned that it was expensive to provide adequate supervision for student workers and that work assignments were sometimes made arbitrarily. Within a few years the school's president admitted, "labor that was instructive was impossible to provide in adequate amounts." By 1880 officials restricted the manual-labor system to only freshmen;

four years later they dropped the requirement altogether.[58]

Like its sister institution in Iowa City, the State Agricultural College experienced a myriad of difficulties in its first several decades of existence. Although Iowa farmers did well during the Civil War, the years following were characterized by hard times, including low farm prices and high operating costs. Nineteenth-century Iowa legislators seemed reluctant to appropriate much money for higher education even in good times, so in times of distress appropriations fell even lower. In 1887 following the passage of the Hatch Act, the federal government established an agricultural experiment station at the college, which gave greater visibility to the institution.

The decades of the 1880s and 1890s would prove decisive for Iowa State Agricultural College in yet another way. In 1884 the state legislature amended the Iowa Code in regard to the school's curriculum. The amendment read: "there shall be adopted and taught at [ISC] a broad, liberal and practical course of study in which the leading branches of learning shall relate to agriculture and the mechanic arts, and which shall also embrace such other branches of learning as will most practically and liberally educate the agricultural and industrial classes." As a result of this change, which broadened the curriculum—and coincided with the departure of President Adonijah S. Welch and Professor of Agriculture Seaman A. Knapp—the enrollment in the agricultural program declined. A few years later college officials dropped the bachelor of scientific agriculture degree program.[59]

The move to do so brought a "stinging attack" from Iowa's leading farm publication, the *Iowa Homestead,* and members of the Iowa Farmers' Alliance. Although some college officials justified the increasing emphasis on a liberal-arts education, the critics persisted. The matter was resolved in 1891 when college officials responded to the farm interests' requests to introduce a short course in agriculture during the winter, and to introduce a "new and distinct" four-year course in agriculture. At the same time, school trustees appointed William S. Beardshear as president and James Wilson as professor of agriculture.[60]

In 1876 Iowa State Teachers College at Cedar Falls became the third state school of higher education to be founded in the nineteenth century. Work to remodel the main building—formerly an orphanage for Civil War soldiers' children—was still under way when the first students arrived in

1876. As a result, "the sound of hammers and saws punctuated the first series of lectures." Nevertheless, with twenty-seven students on hand, the college was under way. The founding of the school coincided with the initiation of certification requirements for Iowa teachers and the recognition of state officials that if instruction was to be improved, potential teachers must have some place to receive training. Although legislators obviously recognized that fact by establishing a teachers' college, support for the school was not overwhelming: The initial bill had been passed "with just one vote to spare" in each house. In its first years of existence, the college received only "pauperish appropriation of funds," and officials found it necessary to work diligently to win more support from the legislature.[61]

By the first decade of the twentieth century, Iowans could take considerable pride in the fact that their state had established a plethora of religious and educational institutions. These developments are not surprising, however, given Iowa's location in the north central region of the country. In effect, this location almost guaranteed that, first, people coming to Iowa in the nineteenth century would be influenced by New Englanders' educational and religious thinking; and, second, that thousands of New Englanders, or their descendants, would arrive in Iowa to help build the very institutions that they cherished.

Religious and educational institutions constructed in Iowa in the 1800s would continue to influence the social fabric of the state. Iowans today still take great pride in their communities and their community institutions, particularly their churches and schools; these institutions are regarded by many as the bedrock of local society, which, along with family, impart proper moral values and training to each new generation. Early Iowans did their work well; educational institutions remain a valued and influential part of present-day society in the Hawkeye State.

8

A Home First and a Business Second:
Agriculture and Farm Life
in the Middle Years

f Iowa's many industries, only agriculture has affected the state totally, visible in every county during every decade of the state's existence. To Iowans even today, agriculture and Iowa often seem synonymous. Agriculture's dominant position within the state, however, has not prevented it from experiencing cycles of boom and bust; in the 1890s, 1930s, and 1980s, the state's farm families suffered disastrous depressions. There have also been less serious, but nevertheless difficult, economic periods in the 1870s and 1920s. At the same time, the early years of the twentieth century were years of prosperity. The study of agriculture alone, however, is not sufficient to understand the entire farm experience. Although agriculture encompasses activities related to land and production, the institution of the farm family also requires attention, including the separate roles of women and chil-

---

Schoolchildren at Crawfordsville Consolidated School in Washington County in 1910 ready to head home in horse-drawn school hacks. Photo courtesy of Wallaces Farmer.

dren. This chapter deals with agriculture and farm life from 1870 to the end of the 1920s. Later chapters cover the subject from the Great Depression to the present.

During the 1870s Iowa entered a new era. The Civil War had served as a watershed between the initial period of settlement and a time of maturity when farms and small towns covered most of the state. Iowa still contained pockets of unsettled land, but for families already on the land, most had moved from subsistence to commercial farming. Transportation, a major problem in the pre–Civil War period, had been greatly expanded with the building of five major railroads across the state; by the 1870s Iowa farmers had railroad connections to all eastern markets. The lack of adequate fencing, also a major difficulty before the Civil War, was solved with the commercial production of barbed wire in the seventies.

Major production patterns had also been determined by the 1870s, as farmers followed the advice to diversify crop production and raise livestock. Even before the Civil War, Iowa agriculturists had urged farmers to "Raise Corn always in preference to Wheat. Learn how to convert Corn into Pork, Beef, and Wool by the cheapest and most economical modes." During the war, farmers had ignored that advice, raising wheat in such quantities that Iowa ranked second nationally in wheat production. In the latter 1860s, however, Dr. Joshua M. Shaffer, secretary of the State Agricultural Society, advised his readers to "break away from a primitive, soil-exhausting cropping system," thus leaving wheat raising to areas to the west. Iowa farmers, he urged, should diversify production.[1]

Iowa farmers would quickly take that advice. Earle Ross has written that farmers in the 1870s would begin to raise cattle, soon moving from grazing to cattle feeding, thus taking advantage of the land's productivity. By the 1880s farmers were traveling to the British Isles to bring back such breeds as Scotch Aberdeen Angus. Hereford cattle were also imported, and by the 1880s Iowa was the center of Hereford importations.[2]

The most significant change, however, would come with farmers' emphasis on corn production. As Ross has pointed out, given the state's "peculiar adaptability" to corn growing, that crop would soon become the state's major agricultural commodity. In the 1870s Illinois ranked first in corn production, but by the following decade Iowa had earned that distinction. Once corn production became pronounced, farmers soon realized the most profitable utilization of corn came in fattening hogs. In the post–Civil War period, given limited demand for corn as food or for industrial use, farmers began to feed more and more of the golden cereal to hogs. Year after year farmers realized the best financial returns when they fed most of their corn crop to hogs. The result was a "phenomenal increase" in swine production and the creation of the "corn-hog complex," which has remained a vital part of Iowa's agriculture.

Although farmers would rank high in the production of corn and hogs, they also raised other products. Given the use of horses for pulling power and transportation, farmers raised large quantities of oats to provide food for the animals. Horse breeding became an important industry in its own right, as by the nineties Iowa was second only to Texas in the number of horses and claimed first place in terms of the animals' value.[3]

Although agricultural production characterized all parts of the state, soon after the Civil War regional specialties appeared. Perhaps most evident, farmers in northeast Iowa had become closely identified with the production of dairy products. Accordingly, the first commercial creamery in the state was established near Manchester in the 1870s. Butter production also became important in the state, but it took some time to standardize the product and eliminate the label of "wild west" butter, given earlier by easterners. Other specialties included grass-seed production in southwestern Iowa, flax production in north central Iowa, and popcorn production in Sac and Ida counties. Regional specialties were most dramatically demonstrated in the 1880s and 1890s when local boosters constructed a series of palaces throughout the state: Sioux Citians built a series of five corn palaces between 1887 and 1891 while citizens in Creston, Ottumwa, and Forest City built bluegrass palaces, coal palaces, and flax palaces respectively.

Although Iowa farmers would experience advantageous conditions during the Civil War, the postwar era was not without problems. A general agricultural depression affected the entire country from the 1870s until almost the turn of the century, bringing financial hardship to farmers everywhere. Iowa farmers experienced low prices for agricultural products, high interest rates, and inconsistent and seemingly unfair railroad rates; they also periodically experienced adverse weather conditions. Some forty to fifty years ago, when historians wrote about the post–Civil War period, they argued that though the economy as a whole was expanding, midwestern farmers failed to share in the fruits of that expansion. They viewed farmers as victims of "land monopolists, loan sharks, greedy railroad owners, unscrupulous commodity speculators, and unethical suppliers and processors." Therefore, farmers stood defenseless against the so-called middlemen or the eastern moneyed interests.[4]

Recent historical studies present a less vindictive view. These studies do not deny that farmers experienced financial distress, but they emphasize that midwestern farmers made important economic gains between 1865 to 1900. Donald Winters writes that "the truth of the matter is that farmers benefitted greatly from those groups accused of exploiting them," and even though farmers suffered, "as a group they enjoyed an improvement in their standard of living comparable to that of the average American."[5] In short, although farmers suffered periodically between 1865 and 1900—as did other Americans—they also benefited from the general expansion of the period.

Although recent scholarship shows that midwestern commercial farmers did benefit from the roles played by railroads, banks, and other institutions in the latter 1800s, it is important to note that farmers felt victimized and took action seeking relief. In the farm protests of the period, Iowa farmers took part but played a rather independent role. Although they joined various movements, they never embraced these groups as totally as did farmers in the Great Plains and in the South. As Leland Sage has observed, in any treatment of this historical period, particularly the 1890s, historians are "constantly challenged" to explain why Iowa farmers "were not swept into the Populist column," as were farmers in the Dakotas, Kansas, Nebraska, and Minnesota. Sage believes the answer lies in the fact that Iowa farmers did not experience the same extreme adversities as farmers in other areas. In short, Iowa farmers suffered, but not to the same extent as farmers elsewhere. Or put another way, "not all states were as secure for orthodox economics and politics as Iowa."[6]

Several factors mitigated the hardships faced by Iowa farmers. First, farmers had taken seriously the advice of earlier agriculturalists to diversify production and raise livestock; therefore, by the 1880s they were producing large quantities of corn, hogs, hay, and beef cattle. Specialties such as dairying in northeastern Iowa also brought economic stability. Iowa's geographical location, moreover, meant a higher level and more uniform pattern of rainfall—and fewer periods of drought—than in the Great

Plains. Also, Leland Sage believes that laws regulating railroad rates in the seventies and eighties provided some relief.[7]

Even in light of less difficult conditions than those suffered elsewhere, Iowa's farm families still responded in large numbers to several protest groups. In the 1870s Iowans flocked to the Patrons of Husbandry, also known as the Grange. The first Iowa unit formed in 1868 at Newton, and by 1873, 1,507 local units existed statewide. At its peak Iowa claimed one hundred thousand Grange members. The Grange, whose declared purpose was to "educate and elevate the American farmer," sponsored monthly meetings and annual Grange picnics, which brought families together for socializing as well as for business purposes. The group also promoted education: At monthly meetings members honed their skills in public speaking and parliamentary law and discussed recently published books. Grange members compiled crop reports, which they disseminated to other farmers.[8]

Although the Grange's main objective was the social and intellectual improvement of the farm population, founder Oliver Hudson Kelley knew that if "pecuniary advantages" were a part of the movement, it would have even greater appeal. The Grange thus set up cooperative enterprises that involved buying elevators, selling farm and household equipment, and even manufacturing farm implements. By 1872 the Iowa Grange controlled one-third of the state's elevators and warehouses. In 1873 the Iowa Grange secretary estimated that farmers saved $2 million by buying cooperative items. He noted that in buying sewing machines, for example, Grange members realized a 40 percent discount, and in buying farm wagons, a 20 percent savings. Following the failure of the manufacturing venture, however, Iowa's Grange membership plummeted. But for a few years the Grange had provided farm families with social opportunities that they sorely needed, and perhaps even with some limited economic relief.[9]

In the 1880s Iowa farmers also joined the National Farmers' Alliance, a group particularly strong in the Upper Mississippi Valley. Once a part of the national group, Iowans then organized the Iowa Alliance in 1881; within two years approximately 150 local groups existed in the state. The alliance continued some practices started by the Grange, such as cooperative marketing and establishing cooperative stores. Earle Ross points out that probably the most effective work of the alliance came in its fight against the barbed-wire combine. As a result, this combine was forced in

1885 to cut its price more than half, which brought the price within the reach of most farmers.[10]

The 1890s would bring forth the most significant agrarian movement of the latter half of the nineteenth century, the People's party, better known as the Populists. In August 1890 former members of what one historian has called "a baffling variety of factions and splinter groups" gathered in Des Moines to organize the Iowa People's party. This protest, the most extreme of the agrarian movement, "reflected the desperation that would no longer tolerate temporizing measures." The Populists called for inflation through national bank notes and free coinage of silver, regulation of corporations, public ownership of utilities, an income tax, and measures for more direct and responsive control of government. The Populists nominated Iowan James B. Weaver (earlier the Greenback-party candidate) as their presidential candidate.[11]

Described as "grim, gray [and] deadly serious," Weaver did not do well in Iowa. Though he garnered over a million votes nationally, he received only 20,595 in Iowa. Iowa's farmers were certainly not past the problems of drought, low prices, and high transportation costs, but perhaps they did not feel their problems sufficiently severe to embrace nontraditional politics. The Populist party would have the greatest appeal for farmers in the Great Plains and in the South, the regions experiencing greatest stress.[12] In 1890, throughout the Midwest and the South, the Populists would elect several governors, one U.S. Senator and numerous U.S. Congressmen.

In a recent study of populism in the Midwest, Jeffrey Ostler analyzes why farmers in Kansas and Nebraska supported the Populist party while Iowa farmers did not. Although Ostler agrees that severe economic problems existed, he argues the explanation lies in the fact that Iowa had a competitive-party system, whereas the other states had only a single-party system. He writes: "In Iowa, where the Democratic Party had become a genuine threat to the Republicans in the mid-1800s, a competitive-party system produced reform in response to Alliance demands, therefore discouraging third-party formation." In Kansas and Nebraska "the one party dominant political system" did not respond to demands for reform, leading the state alliances to organize the People's party.[13]

By 1898 Iowa farmers had returned to their traditional stance. Conservative in their political views, farmers in Iowa had during a period of thirty years joined various agrarian movements but had never been "swept" totally into any one. It is instructive to note that the organization that farmers joined in greatest numbers, the Grange, was the organization most clearly identified with providing social activities for its members. In times of difficulty Iowa farmers had always displayed great faith that good times would soon return. Even in the drought years of 1894 and 1896, Iowans remained optimistic. Perhaps a Warren County farmer best summed up this view in 1898: "Warren County is indeed prosperous. We hear of the return of prosperity, but it is a fact that Warren County has never lost her prosperity."[14]

Often ignored as a part of the American agricultural experience, the activities of the farm family, both socially and economically, are indeed important. Agricultural historians until recently have interpreted their specialty almost solely from the perspectives of land and production; they have rarely viewed (and then only briefly) the farming operation in a holistic way, whereby attention is given to the entire family. In short, historians have viewed agriculture as simply that—the study of major practices or activities stemming directly from the land, thereby either omitting the roles of farm women or casting them in an incidental light. As a result, studies abound on subjects such as cropping patterns, tenancy rates, and land speculation, as well as related areas of transportation and government farm policy. Although these studies are obviously vital in understanding the farm operation, the omission of other areas, such as women's roles, implies that they are less important or perhaps even insignificant. Accordingly, farm families and outsiders alike viewed agriculture as a male occupation, with men and boys performing the most important and most visible work.

In the past two decades, however, an increasing number of scholars have moved beyond the traditional mind-set on agriculture to see farm life in a broader context. Much of this work has dealt with farm women's varied work roles and, therefore, has automatically broadened the focus to the entire family and/or farm operation. Unlike men's work, which was often specialized, women's work, by nature of its diversity, touched every aspect of the farm operation. Women not only carried out domestic and child-rearing tasks in the farmhouse, but typically tended a large garden, raised poultry, carried out or at least assisted with milking chores, and sometimes worked in the field. Farm women's roles could not be studied comphrehensively without considering the entire farm operation, including children, hired hands, and extended family members in the household. In this sense the study of farm women has cast agriculture per se in its proper role: that of being viewed as one facet of farm life, albeit a crucial one, rather than as the totality of that experience.[15] The need to study all dimensions of farm living, however, should not obscure the fact that tasks in day-to-day living were typically gender specific. Men and women demonstrated mutuality in some decision making and in limited work areas, particularly milking and milk processing, but each generally worked apart from his or her spouse.[16]

Gender-specific work typically reached down to children. Daughters learned to keep house, sew, garden, and can by working with their mothers. Sons assisted their fathers with livestock feeding, milking, harvesting, and fence and building repair, thus learning the skills needed to become independent farmers. Historically, farm children made up a vast labor supply that could be contracted or expanded depending on the workload of individual farms and seasonal demands. The presence of children often meant that no money had to be spent on hired help, thus conserving cash.

Diaries and memoirs provide a personal view of the work of farm offspring and clearly reveal that parents expected young sons and daughters to accept major responsibilities. In 1880 Buchanan County farm woman Margaret Miller wrote in her diary that when it was time for spring cleaning, she and her daughters worked out the following arrangement: Margaret did the everyday work of churning, mopping, and baking, and her two daughters, Mary and Letta, did papering of walls and whitewashing of ceilings.[17]

For farm boys parental expectations were the same. Clifford Drury reflected on his work, even as a preteen, on a Sac County farm. When he was twelve and his brother, Grover, was thirteen, "We together took a man's place in the fields, and on the threshing crew." Drury recalled specific tasks as well as the fact that children learned responsibilities early: "My father believed in keeping his children busy as soon as they were able to perform simple tasks. Depending upon the season ... we were usually up at 5:00 or 5:30 a.m. Our first duty was to light the fires in the kitchen and the dining-room stoves. Then we went outside to do the milking, feed and water the horses, and clean out the barns before breakfast."[18] Regardless of sex or age, however, farm life meant many long hours of hard work with few labor-saving machines.

Both males and females did their work according to seasons. Springtime meant planting in the fields and the garden. Summertime brought the heaviest work period for everyone: Men cultivated corn, cut hay, and cared for livestock; women weeded gardens, preserved vegetables and fruits, and tended flocks of chickens. August was threshing time, which meant dirty, hot, hard work for men, and for women, long hours toiling over hot kitchen stoves. In feeding threshers, the farm woman's culinary abilities were on display in the same fashion that the man's work capabilities were reflected in the general appearance of the fields and farmstead. Fall months were generally filled with building maintenance, corn picking, and butchering of hogs and cattle to provide the family's winter meat supply.

Winter months on Iowa's farms, perhaps more than other times, highlighted fundamental gender differences. Though livestock still had to be fed and cows milked, during cold weather men had considerable opportunity to leave the farm, whether to visit neighbors, take part in township activities, or go to town on business or for pleasure. For farm women, child care and meal preparation were pressing daily responsibilities that did not change with the seasons. These responsibilities meant women had fewer opportunities to go to town to shop or socialize. In her diary Emily Hawley Gillespie, an Iowa farm wife who lived near Manchester, wrote repeatedly, "James [her husband] went to town today," while she stayed home.[19]

For farm women like Emily Gillespie, socializing took place, but generally in a more informal manner. Emily wrote about visiting neighbors on a regular basis and sometimes noted that she had sewn for a neighbor or had helped with a neighbor's sick child. Farms in Iowa in the latter nineteenth century were located fairly close together, often within less than a quarter mile of one another, and it was possible for women to walk to neighboring farms for visits, often taking along the youngest child as well as handwork, such as mending.

Diaries of other rural people are filled with references to frequent interactions between families. In 1877 Lydia Moxley, a young Iowa farm wife who lived near Grinnell, kept a diary of her daily activities. Typically she recorded that, several times each week, either she received visits from neighbors or she paid calls on them. The Moxley home was the scene of considerable socializing. In fact, a neighborhood bachelor probably spent too much time there, prompting Lydia to write: "John [Abplanalp] is here as usual." Lydia also recorded that the family frequently went to the United Brethren meeting. On January 14 she wrote they had attended the church meeting in the morning and again in the evening. Unmarried people socialized as well. At Spring Grove in Buchanan County, both before and after the Civil War, young people met on Sunday evenings at the Christian Church for singfests. One man later remembered that "the happiest hours I ever had was with the Spring Grove singers."[20]

Children, often left out of historical studies, can also be viewed in the context of socialization. In her study of Boone County, Nebraska, Deborah Fink has written that "For mothers, having children was a way to partly fill the emotional void created by leaving kin and familiar surroundings in eastern North America or Europe." Mary Hargreaves has observed that on the Great Plains women had large families to "relieve the loneliness" they experienced living on isolated farms.[21] Although Iowa farm sizes were smaller than those in eastern Nebraska—and therefore farms were closer together and less isolated—Iowa farm women probably shared these feelings and found their children's presence comforting. Emily Hawley Gillespie's diary certainly indicates that she treasured her two children, valuing their company and relying on them for emotional support. In short, Iowa farm women in the latter nineteenth century did not lack opportunities to socialize with relatives, neighbors, and friends, but the process usually took place within the home or the rural neighborhood and was often integrated with family responsibilities.

Although farm women's work has traditionally not been viewed as income producing, in reality a great many farm women performed work that resulted in substantial income. Each farm woman routinely raised chickens and then bartered eggs for grocery staples at the local store. Some women also sold chickens for cash. Each family generally kept a herd of cows, which provided milk and cream, the latter being sold or bartered at the local store. Farm women often churned, which frequently provided enough butter both for family and for sale.

Some women did more to qualify as wage earners. Emily Hawley Gillespie not only churned and sold butter but also sold baked goods to neighbors and at one time made bonnets, which sold for a profit of $1.70

each. At another time Gillespie raised turkeys, which she sold for $.75 each. Gillespie, an inveterate record keeper, recorded the family's total income in 1870: Emily's labor (poultry, eggs, sewing), $110.13; James's labor (wheat, hay, hogs), $42.95; mutual labor (butter—James milked and Emily churned—and boarding travelers), $76.21. If viewed in percentages, Emily's income accounted for 48 percent of the year's total income; James's, 19 percent; and mutual labor, 33 percent.[22] Farm receipts and records show that most Iowa farm income came from the sale of hogs, which indicates that 1870 was not a typical year. It is possible that fewer records have been kept on butter making than on the sale of hogs, wheat, corn, and beef cattle—considered to be the most important agricultural products—thus not accurately reflecting the importance of butter as an income-producing or barter item.

Life in the Iowa countryside, at least until World War I, was characterized by both continuity and change. Some aspects of farm life, such as social isolation, would continue for several more decades, and farming remained labor intensive, which meant that often farm folks worked from sunup to sundown. Although farmers had started farming "sitting down" (manufacturers were now adding seats to farm machinery), that practice did not eliminate many of the separate tasks involved in the production of crops or livestock. The work of farm men, women, and children continued to be dictated by the seasons; routines within the rural institutions of church and school reflected the same pattern. As David Danbom has observed, "American rural life in 1900 was in broad outline similar to what it had always been."[23]

At the same time, significant changes appeared that helped lessen social isolation and improve the quality of rural life. By 1900 an increasing number of farm families had telephones, which provided direct communication to neighbors and to town folks. Shortly before 1900 rural free delivery made its first appearance in Iowa; by 1901 Iowa had 292 rural routes. With this service farm families for the first time had daily mail delivery.

As with other aspects of change, these developments had clear gender implications. The general perception was that men used telephones for business, whereas women used telephones for socializing. Although this view seemingly trivialized women's behavior, in reality, it spoke to the particular social needs of farm women, an important consideration. As one farm woman later observed: "What a wonderful thing it was for the farm wife for it let her talk to her neighbors when her work did not permit her to leave the house."[24] With mail delivery farm families could receive daily newspapers, which contained market reports and notices of farm sales, information of interest primarily to male farmers. At the same time, as Roy Atwood has pointed out, rural free delivery was credited with increasing personal correspondence carried out mostly by women. A postal official at Davenport believed that the new system "made it easier for farmers' wives and daughters to 'carry on correspondence with other women whom they may not have seen for years.'" As with the telephone, mail delivery provided women with a means of socializing while remaining on the farm. Even magazines reflected a gender bias. The *Chicago Tribune* reported that new magazines were aimed particularly at rural women.[25]

In the view of some Iowans, however, the implementation of rural free delivery was a mixed blessing. One immediate result was the closing of fourth-class post offices, which often included a small store. Atwood has written, "The loss of the local post offices and the cultural trappings that went with them left many rural families feeling betrayed"—and in some cases more isolated than before. Small-town merchants complained that the mail-order houses, established soon after rural mail delivery began, took away trade. To counteract this effect, local merchants started the home patronage movement, trying to convince rural people that it was to everyone's advantage to shop locally.[26]

For the great majority of rural Iowans, however, life in the first decade of the twentieth century continued much as before. Amelia Grimsehl Hanselman reached adulthood during that decade, and her teen years and early married life serve as a good example of farm women's lives. Amelia's father had emigrated from Germany, and her mother was the daughter of German immigrants. As her great-grandson later wrote in a family history, Amelia's upbringing "had been a unique blend of German culture, including the German language and a distinctively conservative German Lutheran faith." Amelia's family had settled near Lu Verne in northwest Iowa. During her early years Amelia and her family interacted mostly with relatives and other German Lutherans in their rural community. The church played a central role in the family's life, as many social activities revolved around the church and its congregation. Like most children in that neighborhood, Amelia was confirmed in her midteens. At sixteen she was allowed to attend dances, which brought her into contact with non-German and non-Lutheran youths. As the family history makes clear, however, even though young people such as Amelia met new people, "the Germans tended to associate most closely with each other, and it was understood at all times there were to be no romantic attachments to non-Lutherans since such romances would have to be broken unless the other partner was willing to become Lutheran."[27]

Most days on the Grimsehl farm were spent working, but the family did indulge in at least one form of recreation—attending the county fair in Algona. On fair day everyone arose early to hurry through chores. After a quick breakfast the family headed toward town in a surrey; there they boarded the Chicago and North Western train for the trip to Algona. The family history records the day's activities:

> The train trip itself was rather exciting as they sped along through the late summer countryside ... but nothing could compare to the excitement of the fair itself. They walked around all afternoon looking at the exhibits and enjoying the entertainment. Amelia's mother thought it was conceited and wasteful to try for prizes for her own pies, preserves, and garden produce, but they all enjoyed looking at the things the others had entered. By late afternoon it was time to go and everyone was quiet during the ride back to Lu Verne. Already exhausted from the day's activities they all knew that there were still chores waiting to be done at home before supper.[28]

In 1908 Amelia, in keeping with family and community tradition, married Gottlieb Hanselman, who had immigrated with his parents from Germany. Like Amelia, Gottlieb belonged to the German Lutheran Church. The couple married in the church with a reception at home. The family made one purchase—flowers—as everything else, including the wedding dress, was made at home. Later that evening friends and family returned to shivaree the young couple. The next day the entire wedding party went to Algona to have formal wedding pictures taken. Later the same day, at her parents' home, Amelia began packing her things in preparation for the move to her own home.[29]

The young couple began married life on an eighty-acre farm that Gottlieb had purchased for $139 per acre. The farm was located east of

Livermore, placing it a few miles south of Lu Verne. Bridal gifts had been practical, to help the newlyweds begin housekeeping. Both sets of parents had given the Hanselmans laying hens. The move to their own home marked the beginning of many years on the farm; upon retirement they moved to Lu Verne. Throughout their married life they interacted with family and friends from their rural neighborhood. Amelia cherished her German heritage throughout her life.[30]

As the lives of Amelia and Gottlieb Hanselman indicate, the decade and a half before World War I proved to be a prosperous time for farm families throughout the state, and therefore a time for optimism. The term "new agriculture" symbolized that farming had come of age, moving from its pioneer beginnings in the Midwest to a position of dominance and modernization. Optimism about the bright future of agriculture was particularly evident in the Midwest. The press, popular magazines, and political figures all projected the American farmer as an "up-and-coming businessman." Moreover, farmers and nonfarmers alike believed favorable conditions would continue.

As Earle Ross has pointed out, the basis of prosperity for the farm sector was the strong demand for staple products. In the early part of the century the sale of cereals and meats to western Europe was high. Marketing facilities continued to improve in the United States, with specialized shipping practices and services undergoing improvement. Iowa's role in the new agriculture would be a dominant one. By 1916 Ross estimates that of the livestock receipts at the Chicago stockyards, 53 percent were from Iowa. In addition, meat packing had become a major industry in Iowa, particularly in Sioux City, Waterloo, Cedar Rapids, Ottumwa, and Mason City.[31]

The prosperity would also have an impact on farm income and land values. By 1914 the total gross farm income for Iowa was over half a billion. This amount accounted for 8.71 percent of the nation's total; two years later that figure had risen to 9.06 percent. Land values also rose. In 1900 the average price for an acre of Iowa land was $36.35. By 1910 that figure had climbed to $82.58, increasing 127.2 percent. Correspondingly, the value per Iowa farm would rise from $8,023 in 1900 to $17,259 in 1910.[32]

Many of these changes took place between 1909 and 1914, a period known as the Golden Age of American Agriculture, when farmers experienced economic equality or parity with other sectors of the economy. Gilbert Fite explains the development of parity this way: "After considerable study of price relationships, the United States Department of Agriculture [USDA] had determined that in the period 1909 to 1914 prices of farm products were at parity with the prices of nonfarm commodities. That is, during those years a certain farm commodity could be exchanged in the marketplace for a fair amount of nonfarm products. This fair relationship was later dubbed 100 percent of parity." Farmers and others would later look back to this period and use the price relationship between agricultural and nonagricultural products as the benchmark for comparison.[33]

At the same time, the state was moving toward a more comprehensive program to aid Iowa agriculture by passing along the latest findings of agricultural experts at Iowa State College and the USDA Experiment Station in Ames. The roots of the twentieth-century Cooperative Extension Service would go back to these programs as well as to farmers' institutes developed in the late nineteenth century. By 1898 the college had started Farm and Home Excursions, whereby visitors from all parts of the state came to campus to view work done there. Before long this activity had turned into the popular Farm and Home Week intended for both husbands and wives.

In 1902 the college would move to establish a more formal extension service by hiring Perry Greeley Holden. College officials appointed Holden as head of the Agronomy Department, but it was also understood that he would promote farm demonstration work, particularly in the area of corn production. Holden had earlier worked as a professor of agronomy at the University of Illinois and then for Funk Brothers Seed Corn Company. When Holden visited Ames to present a short course for the Funk Company, ISC president William Beardshear heard Holden's presentation. Impressed with his enthusiastic and informative presentation, Beardshear soon offered Holden a position. Once at ISC, Holden began traveling around the state to present material on corn-seed selection and cultivation. One such trip to Orange City resulted in the establishment of the first demonstration farm in Iowa, which, in turn, is viewed as the first extension work in the state.[34]

Holden's success in establishing demonstration plots and giving presentations led him to suggest yet another project. Holden believed strongly that every person who lived in the state was really "a pupil or student of [ISC] and that the college must see to it that every one receives some direct help from the college." This view was implemented when Holden proposed a traveling exhibit that would enable him to take his presentations on corn production statewide. With the support of the Rock Island Railroad, *Wallaces' Farmer,* and other state organizations, Holden put together his traveling exhibit, which he called the Seed Corn Gospel Train. On the train Holden told Iowa's farmers how to select the best seed corn and how to test it; he also demonstrated a germination box. In later excursions Holden dealt with crop rotation, manure handling, and hog raising. From 1904 through 1906 the corn trains traveled eleven thousand miles, reaching ninety-seven of Iowa's ninety-nine counties. College officials estimated that 145,700 people heard Holden's presentations.[35]

While at ISC, Holden initiated another project that also proved popular with the state's farmers. In 1905 at Red Oak he organized the first in a series of short courses on agricultural subjects, presented in different parts of the state by ISC professors. Once farmers began to hear about these programs, college authorities received thousands of requests. In the first winter the college received thirty-seven thousand inquiries about the program. Holden quickly saw the potential of the situation in light of his strong desire to establish a formal extension service. After mobilizing the support of the *Des Moines Register* and *Wallaces' Farmer,* among others, the result was the General Assembly's passage of the Extension Act of 1906. This legislation preceded by eight years the passage of the Smith-Lever Act, which created cooperative extension on a national basis.[36]

Between 1914 and 1929 Iowa's farm families would experience the catastrophic events of world war and a devastating agricultural depression. World War I began in Europe in 1914, and for three years the United States supplied food to European countries; in 1917 America entered the war. The newly established Cooperative Extension Service was mainly responsible for mobilizing Iowa's citizens for the war effort. Extension officials worked tirelessly to organize each of Iowa's ninety-nine counties for extension work. A slogan heard throughout the conflict, "Food will win the war," seemed especially appropriate for Iowa, given its agricultural preeminence.

Iowans quickly supported the war, both through food conservation and greater food production. Home demonstration agents, as a part of Cooperative Extension, presented demonstrations in every county on gardening, canning, raising poultry, butchering, and other aspects of food conservation. Federal officials asked Americans everywhere to conserve on wheat and meat, since these foods could more easily be shipped to the Allies. Town and city residents began to raise gardens and, in turn, canned large quantities of fruits and vegetables. In Buena Vista County citizens planted gardens in the spaces between sidewalks and streets, appropriately termed "front door gardening."[37]

On the farms, production records would also be set. According to extension director Ralph K. Bliss, farmers exceeded the most optimistic estimates. During the war Iowa farmers had increased their production of basic crops—corn, oats, wheat, barley, and rye—by 26 percent over the average yearly production for the ten-year period preceding the war. Hog production also rose, increasing 15 percent between 1917 and 1918.[38]

Shortly after the war ended, however, Iowa farmers would face a reversal of good fortune. In May 1920 the federal government ended wartime agricultural subsidies; agricultural exports also declined as European nations began recovering from the war. Farm prices then began to fall. In his annual report for 1921 Ralph Bliss summed up the difficult situation: "The average farmer grew about 50 acres of corn in 1921. The purchasing power of that 50 acres ... when exchanged for the manufactured articles which the farmer has to buy is just about equal to the purchasing power of 18 acres of corn in 1913 if expended for [clothing, fuel, building materials, and home furnishing goods]."[39]

Iowa farmers also found themselves in trouble because of financial obligations incurred during the war. In response to both patriotic messages and the opportunity to make a greater profit, many farmers purchased additional land on credit. These purchases came at a time when the state was experiencing "an unprecedented land boom." After 1920 farmers were caught in "a cost-price squeeze," whereby they had to continue making payments accrued during prosperous times (and a time of high land prices), even though they had experienced a substantial drop in income. Although Americans often identify the Great Depression only with the 1930s, in agricultural states like Iowa, the agricultural depression actually began in 1920.

Economic difficulties in rural Iowa continued throughout the 1920s, with few efforts to provide relief. The major attempt came in the form of national legislation, the McNary-Haugen Act—which twice passed Congress but was twice vetoed by President Coolidge. Gilbert N. Haugen, a second-generation Norwegian-American congressman from Northwood, cosponsored the bill. First elected to the House in 1898, Haugen had become chairman of the House Agriculture Committee in 1919 and worked unceasingly for passage of the McNary-Haugen Act.[40]

The farm legislation stemmed from the thinking of Illinois businessmen George Peek and Hugh Johnson, who in 1922 wrote a pamphlet expressing their views, *Equality for Agriculture*. They proposed to eliminate agricultural surpluses, thus raising farm prices, by selling the surpluses on two different markets. Commodities sold at home would sell at the domestic market price, but products sold later on the world market would probably sell at a loss. To cover the latter, an equalization fee would be assessed all producers; the plan would be administered by a government corporation. Leland Sage has observed that following the second veto, "the plan had become a political issue that had little to do with its merits. The issue took the form of a question: Should the government *do something* for agriculture?"[41] It had also become clear that nothing of substance would be done to help raise farm prices during the 1920s. As a result, the decade ended much as it had begun: Farmers continued to suffer from low prices with nothing done to reduce the surpluses plaguing American agriculture since the post–Civil War period.

At the same time, changes had taken place in the general area of farm living. The automobile had become an important means of transportation for the farm family. One farm wife, when asked why her family had invested in an automobile rather than in an indoor water system replied, "Well, you can't get to town in a bathtub." This sentiment seemed widespread throughout rural America. By the early twenties farmers in Iowa, along with those in Nebraska, had the highest per-capita ownership of automobiles in the nation. Though automobile ownership obviously brought pleasure to farm people, as David Danbom points out, it also had a negative side in that it "further damaged local institutions that were already in trouble."[42] Rural institutions such as churches and schools were indeed becoming less common. Farm families were still going to church but were attending services in town rather than in the open country.

In effect, in the 1920s many significant changes were occurring in open-country Iowa. With the start of commercial broadcasting in the

1920s, thousands of Iowa farm families purchased radios, which served both an educational and a business purpose, as well as alleviated social isolation. Earlier developments, such as the telephone and rural free delivery, had also reduced social isolation. In short, improved transportation and communication were beginning to erase distinctions between town and country living. As David Danbom has observed, "For better or worse, the countryside was being integrated socially into the urban nation. In its institutions and practices rural America was becoming a part of the larger social whole."[43]

A collective rural mentality also existed concerning the positive and negative features of farm life that produced a certain discontent. By the 1920s Iowa farm families seemed to be of "two minds" about themselves. On one hand, they still subscribed to the view inherent in the definition of agrarianism, "a belief in the moral and economic primacy of farming over other industry." Accordingly, they saw themselves as independent, self-sufficient, and morally superior to others. But at the same time, farm families had come increasingly to recognize the social deficiencies of farm living and clearly wished to share in the conveniences and comforts enjoyed by town and city folks. During the twenties these deficiencies were continually emphasized in popular publications, and by public officials and some agricultural spokesmen who proclaimed that, in contrast to town and city life, farm life was deficient and dull.[44]

A second aspect of this mentality had to do with prosperity, a view that made it even more difficult to continue living without modern conveniences. The Golden Age of Agriculture, when farmers did well financially, had "altered [farmers'] material standards and expectations." David Danbom writes that farmers in the twenties "demanded the same material comforts which magazines advertised for residents of Indianapolis and Chicago." As a result, because their standard of living had improved, during hard times farmers could not "cinch up" their belt as tightly as had their parents.[45] The result was not only unhappiness about the lack of government assistance to agriculture, but also discontent with farm life itself.

From 1870 to 1929 Iowa's farm families had experienced depression, prosperity, and again, in the twenties, another depression. During that sixty-year period Iowa agriculture had become diversified, which brought considerable prosperity and stability to Iowa's farm population. At the same time, given the uncertainty of weather conditions, foreign markets, and domestic situations, farmers had also faced ruinous conditions. While volatile in terms of production and profit, the period from 1870 to 1900 saw limited overall change for farm residents. Families still traveled by horse and buggy, went to town for mail, and did most of their socializing within their rural neighborhoods. By contrast, the period from 1900 to 1929 witnessed a time of major change in communications and transportation, with rural Americans becoming more like their urban counterparts.

Change did not come to rural Iowa without a struggle, however. In what might be called an "agrarian ambiguity," every change, such as rural free delivery, the automobile, and even the radio, brought a twofold response. On one hand, these changes made rural life more comfortable and brought greater satisfaction with farm living; on the other, each change threatened the distinct character of rural life, inherent in agrarianism itself. Rural mail delivery meant that social isolation was disappearing, a negative to some people; moreover, it led to a loss of business for local merchants. The automobile, though embraced totally by some ruralites, meant farm families could bypass rural institutions, thus foreshadowing the death of such entities as the country church. The automobile, in turn, meant better roads, which would allow city folks easy access to the tranquillity of the countryside.

This agrarian ambiguity meant that farm people were always held to a different standard of consumer behavior than were townspeople. Although it seemed understandable that urbanites would adopt modern transportation, communication, and other conveniences as quickly as possible, country people were expected to ponder these decisions and perhaps reject them if they brought fundamental change to the countryside. One recent study presents farm women as exploited by outside interests that urged women to purchase modern appliances to remove some of the drudgery from farm work.[46] While some farm people for various financial or social reasons might have rejected new technology for the home, it seems logical that farm families would have had the same desire as urban families to modernize homes and thus lighten farm women's workloads. For all the rhetoric about keeping the countryside unchanged and untainted by modern influences, farm families, like their urban counterparts, seemed eager to adopt new technology when it meant greater profit and/or greater convenience.

9

Town Life in the Middle Land

I n their studies of state history, historians of Iowa have tended to emphasize agricultural development while paying little attention to life in Iowa towns. Certainly in the period before the Civil War that approach seems justified, given the importance of initially settling the land. But by the 1870s town life was becoming increasingly visible. Even as early as the 1830s river towns appeared, and shortly thereafter small towns followed in the wake of initial agricultural settlement. Life in the smallest towns differed considerably from life in the open country, but at the same time, both town and country living reflected changes in technology, social thinking, and economic activity. An examination of life in Iowa's towns and the ways in which it changed between 1870 and 1930 is vital to an understanding of Iowa's past. As historian Joseph Wall has writ-

Chautauqua Pavilion at Red Oak in 1907. Photo courtesy
of the State Historical Society of Iowa, Des Moines.

153

ten, small-town values "have been taken as the state's values," and almost from the beginning of the state's history "townspeople have exerted an influence far beyond what their numbers would suggest."[1] That way of life would increasingly come to dominate the image Iowa projected to the world as well as the view internalized by Iowans themselves.

Towns that existed in Iowa in 1870, and those that would appear soon after, shared many common physical characteristics. Two general layouts predominated. Generally, county-seat towns, along with some additional communities in southern Iowa, were arranged around a town square. If the community was the county seat, the courthouse—along with several Civil War statues—adorned the square's center. Businesses then arranged themselves neatly along the perimeter.

The second dominant layout was associated with railroad development and more typically affected the western half of the state. As railroads built through eastern Iowa, an area already settled, they linked up existing towns along the right-of-way; as they continued building into western Iowa, however, they expanded into areas where few towns existed. Railroad companies then laid out town sites and promoted the sale of town lots. Railroad towns typically developed with the tracks and depot, along with a lumberyard and hotel, at one end of town, and other businesses located along a main street running perpendicular to the tracks. Though some homes were usually built on both sides of the tracks, the main residential area generally lay at the end of the main street opposite the depot.

Although many observers have used the term "one-horse town" to describe small towns in derogatory fashion, the reference to the horse was appropriate. As Lewis Atherton has written: "The presence of horses was evident everywhere. Droppings in the streets and town stables attracted swarms of flies and narrow-rimmed wheels of wagons and buggies cut gaping ruts during the rainy seasons."[2] The muddy, dung-littered streets not only posed a general health hazard, but presented special problems for women, whose long, full skirts might swish through whatever lay in their path.

Towns in the nineteenth century relied heavily on the horse for transportation. Local merchants used horses to pull their delivery wagons, which often made rounds both morning and afternoon. The local hack carried passengers from the railroad depot to the local hotel. To accommodate horses, town officials constructed watering troughs and hitching posts along the main street. The horse also accounted for the presence of a major business, the livery stable. Often at the end of the main street, or perhaps one block off the square, the livery served as a constant reminder that nineteenth-century residents were dependent on the horse for much of their local transportation and business deliveries. Many residents, moreover, had small horse-and-carriage barns at the rear of their residential lots.

The livery stable was only one business, however, located in Iowa's smaller communities. Each town's business section typically contained one or more general stores, a barbershop, hotel, saloon, and drugstore.

The Frank Bower Building in Lohrville in 1901 with Lohrville Opera House on the second floor. The ads probably tell of coming attractions. Photo courtesy of the State Historical Society of Iowa, Iowa City.

Many towns had several professionals, typically a physician, lawyer, and newspaper editor. Most towns also contained a wide array of artisans or craftsmen.

While nineteenth-century businesses were not generally viewed as gender specific, in effect, most establishments tended to be male dominated and to serve mostly male patrons. Women might clerk or work as bookkeepers for family businesses, but otherwise they were not generally visible in the business world. When men patronized local establishments, they stopped to chat with friends and associates. Lewis Atherton suggests in his study of Middle Border communities that with the exception of millinery shops, men congregated everywhere throughout the business district. Women apparently did not feel comfortable in most establishments, so they hurried through their shopping and headed for home.

That point is well illustrated in Hamlin Garland's short story "A Day's Pleasure." Mrs. Markham, a farm wife, accompanies her husband to town, eagerly looking forward to a day off the farm. Of necessity she brings along her youngest child, a babe in arms. Though her husband has a number of errands, her only destination is the general store, where she quickly completes her shopping. Although she would enjoy browsing in the store, she feels conspicuous and quickly leaves. Waiting for her husband to finish his errands, she has nothing to do but wander around town with an increasingly fussy baby. A local resident notices the forlorn farm woman and comments, "The saloonkeepers, the politicians, and the grocers make it pleasant for the man—so pleasant that he forgets his wife. But the wife is left without a word."[3]

The millinery shop, however, did provide women an opportunity to gather for socializing, learning about new fashions, and sharing a bit of gossip. Moreover, it offered both married and single women a chance to own and operate a business. In effect, the millinery business allowed a few women independence in the business world at a time when they lacked access to most other business areas. It also allowed women the opportunity to travel back East on buying trips and to observe the latest fashions, which they, in turn, shared with their customers. No doubt most female patrons did not have the opportunity to travel widely, and the opportunity to hear about faraway places like St. Louis or Chicago must have added pleasure to their lives.[4]

The presence of numerous diverse businesses in Iowa's towns reflected the fact—at least up to World War I—that for the tens of thousands of Iowans who lived there, life was local in character. Though Iowans certainly read newspapers and magazines covering events elsewhere, most interests and activities centered on or took place in one's own community. Before widespread use of the automobile, people visited the county seat for business or to attend social events like the county fair, but traveling greater distances was not routine.

Accordingly, town residents traded locally for groceries, clothing, and other necessities; the major exception was merchandise ordered through mail-order houses such as Sears, Roebuck, and Company. Advertisements appearing in local newspapers included a wide range of goods such as clothing, shoes, household appliances, and furniture. By 1895 Belle Plaine, with a population of approximately thirty-two hundred, contained twenty-nine merchants, about half of whom advertised regularly in the town's two newspapers. These advertisements indicate that local citizens could buy anything from lumber to pianos to hardware items, making it unnecessary to shop elsewhere. While most merchandise sold in Belle Plaine was probably shipped in by rail, even as late as 1895 the town contained a number of craftsmen, including several blacksmiths as well as a silversmith, marble cutter, broom maker, cheese maker, and harness maker. These workers represented the last producers of custom-made items so common throughout the nineteenth century.[5]

As elsewhere within the Midwest, Belle Plaine's mercantile establishments had begun to advertise brand-name merchandise. According to Lewis Atherton, well before 1900 the open barrels of crackers, rice, and beans had given way to packaged goods bearing individual brands. Patent medicines had led the way, even before the Civil War, in proving that advertising brands could create a market. These medicines proved particularly popular, if for no other reason than that they contained alcohol, especially appealing during times of Prohibition. The growing popularity of brand-name merchandise brought the eventual demise of many local businesses. Customers began to demand Pillsbury flour, for example, rather than flour from the local mill, after reading that the Pillsbury brand had superior baking qualities and greater consistency in quality.[6]

Although life did remain local in Iowa's small towns, the presence of a statewide transportation system brought many economic and social changes. Not only could merchants order goods from urban centers anywhere, but the railroads also made it possible for traveling road shows to appear in towns all over the state. By the 1890s communities like What Cheer began to construct opera houses or theaters. As a result, not only could local residents enjoy traveling performances, but excursion trains allowed patrons from nearby communities such as Belle Plaine, South English, or Montezuma to travel to What Cheer in the afternoon, attend a performance in the opera house, and return home the same evening.[7]

According to John B. Harper, theaters and opera houses "functioned very much as community social centers, the places where nearly everyone came to be entertained, to show off their finest new clothes, and to exchange notes on the latest town scandal." Harper believes that Iowans in the late nineteenth century "took great pride in being regarded as 'cultured.'" The facilities presented a variety of entertainments, including plays, vaudevillian productions, and musical events. As Harper points out, one week patrons might enjoy a Shakespearean play, and the next a popular melodrama, usually in luxurious surroundings. Though exteriors might be plain, the interiors, as the What Cheer facility demonstrated, were plush, with "winding stair cases, ornate moldings, and enormous chandeliers."[8]

Not only did railroads provide outside performers access to countless communities, but residents themselves found traveling to be far easier as Iowa's rail service expanded. By 1910, for example, towns along the Chicago and North Western right-of-way, such as Jefferson, had seven westbound and six eastbound trains daily, making it possible for residents to travel to nearby towns or out of state every day of the week.[9]

In his study of midwestern towns, Lewis Atherton has written that life in the latter half of the nineteenth century was characterized by three institutions: home, church, and school. By 1900 these institutions remained strong, although midwesterners were becoming involved in a wider variety of activities. In towns everywhere men organized Kiwanis, Rotary, and community-booster organizations, while women joined study clubs, General Federated Women's Clubs, or local chapters of the Women's Christian Temperance Union. Atherton referred to this trend toward organizational life as "the twentieth century cult of joining."[10]

Even as Iowans reached out to join countless organizations, the institutions of family, church, and school remained vitally important in town society. Families played a major social role as members came together to celebrate birthdays, holidays, and religious events such as christenings and catechisms. Families played a central role in the socialization of children and in instilling proper morals and religious values in the young. Churches and schools were then seen as buttressing family influence at every turn. Churches, mostly Protestant, held Sunday-school and church services on the Sabbath, midweek prayer meetings, and special services on Easter and Christmas. Public schools were a major institution in 1900, though most consisted of only eight grades and offered few extracurricular activities. For most towns activities such as sports, music, and drama would not appear until high schools were established. Every town also had communitywide activities such as baseball games, Fourth of July celebrations, and traveling circuses. These activities underscored the communal nature of towns, as anyone and everyone, regardless of family or religion, took part.

Yet another trait Atherton ascribed to Middle Border residents was a deep belief in practicality. Although some Iowans may have had aspirations for cultural enhancement, many rejected artistic endeavors for practical reasons. The "Cult of the Immediately Useful and Practical," according to Atherton, proclaimed that behavior was judged by whether or not it had "immediate, useful, practical utilitarianism." The cult, moreover, had several corollaries. The first related to income, proclaiming that "Every art and profession must justify itself financially." This meant that such callings as law, banking, and business, allowing substantial remunerations, were obviously justified; conversely, some occupations, like music making, did not. The second corollary stated that if an action was not immediately useful and practical, women might practice it, but not men. Daughters, therefore, could pursue art and music, but not sons. Atherton points out that young men interested in the fine arts and writing "escaped to the cities" because they found little support or acceptance in the rural areas of middle America.[11]

As the Cult of the Immediately Useful and Practical implied, within town society a gender division clearly existed. Although the doctrine of separate spheres, which described major differences in men and women's lives in the mid-nineteenth century, was less apparent by 1900, it had not completely disappeared. Simply put, females were held to a different set of rules than were males. Men still lived much of their lives in the public world, whereas women were expected to remain at home, tending to their domestic duties. As one woman explained it, even as late as the 1920s women working outside the home were "thought to be not quite decent; working would just not have been right." Interestingly, however, the same woman then qualified her statement: "If a woman worked for someone she knew—like a family member—that work was acceptable."[12] This "qualification" apparently was widely accepted, as both single and married women worked in a myriad of family businesses where they clerked, stocked shelves, and kept books. Most parents, no doubt, viewed their daughter's work as "just helping out," whereas a son performing the same tasks was "learning the business."

Among the many rules governing the life of females were those related to social behavior. Winifred M. Van Etten, growing up in Emmetsburg before the First World War, remembered the taboos governing the behavior of young females, most of which related to sex. These included not parting one's hair on the side, since boys wore their hair that way; not playing cards or dancing; not looking into the open door of a blacksmith shop while walking by; not walking on a street that had a saloon; and not owning a dog. As Van Etten explained, "No nice girl had a dog of her own. The family dog was all right, but as a piece of personal property the dog was taboo." The modest appearance of young women was also crucial. Before going to church, Van Etten explained, she and her sisters had to line up in front of "the east door through which the summer sun sent stabbings of light. If there was the slightest sign of a shadow, back we went to put on another petticoat." Sometimes Van Etten had to wear as many as five at one time.[13] As Van Etten's comments imply, it seemed that, at least socially, the separate spheres of men and women were alive and well in Iowa towns in the early twentieth century.

Increasingly after 1900 town residents came to own automobiles. Although this new invention probably made the greatest difference in the lives of farm people, the horseless carriage also impacted significantly on townspeople. In 1904 Iowa had 155 cars licensed in the entire state. The state legislature determined that in "built-up" sections of cities and towns, the speed limit was "one mile in six minutes." On the open road the first speed limit was "an average rate" of twenty miles an hour.[14] Even though the earliest cars were extremely noisy, emitting a series of small explosions as they lurched along, town residents quickly discovered they led to a far cleaner physical environment than did the old gray mare.

While Iowa towns had many distinguishing features, by 1900 perhaps the most all-encompassing characteristic dealt with religion and
morality. Sidney Mead has observed that by the latter half of the nineteenth century, Protestantism dominated American culture, "setting the
prevailing mores and moral standards by which personal and public, individual and group conduct was judged."[15] Though Iowa certainly had communities with sizable Catholic populations, Protestant churches did pre-
dominate, especially the Methodists, Presbyterians, Congregationalists,
and Baptists, and, in turn, set the prevailing "mores and moral standards"
for their communities.

Accordingly, Tom Morain, in his study of Jefferson in the early twentieth century, writes of the presence of a "Protestant moral code" that governed behavior. That moral code determined it was sinful to play cards,
dance, drink alcoholic beverages, or engage in certain secular activities on
the Sabbath. As Morain writes, in Jefferson "when one worried what
'they' would think or if 'they' would approve, 'they' were Protestants."[16]

The Protestant code was further reflected in Sunday blue laws enacted by the Iowa General Assembly. According to the Iowa Code, Section 5040, "If any person be found on the first day of the week, commonly
called Sunday, engaged in carrying firearms, dancing, hunting, shooting,
horse racing, or in any way disturbing a worshipping assembly or private
family, or in buying or selling property of any kind, or in labor except that
of necessity or charity, he shall be fined." In Jefferson, however, these restrictions soon began to disappear as locals desired to play baseball on
Sunday.[17]

Although life in Iowa's smaller towns conjures up a pleasant, nostal-
gic view of like-minded people, content with their well-ordered lives, social divisions existed within every community. Atherton has written that
each town had its drunkard, its village idiot, and other less-favored individuals. Despite the fact that town residents have often been reluctant to
speak of the existence of social classes within their communities, social
divisions did exist in varying degrees everywhere. In towns served by railroads, the section that lay "on the wrong side of the tracks" implied low
social status for families who lived there. Some individuals who did not
find a comfortable niche within their communities had the opportunity to
leave, but others reluctantly stayed and endured the stigma of poverty, al-

coholism, and out-of-wedlock births. In towns where almost everyone knew everyone else, moving beyond these stigmas was difficult, if not impossible.

There seemed to linger, even from the days of the seventeenth-century Puritans, a sense of the worthy and the unworthy poor. The unfortunate widow, struggling valiantly to raise her fatherless brood, was to be pitied *and* assisted. On the other hand, those who could not rise above poverty because of disabilities, misfortune, or simple inactivity did not deserve either pity or assistance. Town society on the Middle Border, as Atherton has observed, did not tolerate deviance or noncomformity easily. To this day, it seems, residents typically have two views of town life: It was a wonderful place to grow up because everyone was so supportive; or it was a bad place to live because everyone knew your business. The first usually implies acceptance and well-being; the second, nonconformity and rejection.

Like all society, town life was not static. Social and economic events, particularly World War I, would bring change into Iowans' lives; the decade of the twenties would alter life even more. The comfortable, well-ordered, homogeneous existence of Iowans began to fray. By the 1920s, moreover, town life began to come under sharp criticism by popular writers. Sinclair Lewis's *Main Street* is perhaps best recognized for pointing out the monotony and mediocrity of small-town existence. The decade would also bring economic difficulties for the nation's farm families, which, given the symbiotic relationship between town and country, impacted heavily on town business life.

World War I would affect Iowans in many ways, particularly in the area of social change. The war strengthened Iowans' xenophobic feelings and brought repressive measures, such as Governor William Harding's foreign-language ban; German-stock citizens, the largest ethnic group before the war, were particularly vulnerable to antiforeign feelings. The war apparently justified overzealous citizens taking vigilante-type actions, like holding kangaroo courts in which Iowans, usually first- or second-generation immigrants, were threatened with deportation if they did not purchase Liberty bonds. It seemed that in wartime objectionable actions could be tolerated under the guise of being patriotic or promoting Americanism. And the repression, suspicion, and fear created by wartime conditions and actions perhaps made Iowans tolerant of and susceptible to later excesses, such as those inherent in the Ku Klux Klan.

Although the "Great War" is usually presented in broad context—such as the war to end all wars, or the war to save democracy—when examined from a closer perspective, it seems quite different, and local issues suddenly become paramount. Nancy Derr has observed that in Iowa the major impact of the war "was the weakening of the feeling of entitlement to be different, isolated, and idiosyncratic." In short, according to Derr, the war had the effect of "breaking down the spirit of resistance," and forcing "conformity to a narrow standard of behavior." In her study of Iowans during the war, Derr presents examples of their resistence and nonconformity before that conflict. Farmers in southern Iowa resisted improving rural roads and establishing a highway patrol; foreign-stock population, particularly German Americans, continually opposed Prohibition laws; and some Iowans opposed modernization of any sort, believing that the status quo would better serve rural communities.[18]

During the war, town residents everywhere experienced a barrage of pressures. While government officials urged Iowa farmers to produce more wheat, corn, hogs, and livestock, they asked town dwellers to plant victory gardens, canning the fruits and vegetables to help produce and conserve food. Moreover, officials encouraged people everywhere to alter their diets, observing meatless and wheatless days, again to help conserve foods that could be shipped to the Allies. Officials also urged all Iowans to contribute to the Red Cross and purchase Liberty bonds, which provided the main financing for the war. Local newspaper editors sometimes listed names of Liberty-bond purchasers and Red Cross contributors. In Jefferson, editor Vic Lovejoy listed both the names of Red Cross contributors and the amounts they contributed. This practice, of course, had the practical consequence of publicly indicating who had not, thus allowing local residents to assess the patriotism of everyone in Jefferson.[19]

Though town residents everywhere responded enthusiastically to wartime demands, some towns demonstrated more unity than others. Tom Morain has written that in Jefferson the war had the effect of strengthening the town's "sense of community by uniting residents in a common purpose and encouraging sacrifice for the general welfare." That sense of community, no doubt, brought a greater outpouring of support for the war through the purchasing of war bonds and the conservation of food. In Jefferson, as in other communities, not only did residents contribute money to the Red Cross, but women made articles of clothing for soldiers, including sweaters, mufflers, socks, pajamas, and handkerchiefs. To personalize their gifts, women sometimes included their names in the toe of a sock or on paper pinned to a muffler. Occasionally the recipient of the gift responded with a thank-you note. On one occasion, however, a soldier expressed disgruntlement after receiving a pair of knitted socks: "The right one's too big / And the left one don't fit / Who in the hell / Taught you how to knit?"[20]

But not all communities experienced a "coming together" mentality. Iowa towns differed in terms of ethnic composition, and many communities with sizable German-stock population experienced some dissension. Nancy Derr found that in communities such as Lowden—with large numbers of German Americans—that antagonisms created during the war still remained some fifty years later.[21]

Town residents might make sacrifices in regard to food and money, but ultimately the greatest sacrifice came in the form of human lives. America entered the war in April 1917, and the following November Merle Hay was the first Iowan to die in battle. Hay and two other soldiers were killed in a surprise German attack on November 3. The three men's deaths marked the first loss of life for American soldiers in France. Hay had grown up on a farm near Glidden and worked as a farm-machinery repairman before his enlistment in May. During the nineteen months that the United States was at war—from April 6, 1917 to November 11, 1918—approximately two thousand Iowans died.[22]

Following the armistice, if Iowans expected a return to quieter, less contentious times, they were greatly disappointed. Soon after the fighting stopped, Americans everywhere entered a period of national unrest. In 1917 the Bolshevik Revolution took place in Russia, which in turn produced a "red scare" in the United States as Americans feared the spread of socialistic ideas. In 1919 a series of major strikes erupted in American cities as workers protested low wages, a shortage of jobs, and an escalating cost of living; in that year some thirty-six hundred strikes took place involving over 4 million workers. By 1920 the United States Census would indicate that the country contained over 14 million people born in foreign lands, thus helping to fuel even stronger xenophobic fears. Over half of these people, moreover, had come from Catholic countries in southern and eastern Europe, thus threatening the dominance of Protestantism in the United States.[23]

The unrest and fear that first affected the nation's major cities quickly filtered down to America's heartland. Midwesterners, including Iowans, witnessed social change and economic dislocations which, in turn, threatened social values and produced a strong desire to return to an earlier culture and value system. As Americans searched for ways to maintain the status quo and stave off social change, some turned to the Ku Klux Klan. First organized in the South after the Civil War, the Klan experienced a revival in the 1920s, reappearing mainly as an antiforeign, anti-Catholic, anti-Semitic fraternal group. The Klan reached its greatest strength in the mid-1920s, after which it quickly faded. Although historians have determined that the Klan was active in some midwestern states, particularly Indiana, few studies have been done on the Klan in Iowa.

In the most comprehensive study of the Iowa Klan, Kay Johnson writes that though the group was active in Des Moines and many smaller communities, Greenfield was the Klan's stronghold in Iowa. With a population of eighteen hundred, the Greenfield KKK exercised considerable influence in areas of business and politics. Local Klan members built a fifty-thousand-dollar Klavern, or meeting hall, entirely with volunteer labor, the only such Klavern built in the state.[24]

Johnson presents a profile of Klan members in Greenfield during the twenties, noting that members tended to be fairly young, with a median age of thirty-three; two-thirds were under forty. Most Klansmen belonged to the Methodist, Presbyterian, or Church of Christ denominations, and most had lived in Greenfield all their lives. Occupationally, most members fell into three categories: farmers, clerks, and self-employed merchants. The latter category included owners of a clothing store, drugstore, meat market, and barbershop. A third of the Klan members belonged to the Masons, and only three belonged to the American Legion. Greenfield Klan members all fell into the broad category of the middle class, though none of the town's "best citizens" belonged.[25]

Of all aspects of Klan activity, perhaps the most intriguing and perplexing question is, Why did men join? Johnson believes that several social and economic factors explain the Klan's attraction. In the 1920s Iowa's smaller towns were homogeneous in character: In Greenfield, out of eighteen hundred residents, there were fifty-nine immigrants (presumably first generation) and six African Americans. The town did contain a sizable number of Catholics, although many lived outside the community proper. In Johnson's view Greenfield's homogeneity produced monotony, drabness, and boredom. Klan membership offered social activities (some members said they joined for that reason); a sense of superiority in regard to the town's less fortunate citizens; a feeling of exclusivity, given the group's secret rituals; and a sense that members were helping to preserve old values that seemed in danger of being swept away.[26]

At the same time, Greenfield residents' anxiety and fear about declining economic status may have prompted some to join the Klan. The entire state was in the throes of depression throughout much of the twenties, and Greenfield citizens were not immune to these difficulties. Between 1920 and 1925 the value of land and buildings per farm in Adair County had dropped from $34,605 in 1920 to $18,265 in 1925. Paralleling that decline was an increase in the percentage of mortgaged farms, from 33 percent in 1920 to 67.3 percent in 1930.[27] The old order seemed to be changing both socially and economically, and men perhaps viewed the Klan as a way to return to prewar conditions.

By 1925, according to Johnson, the Klan had had a major impact on Greenfield: Townspeople often reacted suspiciously of neighbors and fellow businesspeople; as folks passed one another on the street, they "made it a point not to speak to each other or else muttered under their breaths as they passed." Because there were few blacks or immigrants in Greenfield, Klan members focused their "wrath" on Catholics. Eventually Klan members extended their disfavor to Protestants who had not joined the Klan. In effect, the Klan had divided Greenfield, created suspicion, and "brought riot where once there had been calm." After fleeting success in municipal politics, the Klan disappeared from the community.[28]

Although residents of some communities such as Greenfield may have felt boredom in their lives, from 1900 on, Iowans would experience new forms of entertainment. Increasingly, town residents came to enjoy Chautauqua events. The Tent Chautauqua—so-called because lectures, concerts, and recitals took place under a big tent—began operating in 1903. Chautauqua had limited popularity in cities, but both town and country residents flocked to Chautauqua events, which promoters frequently planned to fit the farm families' work schedule. Often events lasted for a week, known as Chautauqua Week. In Jefferson the first Chautauqua took place in 1905 and soon became so popular that Jefferson residents created the Jefferson Chautauqua Association, purchasing a permanent site and installing camping facilities. Both town and country residents camped on the grounds, taking in the full-week's activities. Events gradually ceased to be religious in nature and changed from the "serious and uplifting to the purely entertaining." Although the Tent Chautauquas were tremendously popular in towns across the country throughout the 1920s, other forms of entertainment, particularly the radio and the motion picture, eventually led to a dwindling attendance at Chautauqua events.[29]

Competing with Chautauqua for some years, and finally eclipsing it, was the motion picture. A major step in developing the moving-picture show came with the opening of the first nickelodeon in Pennsylvania in 1905. From there the industry developed rapidly, and by 1908 hundreds of motion pictures were produced every year. The first productions were silent films, but in the latter 1920s talkies appeared. Theaters soon appeared in the nation's smaller communities. In 1908 the Broadway Electric Theatre opened in Algona, where people who were willing to pay ten cents (half price for children) could see an eclectic collection of short films. Algonians then debated whether movies were "just a fad of which the public would rapidly tire" or if they would have longtime appeal. By the teens, Iowans could watch serials such as *The Perils of Pauline*.[30]

Before long, however, town residents began to question the morality of some films. As Tom Morain has pointed out, even in smaller communities like Jefferson, using "sex to sell a movie was standard practice during the twenties." Newspapers carried movie ads with adjectives such as "lurid," "passionate," or "shocking." Moreover, in Jefferson adolescents used movie stars for role models, trying to imitate their clothing and standards of behavior. Some adults believed movies immoral because young men and women sat together in darkened theaters, and some residents proposed that both males and females should be at least eighteen years old before they could attend a movie. Critics also charged that movies shown on Sunday kept people from attending church.[31]

In the 1920s movies offered lessons in consumption, the same as television would several decades later. Viewers sat in movie theaters everywhere and witnessed the latest in household technology, home decorations, and even clothing styles. One viewer wrote that movies enabled her to "observe a better way of living." Another woman wrote that after attending a movie, she rearranged her home to duplicate what she had seen in the film. Given the presence of movie theaters everywhere, residents in Iowa were exposed to the same influences as were people in Los Angeles, Chicago, or Cincinnati, thus ending both the isolation and distinctiveness of midwestern town society.[32]

By the end of the 1920s, social life in Iowa's towns had undergone major change. Chautauqua serves as a good example of that change, both in Iowa and in other parts of the Midwest. Between 1900 and 1920 Chautauqua events found great favor with town residents, partly because of a moral code which implied that people should participate only in uplifting and morally acceptable activities, and partly because of an absence of other entertainment forms. By the mid-1920s, however, the programs could not compete with the more worldly motion picture, nor with radio programs such as *Amos and Andy*. The passing of Chautauqua was significant in both a real and a symbolic sense: In effect, town society, in which the prevailing moral code had become less stringent and people less socially isolated, found its residents more integrated into a national system of entertainment through both movies and radio.

In his study of Jefferson, Tom Morain has written that the town in 1930 was a far different place from what it had been in 1900. By 1930 Jefferson residents had reached an accommodation with the Protestant code of behavior. Churches were still important, but no longer did they have a "virtual monopoly on social organization." Morain, in fact, writes that while a "church morality" still existed, a "community morality" had also come into existence. The latter dealt with situations not covered by the former. Morain concludes that Jeffersonians were not divided into camps, but rather were comfortable with both sets of rules.[33]

Automobiles also contributed to changes in town society. Although it is unlikely that many residents traveled widely in their leisure time, they did take drives to neighboring towns, both for business and for pleasure, thus helping to end the isolation of communities. Many historians have emphasized the changes in "morals and manners" that came as a result of the automobile, as young people, for the first time, could escape easily the watchful eyes of adults. Certainly those changes affected youth in Iowa as elsewhere.[34]

One way to highlight the changes evident by 1930 is to revisit Main

Street, or the town square, of that year. Gone are the livery stable and horse railings; instead, automobiles are parked around the courthouse square and along main street. In Belle Plaine, for example, by 1925 a filling station and car-repair garage occupied the earlier site of the community livery stable. Two years later Belle Plaine had eight auto-repair shops and three filling stations. Also missing by 1930 are the harness and blacksmith shops. Main Street now has at least one or two movie theaters. Many communities also have cabin camps located along highways to accommodate travelers.[35]

A major change for town society by 1930 came through the public schools. In 1900 many towns still had one- or two-room schools, and many had only six to eight grades. By 1930 high schools had proliferated around the state. High schools not only offered a wide range of courses, but also a greater choice of extracurricular activities. Girls' and boys' sports, especially basketball, had communitywide appeal, with local residents faithfully following "their" team. The local gymnasium became a community center where townspeople—rich and poor, old and young—cheered their teams to victory.

Janice Beran's study of Iowa girls' basketball points to other aspects of the game. For the players themselves, an important consideration was that females had equality with males through the basketball program. As a former coach in the 1920s remembered: "In those days people thought girls should have as many opportunities as boys." Former players interviewed by Beran recalled traveling to other communities and to Des Moines. One explained: "There was not much else to do. It was an opportunity to go out of town, to go to Des Moines, and see the electric lights." The sport also brought increased pride in one's community and school, even if the team was not having a winning season.[36]

While town society was viewed as fairly homogeneous in 1900, by 1930, even in light of a statewide increase in different ethnic groups and African Americans, small towns exhibited greater conformity. Minorities were almost nonexistent in most small and medium-size communities: Increasingly, the largest racial minority, African Americans, would live in cities like Des Moines and Waterloo. Southern and eastern Europeans, the main immigrant groups arriving after 1900, lived mostly in coal-mining communities and in cities. Town society, therefore, was composed primarily of white residents, most of whom were born not only in the United

States, but within Iowa. In Belle Plaine, for example, in 1895 25 percent of the population was foreign-born; by 1925 that number had declined to 15 percent. Of Belle Plaine's native-born population in 1895, 21 percent had been born in Iowa; by 1925 that number had risen to 59 percent.[37] Given the drop in first-generation immigrants, Belle Plaine's population in 1925 had become even more ethnically and culturally homogeneous than thirty years before. State census figures indicate that this situation was typical throughout Iowa's towns.

Iowa towns still reflected strong gender distinctions, but perhaps by 1930 these were less visible than thirty years earlier. Women had been granted the vote in 1920 and so had a political presence not previously evident. (See Chapter 12 for discussion of women's suffrage.) Given the easing of the Protestant moral code, and the move toward organizational life, women were active in a myriad of organizations, including garden clubs, child-study clubs, book clubs, community-improvement clubs, and professional organizations. Women, once routinely active in church and school affairs, began to move out into the wider society after 1900. The doctrine of separate spheres lingered on, but only in faint outline.

By the end of the twenties town residents probably reflected positively on most aspects of their lives. Town living had become more comfortable in a physical sense and more diversified socially. Critics in faraway places might attack the very essence of town living, but those criticisms could be ignored or subsumed by the day-to-day demands of ordinary life. But though town life might have represented the norm for the majority of Iowans in the nineteenth century, urban life, even as early as the 1870s, began to cast a long shadow—a harbinger of things to come.

10

Urban Life in the Hawkeye State

Although Iowa has never contained cities the size of Minneapolis or Omaha, smaller urban areas developed in the state. Though not major metropolises, cities such as Des Moines, Cedar Rapids, and Davenport would experience the full range of problems associated with urban development, including the need to provide adequate housing, install proper sanitation measures, and maintain public order. In Iowa, as elsewhere, each large community would develop a particular character determined by the community's location, its industrial activities, and its population. Iowa's river cities serve as the best example of communities influenced by location. Iowa's eight largest cities during the period from 1870 to 1930—Des Moines, Davenport, Cedar

---

Downtown Des Moines, 300 block on Fourth Street, showing various types of transportation, c. 1915. Photo courtesy State Historical Society of Iowa, Des Moines.

171

Rapids, Sioux City, Council Bluffs, Dubuque, Clinton, and Burlington—
would each develop at a different rate and exhibit a different persona; yet
all communities would contain similar cultural, educational, and service
institutions. For people who called these places home, life would have a
different tempo and ambience than for those who settled in rural areas.

In 1870, with a total population of just under 1.2 million, Iowa had
moved beyond the pioneer stage of settlement. In every part of the state a
visitor might find an abundance of small villages and medium-size towns,
but only six communities with over ten thousand residents. One of the latter would be the capital city of Des Moines, with a population of 12,035
in 1870. Population was heaviest in the eastern part of the state, particularly along the Mississippi River. Accordingly, Dubuque, located along
the "queen of rivers," was Iowa's oldest community (founded in 1833) and
was well on its way to becoming the state's major industrial city. Other
Mississippi communities of note were Clinton, Davenport, Muscatine,
Burlington, and Keokuk. Along the Missouri River, both Sioux City and
Council Bluffs showed early potential for growth.[1]

Even though Iowa's urban centers were obviously destined to increase in size, that growth would take place in a state with a strong antiurban bias. Throughout the nineteenth century, even though an increasing number of rural Americans moved into neighboring cities and towns,
urban areas were seen as places of evil. Among those writing about such
evil was William Holmes McGuffey, who expressed his views through
children's readers. Iowa had its own critics of city life (and proponents of
rural living), including "Uncle Henry" Wallace, who urged young boys
and girls to remain on the farm and not end up on the "scrapheap of life."[2]

Throughout the nineteenth century, as Iowa's population remained
overwhelmingly rural, Iowans firmly espoused agrarianism, the belief in
the superiority of rural life. Accordingly, individuals raised on farms were
superior both physically and morally. Farms produced stable, hardwork-
ing, independent people who therefore constituted the nation's best citizens. On the other hand, the cities, with their vices of gambling, drinking,
dancing, and prostitution, were to be avoided. As Iowa's cities continued
to grow, weary ruralites no doubt cast disapproving eyes on city folk and
their sometimes unacceptable ways.

Suspicion of Iowa's urban areas would be expressed in many ways.

In the 1850s state officials faced the decision of where to place the new land-grant college. Several years earlier the state had created the University of Iowa at Iowa City, and with a view toward economy, some legislators suggested placing the agricultural curriculum within the university. Other legislators responded with astonishment, stating that the Iowa City school was "an urban university." One legislator observed that Iowa City was not the right place for the agricultural school, because "in the heart of a populous city," with "no suitable boarding house where young boys can be under the care and control of a suitable person who would look to their welfare? They would be turned loose after school hours, to all the enticements, vices, and corrupting influences of a city."[3]

Regardless of the general antipathy toward cities, however, the population of urban areas would continue to grow. In 1880 the federal census showed 1,624,615 residents in the Hawkeye State. That figure not only reflected an increase of more than 33 percent over the previous federal census, but also indicated that "the predominately rural state of Iowa had an urban dimension." As Lawrence H. Larsen has pointed out, in 1880, 126,227 members of Iowa's population resided in seven communities of 10,000 or more, "the breaking point used by nineteenth-century demographers to differentiate between large and small cities." These communities were Des Moines (22,408); Dubuque (22,254); Davenport (21,831); Burlington (19,450); Council Bluffs (18,063); Keokuk (12,117); and Cedar Rapids (10,104). At the time, the country contained 227 communities with over 10,000 residents.[4]

In his discussion of Iowa's urban centers, Larsen points out several characteristics of larger communities that set them apart. The cities contained more foreign-born than the state as a whole, which had 15 percent: Des Moines and Keokuk both included 19 percent foreign-born, and Davenport, with a large German-American population, contained 32 percent. Although more African Americans were located in cities than in rural areas, the overall number of blacks in the state remained low. Keokuk had the highest number of blacks—9 percent of the total population—but in other cities the total number was not more than 3 percent.[5]

The religious preference of city dwellers in 1880 also set them apart from rural Iowans. Although the state was predominately Protestant, Catholics made up 34 percent of Dubuque's total population, and 15 percent of the population of Davenport. According to Larsen, only Des

Moines, with 414 Jewish residents, and Davenport, with 50, had significant Jewish populations. However, Iowa contained no synagogues in 1880.[6]

Early in the history of Iowa's largest communities, the city fathers would face problems providing adequate health and sanitation measures and keeping communities clean. As Larsen has pointed out, "hauling away filth" was a major function of the Gilded Age urban governments. Cities contained an average of one horse for every four residents, and "in an eight-hour working day a thousand horses deposited approximately five hundred gallons of urine and ten tons of dung in the streets." Typically, street cleaning involved two steps: The first worker swept dirt into the gutter and a second worker then shoveled the dirt into wagons for transporting to city dumps. Larsen believes that because residents had low expectations regarding cleanliness standards, city efforts were limited: In Davenport, for example, local authorities spent five hundred dollars to clean streets. Some cities used street sweepings to fill potholes; in Cedar Rapids workers dumped debris into the Cedar River.[7]

Garbage pickup presented another problem for urban dwellers. According to Larsen, none of Iowa's largest communities had adequate garbage service. Although Des Moines had specific rules requiring the burying of garbage and disposing of ashes, citizens often ignored them. According to Des Moines's mayor, "The ordinance prohibiting people from depositing ashes, debris, and filth in the streets and alleys is entirely ignored, rendering it impossible at times to get through them with a loaded wagon, and seriously endangering the health of the citizens on the approach of warm weather."[8]

At the same time, city residents believed that fire and police protection were more important than garbage disposal. By 1880 all Iowa cities of ten thousand or more had professional fire departments. In 1878 Burlington's eighteen firefighters had responded to sixty-five alarms, complete with four hose carriages and one hook-and-ladder truck. Police departments also had visibility in urban communities. Policemen wore uniforms—which they paid for themselves—while they worked twelve-hour shifts. Because salaries of police officials in 1880 were considered good compared to national standards—between $480 in Council Bluffs and $600 in Des Moines—these positions were coveted. At the same time, police forces were small; in 1876 Des Moines's force numbered eight. In

1880 there were no merit exams for policemen, and most appointments were political in nature.[9]

Iowa cities continued to grow after the turn of the century, although at uneven rates. Dubuque's population reached 36,290 by 1900, and 38,494 by 1910; Sioux City, given the dramatic expansion of the meat-packing industry in the early 1900s, increased substantially. The Mississippi River cities, with the exception of Dubuque and Davenport, grew more slowly than did interior cities such as Cedar Rapids and Des Moines. Council Bluffs benefited greatly from its role as the eastern terminus of the Union Pacific, a factor that brought three major lines into the city for connection with the Union Pacific. Des Moines, however, realized the greatest population growth: By 1900 the city contained over 62,000 residents, an increase of roughly 40,000 in two decades. The city's selection in 1857 as Iowa's capital had guaranteed longtime economic development.[10]

Even in 1880 Des Moines was a community clearly on the move and destined to remain Iowa's largest city; its development, therefore, is illustrative of the many economic and technological changes experienced by Iowa's urban areas between 1880 and 1930. By the former date, the city contained some of the finest homes in the state, most notably Terrace Hill. Built in 1869 by Des Moines businessman B. F. Allen at a cost of $250,000, Terrace Hill would be purchased in 1884 by Frederick Hubbell, then a leading business and civic figure in the city. In 1877 Hoyt Sherman built a substantial home on Woodland Avenue, now known as Hoyt Sherman Place. Herndon Hall, the home of the Jefferson Polk family, was another of Des Moines's finest homes in the latter nineteenth century. The presence of these elegant structures provides testimony that even in the first five or six decades of settlement, Iowa contained sharp social-class distinctions.

Downtown Des Moines was also expanding as businesses and hotels developed. The basis for one of Des Moines's oldest business establishments appeared in 1874 when the Younker's Dry Goods Store opened. This business would develop into Iowa's most prominent department store as company officials later opened branch stores around the state. The first Younker's operation in Iowa was in Keokuk where Lipman, Samuel, and Marcus Younker opened a dry-goods store in 1856. Later, younger brother Herman, impressed with Des Moines's rapid growth, started a store there. In his memoirs Marcus Younker recalled: "We found ourselves too large for Keokuk. Our business had outgrown the town which, at that time, along with other river-front towns, was on the decline, and ever being ambitious to obtain a firm foothold in the business world, we took out $6,000 of our capital and invested it in a branch store in Des Moines."[11]

Getting to work for employees of Younker's and other local businesses became a little easier in 1888 when electric streetcars began operation and, in turn, began competing with horse-drawn cars. Early in Des Moines's history, most people lived close to their place of work and were able to travel by foot, but as the city expanded, some form of standard transportation was needed. In 1889 all streetcar lines were consolidated and a transfer plan initiated; passengers could ride twelve miles for only five cents. After 1879 residents could also communicate more easily when Western Union opened its first Des Moines telephone exchange.[12]

A major problem in all communities was the poor condition of streets. In Des Moines, until about 1875, streets were simply dirt roads. Although the city spent "thousands of dollars … for cutting and filling, grading, and building many miles of wooden sidewalks," it was not unusual to see wagons and horses mired down in the mud, even on major thoroughfares. In 1878 the city council hired a Chicago civil engineer to recommend a plan for paving the city's streets. City workmen completed the first paving in June 1882 on Walnut Street, from First to Fifth avenues. By 1900 all main downtown streets and alleys, as well as some residential streets, had been paved. City officials had first used cedar blocks, but brick soon became the preferred paving material. Even after streets were hard surfaced, however, there was still the matter of keeping them clean.[13]

Shortly after the turn of the century, the appearance of downtown Des Moines would change considerably as city workers removed the many thirty-five-foot poles that had previously suspended telephone and electric wires above the streets, and put them underground. This move undoubtedly did away with some of the cluttered look that had come to characterize not only Des Moines, but most cities and towns by 1900.[14] In fact, downtown areas even in small communities seemed almost dense with electric and telephone wires and poles stretched from building to building and along major thoroughfares.

Des Moines would continue to grow both population-wise and in terms of local and state attractions. Given its designation as the state capital and its central location, it seemed logical that statewide events be housed there; accordingly, in 1879, the Iowa State Fair would locate there permanently. The fair had taken place in Fairfield in 1854 but then had spent several years "on the road," being held in Muscatine, Iowa City, Clinton, and Cedar Rapids. In 1886 the new state capitol was completed, thus further accentuating Des Moines's role as the capital city.

Des Moines would soon develop numerous medical and educational institutions to serve local and nearby populations. Around the turn of the century, the capital city would become home to several hospitals. In 1893 the Catholic Church would be in the vanguard of providing medical care when the Sisters of Mercy opened Mercy Hospital; in 1901 Iowa Methodist Hospital would open its doors. During the teens and twenties, three more hospitals would appear in Des Moines: Iowa Lutheran in 1914; Des Moines General in 1916; and Broadlawns in 1924. Des Moines would also become home to several institutions of higher learning, providing educational opportunities to mid-Iowans. In 1881 Drake University opened its doors, followed by the opening of Grand View College and Theological Seminary in 1895. A third Des Moines college would begin classes in 1889 when Presbyterians founded Highland Park College; in 1918 it was purchased by the Baptists' Des Moines College and became Des Moines University. In 1908 the Still College of Osteopathy (presently known as the College of Osteopathic Medicine and Surgery) would be established.[15]

World War I impacted on all Iowa communities, but perhaps more so on Des Moines, given the presence of Fort Des Moines and Camp Dodge. At the latter facility, staff trained over one hundred thousand men for military duty. Local residents crowded the downtown areas to cheer recruits as they marched off to war; about a year later residents assembled again to welcome home those who returned. With the announcement of the armistice on November 11, Des Moines erupted in celebration. According to one account, "All stores, offices, places of business, and schools closed. Operators of street cars, buses, and taxis left them standing wherever they happened to be." Residents paraded through the downtown area, singing war songs and waving flags. Before the celebration ended, the German kaiser and General von Hindenburg had been burned in effigy.[16]

In the interwar period Des Moines would see even greater economic and technological change. In 1924 the first Des Moines radio station, WHO, would go on the air; in 1926 the city's first municipal airport would be developed near Altoona; Des Moines's telephone system was changed to a dial system in 1929; and in 1930 citizens would authorize a bond issue to build a new airport along Fleur Drive. By that year Des Moines had changed dramatically from the small community of 12,035 that had existed in 1870. As in other cities, significant changes had taken place in Des Moines's physical appearance, and in the scope of business and social enterprises. The boundaries of the city had continued to expand: In 1890 alone, the city annexed eight surrounding incorporated communities.[17]

After 1900, along with other urban areas, Des Moines would begin developing art associations and, in turn, art museums. This movement, no doubt, rested on several developments. Midwesterners in general were becoming increasingly conscious of a sense of regionalism, which produced pride in the work of area artists and writers; in turn, pride led to the conviction that art should not be limited to eastern cities nor only to a few great artists. Rather, every area and every citizen could enjoy art "as a creative expression of life around them." At the same time, boosterism in Iowa's cities provided motivation for development of cultural institutions as well as rivalry between cities. Whatever the motivation, between 1900 and 1948 art associations and museums would appear in Davenport, Dubuque, Cedar Rapids, Sioux City, and Des Moines. Some cities, like Davenport, would "open one of the first municipally-owned and operated public art galleries in the United States" in 1955.[18] Sioux City would develop a New Deal WPA art center. Des Moines's Art Center would not be built until 1948, but before that the Federated Women's Club of Des Moines, housed at Hoyt Sherman Place, would maintain an art gallery.

Although Iowa's cities would be recognized as centers of enterprise and culture, these same communities would increasingly contain neglected classes of people with special needs. Around the turn of the century economic and social problems in Iowa's urban areas were becoming more evident. In the nation's largest cities, like Chicago, the settlementhouse movement had begun in the 1880s and 1890s to reach out to these special groups, especially immigrants, and the movement would quickly spread to other communities. The settlement-house movement had earlier originated in England, where it served primarily factory workers and their families; in the United States, settlements had responded mostly to the needs of immigrants located in urban areas. Settlement houses, or community houses as they were later known, appeared in Des Moines in the

1890s, and after 1900 in Sioux City and Cedar Rapids. Davenport also contained a community center known as Friendly House. In effect, these institutions served the needs of lower-income residents, many of whom were first- or second-generation immigrants.

In Des Moines the facility eventually known as Roadside Settlement would trace its roots back to the city's Circle of King's Daughters in the Presbyterian Church. This group had as its main project a sewing school for "poor children"; other circles in the Presbyterian Church had projects such as providing food and clothing to needy families and the operation of a day nursery in the church basement. Eventually all circles organized into the King's Daughters Union. In 1894 the group rented a house on Fourth Street, which sheltered projects handled by the various circles; later the King's Daughters Union rented part of a house at the corner of Eighth and Mulberry streets. In 1899, faced with financial problems, a new board of directors was created and the Roadside Settlement House Association was incorporated.[19]

In 1904 the Roadside Settlement board hired Flora Dunlap as its head resident or director. Born in Pickaway County, Ohio, in 1872, Dunlap had graduated from Cincinnati Wesleyan College. Dunlap came from a prosperous family and, like other young women of her social class, was not expected to be employed; at the same time, being a social worker was acceptable to her parents. Dunlap brought firsthand experience to Roadside, having previously lived at Chicago's Hull House; she later observed: "[Hull House] was a stimulating, an absorbing, and a bewildering place in which to live and work." Arriving in Des Moines after being accustomed to a crowded tenement district in Chicago, Dunlap recalled that the "corner of Eighth and Mulberry Streets in Des Moines seemed almost a country village."[20]

Two years later Roadside Settlement moved into a new building located at the corner of Seventh and Scott streets, specifically built for the Roadside program. The new facility included a wide array of services for neighborhood residents, including an auditorium (also used as a gymnasium) with seating for about 350, day nursery, office, library, and two rooms for clubs or classes. The basement housed public baths and a public wash area where neighborhood women could do their families' laundry. The facility also contained living quarters for settlement residents.[21]

At the time the building was constructed, the board of directors had doubts whether American women would be willing to do their laundry in public. Nevertheless, they included washing facilities, with four sets of two tubs each, along with steam driers. Dunlap related that at first few women used the service, but the number gradually increased. In 1912 the settlement added more facilities, including two power washers, an extractor for partly drying clothes, and four new sets of tubs. The mechanical improvements prompted one foreign-born woman, used to heavy physical work, to comment: "Vimmen nowadays is so veak they can no longer vash on a vash board."[22]

During the 1910s, 1920s, and 1930s, Roadside responded to the needs of neighborhood residents. The settlement expanded its services to include classes in sewing, cooking, and manual training. It also served as a station of the Des Moines Public Library and organized activities for boys and girls, including story hour, choruses, and handcraft classes. The settlement opened an employment bureau for women who worked "by the day," a term used for domestic servants. At one point Roadside had 150 women on its employment list. Before the Depression women typically worked for one dollar per day for "indefinite hours," plus lunch and carfare. Even in the 1930s Roadside maintained a short list of "by the day" workers, but there was little demand for the women's services. During World War I settlement workers interpreted war regulations to non-English-speaking groups.[23]

Des Moines would also include several other settlements or community centers. A Jewish community facility, known as the Jewish Branch of Roadside Settlement, would begin in 1907 in the Bremer School neighborhood. During that year evening classes in English would be taught at Bremer School, open to any foreign-born adult. The program was an immediate success, as 114 men and women enrolled the first night. These initial classes in English would eventually lead to a full range of subjects offered as evening classes by the Des Moines school board. In 1910 the Jewish Branch of Roadside would become a separate organization, the Jewish Settlement House. The facility would move again in 1920 and become known as the Jewish Community Center; later the name was changed to the Julia B. Mayer Community Center.[24]

The facility presently known as Willkie House came into existence in 1917 as the Colored Community Service Center, or the War Camp Community Service. The latter name was appropriate because during World

War I the center organized a club for African-American military men stationed at Fort Des Moines. When the war ended, the group—then known as the Negro Community Center—relocated in the old Franklin School. The facility housed a station of the Des Moines Public Library and a Well Baby Clinic maintained by the Public Health Nursing Association. Neighborhood groups met in the facility.[25] In 1922 another facility for African Americans opened at 1622 Walker Street, known as the East Side Community Center.

While Des Moines had the earliest and the greatest number of community centers, both Sioux City and Cedar Rapids had similar facilities. In Sioux City, Italian-American Mary Treglia was a highly visible community activist as well as director of the Sioux City Community House. A rather unlikely candidate for that position because of her second-generation immigrant status, Treglia directed the community center from 1921 to 1959. Along with supervising the traditional community-center activities, such as homemakers' clubs, art programs, teaching English to foreignborn people, and helping them to become naturalized citizens, Treglia also became deeply immersed in communitywide projects. Through her years as center director, Treglia assisted neighborhood families in their fight to keep open a neighborhood school, to provide adequate school transportation for their children, and to provide flood control for their neighborhoods. Treglia frequently assisted neighborhood residents in communicating their needs and wishes to city officials.[26]

In Cedar Rapids a community center would also develop to meet the social and economic needs of a highly diverse population. The person most responsible for the development of the community house, Jane Boyd, had come to Cedar Rapids as an elementary teacher in 1894 to teach at Tyler School. From then until 1918 Boyd did far more than teach first graders. She quickly discovered the Tyler school district included some twenty-two different ethnic groups, including Bohemians, Moravians, Armenians, Swedes, Russian and Polish Jews, and Lebanese. The district was described as "an undesirable section of the city ... [where] the underprivileged and the foreign element settled." During her years as a teacher at Tyler School—from 1894 to 1918—Boyd also served informally as a social worker.[27]

In 1918 the Cedar Rapids school board recognized that Jane Boyd could not continue to perform both roles and released her from teaching to become a full-time social worker. Boyd immediately started numerous projects, such as a milk program for schoolchildren (which she financed herself until undertaken by a local men's service club); a clothing project whereby she maintained a supply of clothing for those in need; and the organizing of numerous groups for neighborhood residents, including the Little Mother's Club for children. As a part of each meeting, participants recited the Pledge of Allegiance. Although this practice was probably viewed as an appropriate patriotic act, the process served a dual purpose: The mothers present (many of whom could not speak English) would repeat the pledge with their children, which helped the mothers learn a few words of English.[28]

In 1921 community activities were centered in one building. First called the Model House, its name was changed to Community House in 1923. Later a Cedar Rapids physician and his wife donated their home for use as a community center. In 1929 the facility was named the Jane Boyd House. Among programs initiated after 1929 was a summer camp for children from low-income homes. Jane Boyd also arranged to "have the mothers ... get a few days of rest there during the summer." Boyd would be active in the Community House and civic affairs until her death in 1932.[29]

The many and varied activities of the settlements and community centers underscore the diversity of life in Iowa's urban centers, and, in turn, the need for private and governmental assistance. Moreover, every community seemed to have its neglected area. Flora Dunlap described the Southeast Bottoms in Des Moines, which existed when she arrived there in 1904: The Bottoms was an area that had "no city water supply, no public sewage disposal, no paved streets." Given the development of railroads in the city, "the southeast bottoms became a district separated from the city by a tangle of tracks on the north and by the river on the south and east." Meat-packing plants located nearby "had not added to its value or desirability as residence property." In Sioux City a similar description could be given of the South Bottoms served by Mary Treglia and her staff, and in Waterloo the black section was cut off from the rest of the community by streets and railroad tracks. The neighborhood in Cedar Rapids served by Jane Boyd was described in similar fashion: "The foreigners and 'the poor' settled on 'the flats' or in 'stump town' in the southern part of the city. The land was cheap in this vicinity, and the T. M. Sinclair Packing Company was conveniently near at hand. Most of the foreigners and the poor were employed there."[30] For those who called these sections home, their lives and the lives of their families were improved immeasurably because of the Mary Treglias, the Jane Boyds, and the Flora Dunlaps.

As cities continued to grow, problems associated with law enforcement became more and more visible. In Sioux City during the late 1800s, William Hewitt writes that "as the city grew, saloons, gambling dens, and houses of prostitution flourished amongst other downtown businesses." Sioux City reformers had first focused on the liquor traffic but had not made much progress until Reverend George C. Haddock arrived in the city. Although Haddock immediately began to crusade for Prohibition, his career was cut short by an assassin's bullet. Quickly Haddock became a martyr for Prohibitionists everywhere, and the shock of Haddock's death had an effect: Sioux City saloons began to close down.[31]

Sioux City reformers then focused their attention on prostitution. As Hewitt points out, however, influential Sioux Citians were divided as to how they should deal with the problem. One group believed that prostitution was inevitable and, therefore, officials could only hope to control it; moral reformers, however, believed that prostitution should be eliminated from the community. After some twenty-five years of reforming efforts, the prostitutes had not gone away. Citizens who favored control rather than elimination of the practice, succeeded in relocating the red-light district from the central business district to the African-American community "and left it near the working-class housing for meat packing plant workers in the South Bottoms."[32] If nothing else, the critics might say, the relocation made the practice less visible in the city. Waterloo would experience somewhat the same situation in that prostitution and other vice operations were eventually relocated in the African-American part of the city.

Sioux City was not the only urban area with vice activity, however. Even in the 1920s a *Des Moines Register* reporter would write about drug use in Des Moines, with an estimated fifteen thousand addicts in the state in 1924. According to George Mills, drug use was evident in various parts of the state, including Sioux City, Mason City, and Davenport. In the same article Mills described Des Moines's red-light district, centered at Fourth and Elm streets south of the loop.[33]

During the 1930s Iowa health officials became concerned over the dramatic rise in venereal diseases, which were often spread through prostitution. The total reported cases of venereal diseases rose from 3,202 in 1930 to 5,031 in 1931, an increase of a little less than 50 percent. The state's health commissioner appealed for help to the American Social Hygiene Association, which, in turn, sent an investigator to the state to locate houses of prostitution; the report, describing the extent of the practice and the location of prostitutes, was sent to the local police department. Although the number of venereal diseases decreased over the next two years, it rose again by 1936.[34]

Iowa's cities between 1870 and 1930, although not large by national standards, would encompass all the economic advantages, cultural pursuits, and technological advances that urban life had to offer; Iowa cities would also confirm some of rural Iowans' worse fears regarding city vices and would include the most visible poverty in the state. Even with the growth of cities, most Iowans, including many city dwellers, would think of the state as a place where rural life predominated and offered the most satisfying existence. Perhaps many city people held this view because they had earlier lived in the country, or in small towns, and had moved to the city only as adults. Perhaps the belief was a carryover from the nineteenth century, with its antiurban bias. Regardless of its origin, agrarianism was alive and well in the cities as well as in the countryside at least up to 1930.

11

Cultural Diversity

B etween 1880 and 1920 Iowa would become home to a growing number of European immigrants and a more slowly expanding minority population. The number of immigrants arriving in the Hawkeye State would reach a peak in 1890;
thereafter, fewer immigrants would arrive, and most would be from southern and eastern Europe rather than from western Europe and the British
Isles. African Americans would also increase in number after 1880, and
many would either settle originally or later relocate in Iowa's larger cities;
Hispanics would begin to arrive during the 1910s. Within the years from
1880 to 1920, certain ethnic or racial groups were often associated with
specific occupations. Coal mining and meat packing were important oc-

---

Boardinghouse in Des Moines in latter 1800s, which prob-
ably served newly arrived immigrants. Photo courtesy of
State Historical Society of Iowa, Des Moines.

cupations for groups such as Italians and eastern Europeans, as well as for African Americans. By World War I the state contained distinct ethnic and racial areas, with the older immigrant groups inhabiting rural localities and the more recent groups residing in the state's larger communities.

By 1900 Iowa had become a state where clusters of first-, second-, and third-generation European Americans could be found everywhere. In effect, every part of the state contained fairly distinct ethnic groups. German Americans remained the largest ethnic group and could be found in all of Iowa's ninety-nine counties. Smaller groups like the Danes were primarily associated with one section of the state, the southwest. Many nationalities would eventually institutionalize their ethnic heritage through the creation of museums and festivals.

From Iowa's first permanent settlement in the 1830s until World War I, German Americans would be regarded as substantial citizens and noted for their agricultural skills; sometimes government officials sought them out as immigrants. But beginning in 1917, when the United States declared war against Germany, the federal government initiated a virulent anti-German campaign whereby all Germans—both soldiers and civilians—were cast as the brutal enemy of Americans. Not surprisingly, Americans altered not only their view of Germans in Germany, but also their perception of German Americans. Following the war declaration in April 1917, the substantial, solid, highly respected German American became a questionable citizen who might harbor more loyalty toward Germany than the United States. In Iowa, as in other midwestern states with high German-American populations, anything German—from foods to breeds of dog to German measles—needed to be renamed. At least one town had its name changed because of anti-German feelings: Germania in Kossuth County became Lakota. At the same time, German measles became liberty measles and sauerkraut became liberty cabbage. Some individuals changed their names to conceal their German ancestry.

In communities with high German-stock populations, German Americans were sometimes put under surveillance for possible disloyal behavior. In the nineteenth century Scott County (which included Davenport) had become closely identified with German Americans, thus almost insuring that once war began, the group would be closely monitored. Census figures show that between one-quarter and one-third of Scott County residents were of German ancestry. Two German-language newspapers were published in Davenport, and German Americans held prominent positions there. Between 1890 and 1917, four German Americans had served as mayor of the city.[1]

During the war Scott County citizens—the same as citizens in other Iowa counties—formed a Council of National Defense, ostensibly to perform patriotic duties such as promoting war-bond sales. Although the council was part of a national organization, its legal authority was never clearly established. The council investigated reported cases of disloyalty, and if individuals were found guilty, they were first fined and then "advised to end all disloyal activities, and usually ordered to ... participate in a patriotic organization." It appears the council often singled out German-American citizens for charges of disloyalty, and some evidence seemed downright silly. On one occasion a German alien was reportedly overheard saying he thought the kaiser was a fine and handsome man. Another person reported that the same German alien never smiled or applauded during a patriotic speech. After a thorough investigation, whereby the council examined the man's naturalization papers, work permit, and even choice of friends, all charges were dropped.[2]

Anti-German feeling also extended into the area of education. Before World War I, German Americans in Davenport had campaigned for years to have the German language taught in the public schools. With the outbreak of war this practice ended and was not reinstated until 1930. Local authorities even went through the public-library holdings and removed books thought to be pro-German. Moreover, one day after the ban on the teaching of the German language, Davenport High School students burned over five hundred German books.[3]

Confrontations involving German Americans also developed in other parts of the state. In northwest Iowa, Lutheran minister Wilhelm Schumann spoke from the pulpit, criticizing the war and the draft. He charged that buying war bonds was "a great humbug," and further, he would not allow a collection for the Red Cross to be taken in his church. Schumann was reported and, under the federal Espionage Act, sentenced to five years in Leavenworth prison for interfering with the war effort. Officials later commuted his sentence to two years.[4]

During the war Iowa Governor William Harding, apparently concerned over what he perceived as a lack of patriotism among the state's foreign-born, issued a proclamation banning the use of any foreign language in a public place, including conversation over telephones, and sermons in houses of worship. Harding believed this action would remove irritations between the foreign-born and others and allow Iowans to be united.

An immediate problem with the language ban concerned church services, as many pastors presented some, if not all, sermons in German. The Reverend Baushoff, pastor of the German Evangelical Church at Denver, defiantly declared he would continue preaching in German. After a visit from a state official, however, the Reverend Bauschoff agreed to preach first in English and later repeat the sermon in German.[5] Harding's proclamation, while probably aimed primarily at Germans, affected all immigrant groups.

Once the war ended, anti-German feeling faded rather quickly, but loyalties to the homeland and to German institutions were never as strong as before. Membership in German organizations, such as the Turners, continued to decline, and fewer and fewer German Americans spoke or even understood German. The war partially accounted for the change, but with each new generation, ties to the homeland became weaker and interest waned in the German language, culture, and traditions.

Unlike the Germans, with their occupational diversity, Scandinavians more often remained within either a rural-agricultural or a rural-industrial setting. Norwegians and Danes were overwhelming agricultural, and occupations for Swedish-American males included both farming and coal mining. For some early Swedish immigrants, such as those in Webster County, the mines offered an opportunity to supplement their income with winter employment. In Boone County some first- and second-generation Swedish immigrants regarded mining as part-time work, whereas others viewed it as a full-time occupation. In Buxton, Swedish-born people made up the second-largest ethnic group. Buxton, in fact, had two suburbs— East Swede Town and West Swede Town—which reflected the large number of Swedish Americans there. Most Swedish-American males in Buxton worked as coal miners, although a few operated businesses.[6]

Charles and Josephine Erickson, a Swedish couple residing in Buxton, illustrate Swedish work patterns. Charles had immigrated to Iowa in the late nineteenth century, settling first at Muchakinock. There he met and married Swedish-born Josephine Carlson; the couple eventually had three children: Alex, Agnes, and Dena. Moving to Buxton when the camp was founded in 1900, four members of the Erickson family worked for Consolidation Coal Company, which operated the Buxton mines: Alex and his father, Charles, worked as miners, while Agnes and Dena worked in the company store. Josephine Carlson contributed to the family income by taking in boarders, mostly young men newly arrived from Sweden. For Charles and Alex, coal mining would be a full-time, lifelong occupation.[7]

As discussed in Chapter 6, once in Iowa, all immigrant groups sought ways to perpetuate their Old World religion and culture, as well as to retain their native language. The Danes, being the last Scandinavian group to settle here, continued to use the Danish language until at least World War I. Before then most Lutheran clergy in Danish-American communities delivered sermons in Danish. As late as 1918 the two institutions that provided the most ministers for Danes in the Midwest—the Theological Department of Grand View College in Des Moines and Trinity Theological Seminary at Blair, Nebraska—were still conducting classes in Danish. As Peter Petersen has pointed out, to older Danes the idea of presenting sermons in English was "almost unbearable." Suggestions for using English rather than Danish were described as "the English disease."[8] After 1920 Danish emigration to the United States would taper off. Today the Danish-American heritage is preserved and interpreted through the Danish Immigrant Museum in Elk Horn.

By 1900 Iowa's immigration patterns were undergoing change. Northern Europeans were still arriving, but emigrants from southern and eastern Europe were also increasing in number. Italians, Croatians, Poles, Lithuanians, and Russians were included in the second phase, with Russians representing the largest group and Italians the second largest. Many newcomers went to work in coal mines, while some settled in cities such as Cedar Rapids, Waterloo, and Sioux City, where they worked in meatpacking plants. Unfortunately, there has been little research done on Russian immigrants in Iowa and only limited work on other eastern-European groups, with the exception of the Italians.[9]

The first Italians in Iowa came from northern Italy and immigrated to escape a life of poverty. In the old country they had typically owned small plots of land, where they did gardening and limited farming. Many had the equivalent of a fourth- or fifth-grade education. Arriving in the United

States with few skills other than agriculture, and with little or no money, Italian males quickly accepted the most available work. In Iowa in the early twentieth century, one such opportunity was coal mining.

Because of poverty Italian Americans quickly made use of sponsors. In effect, a sponsor was usually a relative or friend who had already settled in Iowa and who lent money to another Italian male wishing to emigrate. The experience of sixteen-year-old Italian John Corso illustrates this practice. In 1914 Corso received one hundred dollars from his uncle in Hocking, Iowa. The uncle had written to Italy informing Corso that the coal mines around Hocking were operating, and if Corso was willing to learn the trade, he could get a job. Leaving behind his parents and six brothers and sisters, Corso embarked on a journey that would dramatically change his life. He would join his uncle in Hocking and, for the next thirty years, would work in the Iowa coal industry.[10]

Once located in their new homes, Italian Americans faced many adjustments. Italian males, going to work every day, usually learned English fairly quickly. Their wives, however, at home with children and often associating mostly with other Italian-American women, typically started learning English from their school-age children. Some first-generation women never learned English. One woman remembered that although her immigrant mother never spoke English, she had no trouble shopping, as she always took along samples of foods she needed, such as rice, beans, or coffee.

Due to seasonal layoffs and low wages in the mining industry, Italian-American women often found it necessary to take in boarders to increase the family's income. Usually the boarders were young males, newly arrived from Italy. For two dollars a week, women would provide meals, lodging, and laundry service for the young men. Mary Battani Sertich remembered that her parents, both first-generation Italian Americans, often treated boarders as members of the family. Antonia Cerato explained that she probably charged the young men too little, but she felt she should help them as much as possible, since they were away from their Italian families. The money earned by Italian-American women made a substantial contribution to their household budgets. In some cases, if a woman took in four or five boarders, that income might almost equal her husband's wage.[11]

For Italian-American families, life in a coal camp would have both advantages and disadvantages. Camp housing was cheap at six or eight dollars per month, but camp houses were small, poorly maintained, and without electricity or indoor plumbing. Builders placed houses on corner stones or blocks, with only one layer of flooring and no insulation in the walls. Camp houses were, therefore, drafty and hard to heat. One miner, after leaving his boots directly underneath the coal stove, which he kept burning all night, found the boots frozen to the floor the next morning. Water also proved to be a problem, as in the winter, wells located in the center of the camp froze up and, in the summer, often went dry. One distinct advantage of camp living was cheap medical care provided by a physician either in the camp or in a nearby community. Miners typically arranged with the company to pay $1.50 per month which provided medical care for the miner and his entire family.[12]

For Italian Americans the occupation of coal mining would last for about two generations. By the 1920s Iowa's coal industry had gone into a slump from which it never recovered. Although many mines still existed throughout the late twenties and thirties, the number was dwindling. Following World War II, young men from mining families sometimes attended college under the GI Bill of Rights or found other occupations. For men who had been miners, many remained in the same communities but commuted to work in nearby towns and cities.

While coal mining was an important industry for Italian-American males, many also worked in other occupations, particularly in Des Moines. Most Italian Americans who came there before 1900 had emigrated from northern Italy, whereas after that date most came from southern provinces. The earliest arrivals established small businesses, such as Luigi Jacopetti, who arrived in 1880 and opened a shop where he sharpened scissors and knives. Other immigrants started a candy kitchen, tobacco store, and fruit stand. In 1900 several men started the Italian Importing Company, operating their own truck gardens and selling produce all over the state. In keeping with the tradition of mutual aid so evident among Italians, the company provided assistance to fellow countrymen by helping with travel arrangements and by sending money back to relatives in Italy.[13]

The Italian Americans who arrived after 1900 found a wide variety of jobs available in the Des Moines area. Many went to work on the railroads; others found employment in the brick-and-tile yards or in the city's many retail businesses. Some immigrants managed to save money from their first jobs and eventually opened grocery stores, as well as tailoring shops, shoe-repair shops, and barbershops.[14]

The Italian Americans in Des Moines also concerned themselves with cultural and religious matters. St. Anthony's Roman Catholic Church became a major center for both activities. Several men started publishing the *American Citizen* as a community newspaper; it survived until 1972. Three benevolent societies formed by Italian Americans were Stemma D'Italia, the Garibaldi Club, and Vittoria Lodge. The church, the newspaper, and the lodges all helped local Italian Americans preserve their cultural heritage while also publicizing employment and other economic opportunities within the community.[15]

A third Italian-American community in Iowa began to take shape in Oelwein around 1900 when Italians arrived to work in the yards and shops of the Chicago Great Western Railroad. In 1908 the *Oelwein Register* estimated the number of Italian Americans at two hundred, and seven years later, at five hundred. The Oelwein Italian Americans emigrated from three areas—Venice, Abruzzi-Molise, and Calabria—with the largest number from the latter area. The fact that the Chicago Great Western experienced a constant shortage of workers during the first decade or two of the twentieth century undoubtedly played an important role in the continued migration of Italians to the Oelwein community. Once there, some Italian males began to move into occupations other than railroad work. Six Italian Americans started grocery stores, whereas others started a barbershop, a marble-and-granite works, and a realty company. Many families owned multiple houses, which they apparently rented. A few families owned boardinghouses.[16]

Along with Italians, a limited number of emigrants arrived from eastern-European countries including Croatia, Slovenia, Montenegro, and Poland. The community of Rathbun soon became dominated by Croatians, and many Croats also went to work in the coal mines located in Polk and Dallas counties. Milo Papich, who arrived from Croatia as a ten-year-old boy, later married a woman born in Slovenia who had emigrated to Iowa with her parents. By 1920 the federal census recorded that 1,603 Iowans had been born in Yugoslavia, which then included the former countries of Croatia, Slovenia, and Montenegro.[17]

As the second phase of European immigration diminished during the teens and twenties, Mexican-American immigration to Iowa began to expand. Hispanic migration was greatly affected by World War I. During that conflict, when the flow of European immigration was disrupted, American companies began looking south of the border for workers. Before that only a small number of Hispanics resided in Iowa. Census figures dramatically show how World War I served as a turning point for Mexican immigration: In 1910, 509 first-generation Mexican Americans lived in Iowa; by 1920 that number had risen to 2,560.[18]

In eastern Iowa the Bettendorf Company, which made train equipment, hired many Mexican-American males. The immigrants brought along their families, who were housed in a company town near the plant; there the Mexicans formed a community known as the Holy City. Although various explanations for the name have been given, residents explained that it was called "holy" because a priest had blessed it. When the Bettendorf Company dissolved and Holy City closed down, Mexican Americans remained in the area, where they found other employment.[19]

Within the Bettendorf Mexican-American community, strong communal bonds existed. Residents shared experiences in "gardening, household tasks, work experiences, swimming in the Mississippi (which was at their doorstep), onion topping in the nearby fields ... [celebrating] Mexican Independence Day ... or simply a fiesta for fun." Frances Puente grew up in Holy City and remembered community events: "We had all these parties because somebody was always either being baptized, married or buried and it all amounted to the same thing, except that at burials you didn't have a dance. But you still have the large gatherings, the meal which everyone shared in preparing. It wasn't just the one family. It was everybody."[20] Puente recalled that religious activities were important. On Christmas everyone walked to church together, singing hymns in Spanish. He explained that religion was such an important part of their lives, "it could not be separated. It was just there as much as breathing. It was just a very, very intricate part of our entire lives." He believed that was true of everyone in Holy City.[21]

Within Bettendorf, Mexican Americans formed their own community institutions. David Macias, the first Mexican to arrive there in 1915, became a community organizer and religious and social leader; he was joined in that work by his brother, Manuel, who immigrated later. The Maciases recognized the cultural trauma experienced by their fellow Mexican Americans and helped to ease that through community solidarity and assistance. The brothers helped to create a church for their people, originally worshiping in two boxcars joined together.[22]

Throughout Iowa, Hispanics have worked in a variety of jobs, although for many years the majority labored as migrant farm workers. As a part of this workforce, families lived in communities such as Muscatine, Fort Madison, and Mason City. A small number came to Valley Junction (later known as West Des Moines) in the teens to work for the Rock Island Railroad. Initially, families had to live in abandoned boxcars near the railroad tracks in an area known as Hyde Park.[23]

While the experiences of European settlers would be characterized by considerable economic and social diversity, the experience of African Americans would be less so. Occupationally, black males would work in meat packing and coal mining, while black women continued working primarily as domestics. Increasingly in Iowa, African Americans became city dwellers, with the exception of those who lived in coal-mining camps.

The number of blacks residing in any one coal camp remained fairly small, but Muchakinock and Buxton proved exceptions. In the former community, by 1885 blacks accounted for approximately 66 percent of the total population of thirty-five hundred. In 1900 the Consolidation Coal Company moved its headquarters from Muchakinock to the new camp of Buxton, a distance of about fifteen miles. Buxton took shape within a short time. Buxton quickly attracted national attention for its racially integrated employment and housing practices. Mining officials and workers alike regarded Consolidation as progressive in regard to the quality of workers' housing, community institutions, and modern mining practices. By 1905 Buxton contained roughly fifty-five hundred residents, with African Americans constituting about 55 percent of the total.[24]

Former residents like Marjorie Brown and Dorothy Collier remembered life in Buxton as almost utopian. These women and dozens of other former residents recalled that in Buxton blacks and whites were treated equally in all phases of community life. At the same time, black residents chose to establish institutions of their own, including churches, lodges, and businesses. Buxton also attracted numerous black professionals, including a medical doctor, a lawyer, a pharmacist, and several teachers. Buxton survived for approximately twenty-five years but rapidly declined when Consolidation created two new communities, Haydock and Bucknell, some eighteen miles west of Buxton, then transferred its headquarters to Bucknell. Some Buxton residents moved to the new communities—which survived only until 1928—but many left the area, moving to cities both in and out of Iowa. For years afterward former residents came back to the Buxton site to hold picnics, reminiscing with relatives and friends about what they remembered as a golden time.[25]

The coal industry played a major role in the lives of African Americans between 1880 and 1930. Recruited originally as strikebreakers and later as regular mine workers, thousands of blacks came to Iowa who probably would not have settled here otherwise. In 1900 Mahaska County—the site of Muchakinock—had 1,737 black residents, the second-largest county in terms of black population in the state. With Muchy's demise and Buxton's development, Monroe County—the home of Buxton—had 2,371 black residents by 1918. Only Polk County had a higher number of blacks in 1910, many of whom worked in area coal mines.[26] When Iowa's coal industry began a general decline in the 1920s, correspondingly, the number of blacks employed as miners also declined, with blacks often migrating to urban centers, particularly Des Moines, Waterloo, and Cedar Rapids, as well as to cities outside the state.

By 1930 federal census figures reveal both a relocation and a decline of blacks within Iowa. Population shifts occurred within the state as blacks left the coal camps and possibly other rural areas for larger communities. Black Hawk County (home of Waterloo) had 29 black residents in 1910; 856 in 1920; and by 1930, a total of 1,234. Woodbury County (home of Sioux City) had 317 black residents in 1910, increasing to 1,078 in 1930. Polk County (home of Des Moines) had the largest number of blacks in 1930: 5,713. Lee is Iowa's only county where the black population remained fairly stable from 1880 to 1930. No doubt that county, located in extreme southeastern Iowa along the Mississippi River, served as a longtime entry point for blacks coming from the South. Overall, the total population of African Americans fell from 19,005 in 1920 to 17,380 in 1930.[27]

After 1900, African Americans moving into urban centers gradually established their own communities, but not without difficulty. In Waterloo the first sizable migration of blacks arrived in 1911. In that year Waterloo's white workers had walked off their jobs at the Illinois Central's maintenance-and-repair terminal. In efforts to replace workers, Illinois Central officials induced some of their black employees in Mississippi to come north to Waterloo. One such person, Earl Lee, left Water Valley, Mississippi, in 1913; arriving in Waterloo, he found it necessary to set up housekeeping in a railroad bunk car. Lee's housing arrangement was typical of many of the newly arrived black workers. Waterloo citizens did not look kindly upon Lee and fellow newcomers for several reasons. First, local residents sympathized with the striking workers and therefore resented the presence of men they viewed as strikebreakers. Second, Waterloo newspapers identified "East Siders," which included the newly arrived blacks, with increased lawlessness in the city.[28]

Blacks in Waterloo initially found housing wherever they could afford the rent and, therefore, were not congregated in one part of town. In his study of Waterloo, Robert Neymeyer described the housing as "crowded, dilapidated, and overpriced." Some workers lived in boardinghouses operated by black families; others had to move temporarily into boxcars, much like Earl Lee. Independent households, in which blacks did not take in boarders or share quarters with other families, were unusual. By 1915, however, local realtors had adopted restrictive covenants, and black residents were increasingly forced to reside in a triangular-shaped district of about twenty square blocks bounded by the Illinois Central tracks, Sumner Street, and Mobile Avenue. This development meant that blacks necessarily resided in the same area with pimps and bootleggers.[29]

Blacks in Waterloo soon began building churches, which served as the centers of community life. In 1913 they organized an African Methodist Episcopal Church and before long had raised sufficient funds to hire a minister, Reverend I. W. Bess. The next year local black Baptists organized the Antioch Baptist Church, which received financial assistance from the city's white Baptist churches. In 1918 a local black businessman, J. D. Hopkins, organized the Colored Settlement Association to help establish community programs for blacks and assist them in seeking help from local agencies.[30]

Like black residents elsewhere in Iowa, blacks in Waterloo faced many types of racial discrimination. Robert Neymeyer writes that although there were no Jim Crow laws in Waterloo, a color line existed. Some eating places would not serve blacks, and they found it "convenient" to sit toward the back of buses to avoid hostility or confrontations.[31]

The color line also extended to Waterloo's small professional class, including Vaeletta and Milton Fields. The Fieldses came to Waterloo in the

1920s as newlyweds so Milton could practice law; both were graduates of the University of Iowa. The Fieldses' life in Waterloo was difficult. Milton had no trouble attracting clients, but most had little money to pay legal fees. Given the couple's meager income, Vaeletta realized early in the marriage that she would have to seek employment. Knowing that she would not be hired as a public-school teacher (she had formerly taught in Petersburg, Virginia), she worked in a variety of jobs, including cleaning rest rooms for the telephone company, operating an elevator in a department store, and later working as an assistant to the local YWCA director. Although it is not known how many Waterloo public-school teachers had four-year college degrees in the 1920s, it is probable that, unlike Vaeletta Fields, most did not. The Waterloo school board would hire its first African-American teacher in 1952.[32]

The experience of African Americans in Sioux City would parallel that of blacks in Waterloo. By 1890, 366 blacks had settled there, some opening small businesses, others finding employment as porters and laborers. In the early twentieth century, city officials brought in nearly 500 black workers to install pipelines and build roads and boardwalks. At the time, these laborers, along with domestic and service workers, made up 92.6 percent of the black labor force in the city.[33]

A small number of African Americans gradually opened "barber shops, carpet-cleaning establishments, laundries, [a] dance hall, restaurants, and gambling houses" to become the elite of the black community. In his study of Sioux City's black population, William Hewitt notes that even though these businessmen held an elevated position within the black community, in a wider sense they occupied "low socioeconomic status in comparison to whites, [and] maintained the traditionally established rapport with whites ... either through integrated contacts with whites, or through white business patronage." Hewitt observes that these elites viewed later black arrivals as a threat to the accommodation reached between black elites and the white power structure. In 1910, 305 blacks lived in Sioux City; in 1920, that number had risen to 1,130, with the greatest increase in 1919 and 1920.[34]

With the rise of the Sioux City packinghouses in the second decade of the twentieth century, the black workforce would change considerably. Shortly after 1900 local packinghouse officials imported blacks as strikebreakers, a move that brought hostility and repercussions from white workers. The latter successfully excluded blacks from many jobs until World War I, when labor shortages became crucial. Black workers were then hired in many areas, including the packinghouses. According to Hewitt, during World War I, Sioux City blacks "experienced rapid socioeconomic mobility," and, in turn, could support a higher number of black professionals and entrepreneurs.[35]

After the war blacks continued to work in the Sioux City meat-packing industry. Following a bitter strike, management responded by destroying the union and reemploying only one-fourth of the original strikers. Ironically, after using African Americans as strikebreakers, management reversed its repressive policy and began hiring them along with immigrants because they believed "these workers would split the work force and would be less inclined to offer strong support for the unions." The effect of management's change in policy is dramatically shown through black employment figures: In 1916, 0.6 percent of this group worked in the meat industry; by 1920, that figure had risen to 17.7 percent, and by 1925, to 43.9 percent. Correspondingly, packinghouse employment meant higher wages and greater job security, although new arrivals were forced to live in the South Bottoms close to the packing plants.[36]

William Hewitt has shown, however, that as blacks increased in number and began to improve their socioeconomic status, whites responded in other negative ways. Although white packinghouse employees could not keep blacks out entirely, they did succeed in segregating them into the most undesirable work areas, particularly rendering and the kill floor. By the 1920s Hewitt believes that "racial antipathies and stereotyping" had intensified.[37] Indicative of these attitudes, the Ku Klux Klan marched in Sioux City in 1924.

While Waterloo and Sioux City attracted substantial black populations, by 1900 Des Moines had the largest population of African Americans in the state. Some black families had been attracted to the coal camps surrounding the city, but probably most moved to Des Moines because of its size and, therefore, its greater job opportunities. While many newcomers found jobs, they were typically at the bottom of the employment ladder. One historian has written: "The average black [in Des Moines] held a menial job and could hope for little or no upward mobility socially, economically, or politically. Generally blacks ... received the same treatment as their counterparts in the heavily industrialized cities convulsed by more violent racial tension." At the same time, the black community in Des Moines contained a growing number of black professionals and soon produced a sizable number of community leaders, who through various organizations brought about advancements for the black population as a whole.[38]

Although no studies have been done on African-American employment opportunities in Des Moines during World War I, it seems likely that blacks there made economic gains, the same as elsewhere. Nationwide, 16 percent of the male workforce went into the military, a void filled by black and white women, black males, and Mexican Americans. Wartime mobilization resulted in significant changes for America's black population, perhaps best illustrated by the large migration of Southern blacks to northern cities. There African Americans went to work for railroads, and in packinghouses, coal mines, shipyards, and steel mills.[39]

World War I would impact on Des Moines's black community in yet another way. In 1917 the War Department announced that the city would be the site of a three-month black officers' training camp with 1,250 candidates admitted between the ages of twenty-five and forty. The decision to establish the camp marked the culmination of a long struggle to train black military officers; in the broadest sense, however, the effort can be seen as a "continuation of the movement for full citizenship rights." The campaign to create the camp was national in scope, involving black college administrators, professors, students, and members of the white community.[40]

The move to create a black officers'-training school began in 1916, with national NAACP president Joe E. Springarn initiating the effort. The first goal was to obtain racially integrated training for black men, but when that plan seemed unattainable, officials like Springarn began to push for a segregated camp. Before long blacks themselves assumed leadership of the project. Once under way, reports indicated that conditions in the camp were good and facilities adequate. Colonel C. C. Ballou served as camp commander along with other white officers.[41]

Five months after the initial announcement, 639 successful candidates received commissions, including 9 Iowans. Officers then had a two-week leave after which they reported to one of seven different army camps. Officers were then to train black enlisted men in separate units, later to be formed into the Ninety-second Division in France.[42]

Later in the war federal officials selected another Iowa facility, Camp Dodge, as a site for training black draftees. In the fall of 1917 newly inducted soldiers reported to Camp Dodge, located north of Des Moines; the soldiers arrived from many different states, with the largest numbers from Alabama, Tennessee, and Mississippi; 127 men came from Iowa, mostly from Buxton, Keokuk, and Des Moines. Military officials enforced racial segregation between white and black soldiers, with arrangements made for separate social activities. For blacks, officials opened an army club in an old Des Moines school, which provided a cafeteria, soft-drink stand, game room, barbershop, and auditorium with a moving picture machine. The following summer officials held a second officers'-training school at Camp Dodge.[43]

The military experience of black officers in Des Moines would not be completed without a tragic and controversial episode. In 1918 three black officers were charged and found guilty of assaulting a white girl. They were sentenced to be hanged, a sentence carried out on July 5, 1918. Officials ordered the entire company to witness the hanging. The episode served as a devastating reminder that although blacks in Iowa had won full legal rights almost fifty years earlier, racial prejudices remained strong.[44]

Even before World War I a major move to improve African Americans' social and economic status in Des Moines had been initiated. In 1915 blacks there organized a chapter of the National Association for the Advancement of Colored People (NAACP), a move taken only six years after the national organization had come into existence. The Des Moines chapter, the first in Iowa, had thirty-five charter members; by September of that year membership had grown to two hundred. Prominent African-American attorney Joe S. Brown served as the first president; Brown's wife, Sue M. Brown, also played a central role in chapter activities. Mr. Brown served as the state's district organizer in 1920, resulting in chapters being formed in Council Bluffs, Davenport, Waterloo, and Cedar Rapids.[45]

The work of NAACP members was publicized and promoted by the *Iowa Bystander* (originally the *Iowa State Bystander*), a weekly newspaper published in Des Moines. The paper circulated in black communities throughout the state. The *Bystander* had been founded in 1894 by I. E. Williamson, Billy Colson, and Jack Logan. Typical of black newspaper owners at the time, the three men all had other employment, since the newspaper generated only meager income. As a later editor observed, the paper was founded partly because the local white press did not offer employment for black journalists, and white newspapers "never carried Negro social news." In 1896 J. L. Thompson purchased the paper, making many changes in its news coverage and format. Thompson visited each of Iowa's African-American communities annually, enabling him to print news about communities all over the state. This policy, undoubtedly, increased the paper's appeal to blacks residing outside Des Moines. James B. Norris, Sr., purchased the paper in November 1922.[46]

The NAACP's activities, reported faithfully in the *Bystander,* ranged widely from cooperating with white community leaders in the attempted eradication of racial discrimination and in the promotion of African-American interests, to establishing educational programs for both black adults and young people. Sue Brown, president of the Des Moines NAACP from 1925 to 1930, established a junior chapter, which, in turn, led to the creation of a black YMCA. The NAACP's emphasis on black youth helped reach a milestone in the way the local press depicted blacks. In 1925 a Des Moines dairy featured a black baby in an advertisement. A local NAACP leader believed this was probably the first time that blacks had not been depicted in derogatory fashion in local ads.[47]

In 1925 African Americans helped found the Des Moines Interracial Commission to promote cooperation between blacks and whites, and the following year the group published a fourteen-point "Desiderata of the Des Moines Negroes." The statement made it abundantly clear that though the NAACP and others had made real headway in promoting their goals and eliminating false views about blacks, much work remained. The list called for the abolition of separate bathing beaches, of discriminatory rental and property-selling practices, and of the exclusion of blacks from serving on grand juries. It also called for the hiring of at least one black schoolteacher by the Des Moines school board.[48]

Although the immigrant history of each European group differs in specific detail, overarching observations can be made about the collective immigrant experience in Iowa. Almost all groups came for economic betterment, whether through land ownership or through employment or business opportunities, and all realized that goal in varying degrees. All groups brought along cultural and religious practices; and all sought to perpetuate those practices not only for themselves but also for their progeny. In effect, most groups sought initially to create "little Bohemias," "little Denmarks," or "little Italys" set down in the midst of a strange new land. Individuals in all groups reached out to help family and friends in times of distress and bereavement, both through formal arrangements and through personal assistance. And perhaps equally significant, all groups seemed to view their decision to emigrate as a positive move.

In 1951 Oscar Handlin wrote a groundbreaking history of American immigration entitled *The Uprooted: The Epic Story of the Great Migrations That Made the American People,* wherein he portrayed the experience of European emigrants as shattering, alienating, and disillusioning. Focusing primarily on the urban experience in the Northeast, Handlin's study provided a much-needed work on the subject and helped to initiate a new subfield in American history; his observations, however, do not fit well with the immigrant experience in Iowa.

In general, the immigrant experience here can be regarded as positive, with limited evidence of the alienation or drastic uprooting described by Handlin. Some immigrants, undoubtedly, regretted their decision, and some returned to their homeland. Certainly immigrants felt loneliness and isolation after leaving behind much that was familiar. But for most groups it was possible to bring along and retain some of the past. Immigrants generally continued to speak their native tongue at home, in churches, and at public gatherings, at least until World War I.

Once in Iowa, immigrants tended to settle in clusters with other people from the same country, and sometimes even from the same village. These ethnic clusters, or communities, were present in hundreds of rural neighborhoods as well as in towns and cities. Some entire townships were dominated by people from the same country, sharing the same language, religion, and cultural traditions. For other groups ethnic clustering took place in coal camps. Immigrants everywhere continued to practice the religion they had known in the old country, often building their own churches and sometimes, like the Norwegian Lutherans, bringing pastors over from the homeland to insure that religious thinking not be corrupted by the New World. Newcomers maintained emotional ties with family members in the old country, and some, particularly the Irish, sent money back to families and Catholic parishes to help make life there a little better. Although second-generation immigrants usually fared better economically than the first, hundreds of thousands of first-generation immigrants improved their standard of living in the United States and prospered sufficiently to help their children acquire land, launch a business, or obtain an education.

The major exceptions to this generally positive experience came after 1900. During World War I foreign-born Iowans, particularly Germans, experienced a hostile, suspicious climate in which civil liberties were often violated. For southern and eastern Europeans discrimination was far more widespread, reaching back even into the late nineteenth century; during the twentieth century, groups like Italian Americans experienced discrimination because of their ancestry and their Catholic religion. Italian Americans in coal camps experienced even further discrimination because of their occupation. During the 1920s national immigration laws became more restrictive, primarily aimed at keeping out eastern and southern Europeans and, by the late 1920s had reduced immigration almost to a trickle. By the 1930s and 1940s, however, negativism toward the foreign-born had lessened greatly.

For African Americans, however, that would not be the case. Blacks would not experience a lessening of hostility in the 1930s, nor would they generally share the positive experience of immigrants and the opportunities to improve their socioeconomic positions. Some positive changes would come in World War II, with greater employment opportunities, and in the 1960s, with the creation of a Civil Rights Commission. But in 1930 major barriers remained in the way of equal social and economic opportunities for African Americans.

Regardless of past experiences, Iowa continues to enjoy a rich cultural legacy from the dozens of immigrant groups and the African Americans who have come here searching for a better life. In every part of the state ethnic groups hold festivals to celebrate their heritage; even more visible are the state's major ethnic museums: the Vesterheim (Norwegian) Museum in Decorah; the Danish Immigrant Museum in Elk Horn; and the Czech and Slovak National Museum and Library in Cedar Rapids. Cities like Des Moines contain fraternal lodges, associations, and historical societies, which promote ethnic solidarity and pride and preserve ethnic history. African Americans also celebrate various events and in addition have created the Buxton Iowa Club, which works to preserve the special experience of blacks in that community. Each ethnic or racial group provides a unique contribution to the cultural mosaic that is Iowa.

While members of various ethnic groups eventually assimilated into the mainstream of society, thus reducing their cultural distinctiveness, Iowa would also contain both communal and semicommunal ethnic groups that chose to remain apart from the wider society. Several of these groups would be short-lived, such as the Hungarians who created the colony of New Buda in Decatur County, and a German settlement known as Communia in northeastern Iowa. The Icarians, a French communal society that settled near Corning, survived for some forty years as a secular society. The two most visible groups have been the Old Order Amish, who arrived in the 1840s, settling in Washington and Johnson counties, and the Inspirationalists, who arrived in the 1850s and located in Iowa County. The Inspirationalists characterize themselves primarily as religious communitarians, whereas the Old Order Amish can be described as semicommunal because of heavy emphasis on shared activities and mutual aid.

The Inspirationalists would begin their settlement in Iowa in the 1850s, arriving here some ten years after they emigrated from the German province of Hesse. The group originated in 1714 in what today is southern Germany. There they formalized many religious beliefs and practices, including the one from which they take their name. This central belief was that God would speak directly to them through certain individuals known as *Werkzeugs,* meaning "tools of God." Christian Metz, the most influential *Werkzeug,* had a secretary accompany him at all times to record the testimonies. Often Metz would begin to shake and seem to lose control when receiving an inspiration. Metz described this experience as extremely stressful and was left totally exhausted. Over time the testimonies provided a substantial body of religious literature providing guidance for the Inspirationalists.[49]

In the 1840s the Inspirationalists decided to leave Germany. Membership at the time was estimated at about four hundred members living together on various German estates, and an additional six hundred members scattered throughout Germany, France, and Switzerland. The group first settled around Ebenezer, New York, but remained there only ten years. During that period, however, they fully committed themselves to communal living. Adopting a communal lifestyle meant that all resources were pooled to provide equally for members.

Resettling in Iowa, the Inspirationalists proceeded to develop a well-ordered, religiously centered society. In total, the Inspirationalists laid out six villages, including Amana, Middle Amana, East Amana, West Amana,

High Amana, and South Amana; they also purchased the site of Home-stead. Many craftsmen who had joined the group in Germany were still living, and their skills helped ease the economic transition from Ebenezer. Homestead included a railroad station—along the Rock Island line—so the group immediately had transportation to outside markets. In all, they reconstructed (from Ebenezer days) the woolen mills, meat-processing equipment, and a sawmill operation. Each village also had both an agri-cultural and a livestock program. Members who had selected the Iowa site in 1854 had made a wise decision: With fertile soil, a continuous water supply, and stands of numerous types of timber, the Amana Colonies would soon experience substantial economic success.[50]

Within the village, members would live much as they had lived be-fore. The group built some single homes but also constructed many du-plexes and fourplexes. Families who lived in the latter types of housing were often related. The homes did not contain kitchens, as members ate together in the community kitchens. The Inspirationalists' economic arrangement called for a highly structured assignment of tasks. Young men were usually assigned to work in the agricultural or livestock area, unmarried females worked in the communal kitchens, and married women worked in the gardens. Older women typically were assigned to the nurs-eries. For most children in Amana, an eighth-grade education was the norm.[51]

During the latter 1800s Amanites attended church an average of eleven times a week, including three times on Sunday, every week morn-ing, and once on Wednesday evening. Although the Inspirationalist soci-ety has not been described as a theocracy, in some ways it resembled one. Certainly the church dominated all aspects of society, and the elders and *Werkzeugs* occupied important positions that, in effect, provided both sec-ular and temporal leadership. During the communal stage the Amana Colonies had no sheriff or constable to enforce local laws.[52]

By 1900, although the Amana Colonies were doing well economi-cally, the elders—the main religious figures in each village—faced in-creasing difficulties in enforcing the rules of behavior. As Amana scholar Jonathan Andelson has pointed out, the elders faced a "contradictory prob-lem" that they could not resolve. On one hand they were expected to pre-serve the society by keeping people from leaving. But on the other hand they were also expected to enforce the rules. By 1900 it seemed these two responsibilities were incompatible, for if elders enforced the rules, more people would leave. So, as Andelson points out, the elders began to "look the other way" when rules were violated.[53]

In the 1920s and 1930s the Amana people experienced major economic difficulties. In 1923 a large flour mill and a gristmill burned; the society had no insurance on either facility. During the decade business also declined. With the onset of the Great Depression, society members realized they faced some hard choices. They could give up the luxuries they had slowly acquired, including the hiring of some two hundred outsiders to do the less desirable tasks, and return to the strict ways of their forebears; or they could give up their communal way of life. In 1932 the entire adult membership voted on Amana's future. The issue attracted great attention, with newspapers all over the country covering the event. The situation, indeed, seemed ironic: While some Americans proclaimed capitalism was dead (as a result of devastating economic conditions) and urged citizens to adopt a socialistic government, in America's very heartland a socialistic society seemed about to adopt a system of free enterprise. When the votes were tallied, approximately 75 percent of the membership had voted for an end to communalism.[54]

After 1932 life in Amana changed in some ways, but in countless other ways it remained the same. Members elected a Committee of 45 to formulate a new organization. The result was the creation of two corporations: the Amana Church Society, responsible for the community's religious life, and the Amana Society, which would control business operations. Amanites would be employed for wages, and the earlier practices of providing housing, food, and clothing would be abolished. Each member received at least one share of voting stock, valued at fifty dollars; some members received more, depending on their years of service. The society continued to provide health and burial insurance. Members too old to work were cared for totally by the society.

The transition in Amana from a communal to a noncommunal society came about with surprising tranquillity. Although not all members favored the change, it apparently was carried out with little bitterness and certainly no physical confrontations. The same cannot be said for the demise or changeover of all communitarian societies. Also unlike other groups, many people remained in the Amana Colonies, purchasing the homes in which they had always lived. Since 1932, even though the communal nature of the group has largely disappeared, the Amana Colonies still represent a distinct social and economic entity.

Iowa's second distinctive ethnic society that has chosen to live apart from the wider society is the Old Order Amish. Unlike the Inspirationalists, the Old Order have never been totally communal, but they do carry on numerous traditions that are semicommunal, particularly the practice of mutual aid. When Amish neighbors gather to help another Amish farmer build a new barn, they are practicing mutual aid; they also sometimes provide financial assistance for other Amish families. On the other hand, the Old Order Amish do not hold all property in common; each family owns its own farm, farm machinery, livestock, and all household equipment.

Iowa's Old Order are a group of like-minded individuals who share the same general religious beliefs, have a commitment to an agrarian way of life, and seek to isolate themselves from the outside world. They also practice adult baptism, reject modernism, and believe in nonviolence. The Amish, like many communitarians, seek to curb the individuality of their members. The Old Order are identifiable because their members wear dark, distinctive clothing, which clearly sets them apart from the general population. Of all their distinguishing features, perhaps the most visible is their use of the horse and buggy as a means of transportation. Today in Iowa the Old Order are located around Kalona, Oelwein, Milton, Bloomfield, Riceville, and McIntire. Settlement in the latter two communities was started in the 1970s.

The Amish appeared in Europe in the latter 1600s, taking their name from a Mennonite minister, Jacob Ammann. Soon after, some members began immigrating to the colony of Pennsylvania. During the eighteenth and early nineteenth centuries, members migrated to other locations in the northeastern United States; by the 1840s Amish were settling in the Territory of Iowa. The first Amish families came from Ohio to Lee County, and a few years later other Ohio families settled in Washington County.[55] Once in Iowa, the Amish prospered. Their land selections in Washington, and later Johnson, County proved wise, and more Amish families continued to locate there. Before the 1850s the followers of Jacob Ammann were known only as Amish, but around that time some members took the name Old Order, indicating their rejection of worldly influences, such as modern technology and modern dress. They also rejected separate meeting

houses, preferring to hold church services in their homes. An additional
split would occur in the mid-1920s, when a group called the Beachy
Amish broke away from the Old Order. The Beachy allowed automobiles,
separate meeting houses for religious services, and use of electricity.[56] The
two Beachy Amish settlements in Iowa are near Kalona and Leon.

The Amish way of life in Iowa today approximates in many ways
Iowa's rural life of some sixty or seventy years ago. Most Old Order families live on farms and therefore experience both physical isolation and a
large degree of economic self-sufficiency. Amish farms average around
120 acres, considerably smaller than the statewide average of some 350
acres. The smaller size means the land can still be worked with horses (although some Kalona Amish have tractors) and their numerous children
can assist with farm work. In the past Amish farmers have traditionally rejected use of herbicides and pesticides, but today, apparently, some Amish
are beginning to use some chemicals. The Amish continue to have large
families, perhaps five or six children, as within their society children are
still viewed as economic assets. The Amish also believe they are following God's will in being fruitful.[57]

In every community Amish families are divided into church districts
within which a bishop and several ministers preach and minister to their
members. The Amish come together for Sunday services, listening to
preaching in the morning, sharing lunch, and spending the afternoon visiting. Each church district has about fifteen families, so the group is close-
knit not only because of shared religious beliefs but also from frequent in-
teraction.[58]

Unlike the Inspirationalists, the Old Order Amish have retained their
original structure and have continued to expand in Iowa. Beginning with
one settlement in 1840, the Iowa Old Order now have five separate communities. The major obstacle the Amish have faced is in educating their
young. During much of their time in Iowa, Amish children attended public schools. After World War II, however, the Amish began to resist school
consolidation and eventually set up some private schools. The most difficult period came in Buchanan County in 1961, when area residents considered a proposed school merger between Hazleton and Oelwein. The
Amish became caught up in the situation, which resulted in county school
officials attempting to transport Amish children forcibly to school in Oelwein. In 1967 the educational controversy was settled when the General

Assembly allowed Amish schools certain exemptions, including allowing teachers to have only eighth-grade educations and allowing children to end school at age fourteen. At the same time, Amish schools were to be closely monitored by the Department of Public Instruction to ensure that Amish children were learning basic information.[59]

For the Old Order Amish today, the greatest challenge probably lies in the area of expansion. To carry on their tradition as an agrarian people, the Amish continually need additional farmland for their young. So far that need has been met, but continuing the practice will certainly become more difficult in the years ahead.

12

Social, Economic, and Political Issues in Iowa

The diverse cultural backgrounds of Iowans, so evident in the late nineteenth and early twentieth centuries, would produce various ways of thinking and various modes of behavior. This diverse mentality would be particularly evident in regard to social and political issues. Iowans, therefore, would find themselves severely tested in efforts to reconcile conflicting ethnic and cultural values and to find common solutions to problems that demanded attention during the middle period. The state's struggle to find consensus on the matter of liquor control, the major political issue between 1870 and 1930, serves well as an example of the need for compromise. Prohibition would demand attention as early as the 1840s and continue to plague Iowans until national Prohibition began in 1920. At the same time, during the Progressive Era (1900–17), Iowa officials sought to bring about social and political change within the state, change often resisted by conservatives. Women's suffrage would be yet another divisive political issue in these years, an issue that again underscored Iowans' social and cultural diversity. Beginning in the late 1860s, for almost half a century, women worked to secure enfranchisement through an amendment to the state constitution. The vote for women would finally come through the Nineteenth Amendment to the United States Constitution.

In effect, from 1870 to 1920 Iowans were seeking consensus on major issues that involved various ethnic and cultural viewpoints, different sectional interests (between northern and southern Iowa), and political conflicts between progressives and conservatives. In some ways Prohibition and women's suffrage were part and parcel of the broad movement known as progressivism, yet both had long lives of their own, independent of that movement. Regardless of the interrelationship between issues, Prohibition, progressivism, and women's suffrage would dominate Iowans' social and political thinking for some five decades.

Prohibition would prove to be the most emotional, politically significant, and tenacious of all issues in nineteenth- and twentieth-century Iowa. From the days of statehood to the creation of national Prohibition in 1920, Iowa contained a strong antiliquor element; these forces, moreover, would be highly resourceful in their efforts to abolish the liquor trade. As Dan E. Clark observed shortly before the inauguration of national Prohibition, "almost every known method of regulating the liquor traffic has been given a trial in Iowa during the seventy years since [it became a state]."[1] The issue of Prohibition generally pitted Democrats against Republicans and pietistic religious denominations against liturgical religious groups. In the political arena, Prohibition had a major impact and in two elections, 1889 and 1891, determined the outcome of the gubernatorial races. Between 1847 and 1920, the issue of Prohibition might wane briefly but it would never disappear, as periodically the dry forces gathered steam and demanded the Republican party respond to the dry's demands. Often Prohibition represented the most important political issue of the day.

The first state law regarding Prohibition (or temperance, as it was often known in the nineteenth century) passed the General Assembly in 1847, enacting a local-option law. As with dozens of subsequent Prohibition acts, it was difficult to enforce. In the next decade, however, heartened by the passage of the now famous Maine temperance law in 1851, Iowa's dry forces successfully lobbied the General Assembly for a stronger antiliquor law. This legislation, passed in 1855, was the state's first absolute Prohibition law, thus labeling Iowa a dry state. As with the previous legislation, the new law was frequently violated. Moreover, as they would do so often in later years, the General Assembly soon began tinkering with the 1855 legislation, amending it to exempt from Prohibition "beer, cider from apples or wine from grapes, currants or other fruits grown in this State." Thereafter, because of the diminution of the original legislative intent, an unofficial local-option policy prevailed whereby each community determined its own standard for liquor control. Bootlegging became common as the "prohibition pendulum was swinging far in the direction of lenient enforcement."[2] For the next twenty years, the General Assembly enacted no major prohibition laws.

By the early 1880s, with renewed vigor, Prohibition forces initiated a campaign to amend the state constitution to prohibit the manufacture and sale of intoxicating liquor. This surge of interest rested on the earlier formation of several groups, including the Women's Christian Temperance Union, the Iowa State Temperance Alliance, and the Prohibition party. The General Assembly approved the Prohibition amendment twice (in 1880 and 1882) as required by the state constitution; it was then forwarded to the voters, who quickly approved it. Although the dry forces were jubilant, their victory was short-lived as the Iowa Supreme Court declared the amendment invalid due to a procedural error. The drys then focused their attention on the Republican party, which passed a "stringent prohibitory law" in 1884. Opponents in some communities responded with defiance and even mob violence, but the new law nevertheless greatly reduced the number of establishments where liquor was sold openly; the legislation also "practically abolished" liquor-manufacturing concerns within the state.[3]

The most extreme response to the 1884 legislation took place two years later in Sioux City when Reverend George Haddock, a Methodist minister, was murdered. The fifty-five-year-old pastor had arrived in the rapidly growing river community the previous year to discover a thriving illicit liquor business. Reverend Haddock immediately joined the dry forces to stop the liquor trade. He quickly earned the nickname Informer Haddock, because of efforts to gather information on illegal operations.[4]

Haddock's efforts to document unlawful operations soon paid off, as in case after case judges issued permanent injunctions against the saloons. When Haddock was asked on the witness stand "What is your business?" he responded: "To fight the Devil!" Haddock's zealous efforts on behalf of the drys earned him deep animosity among the city's anti-Prohibition element. Returning home one evening from gathering information on yet another Sioux City saloon, he was mortally wounded. A judge handed down indictments against eight men, and the following year one of the group, Fred Munchrath, was found guilty of manslaughter.[5]

The 1884 campaign for liquor legislation highlighted several important aspects of the Prohibition movement in Iowa. Politically, the Republican party continued to commit itself to a strict Prohibition policy, while the Democrats favored local option. Even though the GOP's support for the issue would wax and wane over time, in general Republicans were viewed as the party supporting Prohibition. The campaign also highlighted sectional differences in regard to the strength of the wets and the drys. A sharp divergence existed between river communities and inland towns. Communities like Sioux City, Davenport, and Dubuque opposed Prohibition, believing it shackled local businesses and stifled future growth. Many river towns, particularly Davenport and Dubuque, contained large numbers of first- and second-generation German Americans and Irish Americans, who were among the strongest foes of the dry forces.

Sectional differences also existed in regard to Prohibition support, as Catholics and Missouri Synod Lutherans—both typically opposed to Prohibition—were concentrated in the northern half of the state, and Methodists were particularly numerous in the southern half. A vote on a state constitutional Prohibition amendment as late as 1917 illustrates this difference. In that year voters in Ringgold County, located in southwestern Iowa, and therefore described as "southern, rural, native-stock, and pietist," approved the constitutional amendment with a vote of 76.7 percent. At the same time, in northeastern Iowa the strongly Catholic river community of Dubuque—composed primarily of German-American and Irish-American residents—cast 80.7 percent of its votes against the prohibition amendment.[6]

The contrast between the wet and dry votes in Ringgold and Dubuque counties also highlights the state's urban-rural split over Prohibition. From the 1840s rural counties, under local option, tended to vote against allowing liquor establishments, and urban communities voted in favor of them. By the decade of the teens the rural-urban split would be even more important in determining the pro and con vote on the liquor question.

The most unwavering aspect in the struggle between wets and drys, however, was the liturgical, pietistic division among Iowa's religious groups. As Laura Derr has written, "The division on the issue of drinking, in [pre–World War I] days, may best be understood by a study of religious differences." Derr was referring to differences between pietists and liturgicals. The pietists had arrived here first, represented mainly by native-born settlers from the northeastern United States, and belonging to mainline churches, particularly the Methodists, Baptists, Congregationalists, Presbyterians, and Disciples of Christ. The pietist churches represented the dominant culture in America, emphasizing what they believed to be "right behavior" and deemphasizing dogma and ritual. Pietists were evangelistic and reformist in nature, believing that "one's own faith necessitated witnessing, preaching, and living an exemplary life." Each individual was responsible for his or her own behavior and thus had the ability to change society as a whole. Accordingly, pietists had no problem accepting—even promoting—the state's role in improving its citizenry through issues such as Prohibition. By the World War I era pietists outnumbered liturgicals in Iowa by three to two.[7]

Liturgicals, composed primarily of Roman Catholics, German Lutherans, and Episcopalians, "found the significance of belief" in the sacraments and rituals of their faiths. Liturgicals stressed "the concept of a community of true believers, within which one was safe and saved, so long as one adhered to, or returned to, the rituals of atonement and worship." Rather than an individualist approach to the deity, liturgicals believed that one's relationship to God was "mediated by the church, its hierarchy and rituals." At the same time, liturgicals rejected a reformist government that attempted to prohibit or limit one's behavior, such as controlling access to alcohol. The liturgicals believed, rather, that the actual practice of drinking such beverages was not in itself harmful and would be controlled within the community. Unlike the pietists, who were composed of diverse ethnic groups, the liturgicals—through the Catholic and Lutheran churches—were dominated by German-stock and Irish-stock members, particularly the former. Of all foreign-stock groups, German Americans were the most vocal in their struggle against Prohibition.[8] The opposing views of pietists and liturgicals would remain evident as Iowans continued to struggle with "the liquor question" for the next three decades.

By the late 1880s the liquor question would affect the state in yet another way. In 1889 many Iowa voters, becoming increasingly unhappy with Prohibition, elected Democrat Horace Boies as governor. The election of a Democrat as chief executive ended a thirty-two-year string of Republican gubernatorial victories. Although Prohibition played a key role in the election, Leland Sage believes that Boies's designation as a Democrat deserves some qualification. Sage points out that the governor, formerly a Waterloo attorney, believed in and practiced temperance, but opposed Prohibition on the grounds that "it would deprive persons of their property rights without remuneration, and invade their personal rights." Also, because of Boies's opposition to a high tariff and his "lukewarm" support of the free silver idea (two major political issues at the time), Sage sees him as a political independent rather than as a fully committed Democrat.[9] Boies would win reelection in 1891.

To Republicans, Boies's victory brought a strong message: Iowans were unhappy with Prohibition, and this could translate into more losses at the polls. Republicans then "softened" their views on local option and won back the governorship in 1893. The following year the legislature passed the Mulct Law, which did not repeal the 1884 legislation but did add a local-option measure. The Mulct Law was one of the strangest laws in Iowa history. Under the legislation, Iowa counties could decide for themselves whether to be wet or dry; saloons in wet counties would then "be allowed to violate the provisions of the state [1884] prohibition law" in return for a six-hundred-dollar fine paid to the county government. This arrangement proved popular, as by 1906 forty-three out of Iowa's ninety-nine counties allowed taverns to operate.[10]

Between 1894 and the implementation of the Eighteenth Amendment, Iowa's legislature continued to introduce an almost bewildering array of Prohibition legislation. Indicative of the interest in the issue, at least nineteen bills were introduced in 1909 alone. One unsuccessful bill called for the state to be divided into two districts, with a liquor law enforcement commissioner for each district and up to ten deputies for each commissioner. In 1909 the General Assembly passed the Moon Law, which restricted the authorized number of saloons to one for every one thousand inhabitants. The law had some effect, as between 1908 and 1912 the number of saloons in the state fell from over 1,600 to about 740. In 1915 Iowans pushed for a third major dry offensive, resulting in the passage of yet another total prohibitory law. As Dan Clark has noted, "Gradually the saloon in Iowa was being crowded to the wall," as Iowans became increasingly unhappy with public saloons. According to the 1915 law, Iowans could no longer "legally" violate the law; instead, the General Assembly reestablished absolute prohibition.[11]

The period of national Prohibition, beginning in 1920, provides yet another stormy chapter in Iowa's liquor history. The most popular accounts deal with bootlegging, particularly the manufacturing of rye whiskey by Templeton-area farmers, known appropriately as Templeton rye. With repeal of the Eighteenth Amendment in the 1930s, Iowa's state officials once again faced the need for liquor legislation. During much of the time between 1933 and 1963, when liquor-by-the-drink became legal in Iowa, a state liquor commission regulated the sale of packaged liquor through state-owned liquor stores. Increasingly, the "liquor question" came to be viewed as a struggle between rural and urban interests—and therefore between urban Democrats and rural Republicans—rather than between pietistic and liturgical forces.

During some six decades, however, the struggle over Prohibition dominated legislative sessions, influenced gubernatorial elections, brought forth civil disobedience, and aroused passions more consistently than any other issue. The struggle over the liquor question was, as one historian put it, "the one problem which lay closest to Iowans' hearts."[12]

During the period in which wets and drys struggled over liquor control, Iowans, along with other Americans, involved themselves in less emotional but broader reforms known collectively as the progressive movement. The Progressive Era (1900–1917) constituted a many-sided reform movement that involved economic, political, and social issues and affected government at every level. Numerous causes existed for the eruption of reform even before 1900, including a devastating depression in the 1890s, with much labor strife, an ever-increasing number of immigrants pouring into the nation's cities, and the problems of the cities themselves in coping with expanding populations and increasing poverty, crime, and disease. During the same decade the United States became the leading manufacturing nation in the world, highlighting the prosperity of a few and the poverty of many. It seemed that not everyone was enjoying the fruits of the new industrialism.

The major focus of progressives, however, was the corporations, which held great political power by 1900. As one source put it, "In the minds of many, industrialists had become the nation's new monsters, controlling markets, wages, and prices in order to maximize their profits."[13] To reformers, legislation seemed the logical response to curb corporate power and deal with the inequities and corruptions of the time.

Even in rural states like Iowa, citizens believed reform necessary to curb corporate power and to safeguard citizens' health and welfare. However, as Leland Sage has pointed out, "the theories of government" regarding progress and reform "had nothing to do with the origins of progressivism in Iowa." Rather, the movement stemmed from a split in the dominant Republican party and "was rooted in practical politics."[14]

Progressivism in Iowa was essentially the story of Republican-party politics, since that party held almost total political power both before and during the progressive years. As Leland Sage has observed, few midwestern states "could match the Iowa story of one party domination over a forty-year period." Not only were all governors Republican between 1858 and 1900—with the exception of Horace Boies—but only occasionally did Iowans elect a Democrat to the General Assembly or to the national Congress. Republicans also typically controlled county courthouses. This success would prompt Jonathan Dolliver, a U.S. Senator from Fort Dodge, to issue his oft-repeated comment: "Hell would go Methodist before Iowa went Democratic."[15]

The Republicans' overwhelming success in Iowa would not, however, result in copacetic relations between party members. By 1900 Iowa Republicans would find themselves split into two camps: the conservatives, labeled as the "stand-patters," and the insurgents or progressives. Thomas Ross believes the gubernatorial race of 1897 was "the seedtime" for the rupture between the two groups. In that year the party nominated Leslie M. Shaw of Denison as its gubernatorial candidate, but at the same time another Republican, Albert B. Cummins of Des Moines, served notice he was interested in obtaining the senatorial nomination in 1900. Some party realignment took place among the powerful conservatives in an effort to block Cummins's Senate aspirations, as the latter was considered too liberal for many of the stand-patters' tastes. From then on, according to Ross, "The split within the [Republican] party grew wider and wider."[16]

Albert B. Cummins would soon be most clearly identified as "the front man" for the emerging progressive wing of the party. Cummins had begun his law practice in Des Moines some twenty years earlier, a practice that eventually produced considerable wealth. Although some historians have portrayed Cummins as an agrarian crusader and supporter of the working class, Leland Sage discounts this view, describing Cummins as a practical person supported primarily by "urban, middle-class, fairly well-to-do businessmen, lawyers and reformed minded editors." In a personal vein, Sage views Cummins as anything but a man of the people, describing him as "rather aloof, fastidious ... , of elegant tastes and patrician manner ... and a member of Des Moines's most exclusive clubs."[17]

In 1901 Cummins won the governorship of Iowa and thus occupied a most favorable position to influence party policy. Cummins's inaugural address foreshadowed the many reform measures that would receive attention in the next decade. Cummins's address, one historian has written, "breathed a new spirit into Iowa government." Accordingly, for the next twelve years Iowa's General Assembly produced a wide range of reform measures that paralleled progressive reform actions elsewhere.[18]

The railroads, as Iowa's largest corporations, would be the initial focus of state progressives. Iowa's farmers had long protested the railroads' unfair practices and sometimes excessive rates. In response Iowa officials in 1870 had created the State Railroad Commission to regulate Iowa's roads; in practice, however, the commission had little or no authority. By 1900 Iowa progressives were focusing on four railroad issues: determining more equitable tax rates (so railroads would pay their fair share of state taxes); increasing the power and authority of the State Railroad Commission; eliminating the free-pass system; and establishing the two-cent fare, or more reasonable passenger fares.[19]

Between 1902 and 1907 Iowa's General Assembly responded to progressive concerns by passing a number of railroad laws. The first law, in 1902, changed the way in which the railroads' taxes were determined, pro-

viding "more equitable taxation of the railroads." The law ended the secret nature of the tax-assessment proceedings and required railroads to report their gross and net incomes, along with other pertinent information,
to state officials. As a result, in the Cummins's administrations alone the
roads paid $39,000 additional state taxes and $405,000 additional county
taxes.[20]

Other important railroad laws strengthened the regulatory power of
the State Railroad Commission and placed limits on passenger rates. The
first action gave the commission power to inspect railroad property with
regard to public safety, and the right to appeal to the Interstate Commerce
Commission if railroads were accused of charging unfair rates. In 1907
legislators passed a bill regulating passenger fares, which divided Iowa's
roads into three classes, depending on their earnings per mile, and then
imposed limits on passenger rates for each class. Although not strictly an
enactment of a two-cent passenger rate, the bill required rates of not more
than three cents per mile for "class C" roads. Later legislation prohibited
railroad-corporation contributions to political campaigns.[21]

The most visible and vigorously contested issue, however, dealt with
the railroads' liberal policy of handing out free passes to politicians and
others to obtain political favors or to secure business. In 1906 and 1907
the General Assembly passed legislation mandating that railroads give
free passes only to employees and their families, or for charitable work.
The second law forced the railroads to maintain a list of free-pass recipi-
ents, a requirement that effectively ended the practice. With the enactment
of these two bills, as well as previous legislation, "the victory over the
railroads was complete."[22]

During the Progressive Era, Iowa legislators also made important
changes in election procedures, particularly in the matter of "wearying"
annual elections. In 1902 state officials secured an amendment requiring
biennial elections, which, in effect, eliminated the need for any state elections in odd-numbered years and thus placed all elections in even-numbered years. The change meant the terms of some officials were extended
an extra year to accommodate the new schedule.

The greatest triumph in the area of election procedures, however,
came with the establishment of Iowa's direct primary, called by one historian "the supreme triumph of the progressives." As elsewhere, Iowa
progressives believed the caucus-and-convention system of choosing
party nominees was open to manipulation by party bosses and should be

changed. Under the old system, according to one study, as few as three individuals—the committeeman and two friends—could control precinct
nominations for delegates to the county convention. The committeeman
would appoint one of his cohorts to the chair; then one of the two not
presiding would move that the chair name a three-person committee to select delegates, and the other friend would second the motion. The chair
would then declare the motion passed and appoint his two friends and a
third person to be delegates.[23]

According to a former legislator, Emory H. English, as more party
members began to attend precinct caucuses, the chairperson and his
friends sometimes used other devices to maintain control: "One method
was to advertise that the caucus would be held at eight o'clock, but the
precinct committeeman and his friends would meet at seven-thirty, set the
clock ahead, transact the business, and adjourn before the larger group of
voters arrived. Another method was to set up a counter attraction such as
a fire at the time scheduled for the caucus."[24] The direct primary was
strongly opposed by railroad officials, who feared a loss of influence in selecting candidates. The railroads not only owned vast properties but employed thousands of workers all over the state. According to one source,
"in every community the more able lawyers and most competent doctors
were retained by them." The free pass was an important weapon for the
railroads, and they awarded it to "county and state officials and commit-
teemen, members of congress, judges, convention delegates, and newspa-
permen, as well as all prominent citizens who could contribute HELPFUL
political support." Even with opposition, legislators continued to introduce direct primary legislation for eleven years. Finally, in 1907, the General Assembly approved "a full-fledged direct primary act." The bill provided for a primary election on the first Monday in June in even-numbered
years.[25]

Iowa progressives would also impose regulation in other areas. In
1906 and 1907 the General Assembly enacted laws that related to the activities of the state's insurance industry. These included requiring fire-
insurance companies to use uniform policy forms that cut down on fraud.
Progressives, after several attempts, finally succeeded in 1913 in creating
a department of insurance with an insurance commissioner. Regulation
would also extend into two additional areas when legislators passed both
pure-food and pure-drug bills in 1906 and 1907.

Progressives next turned their attention to education. In 1909 the legislature created a State Board of Education to govern Iowa's three state schools of higher education, replacing individual boards for each school. The legislature also created the Department of Public Instruction, which would have authority over the state's rural, elementary, and high schools. A longtime concern of state officials was a compulsory school law, and as early as 1902 the General Assembly determined that children between the ages of seven and fourteen would attend school for a period of twelve consecutive weeks of every school year. Two years later the legislators extended the time to fourteen consecutive weeks of school annually.[26]

By 1915, after unsuccessfully considering issues such as child labor and the creation of an industrial reformatory for women, the progressive impulse seems to have faded. By then a world war raged in Europe, and though the nation was officially neutral, problems of foreign relations began to overshadow domestic interests. Iowa progressives, although not accomplishing all their objectives, could take great pride in their record. As one historian has observed: "Judged by what it actually accomplished, directly or indirectly, Progressivism would seem undeniably to have been a success in Iowa."[27]

In the midteens, as the Iowa progressive spirit waned, yet another reform issue would become highly visible. The enfranchisement of women had long been of interest to a small but growing number of Iowans. Although countless women's-suffrage amendments had been introduced in the General Assembly over a period of some fifty years, each amendment had failed to pass both houses in two consecutive sessions, thereby failing enactment. Finally, in 1915, women's-suffrage supporters had cause to celebrate: Both houses of the General Assembly had twice approved the women's-suffrage amendment and had set the June primary of the following year for a vote by the general electorate. The jubilation was short-lived, however, as the suffrage amendment went down to defeat by a margin of 10,141 votes.[28]

The story of the struggle to enfranchise women would actually begin with the inception of the women's-rights movement in 1848. In that year some two hundred women, including Elizabeth Cady Stanton and Lucretia Mott, held a women's-rights convention in Seneca Falls, New York, where they issued a declaration listing grievances and demands for change. Women's suffrage was one demand, although not the major one,

*A women's suffrage group at the Callanan home in
Des Moines in the 1890s. Photo courtesy of the
State Historical Society,
Des Moines.*

as delegates were most concerned about married women's right to own property. Suffrage was, however, the most controversial issue at the convention. Soon after the Civil War women's-rights advocates would focus on suffrage as their major goal, stressing that the right to vote would give them the power to change other aspects of their lives.

Iowa suffragists began to organize and speak out on the issue of female enfranchisement in the latter 1860s. As elsewhere, women in Iowa soon discovered that their cause seemed always eclipsed by the issue of black male suffrage. In 1868 Iowans would amend the state constitution to grant black males the vote (by striking out the word "white" in Article 2: Right of Suffrage). Supporters of women's suffrage argued unsuccessfully that their issue should be included as a part of the black-suffrage amendment (by crossing out the word "male" in the same phrase). Two years later, in keeping with the general reform mood of the times, both houses of the General Assembly passed a women's-suffrage amendment. In 1872, when the amendment came before the legislature a second time, interest had waned and it failed to pass. These failures emphasized women's inequality and prompted some individuals to begin a statewide educational campaign. That effort included organizing local suffrage clubs and petitioning state legislators to reconsider the suffrage issue. In 1870 women organized a statewide group, the Iowa Woman Suffrage Association, later renamed the Iowa Equal Suffrage Association.

Although the majority of Iowans in the 1870s were not predisposed to support women's suffrage anyway, an event in New York City gave antisuffragists further ammunition. In 1871 and 1872 Victoria Woodhull, a thirty-three-year-old journalist and stockbroker, became involved in the women's-suffrage movement. After she had attracted considerable attention in the movement, it became clear that Woodhull was a proponent of sexual freedom and birth control, two shocking confessions in the nineteenth century. Antisuffragists immediately labeled Woodhull's views "free love" and charged that all suffragists were tainted by Woodhull's thinking. Clearly, Woodhull did not speak for the suffrage movement, nor did the rank and file agree with her. But for the next thirty-some years suffragists everywhere had to contend with the charge that they shared Woodhull's "scandalous views."[29]

The issue of free love, as wielded by antisuffragists, would create dissension among Iowa suffragists as they debated a proper response. Annie Savery, a founding member of the Iowa Woman Suffrage Association and soon "the leading spokeswoman for the woman suffrage forces in Iowa," would become a casualty of the Woodhull controversy. Savery defended Woodhull's right to express her views, no matter how unpopular. Following that defense, Iowa suffrage supporters ostracized Savery and attempted to shut her out of the movement.[30]

During the 1870s and 1880s, as more local suffrage clubs began to organize and as suffragists became more vocal, opposition did not diminish. According to Ruth Gallaher, most Iowa newspapers opposed the movement, although some gave it publicity. The Iowa suffragists' own publication, *The Woman's Standard,* noted at its inception that only one state newspaper, *The Keokuk Constitution,* favored their cause. One German-language newspaper opposed the entire movement "because the editor believed only bad women would vote if they were given the ballot."[31]

Although the suffragists had foes, they also had allies, mainly the state's stalwart antiliquor groups. In 1877 and again in 1879 the State Temperance Convention stated their support for women's suffrage "as a means of enabling women to aid in the protection of the homes." In general, the dry forces, including the Women's Christian Temperance Union, would remain strong advocates of the vote for women. Although the support of both groups obviously swelled the suffragists' ranks, that support also convinced anti-Prohibitionists that enfranchised women would be only too happy to vote for liquor regulation. To some wets, all women were natural opponents to the liquor trade, and the close association between suffragists and the drys strengthened the wets' resolve to defeat any effort to give women the vote.[32]

In 1894 the lobbying efforts of suffrage forces secured at least a partial victory when the General Assembly passed legislation giving women the right to vote at municipal and school elections "involving the issuing of bonds, borrowing money, or increasing the tax levy." The efforts of women had paid off, as four years earlier they had concentrated their efforts on school and municipal suffrage. By 1894 women were conducting "an unusually active campaign," and as many as fifty petitions a day were presented in the Senate.[33]

The partial suffrage victory in Iowa underscored a growing change nationally in regard to the movement. By 1890 the issue of enfranchising women had become respectable as the nation's largest women's organizations (particularly the National Federated Women's Club and the Women's Christian Temperance Union [WCTU]) supported women's suffrage. No longer was it improper for women to address public gatherings or political meetings in support of the suffrage cause. By the 1890s the first generation of college-educated women—many like Jane Addams, who founded Hull House in Chicago—were adding their support to the suffrage movement.

General attitudes toward women's suffrage also began to change in Iowa as public officials like Albert B. Cummins spoke out in support of the issue. Ruth Gallaher believes that between 1890 and 1910 newspapers began to take a more favorable stance toward the issue, and most important, women were demonstrating more self-confidence in their own suffrage activities. Some males had always supported votes for women, and in 1910 a group of Des Moines men formed the Men's League for Woman Suffrage. The group included well-known public and business leaders, such as Henry Wallace, Edgar R. Harlan, E. T. Meredith, and Harvey Ingham.[34]

The women active in the Iowa suffrage movement shared social traits with national leaders. Both groups were typically white, native-born, Protestant, well educated, frequently unmarried, and often working to support themselves. If women were married, they usually had the financial means to hire domestic and child-care assistance. Many suffragist leaders were "strikingly well educated": Anna Lawther, president of the Iowa Equal Suffrage Association (IESA) for a time, graduated from Sarah Lawrence College; ISEA executive board member Jesse Taft earned a Ph.D. from the University of Chicago; Effie McCollom Jones, pastor of the Univeralist Church in Waterloo, had acquired a doctor of divinity degree.[35] Flora Dunlap, president of the IESA in 1916, was a professionally trained social worker.

Carrie Chapman Catt, the most visible leader of the national movement by the early 1900s, shared many of these same traits. Born in Wisconsin in 1859, Carrie Lane grew up on a farm near Charles City. She graduated from Iowa State College, the only woman in her class, then taught school in Mason City; later she became the first woman superintendent of schools there. She married Leo Chapman, a newspaper editor in Mason City, and helped him edit the paper. Following Chapman's death, Carrie married a former college classmate, George Catt; her husband's wealth enabled her to work for the suffrage movement several months of every year. Catt began in 1889 to help organize suffrage clubs and in 1900 was elected president of the National American Woman Suffrage Association (NAWSA), the largest national suffrage organization. She left that post in 1905 due to her husband's poor health. Because of her longtime association with Iowa, Catt is regarded by many as an Iowan.

At the same time that Iowa's suffrage supporters were becoming better organized, antisuffragists were expressing their views through speeches, letters to newspapers, and legislative petitions. In general, the views of the antis in Iowa paralleled those of antis in other states. Among the major arguments was the notion that political participation would taint women and "pull them down" to the level of men. Rather, women should be satisfied to remain in the home—and away from politics—because they could be far more effective where they reigned over domestic matters. Other antis asserted that as women formed independent political views — and possibly disagreed with their husands—the vote might create dissension in the home. Some antis grumbled that the suffrage movement consisted only of poor housekeepers and discontented women.[36]

By 1913 the many years of work by suffragist forces would begin to pay dividends when both houses of the General Assembly passed the equal-suffrage amendment. Two years later they again passed the amendment before presenting it to the general electorate. Both suffragists and antisuffragists swung into action, each determined to win the referendum. Flora Dunlap, president of the Iowa Equal Suffrage Association, directed that group's efforts. Carrie Chapman Catt, once again president of the NAWSA, advised Iowa supporters to organize everywhere throughout the state, canvassing in every town regardless of size. Accordingly, workers set about appointing chairpersons in each precinct and county, then training speakers, raising money, and organizing a letter-writing campaign to local newspapers.[37] Catt and other national suffragist leaders campaigned throughout Iowa in the weeks just before the primary. Speaking in Sioux City on April 19, 1916, Catt declared that women needed the ballot "to make them effective reformers. 'We are opening a new world and getting a vision of reforms needed in the world.'"[38] On June 5, following many months of intense campaigning, adult males in Iowa trooped to the polls to decide the fate of the women's suffrage amendment.

When the votes were tallied, the suffrage forces had come up short: 162,849 Iowans had voted for the amendment, 172,990 had voted against it. River counties with high numbers of German-stock residents had voted most strongly against the measure, particularly Dubuque, Clinton, Scott, Des Moines, and Clayton. Carrie Chapman Catt believed that liquor interests had worked hard to defeat the measure and that ballot fraud was also involved. There was little doubt about Catt's first assertion: Iowa's brewers and liquor dealers had played a visible role in the campaign. Not so clear-cut was the matter of fraud. The IESA, informed by its lawyers that there was no way to "rectify the error," since it involved a constitutional amendment, had decided to forgo any formal investigation. The WCTU, a strong suffrage organization in the state, initiated an investigation of election procedures and official returns in forty-four counties. Four months later the WCTU reported in a two-hundred-page document that they could "draw but one conclusion ... namely that they were defrauded out of their right to the ballot."[39]

The failure to gain complete suffrage for women was one more bitter defeat in a long line of defeats stretching back to 1870. Women had learned that other issues seemed always to preempt the women's vote. In 1868 the issue had been suffrage for black males; in the 1890s it had been efforts to gain a total Prohibition law; in 1916 Iowa voters—whether because of antisuffrage arguments, efforts by the liquor forces, or voter fraud—had once again refused to grant suffrage equality to nearly one-half the state's population. In the nearly fifty years that suffragists had struggled to gain the vote, "very little," it seemed, "was required to divert the attention of most [state officials] from the suffrage issue."[40]

Following the 1916 vote, attention shifted to the nation's capital, where officials of the NAWSA began waging an all-out battle to amend the United States Constitution, thus providing suffrage for all American women. Carrie Chapman Catt, described as a superb organizer, orchestrated that campaign. As a person who had dedicated much of her adult life to winning the vote for women, Catt, as president of the NAWSA, formulated her "winning plan." This approach involved working at both the national and state levels. In effect, in state capitals and in Washington, D.C., women lobbied politicians, wrote letters, and organized rallies. In 1919 the NAWSA forces proclaimed a major victory, for by then both the Senate and the House of Representatives had passed the Nineteenth Amendment. A short time later the measure went to the individual states for approval; by August 26, 1920, a sufficient number of states had ratified, including Iowa. The following day Mrs. Jens G. Thuesen voted in a rural-school-reorganization election near Cedar Falls. Mrs. Thuesen was the first woman to vote in Iowa following passage of the Nineteenth Amendment, and possibly the first woman in the nation to vote under the new amendment. The long, hard battle had finally been won.[41]

By 1916 the political climate in Iowa had changed dramatically. Progressivism had faded, and though Republicans still controlled the governorship, the man elected to that office in 1916 was not a typical party member: William L. Harding was neither a Prohibitionist nor a supporter of women's suffrage. In fact, he could be labeled a "stand-patter" in regard to other issues, such as his opposition to improvement of state roads.

Harding would be elected to a second term in 1918, and by that time the nation would be engulfed in a world war. When he left office in 1921, both prohibition and women's suffrage had become the law of the land due to amendments eighteen and nineteen of the United States Constitution.

Within Iowa the interrelationship between progressivism, Prohibition, and women's suffrage is difficult to determine. Certainly from the national perspective progressivism proved the dominant movement, but within Iowa the issues of Prohibition and women's suffrage, particularly the former, commanded more attention and evoked more emotion. Although both Prohibition and women's suffrage should be viewed in their relationship to Iowa's progressive movement, it is difficult to determine precisely how they were impacted by progressivism. The Prohibition movement waxed and waned between the 1850s and 1920, clearly possessing a life of its own. Although the spirit of progressivism may be linked to national Prohibition, it is not so easy to see that association in Iowa. The women's-suffrage movement also had a life of its own, long before the spirit of progressivism made an appearance here. Although perhaps buoyed by that general spirit, Iowa women, like women elsewhere, stood mainly alone in their struggle to gain the vote.

Between the 1870s and the 1920s, however, Iowa had undergone considerable social and economic change. Progressive Era changes brought greater involvement of the general electorate in the processes of government, the direct primary being the most obvious example. The welfare of the average citizen was protected to a greater degree than before through the passage of pure-food-and-drug legislation. And the state's largest corporations, the railroads, had come under additional control, experiencing a diminution of political influence through elimination of the railroad free-pass system. By 1920 the progressive spirit had waned, but "the fruits of Iowa progressivism" would remain for years to come.

13

Economic Development: Iowa's Industries and Industrial Workers

I n the latter nineteenth and early twentieth centuries, Iowa's image in the world was that of a rural state where pastoral scenes abounded. Within the state, however, a diversified economy was getting under way. From the beginning of settlement, vital developments had been taking place that would serve as prerequisites and vital support systems for industrial expansion. As discussed in previous chapters, the state had experienced the construction of a statewide system of railroads, the growth and diversification of agriculture, the expansion of urban centers,

---

The Ducey family—Charles, John, Jennifer Buch, Alberta, Mamie, and Dave—posed outside their home at the mining camp of Brazil in the 1890s. Photo courtesy of the State Historical Society of Iowa, Iowa City.

and the immigration of tens of thousands of foreign-born; all these developments made it possible for a wide range of industrial operations to follow.

In Iowa agricultural-related industries would dominate, but non-farm-related manufacturing would also appear. Although most larger firms would be located in one of Iowa's seven or eight largest cities, several thousands of industries could be found in smaller communities. Within these many firms would be a diverse workforce composed of both native-born and foreign-born persons; female workers, always a part of the state's labor force, would become increasingly visible after 1900. The state would also experience considerable union activity, particularly after the 1920s.

In 1870 Iowans appeared poised for major economic change. The necessary prerequisites for industrial development—transportation, labor, and raw materials—were present in the state. Moreover, Iowa was home to numerous individuals, mostly in river communities, who had sufficient capital to initiate new enterprises. Also by 1870 Iowa's population was expanding rapidly. In 1860, one year before the outbreak of war, Iowa contained 674,913 people; ten years later that number had jumped dramatically to over 1 million. Most people, moreover, lived in the eastern half of the state, many in counties along the Mississippi River. Scott County, for example, had 38,594 residents, whereas Dubuque County had 38,969.[1] With the exception of Des Moines and Cedar Rapids, the largest centers of population lay either along the Mississippi or, to a lesser degree, along the Missouri River. Given the presence of sufficient labor and the concentration of that labor in specific areas, Iowa was well suited for development of large industrial operations. By the seventies Iowa had moved a long way from its initial frontier status.

Given Iowa's preeminence as an agricultural state with high pork production, the early appearance of pork-packing plants seemed a natural development. All major Mississippi River cities contained these operations before 1870, but after that date the production plants established at interior locations quickly surpassed those along the river.[2] In their study of Iowa's meat-packing industry, H. H. McCarty and C. W. Thompson describe the rise of interior packing centers as "meteoric."[3]

The Sinclair Company of Cedar Rapids was the first pork-packing plant to begin in Iowa after the completion of the east-west railroads. In 1871 Thomas M. Sinclair, a young man from Belfast, Ireland, started the Sinclair operation. Sinclair had several relatives who were also active in the meat-packing business: One brother handled company affairs in New York, while other family members handled business in Great Britain. By 1871, in fact, the Sinclair family had almost forty years' experience in meat packing. That experience would pay dividends as the plant quickly became Cedar Rapids's leading industry; moreover, by 1874 Cedar Rapids was first among Iowa packing centers, and four years later the company ranked eighth among the nation's packers. In the 1880s the plant added a beef kill and butterine manufacture (a butter substitute similar to oleo-margarine), but the pork operation remained a major interest. Recognizing the need for a national marketing system, Sinclair in 1913 became affili-ated with what is today Wilson and Company of Chicago.[4]

A second meat-packing operation, John Morrell and Company, es-tablished itself in Ottumwa in 1878. The Morrell Company had originated in England in the 1820s and then expanded to the United States; by the 1870s, with an office in Chicago, the firm desired to move farther west to be closer to the source of their raw material. A family member, Thomas Foster, traveled through Iowa and Minnesota looking for possible sites and finally decided on Ottumwa. Foster wired the main office that the city met all requirements: It had a sufficient labor force, a water source (the Des Moines River flowed through the city), a railroad, and most impor-tant, it was located in the middle of prosperous farm country where the company could obtain its supply of hogs.[5] It was no accident that com-munities emerging as interior packing centers, such as Cedar Rapids and Ottumwa, developed along rivers, given the particular needs of the indus-try. The rivers allowed for some shipping, provided ice for winter opera-tions, and allowed a place to dispose of waste.[6]

In Ottumwa the company would soon diversify its operation and quickly become the city's major employer. Diversification included adding beef and mutton departments (to the original pork-packing opera-tion), and later the canning of meats and the production of other food lines. As Ottumwa's largest employer, company influence was felt every-where in the community. Even as late as the 1930s, a Works Progress Administration writer would comment: "The economic life of [Ottumwa] depends on the processing of pork."[7]

While other cities, such as Waterloo, Des Moines, and Mason City, would develop important meat-packing operations, Sioux City eventually dominated the industry in Iowa. The first packing there began as a sideline to a general mercantile business, as had frequently happened in Mississippi River towns. The Sioux City industry started when a boatload of wheat sank in the Missouri River. Seeing a potential profit, local merchant James E. Booge purchased the water-soaked wheat, and, learning it was good only for animal feed, purchased several hundred hogs to eat the grain. Finding there was little market for live hogs, Booge began to slaughter the hogs and sell the meat. He soon decided to devote his attention fully to the meat-packing business, organizing the James E. Booge and Sons Packing Company and building the first "genuine packing plant" in Sioux City. Other Sioux City businessmen soon recognized the opportunity provided by meat packing and in 1883 organized the first Union Stock Yards. A second operation, the Central Stock Yards, soon followed. In 1884 the two centers merged into the Union Stock Yards Company.[8]

By 1887 Sioux City's packing industry had been launched. By then Booge's company was an apparent success and the stockyards were open. These developments, in turn, attracted other meat packers, including two Chicago firms, Robert D. Fowler and William H. Silberhorn. Early in the next decade the first of the big Chicago packers, Cudahy, arrived in Sioux City. Between 1897 and 1901 Cudahy expanded its Sioux City operation, processing not only pork, but also beef and mutton. The plant added the lines of soap, lard, axle grease, and glue by-products; officials also experimented with local distribution by running a refrigerator car to Perry to deliver fresh meat to retailers there. Eventually Armour and Company and the Swift Company would begin operations in Sioux City, leading to what Sioux Citians recognized as "the three 'greats'" in the local packing industry.[9]

As activities in Sioux City, Cedar Rapids, and Ottumwa indicate—as well as countless other communities not discussed here—meat packing in Iowa was vitally important to the state's economy. McCarty and Thompson observed in 1929 that "one-tenth of all Iowa factory workers were employed in these plants and the meat-packing industry reported a larger 'manufacturing income' than any other Iowa industry." The number of persons on the payrolls of meat-packing firms totaled 9,780. According to the same study, only one Iowa factory industry, the railroad shops, had

The Sioux City Union Stock Yards in 1894. Photo courtesy of the Sioux City Public Museum.

more employees, with 10,801 workers in 1929. From 1914 to 1923 Iowa had risen from a tenth-place national ranking in the meat-packing industry to fourth place, and remained there through 1929.[10]

It is not surprising, then, that between 1870 and 1940 the category of "food and kindred products"—which included meat packing—ranked first among Iowa's manufacturing activities. By 1925 the value of products in that category would reach $430,430,134, and the various industries would include 19,755 wage earners. In addition to meat packing, food and kindred products also included butter and cheese; corn syrup, corn oil, and starch; flour-mill and grain-mill products; canning products; poultry killing and dressing; and candy products.[11]

A second industry included in the same manufacturing category was the oats-processing industry. In the 1870s two Scotsmen in Cedar Rapids would start the firm eventually known as Quaker Oats. John and Robert

Stuart had first settled near Ingersoll in Ontario, Canada, where they had set up an oatmeal mill. Believing they could do better in the United States, the Stuarts selected Cedar Rapids as the site of a new plant. Early in the venture, the Stuarts took in a partner, George Douglas, also a Scottish emigrant. Douglas had come to the United States to practice his craft of stone-masonry and had earlier built many railroad abutments and bridges. The first oatmeal plant in Cedar Rapids was the North Star Oatmeal Mill, established in 1870. Shortly after initiating this venture, Robert Stuart and Douglas moved to Chicago, where they established yet another mill. Although that operation lasted only a short time, the two men continued to maintain their general office in Chicago. Robert Stuart would also acquire mills in other cities, but the Cedar Rapids plant remained an important part of the company's operation.[12]

The Scotsmen would do more, however, than increase the amount of oatmeal milled in the country: They would help create a greater demand for the product. In the late nineteenth century many Americans believed that oats were for horses, not humans. According to one source, "the spectacle of Americans eating oats provoked uproarious merriment in the hearts of cartoonists and editors." In 1910 an artist for *Cosmopolitan Magazine* depicted as much in a cartoon, which Harrison J. Thornton has described in the following manner: "a Yankee farmer on eating oats for breakfast would prance around his barnyard, drink from the horses' trough, hitch himself to the buggy, careen in high fettle over the pasture, and stand at the hitching post while his wife groomed him with a currycomb." But the Stuarts and Douglas were not to be put off by this view; along with several other oatmeal manufacturers, they gradually convinced the American public, especially immigrants who were short on money, that oatmeal was a good bargain, being both cheap and filling.[13]

In addition to food items, Iowans also manufactured hundreds of other products that fell into the following general categories, listed in order of their economic importance: iron and steel and their by-products; railroad repair and construction; lumber and its remanufactures; printing and publishing; chemicals and allied products; textiles and their products; stone, brick, and glass; land vehicles; metal and metal products other than iron and steel; leather and its finished products; tobacco manufactures; liquor and beverages. The census also listed the category of "miscellaneous industries," which included a wide array of products such as washing machines, buttons, agricultural implements, and playground equipment.[14]

One miscellaneous operation, the manufacture of agricultural implements, would begin here around the turn of the century and eventually contribute significantly to the state's economy. The production of tractors would become a vital part of Iowa's economy after 1900, but the first success in producing a tractor came in 1892, when German-American John Froelich, described as a "farmer-tinkerer" in Clayton County, succeeded in attaching a gasoline engine to a farm implement, which allowed the unit to go both forward and backward. Froelich, perhaps not realizing the potential value of his invention, sold it to the Waterloo Gas Traction Engine Company in 1893.[15]

Little progress would be made in the development of the tractor until two engineering students at the University of Wisconsin, Charles W. Hart (an Iowa native) and Charles H. Parr, began experimenting with automotive farm machinery; in 1900 they moved to Charles City, where they began building internal-combustion traction engines. A Mason City farmer purchased the first unit—completed in the winter of 1900–1901—and "proved that it was practical for farm use." The next year the Hart-Parr Company manufactured fifteen tractors, and in 1907 the two men adopted the name "tractor" for their invention. The firm continued to expand and in 1929 merged with three other farm-implement manufacturers to form the Oliver Corporation.[16]

At the same time that Hart and Parr were active in Charles City, the John Deere Company became involved in the production of tractors. In 1918 the company purchased the Waterloo Gas Traction Engine Company. The history of the Deere Company would actually reach back to 1837, when John Deere himself invented a plow that would scour when used in prairie soil. Before Deere's invention farmers had to carry a paddle to scrape off the sticky soil that clung to the plowshare. Deere's invention—using a piece of polished steel—made scraping unnecessary. Deere's new plow was a great success, and within ten years he had produced almost a thousand of them. Deere later moved his operation to Moline, Illinois, and the company grew steadily: By 1895 it was a prominent national enterprise.

When the John Deere Company acquired the Waterloo tractor works in 1918, the company had already expanded the number of farm implements it produced, including corn planters, cultivators, and harrows. In fact, the oldest Deere company in Iowa was started in Ottumwa in 1900 as the Dain Manufacturing Company. Deere purchased the Dain operation and by the 1950s was manufacturing hay balers, side-delivery rakes, forage choppers, and other equipment at the plant.

During the twenties, thirties, and forties Deere would continue to expand in Iowa. Their first acquisition, the tractor works, had become by the 1950s the largest single-unit tractor factory in the world. By that decade the factory produced all of Deere's large-wheeled tractors. In 1947 the company established a new line of small tractors at Dubuque, known as the Dubuque Tractor Works. The same year, John Deere purchased the Des Moines Ordnance Plant located in Ankeny, a facility started during World War II. In the fifties the plant's production included corn and cotton pickers.

Even though farm-related industries—involved in either the processing of farm products or the manufacturing of products used on the farm—have dominated the state's economy, a sizable number of large nonfarm-related industries have also developed here. One of these, the Maytag Company, would be the creation of Frederick L. Maytag, a second-generation German American, born in 1857. From an early age Maytag displayed entrepreneurial talent. At sixteen he set up a threshing-machine operation, doing custom work for local farmers; some seven years later he purchased a team of horses and delivered coal in the area. In 1880 he went to work for a local implement store and for a short time owned one-half the business. Maytag's first effort at manufacturing came with the development of the self-feeding band-cutter attachment for threshing machines. Before the invention the metal bands that wrapped around the grain bundles had to be cut by hand, then fed into the threshing-machine cylinders. The new device simplified the operation and made it safer.[17]

Maytag would eventually become best known for producing washing machines, but before that he tried his hand at manufacturing automobiles. In 1909 Maytag helped finance an automobile-manufacturing business in Waterloo; the company put out a variety of models.[18] The same year that Maytag became involved with the short-lived foray into auto manufacturing, he also began manufacturing washing machines. The first power machine with a belt-driven pulley appeared in 1909. Five years later Maytag introduced a two-cycle gasoline engine to replace the electric engine.

Soon the sales of Maytag's gasoline-powered machines accounted for more than half the company's sales. From the teens on, the company made continual improvements in its washers, such as the development of an aluminum tub and the placement of the agitator on the bottom of the tub, rather than attached to the lid. According to a biography of Maytag, this principle, known as the gyrofoam action, revolutionized the washing-machine industry.[19] From the beginning of its washing-machine era, Maytag earned a reputation for quality and dependability.

While a limited number of towns, such as Newton, developed major industries, dozens of similar-sized communities also attracted manufacturing firms, although usually smaller and of shorter duration. By the early 1900s communities in every part of Iowa were pushing hard to attract new industries. One such community was Perry, located in central Iowa.

By 1910 Perry's population totaled about five thousand, and the town seemed well situated for the development of industry. Of vital importance, the community had excellent transportation facilities, serving as a division point for the Chicago, Milwaukee, St. Paul & Pacific Railroad, as well as being served by several other rail lines; Perry was also connected to other central-Iowa communities by an interurban line. During the teens Perry was the site of a number of industries, including two washing-machine factories, a milk condensery, a corset factory, a canning factory, an ice plant, a chalk-channel manufacturer, and a car manufacturer. Like similar communities at the time, Perry's citizens worked hard to attract additional industry. A major recruiting effort took place in 1912, when Perry officials worked tirelessly to lure an iron-and-steel plant away from Marshalltown. As Deborah Fink has pointed out, "Everyone in Perry seemed to be obsessed with industrial development in the years from 1910 to 1915."[20]

As with other communities, Perry's ability both to attract and to retain companies would wax and wane. Although officials would fail to attract the iron-and-steel plant, by the end of the decade the town still claimed the two washing-machine plants, the milk condensery, and two new firms, a steel-plow-shovel manufacturer and a seasonal corn-canning plant.[21] No doubt, given the state's agricultural difficulties in the twenties—and their subsequent effect on the state's total economy—the boosterism of the 1910s had been dampened considerably in Perry and elsewhere.

As the experiences in Newton and Perry indicate, even despite the economic downturn in the twenties, Iowa manufacturing would grow fairly steadily between 1870 and the 1930s. In 1870 the state contained 6,566 manufacturing establishments; that number would increase to 6,921 establishments in 1880 and 7,440 in 1890. In 1900, however, the number would drop to 4,859 firms. It would begin to rise again in 1909 and reach its peak during World War I. In 1921 the number of manufacturing establishments dropped by approximately 2,000 to 3,527, and by 1925 it had declined further to 3,270. The number of wage earners would parallel those increases and decreases. By 1925 Iowa had 74,976 wage earners working in manufacturing establishments as compared to 25,032 workers in 1870. By 1934, 75,293 persons would be engaged in Iowa manufacturing.[22]

Along with manufacturing, Iowa contained the major extractive industry of coal mining. Although railroads made it possible after 1870 to ship Iowa products all over the eastern United States, they had demands of their own, such as acquiring coal to fuel their locomotives. That need was met in Iowa by opening hundreds of coal mines, particularly in the central and south central sections of the state. Although the first coal mining was done in southeastern Iowa in the 1840s, the industry did not become economically significant until after railroads became the major consumer. Wesley Redhead, an English emigrant, helped develop one of the first major operations, the Black Diamond Mine, in Des Moines in 1873; within a few years the mine employed 150 men. Lucas County also became the site of extensive coal mining in the 1870s, when the Whitebreast Fuel Company was established there. In effect, as railroad mileage expanded in the Hawkeye State, the number of coal mines increased accordingly. By 1880 state mine officials listed 450 underground coal mines operating in the state, with a total of 6,028 miners. The peak of production was reached during World War I, when some 18,000 Iowa miners produced over 9 million tons of coal.[23]

As the Iowa coal industry got under way, two types of mines developed: shipping and local. Shipping mines were the largest operations, commonly known as captive mines. Each was generally owned or controlled by a particular railroad, which was then assured of a continuous supply of coal. Buxton contained the largest captive mines, which provided coal to the Chicago and North Western Railroad. Because shipping

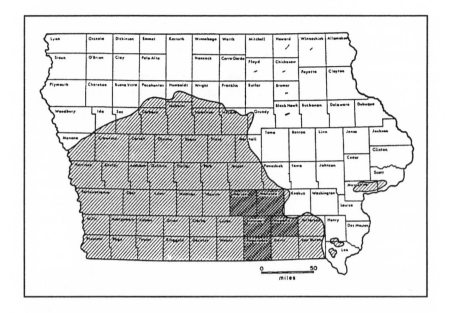

Shaded area is underlain with coal. From Leland Sage,
A History of Iowa.

mines had fewer shutdowns than did local mines, shipping-mine employees earned somewhat higher wages. Although there has been no comprehensive examination of coal miners' incomes in Iowa, studies of Buxton,
Beacon, Cincinnati, and Seymour provide limited data. Buxton miners in
1914 earned an average of $499, whereas the 1914 income of miners in
the latter three communities averaged $466.[24]

In contrast to shipping mines, local mines produced coal only on a
seasonal basis and were the most numerous in Iowa. Some Iowa coal was
used for industrial purposes, but given the small number of industrial
firms here—as compared to states in the northeast—coal sales remained
limited. Iowa households used coal only for heating and so purchased no
coal during warm weather. Given the seasonal demand for coal, most local mines shut down in April and did not reopen until October. Miners,
therefore, had to seek short-term work in other areas or remain unem-

ployed for several months. Some miners developed dual occupations that accommodated the seasonal mining schedule; others purchased acreages, which they worked during the summer.

The development of the coal industry in Iowa had a major impact on the state's economy. Smaller towns, such as Mystic and Hiteman, and even larger communities, like Albia and Ottumwa, benefited greatly from the presence of coal-mining families. The presence of dozens of unincorporated coal camps throughout central and southern Iowa also meant business for merchants located in nearby, larger communities. Although most coal camps had company stores, there were always items that could be purchased only in larger mercantile establishments.

The coal industry influenced Iowa in other important ways. Eastern and southern Europeans emigrated to Iowa because here they could find immediate employment in the mines. Whereas northern Europeans and residents of the British Isles were often attracted by opportunities in agriculture, thousands of other Europeans came here to work as miners. Emigrants from countries such as Croatia and Italy often had limited financial resources, and they came eager to find work and improve their economic lot. The money earned by thousands of immigrant miners not only supported them and their families, but also helped sustain the economic life of countless Iowa communities.

Even though coal mining attracted thousands of people to Iowa, the industry was destined to be short-lived for several reasons. Of major importance was the fact that in the 1920s Iowa railroads began purchasing coal from out-of-state producers, some from as far away as Kentucky. Ironically, the railroads had first brought expansion to the coal industry, and in the twenties the railroads initiated the industry's decline. Furthermore, Iowa operators had to accept the fact that Iowa's coal formations mitigated against large-scale development. Because Iowa's coal deposits often lay tilted rather than horizontal, it was difficult to develop larger, more profitable operations. Other changes also affected coal sales, such as the growing acceptance of fuel oil, natural gas, and electricity for heating homes and offices.[25]

In many areas coal mining would be a two-generation, or at most three-generation, occupation. The sons of men who came from Italy or Croatia around 1900 would go to work in the mines in the 1920s. But their sons (the third generation), many of whom served in the military in World War II, found it more pleasant to work aboveground. As mining camps closed down, operators routinely sold the houses for fifty dollars each; the houses were then hauled into nearby communities, placed on concrete foundations, and sold to local residents. Some families remained in camps, such as Moran, and the men commuted to work in nearby Ames or Des Moines. Coal mining had remained a vital industry in Iowa for over seventy years, but by 1950 only 158 mines remained (including 63 strip mines), with 1,478 employees.[26]

Although the discussion here of Iowa's economic life has focused mainly on manufacturing and mining, it should be noted that many businesses in Iowa rank among the largest enterprises in the state. The most notable, the insurance industry, has a strong presence in many parts of the state, particularly in Des Moines. Frederick Hubbell would start Iowa's first insurance company in Des Moines in 1867, the Equitable Life Insurance Company of Iowa. The second insurance company to form in Iowa, known today as the Principal Financial Group, began in Des Moines as the Bankers Life Association. Initially the company provided insurance for bankers and their employees but soon expanded its services. By the 1950s Des Moines would be recognized as one of the major insurance centers in the nation. Today the Principal Financial Group is one of the state's leading employers.

The foregoing history of Iowa's industries is important for an understanding of the state's economic development, but equally important is the story of the industrial workers. The laborers who mined the coal, slaughtered the beef, and processed the grain had backgrounds and experiences that often set them apart from agriculturalists, the state's main occupational group. Industrial workers typically performed their tasks under difficult conditions, working long hours for low pay and little job security. Frequently they and their families lived in the poorest sections of town. When worker groups attempted to improve their lives through union organizing, their efforts were often met with hostility from management. Ralph Scharnau's description of Dubuque's workforce in 1885 reflects the difficulties workers faced everywhere:

> The typical Dubuque worker ... labored ten hours per day, six days per week. Work place routines often included close supervision with few rest periods. ... Without work place health and safety codes, working-class neighborhoods buzzed with

grisly accounts of death, maiming, and other job-related in-
juries and diseases from unguarded machinery, fires, explosions, bad ventilation, and other unsanitary conditions.[27]

Wages for Iowa's laboring force are difficult to determine, particularly wages in specific occupational areas. According to a University of
Iowa study in 1935, the average annual wages in manufacturing were as
follows: 1910, $549; 1915, $749; 1920, $1,417; 1925, $1,242; 1930,
$1,190. The peak income of $1,417 no doubt resulted from higher wages
paid during World War I, when labor was scarce due to men in the military.[28]

Although workers exhibited considerable diversity in their cultural
backgrounds and work experiences, some generalizations can be made regarding place of origin. In coal mining before 1900, most miners were
from western Europe (particularly Sweden) or from England or Wales;
after 1900 Iowa's mining population included an increasing number of
southern and eastern Europeans. The latter development led to the presence of Italians, Croatians, Slovenians, Serbs, Poles, and Russians in coal
camps. The industry also included a small group of African Americans
who were first recruited by coal operators in the 1880s.

In the meat-packing industry the background of workers also varied,
depending upon location. Eastern Europeans, including Lithuanians, Russians, and Poles, as well as Syrians, had come to work in Sioux City's
meat-packing industry after 1900. On the other hand, most workers at the
John Morrell plant in Ottumwa were native-born and shared a common
background. Wilson J. Warren writes that the Ottumwa workers "shared a
cohesive class and cultural identity which included living in the same
neighborhood and belonging to common religious and associational organizations." Warren explains that ethnic and neighborhood ties had been
apparent since 1900, as 60 percent of employees at Morrell had native-
born parents. Like Ottumwa's labor force, Dubuque's workers had considerable homogeneity, as many were Catholic and had either German or
Irish backgrounds.[29]

Although immigrants constituted a major source of labor, Iowa's
workforce has always included people who migrated from the farm to the
city. Particularly when economic depressions struck, farm people often
moved to town looking for employment. The Iowa census figures of 1900

and 1910 provide an example of this migration: Between those years, seventy-one counties in Iowa lost population, but twenty-eight counties, mostly with urban centers, gained population, thus indicating some farm residents had become urban dwellers.[30]

As the backgrounds of workers varied, so did industrial working conditions. In *Solidarity and Survival: An Oral History of Iowa Labor in the Twentieth Century,* Shelton Stromquist provides a rich collection of interviews with wage earners who gave countless testimony on all aspects of their work.[31] Working conditions in the meat-packing industry proved especially difficult because of the lifting of heavy carcasses and the fact that workers often moved between hot and cold work areas. Richard Lowry remembered the drastic change in temperature when he worked at Tobin Packing Company in Fort Dodge. Lowry started the day "breaking" and packing hogs where "you'd be in this cold room and work until ten, eleven o'clock in the morning, or maybe noon ... and then [because you were going to work on the kill floor] you would hurry up to the locker room and shuck off your clothes and get into something as little as possible and run out on that steamy hot kill floor and work the rest of the day." Lowry explained that rosin was used in the process of dehairing the hog carcasses, and as he worked on a carcass and pulled it around, "My fingernails would fall off. You'd dig your fingers in those hot ears, and after a week or so you didn't have no fingernails."[32]

Although many factors accounted for workers' support or rejection of unionization, plant conditions obviously played a part, sometimes in a rather unlikely way. Richard Lindner worked in the kill department of the Tobin plant in the 1930s. He recalled one instance that predisposed him toward joining the union: "When I worked on the kill we'd work eight, ten, sometimes, eleven hours. You stand up there on that chain, you know, with the hogs going by, and you stand there three or four hours and have to go to the toilet. The one thing I distinctly remember was I asked our foreman for relief to go to the toliet. And he asked me what I done when I was a baby. They made a union man out of me by pulling those kind of things."[33]

Previous employment also played a part in workers' willingness to join unions, particularly in the thirties. Don Harris, the first national director of the CIO's Packinghouse Workers' Organizing Committee, related the role played by former United Mine Workers:

> As the mines closed down ... the miners went to work in other
> places such as Maytag at Newton. And it was the mine work-
> ers ... that organized that plant. This happened time after time
> in packing plants, in all kinds of plants all over Iowa. It was old
> [UMW members], or it was their kids whom they had brought
> up in a union family and taught the value of trade unionism and
> had imbedded it in their minds and souls.[34]

At the same time, another group of workers came into the industrial
plants with no union experience and often predisposed against them. As
Shelton Stromquist has pointed out, farm youths "brought with them a
sense of independence and pride that did not easily adapt to 'being told
what to do and how to do it.' Others stayed on the farm but worked in a
factory. They proved harder to organize." Richard Lindner recalled that
when he went to work in Fort Dodge, he observed efforts to organize the
CIO: "All of us Fort Dodgers didn't know a damn thing about unions, and
they didn't make enough effort to educate us in the right way."[35] Lindner
joined a company union, the Employees' Benefit Association, which the
company offered in response to organizing efforts by the CIO.

Sometimes ethnic groups played important roles in union organizing.
In his study of the unionization of Sioux City's packinghouses in the thirties, Roger Horowitz explains that of the many ethnic groups who worked
there and supported unionization, the Russian emigrants played the most
vital role. Horowitz writes that the Russians, because of "their sheer numbers in unskilled production jobs and their readiness to support unionism,
provided the linchpin of ethnic support for the CIO drive."[36]

Union organizing proceeded unevenly throughout Iowa industries
and even within separate plants in the same industry. Craft workers such
as machinists, printers, and building tradesmen had earlier dominated
nineteenth-century labor activity. The state's first craft union, Typograph-
ical Union No. 22, was chartered as early as 1855 in Dubuque. In the next
thirty years Dubuque included unions for "cigarmakers, locomotive fireen
and engineers, tailors, and blacksmiths." Ralph Scharnau writes: "These
skilled unions, small and poorly organized, protected their membership
and shunned independent politics."[37]

The Knights of Labor would be the first inclusive labor organization,
attempting to bring workers from all occupations into one large union. The
Knights, a national organization, began to organize in Dubuque in 1885

and in two years claimed a membership there of twenty-five hundred. By 1888 they had reached their statewide peak membership of thirty thousand. The Knights set up cooperative enterprises, including an overalls factory in Cedar Rapids, and also moved into the political arena, lobbying to improve working conditions and wages for industrial workers. According to Scharnau, the creation of the Iowa Bureau of Labor Statistics in 1884 can be credited to "sustained" lobbying of the Knights of Labor. By 1890, however, the organization was rapidly disintegrating.[38]

The United Mine Workers of America constituted the largest trade union in the state from the 1890s until the 1920s. Miners organized the UMW in 1890, and the Iowa coalfields, known as District 13, quickly became unionized. In 1899 Iowa miners won a major victory when they secured the eight-hour day. Iowa miners had additional concerns, however, including higher wages, acceptance of union checkweighmen, and elimination of restrictive company-store policies. Checkweighmen appointed by the union were considered necessary to guarantee each miner full credit when coal cars were weighed. Although the UMW would lose membership as Iowa's coal industry declined, in earlier years it was a highly constructive force in the lives of miners and their families. Until 1905 union leadership dealt mainly with "bread and butter issues" such as wages and hours, but later, union officials worked to create death benefits, medical care, and better housing.

In the 1930s union organizing in other industries would take on new life. Of vital importance was the passage of the National Labor Relations Act (or Wagner Act) in 1935 which, in effect, legitimized unionization. This legislation gave workers the right to unionize and bargain collectively with management. Elections of bargaining units and agents were to be supervised and authority given to a federal board to issue cease-and-desist orders against unfair practices by management. A second important development was the creation of the Committee of Industrial Organizations in 1935, which set about organizing industrial—as opposed to craft—plants. The CIO organized all plant workers into one large union rather than into smaller unions for separate work specialties. The passage of the Wagner Act and the formation of the CIO proved absolutely crucial to the development of labor unions in Iowa, because before the 1930s workers in Iowa's two most important industries, meat packing and farm-machinery production, faced "a fierce anti-union spirit among employers."

That antiunion spirit had succeeded in "stifling the spread of industrial unionism before the 1930s."[39]

Given the federal legislation and the presence of the Committee of Industrial Organizations (or the Congress of Industrial Organizations, as it was known after 1938), union organizing got under way in packing plants across the state. Before those changes union activity had been sporadic and often ineffective. At the Morrell plant in Ottumwa, for example, in the early 1900s the Amalgamated Meat Cutters and Butcher Workmen of North America had a local with a membership of about thirty skilled men out of a workforce of one thousand. Between 1922 and 1937 the company had instigated welfare capitalist measures in an effort to avert unionization. In 1937, however, with changes in the law and the assistance from the CIO, Morrell employees succeeded in making the Packinghouse Workers Organizing Committee of the CIO their bargaining representative.[40]

In Sioux City, packing plants were also being organized. As Roger Horowitz points out, in the late 1930s and early 1940s, with the assistance of the CIO and the affiliated Packinghouse Workers Organizing Committee (PWOC), "local union activities were able to overcome the determined resistance of the packing companies." Like the Morrell plant, the Sioux City packing plants had been organized earlier, with unions present in World War I, but these had collapsed during nationwide strikes in 1921–22. Although Sioux City workers had managed to establish union locals in three major plants in 1934, the industrywide organizing would come in the latter 1930s with assistance from the CIO. The result was that by 1943 more than two thousand employees of the packinghouse industry in Sioux City belonged to the PWOC.[41]

Although workers in Iowa's manufacturing sector were primarily male, women would play an increasingly important role in the state's labor force. Overall, the percentage of female workers in Iowa increased slowly from 1870 to 1930; the greatest increase would come later, during and after World War II. In 1870 females accounted for approximately 6 percent of Iowa's labor force; by 1890 that number had risen to approximately 12 percent; and in 1910 and 1920 the rate hovered around 16 percent. By 1930 the percentage of females in Iowa's labor force had risen just slightly, to 17 percent. In the period under discussion, therefore, the rate of female employment increased approximately 11 percent within the total labor force.[42]

Although females would work in a number of capacities, many jobs would be viewed as exclusively or primarily female occupations. One such occupation, domestic servant, included in 1910 more female workers—24,097—than any other category. By 1930 domestic service would rank second, with 21,447 females. From 1910 to 1930 other categories of employment that ranked high for females were teacher, store saleswoman, stenographer-typist, and bookkeeper-cashier-accountant. Only the position of accountant was not viewed as predominantly or exclusively female.[43] By the 1920s, within the manufacturing category of "food and kindred products" (the largest manufacturing classification in the state), females were often clustered in confectionary or candy-making plants.

The category of "store saleswoman" would eventually become an important one for women wage earners. In his history of the Younker Brothers Department Store, Joseph Rosenfield writes that in 1881 Younker's in Des Moines hired its first female employee, Mary McCann. Mrs. McCann was, indeed, the first woman hired by any store in Des Moines. Initially, Mary McCann's experience at the department store was discouraging. Rosenfield writes that the "male employees of the store greeted her in the same manner as they would have greeted the bubonic plague. They were jealous of her and afraid of her and, for some time, made her life quite miserable." Rosenfield explained that although Mrs. McCann was a timid woman and spent most of her time in the rear of the store, she "stuck to her guns and, within a few years, many women were employed in stores all over the city of Des Moines."[44]

Although the total number of Iowa's female wage earners would increase from 1870 to 1930, that increase would not be reflected in the number of women working in manufacturing and mechanical industries. In 1910 females accounted for 15.5 percent of jobs in that category; by 1920, however, that percentage had decreased to 10.4 percent, and by 1930 decreased still further to 8.6 percent. Along with these dwindling percentages, the total number of women working in this category would decrease as well.[45]

One nonmanufacturing area, commercial laundry work, allows a closer look at female employment in 1915. In that year the Iowa Bureau of Labor Statistics conducted an investigation of 1,296 women working in commercial laundries. The bureau, particularly concerned with working conditions, selected commercial laundry work because of its physical demands and uncomfortable work environment. The study included women in commercial laundries in all cities with a population above six thousand; women made up about 70 percent of the workforce in the laundries surveyed. The report stated: "Ordinarily the humidity of the room is high and oft-times the drainage poor, causing damp and wet clothing and feet." Within the industry there were twenty-five different classes of work, including flatwork machine operators, and shakers and tumblers. The latter workers received the clothing just out of the extractor, which left them "packed in hard and tangled masses." According to the bureau's report, "The [laundry] pieces are picked out one at a time, snapped or shaken violently which requires a peculiar swaying motion of the body in a somewhat stooped position and a constant use of the muscles of the arms, back and chest."[46]

Although no statewide studies have been conducted on wages and hours of female workers, fragmentary data from individual communities and industries are available. Ralph Scharnau estimates that in the latter 1800s in Dubuque, women received about one-third to one-half the pay received by males. This figure corresponds with national studies on women's wages in the first quarter of the twentieth century. The Bureau of Labor Statistics found that among laundry employees surveyed in 1915, the weekly wage ranged from $4.50 to $20.00; only three women, however, earned the higher amount. The weekly wage for most females was between $6.00 and $10.00. If the typical employee worked throughout the year—and earned $8.00 per week—the total yearly income would have been about $416.00. That amount is significantly less than the $749.00 average yearly wage of manufacturing workers where males predominated.[47]

Among laundry employees, hours of work per week started at 42.5 for a few workers, but typically ranged between 55 and 57 hours per week for most workers; about forty women worked 60 hours per week. Since Iowa had no law limiting females' hours of work (as did a number of states), the hours were determined "by the character of the work and the inclination of the employers."[48]

The story of Iowa's industrial development between 1870 and 1930 has been characterized by fairly even development of the industrial sector as new firms appeared regularly throughout the period. Many of the larger concerns started out as independent local operations and eventually allied with, or were taken over by, national firms. Although the number of industries present by 1930 numbered in the thousands, the most visible were still within two general categories: meat packing and farm-machinery production. Iowa's industries have not, for the most part, been concentrated in major urban centers. As the experience of the Maytag Company at Newton suggests, medium-size towns all over the state attracted industrial operations. Iowa's industries, moreover, would generally be smaller than those in eastern states.

The story of Iowa's workers, however, has taken many twists and turns: Employees faced not only difficult working conditions but often hostility from management as well as apathy from certain segments of the working class. Most early efforts at unionizing produced only limited, short-term success. Before the 1930s two significant efforts to unionize Iowans came with the Knights of Labor and the United Mine Workers, with members of the latter group playing a major role in organizing other industries in the 1930s. That decade, particularly with the help of the federal government, brought new vigor to efforts to unionize, a vigor that would be sustained throughout World War II.

III

The Recent Years

Depression, War, and a Balanced Economy

14

The 1930s: A Time of Trial

I n 1932, an Iowa State College professor wrote: "Nature has never treated the farmer more generously, yet our economic system could hardly treat him worse."[1] That terse statement aptly summed up the predicament facing rural Iowans in 1932. Although Iowa farmers harvested their largest corn crop ever, many faced agricultural ruin because of low prices and large debts. Iowa farmers responded to the hard times with uncharacteristic militancy, first engaging in a "Cow War" and then employing a farm strike. In 1934 and 1936 conditions worsened as farm families experienced extreme drought. Local responses would bring little relief, but like farmers elsewhere, Iowans benefited from the Agricultural Adjustment Act of 1933. Throughout the "dirty thirties," not only did Iowa farm families suffer devastating losses, but Iowans in cities and towns experienced high unemployment with many adults going on relief or seeking work on Works Progress Administration (WPA) projects. By

---

*Farmers Holiday Association members carry out a
blockade near Sioux City in 1932. Photo courtesy
of the State Historical Society, Des Moines.*

1937 Iowans began to feel some relief, but like many Americans, they did not realize complete recovery until the beginning of World War II.

Though many Americans experienced prosperity in the 1920s, most Iowans were not so fortunate. Government subsidies and high demand kept farm prices up during World War I and for a short time after, but by mid-1920 the situation had been reversed. In May the federal government withdrew agricultural price supports with the result that farm prices were cut almost in half. Farm families struggled throughout the remainder of the decade, many facing foreclosure. Small-town businesses and banks suffered accordingly. Between 1921 and 1929 Iowa led the nation in bank suspensions, with a total of 457.[2]

Although the stock-market crash occurred in 1929, Iowans did not feel the full brunt of the Great Depression until two years later. In 1932 farmers harvested a record corn crop, but it soon became apparent that the bumper harvest would not bring prosperity. In November hogs were selling for three dollars per hundred; beef cattle, five dollars; corn, ten cents a bushel; and oats, seven cents a bushel. In effect, farm products were selling for about one-half or even one-third of their 1922-29 average. One Iowa State economist put it this way: "the purchasing power of the farmer's products now is only 52 percent of pre-war; the farmer's capacity to pay has been cut in half. When he takes a load of hogs or corn to town and sells it to meet his running expenses, the money he receives for the load will go only half as far as it used to go."[3] At the same time, the cost of necessities purchased by farmers declined only slightly or remained the same.

Farmers also suffered from high fixed costs. During World War I, many farmers had purchased additional land, paying some cash and securing the remainder of the cost through mortgages on their original holdings. Land prices were high during the war, but they did not remain so during the 1920s. As the price of land fell, farmers still had the same high payments on their recently purchased land. One Iowa State College economist compared the farm situation in 1932 to that of the 1890s depression: A. G. Black pointed out that in 1896 the average cost of corn in Story County was $.13 a bushel; hogs sold at $2.98 a hundred. But at the same time, the "average mortgage debt per mortgaged acre" in Story County was $15.99. In contrast, in 1932 the average mortgage debt per mortgaged acre in Story County was $86.50, five times that in 1896. This was a significant figure, as in 1932, 58 percent of all Iowa farmers were mortgaged. The unavoidable effect was an increasing number of farm foreclosures. According to an ISC study, in six representative Iowa counties, from January to September of 1932, 257 farms were sold at foreclosure sales. In the previous year in the same six counties, 90 farms had been sold.[4]

Although Iowa's farm population has traditionally not displayed much militancy during times of economic distress, the early 1930s proved an exception. Iowa farmers protested several government programs, and some joined the Farmers Holiday Association. The two most important examples of collective action taken by Iowa farmers were the so-called Cow War and the farm strike, though the number of farmers involved in the latter was only a small minority of the state's total farmers. Later, farmers in northwestern Iowa attempted to prevent judges from executing foreclosure sales.

During the Cow War, Iowa farmers reacted militantly in response to the testing of cattle for bovine tuberculosis. Veterinarians had long suspected that tuberculosis in cattle could lead to tuberculosis in humans, a suspicion that prompted the passage of a law requiring testing of dairy herds in the state. Testing for TB in cattle began in 1917, at first on a voluntary basis. By 1923 the "area-plan law" went into effect, which determined that when a majority of farmers in a given area requested the test, it would become mandatory for the entire county. By the end of the decade officials had made the test compulsory throughout the state. When an animal was condemned, the federal government reimbursed the owner for one-third the cost, the state provided reimbursement for another third, leaving the owner with one-third of the replacement cost.[5]

In ordinary times the testing program would probably have caused little opposition, but the twenties and early thirties were not ordinary times. Farmers, hard-pressed to survive anyway, found the testing and subsequent condemnation of cattle increasingly alarming. Some farmers believed veterinarians were "in cahoots" with meat packers in Chicago. A retired farmer in Tama County repeated this charge in 1976, almost fifty years after the testing episode. The elderly man asserted that he and many friends "knew" the vets were condemning healthy cattle, shipping them to meat packers in Chicago in return for a kickback. The man hesitantly brought forth a fading snapshot, which showed about a dozen farmers in front of a barn; hanging from the top of the structure was a dummy figure with the letters "ISC Vet" painted on its chest. The farmers had hanged in effigy an Iowa State College vet to show their extreme hostility toward what they perceived to be an unfair practice.[6]

Opposition to the testing program seemed to center in eastern Iowa, where many farmers belonged to the Farmers' Protective Association, a group formed specifically to oppose the testing law. Farmers based their opposition on several factors, including their belief that the test was unreliable and did not protect public health as state officials insisted. Moreover, farmers had been accustomed to local veterinarians doing the testing, men whom they knew and trusted. Under the compulsory law, however, outside vets did much of the work. Farmers showed their opposition to compulsory testing in two ways: They sought to replace the compulsory law with a voluntary one, and they began organizing committees to prevent state veterinarians from carrying out testing programs.

The first organized opposition to testing took place in February 1931. Plans called for participating farmers to arrive at a testing site in the hope that their very presence would discourage veterinarians from proceeding with their work. The farmers succeeded in at least a few instances, including one in Cedar County when a group of five hundred farmers prevented vets from testing cattle on the farm of Jake Butterodt. The following day more groups of farmers prevented testing on five other farms in the area. A short time later a number of farmers traveled to Des Moines to present their case to the legislature; one source estimated the group at twenty-five hundred. Farmers met with state officials and many farmers made speeches in the House Chamber of the capitol, arguing for the passage of the Davis bill, which was designed to allow for voluntary rather than compulsory cattle testing.[7]

The man most visible in the farm protests of the early thirties was Milo Reno. An Iowan who had farmed for some years and trained for the ministry, Reno had been a leader in the McNary-Haugen campaign in the twenties. The former preacher delighted in attacking many traditional aspects of agriculture, including extension personnel and professors at Iowa State College. Reno accused ISC of "distracting the attention of the farmer 'from the real solution of his problems' and of preparing him to accept 'the lowly position of the peasant.'" He believed the approaches of the "academic theorists" were worthless in solving the practical problems facing the state's farmers. Often he advised the academics: "Try to run a farm of your own." In 1931 Reno became head of the national Farmers Holiday Association.[8]

Farm unrest continued throughout the summer and the fall. In September two veterinarians, backed up by sixty-five law-enforcement agents, arrived at the farm of Jake Lenker, fourteen miles south of Tipton, intent on testing Lenker's cattle. According to longtime political reporter, George Mills, the four hundred farmers who gathered at the Lenker farm "were in an ugly mood." Lenker himself defied the vets to take action, declaring: "They'll test my cattle over my dead body." The farmers quickly turned their wrath against the state veterinarian's car, which they "filled ... with mud, broke the gasoline line, slashed the tires and smashed the windows." The veterinarians, badly outnumbered, wisely retreated, but the next day Governor Dan Turner reacted decisively by declaring martial law in Cedar County and calling out the National Guard. The Guard, nineteen hundred strong, "fanned out from Tipton, convoying the vets to the protestors' farms. They mounted machine guns along the roads. Armed outposts were set up." According to Mills, "There was no way the farmers could win, and they knew it." For all practical purposes, the incident at the Lenker farm ended the Cow War, and the only casualty was one guardsman who accidentally shot himself in the foot. The law had been enforced, but the operation was expensive: Officials estimated the cost at twenty-five hundred dollars per day.[9]

Although the Cow War attracted considerable attention in places like Cedar County, most Iowa farmers did not support the protest. What the militant outbreaks did indicate was that Iowa farmers were badly affected by the Depression and they resented the "far-reaching hand of government, colleges, and other centralized agencies, especially at a time of falling prices." In typical fashion, Milo Reno expressed this frustration by describing the state veterinarian as "Any little shyster who has come out of a certain college in the state [and] can go on a farmer's property and conduct a test which is more apt to be wrong than right."[10]

The Cow War did help pave the way, however, for the farm strike. Reno himself had talked about such a strike in 1927 when he announced before a farm committee, "If we cannot obtain justice by legislation, the time will have arrived when no other course remains than organized refusal to deliver the products of the farm at less than production costs."

Members of the Farmers Union passed a resolution at their 1931 annual meeting "asking for 'a farmers' buying, selling and tax-paying strike,'" unless state officials enacted what Farmers Union members perceived to be the necessary remedial legislation.[11]

On May 2, 1932, farmers organized the Farmers Holiday Association in Des Moines. The logical choice for president—a nearly unanimous one—was Milo Reno. The group elected John Bosch of Minnesota as vice president. The farmers were then ready for action, which Leland Sage has described in the following way: "The key decision summing up all their planning, and their emotions as well, was one which set July 4 as the beginning date for a withholding action, to run for thirty days or until 'cost of production' was achieved." As Sage points out, the term "cost of production" was never explained; equally vague was "what methods were to be used to force somebody to grant it to them." Participants selected the slogan: "Stay at Home—Buy Nothing—Sell Nothing," and adopted the name "Farmers Holiday," modeled after early bank holidays.[12]

At first organizers intended that the farm strike would keep farm products off the market. The area around Sioux City soon became a focal point for this action as Farmers Holiday members attempted to prevent farmers there from marketing their milk, cream, and hogs. Though participating farmers hoped the protest would be peaceful, violence occurred almost immediately. As one study described it, "Roads were blockaded, fist fights broke out, arrests were made, and gun toting, exhortation, vituperation, picketing, storming of jails and capitol buildings, and stopping of trains and automobiles were among the other events that took place."[13] No doubt the presence of the stockyards made Sioux City a logical place for farm-strike participants to congregate. Pickets barricaded roads, trying to convince farmers to return home and support the farm strike. When the pickets failed, they sometimes confiscated and destroyed farmers' produce. At one point picketers stopped a truck carrying butter, and then spread the butter on a section of Highway 75 for a 200-yard stretch. A Plymouth County resident, Ralph Rippey, remembered: "They smeared it all over the pavement. I came along in my car and went into the ditch. There were tubs of butter. ... Every time you hit a slick place, off you would go, like that."[14]

Most pickets were carried out without physical harm, but there were exceptions. A few shots were fired by both picketers and area farmers, but in only one case did a fatality occur. On that occasion strikers ordered a young driver to stop, observing milk cans in the back of his truck. When the driver attempted to run the barricade, a farmer fired at the vehicle, stating later that he intended to hit the windshield above the young man's head. Instead the bullet hit the driver in the head, killing him instantly. An observer recalled what followed: "A bunch of picketers leaped up on the back of the truck to empty the milk cans. And what do you suppose they found in the cans—not milk but bootleg whiskey? That damned-fool kid, if he'd only stopped and told them that he had whiskey not milk in those cans, they'd have let him through."[15] In 1932 bootlegging was illegal. Ironically, the young man's death resulted not from breaking the law through bootlegging, but because picketers were determined to halt legitimate milk deliveries.

Although efforts by Farmers Holiday members continued, both in Iowa and in several nearby states, the action produced little change in the farm situation. The *Des Moines Register* reported that the marketing of hogs did not go down as a result of the strike. Before picketing began, Iowa farmers marketed approximately 750,000 hogs. In August, a month after picketing had started, approximately 804,000 head were marketed, and in September the number totaled 787,000. Nor did strike efforts raise farm prices. John Shover concluded, after a careful study of the Farmers Holiday Association, that the group failed basically for two reasons: lack of discipline among members and lack of adequate economic planning.[16]

Even though the farm strike produced little change in farm prices, many Iowans continued to show their extreme frustration. In September 1932 governors from the midwestern states met in Sioux City to consider farm problems. The governors planned to draft a program "calling for tariff equality, currency expansion, more agricultural credit at lower interest rates, a moratorium on debts, and surplus-control legislation." Local farmers turned out, about five thousand strong, to parade through the city. *Des Moines Register* farm editor Jim Russell wrote: "Displaying the American flag, truckload after truckload of farmers paraded through the streets thronged with the largest crowd that Sioux City had known since Lindbergh was here."[17]

The September meeting in Sioux City had also introduced another element into the farm situation: communist agitators in Iowa. In an effort by the Communist Party of America to infiltrate the Farmers Holiday movement, three party members—Harold Ware; his mother, Ella Reeve Bloor (popularly known as Mother Bloor); and Lem Harris—arrived in Sioux City. These individuals, believing that a peasant economy existed in the Midwest, hoped to "take charge of the program of stimulating the protest movement in the hope that the traditional capitalistic system of farming could be destroyed." Although the party members had little impact on the Sioux City situation, they did convince farmers to call a Farmers National Relief Conference in Washington later that year.[18]

By January of the following year, Iowa farmers were still not getting any relief. Farm prices remained extremely low, with corn bringing only fourteen to fifteen cents a bushel in Sioux City. In March frustrated and angry farmers "invaded" the Iowa legislature. Although that body had been in session for only two weeks, farmers believed members had done little to provide relief. According to George Mills, the farmers carried pitchforks and completely stopped all proceedings in both houses of the General Assembly. The farmers stated they were looking for state senator Mike Fisch, a Le Mars Democrat, because they were unhappy with a bill Fisch had sponsored. The farmers announced loudly they were going to hang Fisch over a railing in the rotunda. Mills reported that Fisch "wisely retreated by climbing up into the Statehouse golden dome."[19]

The following month farmers in northwest Iowa again gained national attention when the most dramatic event of the decade took place in Le Mars. Realizing that the farm strike had not worked, some farmers believed more drastic action was needed. Farmers were particularly upset about the high rate of foreclosures taking place throughout the state. Apparently a small group of farmers around Le Mars believed they could stop such action if they showed up at foreclosure sales. On April 27 Morris Cope and Art Bock of Hinton along with a small group of farmers who called themselves the Seventy-sixers and the Minute Men arrived in Primghar, the county seat of O'Brien County, determined to prevent the foreclosure sale of John Shaffer's 160-acre farm. Somehow O'Brien County sheriff Ed Leemkiul heard about the plans, swore in twenty-two deputies, armed them with pickax handles, and met the farmers at the courthouse. Based on interviews with some participants many years later, George Mills constructed the following account:

> The farmers crowded into the courthouse. Barring their way up the stairs were the waiting deputies, three on each step. Somebody came down the

stairs and shouted: "Everybody out, fellows. We've made a settlement."
Cope yelled: "Everybody stop where you are! There's something
wrong here." Then came the cry: "They're selling the man's farm from
the balcony!"

The farmers charged the stairs and ran into a storm of flailing handles. Eight or 10 farmers were injured, most not seriously, according to
reports. But Cope took a hard rap on the head. "A deputy hit me over the
head and fractured my skull," he said. "I bled out of my nose and ears."[20]

Ignoring the protests, officials sold the Shaffer farm for seventy-four hundred dollars to a Primghar attorney. In a last, defiant act, the farmers demanded that the attorney come outside and kiss the American flag.

Despite his aching head, Morris Cope told the farmers: "Now what
we should do, instead of going around fighting deputies, getting our skulls
fractured, we should go in a body down to Le Mars. We should ask Judge
Bradley to give us the benefit of the doubt." Later that same afternoon
some three hundred to four hundred farmers assembled at the Le Mars
baseball field. Cope suggested: "Let's go up and throw the fear of God into
Bradley." To the farmers, agitated over the difficult economic depression,
some fortified with alcohol, Cope's suggestion seemed to make sense.[21]

Pressing into the courtroom, the farmers apparently demanded that
Judge Bradley cease signing foreclosures. The fifty-four-year-old judge
replied: "I don't have to listen to you farmers." Several farmers swarmed
around the judge, pulling him from his chair and dragging him outside the
courtroom. One farmer had brought along a rope, which was dangled in
the judge's face. Bradley later testified that "Six or eight men rushed at the
bench, dragged me through the courtroom and down the front steps of the
courthouse. I fell on the steps and someone kicked me." The judge's ordeal ended several miles outside of Le Mars, but not until the farmers had
removed the judge's trousers, threatened him with mutilation, and placed
a noose around his neck. They then demanded that he promise not to sign
any more foreclosure decrees. The judge refused. Several men later admitted they admired the judge's courage in the face of the potential lynching. The event ended quickly after the "seven or eight men most active in
the abduction 'leaped into an auto and sped away.'"[22]

The same day, Plymouth County sheriff Ralph Rippey notified Governor Clyde Herring that the situation was beyond the control of local
civilian authorities. Herring, in turn, called out the National Guard and declared martial law in Plymouth County; by May 6, 1933, 155 individuals

had been arrested as a result of their participation in the foreclosure action. Several farmers served three months in jail. In interviews with George Mills, two participants in the Bradley affair, Martin Rosburg and Morris Cope, expressed regret at having taking action against the judge but felt no remorse for their attempts to help local farmers. Cope declared: "Our troubles forced the people in the East to look this far west to see what was happening. It all helped. I thought it was good. What we wanted was the cost of production."[23]

The Judge Bradley incident marked the end of the violence and intimidation carried out by a small number of Iowa farmers. The latter point is significant, as only a limited number of farmers in any community supported the Farmers Holiday Association or took part in the protests. In Plymouth County the local newspaper estimated that no more than 10 percent of the farmers took part in Farmers Holiday activities. By November of 1933 the federal government (under the Agricultural Adjustment Act) had begun to extend corn loans to farmers to give some relief. That action was soon followed by agreements between individual farmers and the Agricultural Adjustment Administration, which again helped alleviate some financial distress. These federal policy changes marked the end of the Farmers Holiday Association. The conditions that had led to militant responses by Iowa farmers were slowly fading away; farm prices were rising and farmers (through government payments) had more purchasing power. A dark period in Iowa's history had come to an end.[24]

While rural Iowans were intensely interested in the AAA because of its impact on agriculture, they were also interested for another reason: The man selected as secretary of agriculture in 1933 was a native Iowan. Henry Agard Wallace, as editor of *Wallaces' Farmer,* had been one of the most visible agricultural spokesmen in the Midwest during the 1920s and early 1930s. Wallace came by his agricultural interests naturally, as his grandfather, "Uncle Henry," and father, Henry Cantwell, had been involved in a wide range of agricultural activities, both regionally and nationally. The two men had started publishing the farm journal that eventually would carry the family name. Henry Cantwell Wallace had also served as secretary of agriculture in the Harding administration. Henry Agard Wallace, interested in agricultural experimentation since boyhood—and having a plethora of related interests in tariffs, agricultural economics, and world trade among others—seemed the logical choice for the head position within the United States Department of Agriculture. In turn, Wallace played a crucial role in determining the New Deal's agricultural policy.

While farmers themselves faced difficult conditions, having to work harder all the time to maintain their operations, farm women contributed significant, often crucial, labor to the family farm. Traditionally, farm life in any period has been evaluated in agricultural terms—acres under cultivation, farm prices, and government farm programs—and often has not taken into account the labor and contributions of all family members. No adequate assessment of the farm sector during the Great Depression is possible without considering farm women's responsibilities and contributions. During the 1930s farmers' wives labored unceasingly to produce their family's food supply and to raise extra farm products that were either sold for income or bartered to reduce expenditures.

According to a federal report in 1935–36, the value of home-produced goods nationally for families of moderate means made up 45 percent of net family-farm income. This report seemed to typify the Iowa situation, as the Farm Security Administration reported in 1938 that of those farm families receiving Farm Security assistance, the average Iowa farm family produced food and fuel at home worth $352.63 while spending an average of $325.67 in cash. In general, women's home production has been estimated at 40 to 50 percent of the total household budget.[25]

Iowa farm women missed no opportunity to improve the financial conditions of their families. In 1933 *Wallaces' Farmer* ran a contest on "Swelling the Family Income" and invited farm women to share the ways in which they had done so. Many women wrote they had increased the "direct sale of poultry and dairy products" to town customers but also had sold such disparate items as pimento and celery plants, braided rugs, canaries, Persian cats, and black walnuts. Farm women also offered services such as mending, sewing, baby-sitting, and catering meals.[26]

Iowa farm women also continued to perform the same tasks they had done for decades, most of which contributed food to the family as well as provided sources of income. Women were typically involved in milking, separating, and churning butter. Farm women traditionally raised substantial gardens, many of which were enlarged during the 1930s. The latter work was especially difficult, since large areas of Iowa experienced devastating drought in 1934 and 1936. The shortage of rainfall meant women had to rig up special devices to water gardens. Farm women also often raised poultry, which, along with the subsequent egg production, provided both food for the family and income. In 1933, 17 percent of Iowa's farm income came from the sale of butter, 7 percent came from eggs, and 5 percent came from poultry. Together this accounted for just under 30 percent of total farm income. The income from butter, in fact, had increased from 12 percent in 1924 to 17 percent a decade later.[27]

While farm families faced great difficulties in the thirties, town and city dwellers faced equally trying, if different, circumstances. In 1970 Studs Terkel published his oral history of Americans' experiences during the Great Depression. He included some twelve interviews with Iowans, some of whom were city dwellers. One informant, Slim Collier of Waterloo, remembered his father's being laid off as a tool-and-die maker for John Deere and the changes that circumstance brought to his family. Seven years old at the time, Collier recalled: "All of a sudden, my father, who I saw only rarely, was around all the time. That was quite a shock. I suddenly became disciplined by him instead of my mother. The old woodshed was used extensively in those days." Collier's father had an extremely difficult time because he was "the kind of man who had to be active. He'd invent work for himself." One time when Collier found a dollar, his father "gravely [took] charge of it ... doling it out to me a dime at a time."[28]

Unemployment or reduced wages and hours affected thousands of families living in Iowa's cities. In Dubuque, between 1927 and 1934, thirty firms employing twenty-two hundred workers closed up or left town. At the same time, only thirteen new businesses opened, with a total of three hundred employees. The shops maintained by the railroads experienced dramatic cutbacks; in 1931 they employed six hundred, but by 1934 that number had dropped to twenty-five.[29]

As a result of widespread unemployment, many Iowa families either went on direct relief or the family breadwinners went to work on federal projects sponsored by the Works Progress Administration. In Dubuque, Eagle Point Park and a Mississippi River lock and dam were the two major WPA projects. Ralph Scharnau writes that in Dubuque County, "as many as 1,200 people worked one, two, or three days per week on a variety of WPA projects." At the same time, Iowans worked on writing and art

projects. The federal government hired unemployed artists (through programs such as the Works Progress Administration, the Public Works of Art
Project, and the Treasury Relief Art Project) to paint murals in the interiors of public buildings; the project completed some fifty murals. The art-
work graced buildings in both cities and towns, including Cedar Rapids,
Des Moines, Mount Ayr, Corning, and Ames.[30]

Large numbers of businesspeople in the state also lost their liveli-
hood. Frank and Rome Hentges were brothers who operated a total of five
clothing stores in Iowa and South Dakota. Interviewed by Terkel in Le
Mars, the brothers related they had been forced to close all their stores
around 1933; none was ever reopened. When asked what they had done
since that time, one brother replied with a laugh: "Sit around."[31]

Not even entertainers escaped the effects of the Depression. The
Toby Tent Players had been an Iowa institution since 1925; during its first
ten years, the group toured only Iowa towns, but later the players expanded their performances throughout the Middle West. Neil Schaffner recalled that his company had an extremely difficult time attracting patrons
during the thirties, so he tried all kinds of "dodges." Once he paid ten dollars to have someone launch a balloon in front of the Toby tent. The as-
cension was made, but the balloon drifted off five miles into the country.
The crowd followed the balloon, never returning to pay admission for the
show. But Schaffner did discover one good technique to bring in depres-
sion-stricken Iowans: At Burlington he agreed to give merchants all the
tickets they wanted for one hundred dollars (each merchant paid one dollar). In turn, they dispensed the tickets free to their patrons, who, in addition to the ticket, paid only ten cents to see the Toby show.[32]

Of all Iowans, African Americans experienced the greatest difficulty
finding work during the Depression. Making up less than 1 percent of the
total state population, blacks were clustered in the ranks of unskilled and
semiskilled workers. In Sioux City, Waterloo, and Ottumwa, black men
found some work in the slaughtering and meat-packing plants. Railroads
hired black males, but typically only as porters and waiters rather than in
the higher-paying positions of engineers and conductors. According to the
census of 1930, railroads in Iowa employed the following black workers:
nine brakemen, six firemen, five foremen, five switchmen and flagmen,
and one inspector.[33] The experience of Iowa's black population paralleled
that of blacks elsewhere in that they were impacted earlier by the Depres-

sion than were whites. In Chicago, for example, blacks in 1931 made up 4 percent of the population but 16 percent of those out of work.

In Manly during the thirties, black railroad workers lost their jobs more frequently than did white workers, an action that stemmed from two conditions: First, African-American workers had been unable to join all-white unions—which, in turn, protected its white members during lay-offs—and second, diesel engines began to replace steam engines, thus bringing further cutbacks. About thirty black workers left Manly in the thirties, with some seeking work in nearby Mason City. There they were refused higher-paying jobs in cement plants and packinghouses and were forced to take "traditional jobs" for blacks, such as bellhops or laborers in the car washes.[34]

Marjorie Brown, an African-American woman, remembered vividly the difficulties she and her husband, William, experienced during the 1930s. The Browns had lived in several Iowa communities but in 1934 moved to Cedar Rapids. Even though William Brown was a college graduate, he could not find employment for two years. Marjorie then went to work to support the family. She remembered the Depression as "one of the bitterest periods of my life. ... I'm one of the people who ... watched the house full of furniture be taken to be reclaimed. ... I have worked seven days a week doing housework, and that includes washing, ironing, and cooking—and believe me, we did do windows—for five dollars a week."[35]

For black women throughout Iowa, Marjorie Brown's experience was probably typical. Married black women had always worked outside the home in higher numbers than their white counterparts, and the Great Depression intensified that practice. Although some black women continued to work as domestics—their major occupational category—many were laid off as the Depression intensified. In Chicago the unemployment rate for black women soared to 50 percent. For many black families in Iowa, the five-dollar weekly wages women like Marjorie Brown brought home kept the family intact.

For all unemployed Iowans, housing was frequently difficult to secure. Dorothy Takach of Cedar Rapids remembered that as a youngster, home for her family meant two railroad boxcars. Because her father worked for the railroad and was on call twenty-four hours a day, the railroad provided the family with two facilities. Takach described it as "a grand thing—two 40-foot long boxcars set side by side, partitioned into ll-by-9-foot rooms, a gable roof over it and packing cases at the door for porches."[36]

Finding fuel also posed problems. One might cut down on food and go for a day or two without eating, but in bitterly cold weather some heat was a necessity. One Des Moines couple supplemented their purchases of coal with trips to the city dump in search of wood. The woman related that with wood one of them had to get up two or three times a night and fire up. With coal they could bank the stove and sleep uninterrupted. Many evenings the couple went to bed at dark to save fuel and electricity. Another Des Moines woman recalled: "One of the saddest things I remember was the plight of a family across the street from us. They were reduced to smashing their wood furniture and burning it for heat."[37]

Clothing one's family often required ingenuity on the part of homemakers. Women used flour and feed sacks to make dresses and underwear, and countless Iowans remembered seeing young girls with "Mother's Best" across the seat of their bloomers. One woman in Grinnell, in need of coats for several children, remembered the good upholstery in a car hauled to the city dump. She retrieved the seat cushions and removed the velour material; after washing the material she managed to make several coats for her children. A fairly common practice was family members sharing the same pair of shoes: If one person went to town, the other person stayed home. Moreover, laundry was attended to frequently when children had only one pair of stockings. Mrs. D. O. Beckman of Perry recalled that she washed "every evening the 'one and only pair of stockings' each of [her] children had," then dried them behind the heating stove so they would be wearable in the morning. Mrs. Hester Wells of Grinnell recalled that one man, needing five dollars for shoes for his two children, went to the cemetery where his infant son had been buried, dug up the body, and reburied it in the garden. That allowed him to sell the cemetery plot for five dollars and buy shoes for his two living children.[38]

While finding sufficient food, clothing, and shelter for one's family could be exceedingly difficult, the basic problem of unemployment also took a heavy emotional toll. A Council Bluffs woman explained: "No one would believe how we existed up until 1941 when my husband got a steady job with the railroad ... We were always in debt. I hid behind doors and never hardly answered a knock. [I] learned to tell little white lies and lay awake nights and cried alot."[39]

During the Depression the view existed that there should be only one job per family. Therefore, if a married woman worked outside the home, she was regarded as holding a job that really belonged to a man. The result was that some women who had jobs and wanted to marry simply kept the wedding secret. If the woman became pregnant, she quickly produced the marriage certificate.

Although women suffered greatly from the economic hardships of the Depression, perhaps men suffered the most grievous psychological damage. Americans have historically believed that work is necessary for self-respect; men have traditionally defined themselves by their work and by their success within their occupation. Caroline Bird entitled her book on the Depression, *The Invisible Scar,* because that experience left millions of Americans affected deeply in a psychological sense. She wrote that unemployed men often left home in the morning and remained away all day, telling their wives they actually had been working. Women found it easier to cope, perhaps, because their daily routine changed less than did their husbands'. A woman might have to scrimp and save, but she still had the same routine of washing, ironing, preparing meals, doing dishes, and providing child care.[40]

As hard times continued, the Works Progress Administration determined in 1937 to look at "the personal side" of the Depression. The agency selected Dubuque for study because of the city's size and its industrial background. The WPA researchers believed that "the statistics of unemployment and relief measure the magnitude of distress with … efficiency … but they do not show what it means to the individual to be out of work or on relief—they leave untold the personal side." In an attempt to tell "the personal side," researchers collected 103 histories from Dubuque residents in 1937 and 1938; later they selected 45 accounts for publication.[41]

Although the forty-five families experienced a wide range of difficulties, there were important commonalities: Most families had "very reluctantly" gone on relief; some had waited until the cupboard was literally bare before asking for help, and many had first sought assistance from family members. In most families the male breadwinner had strongly preferred to work for a private employer rather than on a relief project. Most families planted large gardens that produced a substantial part of their food supply. Many families had moved several times, each time seeking cheaper rent.

Claud and Martha Park and their three children provide one case study of how Dubuque citizens coped with unemployment. Claud and Martha married in 1924, and for the next seven years Claud had steady employment. In 1931, however, he was laid off his job as spray painter at the Iowa Foundry and for the next five years could find only irregular employment. With little money coming in, the Parks borrowed from Claud's parents and also borrowed on an insurance policy. But by December 1932, as the temperature hovered around zero and with credit at the local store about to be cut off, "the situation had become desperate." Moreover, Mrs. Park was pregnant. After talking the situation over, the couple decided they had no alternative but to apply for relief, yet they both felt they would be "disgraced." The report explained: "Mrs. Park bitterly opposed going on relief," but during the night Claud got 'scared about the kids,' and thought 'we can't let the kids starve just because we are proud.' The next morning, without telling his wife his intentions, he went to the courthouse and made application for relief." Claud Park recounted taking the painful last step: "I must have walked around the block over a dozen times—it was 10 below zero, but I didn't know it." Finally he summoned his courage and entered the office.[42]

During the Depression low-income housing in urban areas would also receive attention. Given the federal housing programs enacted in the thirties—such as the Home Owners' Loan Corporation—Iowans formed several groups to supervise and carry out low-income housing surveys in eighteen Iowa cities. These surveys were conducted under the auspices of the Federal Emergency Relief Administration for three reasons: (1) to give residents of each surveyed city "a factual picture of the housing and living conditions of the economic lower half of their people, with a view to developing ways to improve these conditions"; (2) to provide federal officials with a "research portrayal" of housing conditions in these cities; and (3) to provide a scientific basis for housing and city-planning programs for the Iowa State Planning Board, which, in turn, had responsibility for pursuing remedial action.[43]

The survey reports included both photographs and written descriptions of housing; these reports, particularly of Dubuque (1934) and Des Moines (1935), left little doubt that ghetto-type conditions existed in Iowa's urban areas. Though housing conditions deteriorated for many families as a result of the Depression, the surveys made clear that some families had lived in shacklike dwellings for more than eight to ten years, obviously preceding the Depression. The worst housing was in Des Moines, often in view of the state capitol.[44]

The Depression years were not totally bleak for Iowa's economy, however, as some important new industries originated in that decade. Collins Radio Company in Cedar Rapids, started by Arthur A. Collins in 1933, would develop into one of the largest industrial firms by the 1950s. As a young boy, Collins was fascinated with radios and made his first transmitter from a Quaker Oats box, a spark coil from a Model T, and other parts from a rural telephone office. Collins attended both Coe College in Cedar Rapids and Amhurst but at age twenty-three, believing he could produce better radio equipment than that on the market, incorporated the Collins Radio Company. As with so many firms, World War II brought great expansion to the company; by 1941 Collins had set up offices in New York City. The company continued to expand after the war, and by the mid-1950s the firm had ten plants in Cedar Rapids as well as branches in other American cities, in Canada, and in England. The company produced radio communication and navigation equipment, broadcast transmitters, aircraft instruments, and amateur communication equipment.[45]

Another firm destined to become a major Iowa manufacturing concern began in the 1930s in the Amana Colonies. In 1934 Amana resident George Foerstner and two friends hit upon the idea of building a beer cooler. Foerstner then took over the Middle Amana Woolen Mill and began to produce meat cases and coolers. Two years later the Amana Society assumed control of the operation and soon became the largest manufacturer of cold-storage locker plants in the country. In 1945 the company became the first to manufacture upright home freezers. Although the firm retained the name Amana, by 1950 it had been sold to private investors outside the colonies. Today the brand name Amana, along with brands such as Maytag, are known worldwide for dependability and quality.

By 1937 economic conditions had improved for both rural and urban dwellers in Iowa. The Agricultural Adjustment Act, passed in 1933, had brought improved conditions for Iowa's farm families. In 1932 national farm income had totaled $5.5 billion, and that amount had risen to nearly $8.7 billion in 1935.[46] Though participation in the AAA was voluntary, approximately 75 percent of Iowa farmers took part. Many Iowans talked in terms of the Depression coming to an end in 1938.

Although the Depression years had been difficult, these same years had included some positive change, as well. During the thirties some farm families had experienced an improvement in the quality of rural life. The same percentage of farm families had automobiles in 1940 as in 1930 (90.2 percent), but cars had become sturdier and more dependable. More important, however, the miles of hard-surfaced or graveled roads greatly increased in the state. By 1940, 57 percent of Iowa's farm families lived along improved roads. Farm families were able to travel to town more easily and were able to visit neighbors and friends more often. In effect, farm families were becoming more like town families in their social and leisure-time activities.[47]

Perhaps the greatest change for farm residents came with the Rural Electric Association in 1935. To farm women, especially, getting electricity meant major changes. Iowa poet and author James Hearst, himself a farm dweller, described the transformation: "Farm life took on a new dimension. Not even the telephone changed our way of living, thinking, and acting as much as the coming of electricity. This break with the past seemed an entrance to the modern world."[48] Farm women themselves described the change in glowing terms. One woman wrote *Wallaces' Farmer* that she viewed electricity as giving her a "houseful of servants—servants that carry water, sweep rugs, help with washing and ironing and preparing of meals." A farm wife from Tama County expressed her appreciation this way: "The good fairy, electricity, has waved her magic wand across my path and now I lead a charmed life. ... No water to be carried uphill; no waste water to be carried out; no kerosene lamps to be cleaned and filled; no hand scorching sadirons to be used; no fuel to clutter up my kitchen in pails and boxes; no ashes to be swept up and carried out. ... It seems too good to be true."[49]

By 1939, like Americans everywhere, Iowans were experiencing a return of prosperity but also were becoming increasingly apprehensive about events in Europe. That year Hitler's armies moved into Poland, officially marking the beginning of World War II. Like the First World War, Iowa farm families would profit substantially from World War II, but in the process the calamity would change their lives in major ways.

15

World War II and the Years Beyond

W hen the Japanese carried out a surprise attack on Pearl Harbor on December 7, 1941, Americans had little indication they would face almost four long years of war. Nor did Americans realize that the war would serve as a major economic and social divide between the world they knew in the late 1930s and the world they would come to know in the years beyond. In Iowa, World War II impacted on every aspect of life as Iowans entered the

During World War II many women performed outside farm chores. Here Mrs. Luther Severtson of rural Boone County is hoisting hay. Photo courtesy of Wallaces Farmer.

military, worked in war industries, and labored to achieve record agricultural production. Once the war ended, Iowans continued to experience major change as the state became increasingly urbanized and industrialized. Agriculture clearly remained the most important single industry but experienced hard times during much of the 1950s. Iowans also experienced more geographic mobility as rural people moved to the cities. Although some change was inevitable even without war, that conflict must be regarded as a major watershed in Iowa history. By the end of the fifties, Iowans found themselves experiencing a social and economic transformation as rural and urban interests became equally significant.

With the outbreak of war in Europe in 1939, Iowans were well on their way to recovering from the Great Depression. Agriculture, the most visible victim of the Depression, was rebounding rapidly, the state's total cash farm income having increased by $60 million between 1938 and 1939 alone. Other changes were also apparent as the state's farmers began to mechanize; in 1939 Iowa farmers had the most tractors of any state in the nation, with 135,000 units. Farmers increasingly were using hybrid seed corn, and by 1940 about half of the state's corn crop was picked mechanically. Also, more and more farms were getting electricity as a result of the Rural Electrification Administration, formed in 1935. Although the war would indeed result in far greater agricultural production, the latter 1930s marked the beginning of economic recovery for Iowa's farm families.[1]

Given Iowa's status as a major agricultural state, state officials began in 1940 to mobilize for increased production. As the key agricultural organization, the Iowa Cooperative Extension Service would have major responsibility for that task. Extension director Ralph K. Bliss had served as head of the service through World War I and thus brought valuable experience to his work in the Second World War. Getting information to farm families had been a major problem in World War I, and to solve that, Bliss had appointed one farm person in each township to serve as a War Food Production Cooperator. Each cooperator, in turn, contacted sixteen other families in the township. This statewide communications network remained in place and was used again during World War II. In 1941 Bliss estimated that USDA information from Washington could be passed on to almost every Iowa farm family within one week.[2]

In April 1941 USDA secretary Claude Wickard declared "Food will win the war and write the peace," a motto heard over and over during the next four years. Even in 1941 Iowa farmers seemed to be doing their part to support Wickard's statement, as open-country Iowans produced more livestock, milk, and eggs in 1941 than ever before. During the war the extension service, primarily through county agents and home-demonstration agents, worked hard to promote the government's goals of producing even more food, conserving food, and encouraging people to support the war effort through purchase of war bonds. In effect, extension personnel wore many caps during the duration.

Throughout the war Iowa's farm sector achieved production records. Each year from 1941 to 1945 farm families produced more than in the previous year. Sometimes extension personnel devised slogans to promote their goals; a particularly descriptive one, "An extra squirt from every cow," was meant to encourage dairy farmers to do their part for the war effort. Midway through the war Bliss wrote in his annual report: "The fields and feedlots of Iowa produced 640 million bushels of corn, 39 million bushels of soybeans, 21 million head of hogs, 7 million pounds of milk, 70 million chickens and 326 million dozens of eggs; all new production records set in 1943." At war's end Iowa's farm production was 50 percent higher than in World War I.[3]

A major problem confronting the state's farmers was a labor shortage, particularly in 1943 and 1944. Extension personnel had responsibility for intrastate-labor and farm-labor placements, and each county had several labor centers. In Marshall County every town had a labor center where officials handled local registration and placement of workers. Labor needs obviously varied across the state: Lee County officials, for instance, needed seasonal help to harvest crops such as strawberries, cucumbers, and tomatoes, whereas in northwestern Iowa the harvesting of small grains and corn was vital.

Iowa farmers also had labor assistance from foreign nationals and prisoners of war. Beginning in 1942, Mexican nationals began to arrive in Iowa, and the next year they were joined by workers from Jamaica. Farmers would receive the greatest assistance, however, from German prisoners of war who began to arrive here in 1944. Iowa officials established two prisoner base camps, at Algona and Clarinda. One and a half miles west of the city limits, the Algona camp contained 286 acres and could house up to three thousand prisoners as well as 500 military guards. The facility included frame barracks, mess halls, an electric distribution system, and water and sewage facilities.[4]

In addition to the two base camps, officials established nine branch or side camps. In turn, the branch camps sent contingents of workers out to surrounding communities. The Eldora branch or side camp, for example, sent workers to Hampton, Reinbeck, Grundy Center, and Ackley. There prisoners worked in canning and hemp plants, did agricultural work, and assisted with construction of a rural electrification line.[5]

County extension reports indicate that, generally, Iowa farmers were pleased with the prisoners' work. In 1944 the Page County extension agent reported that "12,491 man days of prisoner labor were used ... by some 60 different farmer employers." In effect, each farmer negotiated a contract with camp officials for the labor. The Kossuth County agent reported that prisoners typically worked in groups of three to five to shock and thresh grain, make hay, and pull weeds. The Fremont County agent estimated that in 1945 the prisoners' labor "would be equivalent to every farmer in Fremont County using one prisoner for a period of about 10 days' time." Later in the war, Italian and Japanese prisoners would also be sent to Iowa.[6]

The arrival of German prisoners in rural Iowa aroused considerable interest. In July 1944 the *Kossuth County Advance* carried a firsthand account of the arrival of more than one thousand German prisoners at Algona: "Some of the prisoners looked no more than 15 or 16 years old, and others looked 40 or better. They were well behaved and marched in unison." A few months later a reporter from the same paper observed four hundred prisoners arriving at Algona; the additional months of war had obviously taken a toll: "They were a non-descript group. Clad in dirty, some ragged, remainders of what had at one time been uniforms, all of them filthy, all of them appearing exhausted, weary, weak. ... These German prisoners of war were a beaten and subdued ... group of boys and old men." The reporter added that all prisoners appeared "unshaven, unkempt, dirty, lousy, many of them so filthy that sores appeared on their bodies."[7]

Given the dual pressures of labor shortages and the need for increased production, farmers quickly adopted new machinery wherever available. In many cases, however, they had to "make do" with what they had. When International Harvester made one automatic hay baler available in Polk County, sixty-four people applied for it. The Polk County USDA's War Board convinced "nine or 10 farmers to take turns using the machine so it would run day and night." Overall during the war, farmers shifted from human labor to machines whenever possible. That shift, along with better equipment and increased use of chemical fertilizer, pesticides, and hybrid seed corn (by 1943 almost 100 percent of Iowa farmers used hybrid seed) made greater production possible. Increased use of mechanization, however, also meant fewer farmers and less need for farm workers. In 1940 Iowa contained 212,318 farms; by 1945 that number had decreased by 3,300.[8]

During the war large numbers of Iowans served in the armed forces. As countless numbers of veterans have stated, World War II was the good war. Antiwar sentiment existed before Pearl Harbor, but Americans quickly became united behind the war effort. By 1944 state officials estimated that 261,000 men and 4,000 women were in the military. Of that number nearly 8,400 lost their lives. The war brought even further mobility as an estimated 24,000 Iowans left the state looking for defense-related work. The casualties of war would also involve those on disability: By March 1946, 19,948 World War II veterans were receiving disability pensions.[9]

The greatest sacrifice for an Iowa family came with the death of five Sullivan brothers from Waterloo. Joseph, Francis, Albert, George, and Madison Sullivan all served aboard the USS *Juneau*. On November 13, 1942, the Japanese torpedoed their ship. Out of 728 crewmen aboard the *Juneau*, only ten were still alive when rescued several days later.[10]

During the war Iowa had four military training centers: the naval training base in Ottumwa, the B-17 training base in Sioux City, the Women's Army Corps training base in Des Moines, and the Women Accepted for Volunteer Emergency Services training base in Cedar Falls. SPARs, members of the United States Coast Guard Women's Reserve, would also train at Cedar Falls for a short time. Though Iowa had been home to army posts and training centers for males dating back to territorial days, training centers for females placed Iowa in the vanguard of women's military experience.

On November 23, 1942, Congress created the SPARs and Iowa State Teachers College (now University of Northern Iowa) became a training center for the first group of 150 women who enlisted. Their first instructors were male and female naval officers rather than coast-guard personnel. SPAR officers arrived later and taught "the usual military courses—rates and ranks, insignia, nautical terms and customs and courtesies" along with coast-guard history. When the women completed four weeks of training at Cedar Falls, they held the rank of seamen second class.[11]

Mary Jane Klein was among the women SPARs trained in Cedar Falls. She later recalled that the first day at boot camp was relaxed, but at 0530 the next morning the recruits "heard a shrill whistle and a booming voice give forth with 'hit the deck.'" Klein also recalled another activity during an Iowa winter: "Frozen in my mind are the chilling memories of the fire drills at 0200 or any hour before dawn, as I picture the long line of pajamas and robes planted in two feet of snow like stalks of corn, while the officers pretended that the dormitory was afire."[12]

Iowa also served as the site of a WAVEs training school located at Iowa State Teachers College. The first group arrived in December 1942, and for the next twenty-nine months some 14,000 women spent six weeks in training at Cedar Falls, occupying Bartlett Hall. Women served as hospital technicians, mechanics, parachute riggers, aviation mechanics, chauffeurs, messengers, photographers, clerks, meteorologist's assistants, and other special workers. Each WAVE was to replace a man for sea duty. Initially the navy tried to condense eight weeks of training into four but soon decided that six weeks was more reasonable.[13]

The largest Iowa military training center for women was Fort Des Moines, which served as the first training center for Women's Army Auxiliary Corps recruits. The initial contingent of 450 women arrived in Des Moines in July 1942; the women had been carefully selected out of a total group of 150,000 applicants. On August 4, 1943, WAAC Director Oveta Culp Hobby administered an oath to the women that transformed the WAACs into the Women's Army Corp (WACs), making them a part of the United States Army.

Once under way, the camp soon included 11,000 trainees. As new recruits arrived, additional city facilities, including the Coliseum and three buildings on the Drake campus, were used for training purposes. Women were also quartered in Des Moines hotels such as the Plaza, Savery, and Chamberlain. During the base's four-and-a-half-year tenure, 72,141 women received training there. In December 1945 the training program officially ended, and Fort Des Moines became one of six separation centers for WACs.

Charity Adams was among the first group of women to arrive at Fort Des Moines on July 19, 1942, to begin officers' training school. Adams remembered the fort as being "so beautiful and well kept, one would never think of it as military." Born and raised in Columbia, South Carolina, Adams was one of thirty-nine African-American women who made up the Third Platoon of the First Company of the First Training Regiment. Although raised in the South, Adams was astounded when on the first day a young male officer announced: "Will all the colored girls move over on this side?" Adams recalled that "there was a moment of stunned silence, for even in the United States in the forties it did not occur to us that this could happen." Soldiers then escorted the women to their segregated barracks. Adams became the first African-American woman to receive a commission in the WAACs and remained at Fort Des Moines for almost three years.[14]

World War II would also bring great change to Des Moines and other major cities through the expansion of industrial facilities. Hundreds of Iowa firms converted to wartime production, and many new firms were established as a result of wartime needs. In Waterloo seventeen war plants employed more than 14,000 workers, 10,000 male and 4,000 female. The John Deere Tractor Company employed the largest number, 5,763, to make tractors, aircraft parts, and tank transmissions and final drives. The second-largest firm, Rath Packing Company, employed 4,756 workers to produce boneless beef, processed meats, and lard for the military and for the Lend-Lease program. Other Waterloo firms produced a wide variety of products, including service tools for the army and navy, army cot covers, military clothing, tow targets for the army air force, and platform trailers for the Seabees.[15]

Other Iowa cities and towns shared Waterloo's experience as new defense companies came into existence and existing companies switched to war production. In Newton the Maytag Company produced fighter-plane parts; in Ankeny, an ammunition plant employed some 18,000 workers who loaded .30- to .50-caliber bullets; in Burlington 12,000 workers loaded artillery shells and large aerial bombs. In Muscatine, Roy Carver bought an empty sauerkraut factory to build pumps, the result of a military contract he had been awarded. That business would provide the financial base for the future Bandag, Inc., a multimillion-dollar tire retreading company. Some firms received a financial boost from government contracts that led to major expansion both during and after the war. Weitz Construction built two large, multimillion dollar munitions plants in Iowa and Wisconsin and grain alcohol plants in Iowa. Today the company is one of the largest construction firms in the state.[16]

The impact of World War II on Iowa's economic status was major. In 1939, according to a postwar study, Iowa contained 2,541 industrial establishments with 64,773 workers; the value added by that manufacturing was $243,390,000. By 1947 the number of industrial firms had increased to 2,965 with 112,490 workers, and the value added by that production was $671,100,000. The federal government estimated that 154 new facilities were started in Iowa during World War II.[17] Moreover, the war acted as an impetus for the later creation of additional industries.

Along with food, ammunition, and army clothing, rope was also needed by the military. When hemp, the raw material used to make the product, could no longer be imported, Iowa farmers were urged to grow it. In January 1943 the *Kossuth County Advance* reported that "hemp is a cash crop, paying good money per acre—a better return than any other cash crop." In the Humboldt area some farmers realized as much as $200 an acre for their efforts. By 1943 the government had established eleven hemp-processing mills in Iowa, at a cost of about $4 million, where workers separated the fiber from the stalk. The fibers were then sent to factories in the eastern United States for processing into rope.[18]

Given current attitudes about marijuana use, and its illegal status, an amusing sidelight of hemp production concerns the wartime workers' view of the substance as a mind-altering drug. Harold Ennis, night foreman at the Humboldt plant during the war, recalled that the eighty workers "were so naive they didn't question a government official's explanation that marijuana grown in the United States could not be smoked." Ennis contends that with that explanation, workers simply dismissed the possibility of smoking the plant. He added that the No Smoking signs around the plant referred to cigarette smoking only![19]

A major change occurred in the labor force during the war as women went to work in larger numbers than ever before. Although the percentage of Iowa women working outside the home had been increasing since 1900 (except for the decade between 1910 and 1920), the greatest increase would come during World War II: Between 1940 and 1944 the number of working women increased 56 percent. Iowa women, like their counterparts elsewhere, would be employed in almost every capacity. Women worked in the hemp plants in northwest Iowa, making up 20 percent of the labor force at the Algona plant.[20] In Waterloo, women began to drive city buses. In Burlington, women worked in an ammunitions plant.[21]

A group of seventeen women in Clinton replaced Chicago and North Western Railroad workers. Known as "WIPEs," the women cleaned the locomotives with live steam, loaded sand into the sand domes (used for driver-wheel traction), and did work in the roundhouse. The Chicago and North Western issued numerous news releases, complete with photos of the women dressed in greasy coveralls and railroad caps working on the huge engines. Captions typically compared the women's cleaning of engines to their traditional work. In May 1943 a caption read: "Beauty treatment for an iron horse is a far cry from the facials Mrs. Edith Bennis, former beauty operator, used to give. Mrs. Bennis, whose husband is working on an army construction project in Alaska, gives a facial here to a 1600 North Western locomotive. She has since been promoted to turn table operator in the round house."[22]

For African-American women the war would also bring change. Both black males and females, in fact, found employment in higher-paying jobs, often left vacant by men going into the military. The greatest increase in black women's employment would come in industries such as shipbuilding in Seattle; many women also moved to Detroit to work in defense plants such as Willow Run. And for black women everywhere, wartime opportunities meant moving out of domestic work into higher-paying positions. Although no studies have been done on the subject, given these opportunities nationwide, it seems fair to assume that African Americans in Iowa also found considerable opportunities for job advancement. Some blacks probably moved outside the state to find work during the war, but census figures do not reflect out-migration: In 1940 blacks totaled 16,694 and in 1950, 19,692.[23] It seems likely that in Iowa some blacks moved here to take advantage of wartime jobs, and some blacks moved from small Iowa communities into urban areas such as Des Moines and Davenport.

Iowa women went to work for a variety of reasons. Many were motivated to work outside the home for financial gain, while others responded to the government's emotional, patriotic appeals for war workers. Early in the war the federal government believed it could meet the labor demands through its traditional labor supply. But by 1943, as more and more men were drafted, it became clear that new sources of labor were needed. The government then began a campaign to attract more women into the labor market, including married women with children. Slogans abounded such as "The More Women at Work—The Sooner We'll Win."

The War Manpower Commission, responsible for mobilizing sufficient labor for the war industries, faced a challenge, however, in recruiting women. As Glenda Riley has pointed out, throughout American history women were regarded as a flexible labor supply "to be pulled out of the home when needed and pushed back in when not." A difficulty in the 1940s was that for some time women had been lectured that their major responsibilities were as wives and mothers, which necessitated full-time homemaking. As Riley points out, the government then had to "recast the image of women as potential workers."[24] The main recruitment came through the use of the image of Rosie the Riveter, an attractive young woman with a kerchief on her head. The song "Rosie the Riveter" was heard frequently, and Rosie's picture adorned posters everywhere.

While thousands of Iowans were directly involved in World War II through the military or war-defense work, even more people made contributions through buying war bonds, planting victory gardens, and conducting paper drives. Every community held war-bond rallies where donated items were auctioned off, with proceeds going to buy bonds. In Des Moines, city officials kicked off the fifth war-loan drive (with a goal of $51,115,000) in spectacular fashion by creating a mock battle. The battle began as fifteen civil-air-patrol planes "roared over 'third army' headquarters on Locust Street between Sixth Avenue and Seventh Street in a 'bombing foray.'" One hundred soldiers from Camp Dodge defended the area after they had "barricaded the street with sandbags, brought in jeeps, command cars, an armored car and an ambulance." The mock battle lasted for some twenty minutes as planes made two runs, dropping bombs made of two ounces of flour wrapped in thin paper.[25]

In Iowa's rural areas young people as well as adults contributed to the war effort. Boys' and girls' 4-H groups worked to promote the sale of bonds and stamps, assisting with local bond rallies, and canvassing their neighborhoods to secure pledges to buy bonds. 4-H members themselves bought bonds and stamps. Between July 1 and September 1, 1944, Kossuth

County 4-H girls bought almost $4,000 in war bonds. In Johnson County eleven different 4-H girls' clubs held auctions where they sold baked goods and dressed poultry. They received a total credit of $503,925 in war bonds.[26]

While most Iowans openly engaged in activities that supported the war, one group on a college campus had to maintain secrecy. Iowa State College played a role in the Manhattan Project, which developed the atom bomb. Early in the war, when scientists began working on the bomb, they faced a shortage of high-quality purified uranium. Two scientists on the ISC campus, Harley Wilhelm and William Keller, decided they would try to produce the material. According to a recent account, the two men "took a small iron pipe with a cap and sealed it at the bottom. They lined the container with magnesium oxide and poured in calcium and uranium tetrafluoride. They hooked up a Champion spark plug to spark an intense heating process." Wilhelm observed: "We opened it up and we had two ounces of nice pure uranium metal." Wilhelm then notified ISC professor Frank Spedding, head of the chemistry department and an expert in rare metals, who notified Arthur Compton at the University of Chicago. Soon a group at Iowa State College was producing more uranium. The group carried out their work in a former women's gym on the ISC campus. Wilhelm estimated that in total, the Ames group produced about one thousand tons of high-quality uranium. This research led to the establishment of the Ames Laboratory at ISU, which continues to do research related to energy problems.[27]

After almost four years of death and destruction, World War II came to an end and Iowans prepared for the transition to a peacetime society. Men and women returned from military life, many to resume the activities they had known before the war. For thousands of returning veterans, however, a brighter future lay ahead because of federal legislation passed in 1944: The GI Bill of Rights offered financial support so veterans could work for a college degree. Nationally, by 1946, almost one out of every two students was on the GI Bill.[28] In Iowa, institutions of higher learning built temporary housing units for returning GIs and their families, some of which still stand today. As a result many males did not go back to the farm, the coal mines, or the factories, but rather pursued careers as teachers, engineers, or accountants.

In the immediate years after the war, Iowans gratefully forgot about shortages and rationing. Housewives eagerly looked forward to purchasing new refrigerators and other household appliances unavailable throughout the duration. Farm families who had failed to receive electricity before the war looked forward to the renewed construction of rural electrification lines. After the war many farm families had sufficient funds to remodel homes or construct new ones. And Iowa families everywhere could purchase sugar, gasoline, and even shoes without ration stamps.

By 1950 the nation would find itself in another military struggle, but the Korean War seemed to have only minimal impact on the state as a whole. In fact, it is hard to find much mention of the conflict in most popular publications. Apparently more important to Iowans were topics such as the weather, the price of corn and hogs, increases in industrial employment, school consolidation, and the political issue of reapportionment of the state legislature. Aside from specific concerns, however, the decade of the 1950s represented a transitional time when urban population outstripped rural population and urban interests increasingly took precedence over rural concerns. That transition would become increasingly visible throughout the decade.

Even though rural influence would decline during the fifties, Iowa agriculture remained the dominant economic consideration throughout the state. Iowa farmers prospered during World War II, and that prosperity continued into the early 1950s. By 1953, however, farm organizations such as Iowa's Cooperative Extension were lamenting the dismal outlook for the state's farm families. Agricultural economists at Iowa State College issued *The Iowa Basebook for Agricultural Adjustment,* which expressed puzzlement over the fact that while the general economy was improving, agriculture was experiencing a downturn. The report stated that "agriculture was out of adjustment with the rest of the national economy; resources elsewhere in the economy were earning increasing returns while returns to resources in agriculture were decreasing."[29] By 1956 hog prices were about half of what economists believed to be a fair price, and returns on feeder cattle "could hardly pay [the farmer's] feed bill for the 12- to 18-month fattening period."[30]

By mid-decade everyone from the governor to small-town businessmen expressed growing concern over the depressed state of agriculture. In 1955, as a result of protest meetings, farmers in southwest Iowa and northwest Missouri organized a new agricultural group, the National Farm Organization. Formally organized in October, by December the organization claimed a dues-paying membership of fifty-five thousand.[31] By 1956 some Iowans were even speculating that a "farm revolt" was in the making for the presidential election. Although that revolt did not materialize, farm protest was evident throughout the state.

Frequent drought throughout the fifties further aggravated agricultural problems. By 1956 farmers in various parts of Iowa had experienced drought for four consecutive years, and as always, agricultural conditions impacted all other economic activities. As one publication explained it: "In a preeminently farming area, a medium-poor agricultural year can be expected to affect general business activity like a stubborn head cold—it just spoils everything, and drags on and on." Poor agricultural conditions would continue until the end of the decade.[32]

During 1953, the first year of the agricultural downturn, a seemingly insignificant issue surfaced but attracted so much attention that one Iowa journalist called it "this year's Number 1 legislative problem." The issue was legalizing the sale of yellow oleomargarine and repealing a tax on the product. Many Iowans, especially those living in larger communities, probably tended to dismiss the whole matter as somewhat silly, but to the state's dairy farmers it was of extreme importance. Complicating the issue further was the fact that four of the states surrounding Iowa sold yellow oleo, so Iowans often purchased the product out of state. Merchants in border communities complained they lost sixteen thousand dollars in sales annually. The issues of legalizing yellow-colored oleo and repealing the five- cents-per-pound tax on margarine took up one hundred days of debate in the General Assembly in 1953 and attracted widespread attention.[33]

The oleomargarine controversy had plagued Iowa's dairy farmers since the product had first been introduced around 1880. By 1886 Iowa's General Assembly passed legislation regulating "the manufacture, packing, sales and serving" of the product. Later legislation included an "anti-yellow color" law and restrictions on names for the product "that suggested any connection ... with a cow, dairy, or creamery." In 1931, with the state mired in a depression, legislators passed a five-cents-per-pound tax on oleo intended to raise revenue for the state's general fund. The first year of the legislation resulted in $165,724 from the sale of 3,319,911 pounds of oleo.[34]

In 1953 the Fifty-Fifth General Assembly took up the issue of legalizing yellow oleo and repealing the five-cent tax. Debates became emotional, even "acrimonious." Supporters of dairy farmers claimed that because people buying oleo might think they were actually getting butter, they [the legislators] were simply "trying to ... protect the consumer from getting cheated." The debate reached a particularly emotional moment when the representative from Anamosa, presumably speaking for all fifteen thousand persons in prisons, mental hospitals, and other facilities, including the prison facility in his hometown, asked: "Do you want oleo forced on people who have no choice in what they eat, many of whom cannot read or write? Or are deaf or cannot see?" As George Mills reported: "After weeks of struggle, the 1953 Legislature voted to legalize yellow oleo."[35]

The oleo legislation, allowing margarine to compete on equal terms with butter, represented a victory for the growing urban forces in Iowa and, as such, underscored the most significant change under way in Iowa in the 1950s. In that decade Iowa's population ceased to be primarily rural. As Leland Sage has pointed out, 1956 was "a watershed year in Iowa history, the memorable year in which the charts showed the ascending urban line and the descending rural line bisecting each other." Iowa's estimated population in 1956 revealed 1,362,000 urban residents, compared to 1,360,375 Iowans living on farms and in communities of 2,500 or fewer. Federal census figures in 1960 reinforced that shift, as 47 percent of Iowans were then classified as rural and 53 percent urban.[36]

Population shifts from rural to urban had been moderate but fairly steady since the latter nineteenth century. In 1880, 84.8 percent of Iowans lived in rural areas, which included towns of fewer than 2,500.[37] Following that date the number of rural residents would gradually decline, although Iowa would remain more rural than the nation as a whole, which in 1920 showed an urban majority. As farms increased in size and became more mechanized, the number of farm residents declined, and some farm residents relocated in cities and towns. With mechanization, moreover, fewer farms needed hired help, which necessitated a further drop in farm population. World War II also had a major impact on the state's demographics as the *Des Moines Sunday Register* reported:

> Between 1940 and 1950, the larger centers in Iowa almost without exception gained in population. The rural areas and small towns lost. The war was a major factor in the population shift. High wages and good working conditions in war plants attracted thousands of rural people to

the cities, both inside Iowa and in other cities. Most of the migration was permanent. Also, many of the farm youths who served in the armed forces haven't returned to the farm to live.[38]

Hand in glove with growing urbanization was increasing industrial development. As a result of World War II, Iowa witnessed an increase in the number of industrial operations, but that sector did not continue to expand spontaneously; by 1947 business and economic leaders were expressing concern over the state's lagging industrial development, compared to the national average. State officials and community leaders then began an intensive effort to reverse the trend; throughout the fifties, reports abounded on both the expansion of older industries and the establishment of new ones. The Iowa Development Commission reported in 1955 that the state had 3,736 manufacturing plants, and almost 1,000 plants had been established since 1945. While 37.7 percent of these operations were located in Iowa's thirteen largest cities, 2,023 industries were found in communities with a population under ten thousand.[39]

Most of Iowa's industrial activity continued to be centered in the fields of meat packing and production of farm equipment. Almost every major city in the state had a meat-packing operation, whereas Sioux City had four major firms. John Deere, with plants in Ottumwa, Dubuque, Ankeny, and Waterloo, ranked as the state's largest industrial employer, with a total of approximately ninety-five hundred workers.

In keeping with officials' determination to bring more industry to the state, by 1956 sixty-two communities had drawn up industrial-development programs and had lands set aside and commissions established to "make each community the most attractive location possible for new industrial plants." In his message to the Fifty-Seventh General Assembly, Governor Herschel Loveless described Iowa as the "'twin empire' state with balanced agriculture and industry." He added that in 1955–56, the state experienced its greatest industrial growth as 183 new operations got under way involving ten thousand new jobs.[40]

Throughout the fifties the Iowa Development Commission ran "testimonial-type" advertisements in newspapers and magazines emphasizing Iowa's successful business operations and favorable environment for economic growth. These ads, as well as statements by political and business leaders, stressed that Iowa's economy was indeed diversified and also balanced between agriculture and industry. Public officials seemed to be proclaiming: Iowa is on the move, and moving in the right direction! Indicative of that spirit, a popular magazine carried articles on Iowa's different communities, such as Waterloo, where the headlines announced: "Waterloo: The Story of Iowa's Industrial Giant, a City Where Tractors Are Born and Hogs Die on the Assembly Line."[41]

While industrial development was a natural parallel to increased urban growth, a further parallel came in the form of political change. From 1856, when the first Republican governor had been elected, until the mid-1950s, only three Democrats had occupied the governorship. In effect, rural Iowans repeatedly voted Republican. In the 1950s, however, the Republicans, heavily influenced by the Iowa Manufacturers Association and the American Farm Bureau Federation, would face real challenges from Democrats in urban areas. Those challenges would continue until by the 1960s Iowa Democrats were well on their way to creating a balanced two-party system.

The first major evidence of change came in 1956, when Democrat Herschel Loveless defeated Republican Leo Hoegh for the governorship. Changes, however, had also been underway in Des Moines, where in 1948 Democrats became the majority party in the Polk County courthouse. According to James Larew in his study of the Democratic party in Iowa, starting in the 1950s the Democrats "developed organizational strategies and techniques in urban politics which led to the establishment of their first solid political base in Iowa's most populous city, Des Moines." The Democrats then expanded their appeal to the rest of the state.[42]

The 1956 gubernatorial campaign involved several major issues. As attorney general in 1953–54, incumbent Hoegh had vigorously enforced the state's liquor laws, which prohibited liquor-by-the-drink. The issue involved a rural-urban split as urban communities generally favored liberalizing the state's liquor laws. Six of Iowa's largest cities were along the state's borders, where, businessmen lamented, Iowans crossed state lines to drink, thus depriving Iowa businessmen of profits.

Not all issues divided along rural-urban lines, including tax issues, which played a significant part in the campaign. During his first term Hoegh had strongly urged an increase in state aid to public schools, more money for higher education, and a bonus for Korean War veterans. In his budget message in 1954, the governor proposed spending almost $24 million more than in the previous budget. The major tax issue, however, involved raising the state's 2 percent sales tax to 2.5 percent, a bill that

Hoegh had signed into law. Larew explains that "Loveless made good use of the issue and stung Governor Hoegh with a campaign epithet: 'High Tax Hoegh.'" All the additional spending, moreover, came during a time when Iowa's farmers, the state's largest economic group, were experiencing hard times.[43]

Yet another major concern to farmers and small-town residents in the fifties was the matter of school consolidation. Public education had been of vital importance to Iowans since territorial days, and in the 1950s demographic change would affect the state's smaller school districts. During that decade the legislature made significant changes in regard to school consolidation, funding, and control. Although all these areas were important, consolidation was the most visible—and emotional—issue. Most small-town residents undoubtedly viewed consolidation as designed to favor urban interests at the expense of smaller communities. During the fifties state officials would strongly promote larger school districts.

The trend toward increased school consolidation had been evident since the latter 1800s. In the nineteenth century Iowa had some 12,600 rural schools, mostly supported by local property-tax levies. These schools varied dramatically in size and quality of instruction; a few schools had only one student, while about one-fourth of the schools had fewer than ten students. As Joseph Wall has pointed out, a single township might have anywhere from thirty-five to forty-five school-board members administering eight or nine schools for a total of thirty to forty students.[44]

In 1897 a major change was initiated when Buffalo Township in Winnebago County created the first consolidated township school in Buffalo Center. The action of township officials rested on recent legislation that authorized consolidation "when there will be a saving of expense and the children will also thereby secure increased advantages." As township officials began closing country schools, they then transported children to the new town school in six horse-drawn hacks. A limited number of districts followed suit; by 1921 there were 439 consolidated school districts in the state.[45]

In 1953 further changes in public education ensued when the state legislature took what one historian has called "two heroic steps" regarding public education: They first created the Board of Public Instruction, a nine-member bipartisan group with power to appoint the state superintendent of public instruction (thus removing the office from political pressure). The state superintendent had authority to supervise the state's secondary-school program. The legislature then replaced the 1897 consolidation law with the Community School District Act, declaring two years later that every "unit in the state must become a part of a high school district by July 1, 1962" (later modified to July 1, 1966). Every new district, moreover, had to have at least three hundred pupils, thus insuring, legislators believed, that a larger number of courses would be offered and teachers would be more qualified than before.[46]

The push for school consolidation continued in 1955 as the State Department of Public Instruction asked the legislature for $11 million to be used as "incentive aid." The money would be used to "encourage the formation of larger school administrative units." The department also requested that the minimum number of students in a reorganized district school be raised from three hundred to six hundred. The legislature failed to grant either request.[47]

By the 1950s advocates and opponents of school consolidation were making their views known, including Iowa's governor. In his message to the legislature in 1957, shortly before leaving office, Governor Hoegh noted that continuing school mergers had reduced districts from 4,417 in June 1954 to 3,600 by the end of 1956, but he believed that more incentives were needed to speed up the consolidation process.[48] Advocates of school consolidation argued that mergers would result in better educational opportunities for all children, including improved instruction, less-expensive schools, better equipment, more modern schools, and the offering of more extracurricular activities.

Though the state certainly had citizens who agreed with Governor Hoegh, thousands of small-town residents did not and responded with considerable emotion. Advocates of larger schools might believe that they were helping Iowa's students deal more effectively with the modern world, but small-town dwellers typically envisioned only negative results, such as the stifling of individual thought. To many, small schools represented the "last stronghold of democracy close to the people." Advocates of small schools argued that they allowed for individual attention and that small districts were among the "most efficiently operated democratic government units in the world."[49]

Small-school advocates also believed that the social consequences of larger schools could be devastating, possibly resulting in the "destruction of the small town in America." But the movement to larger schools obviously would have economic consequences also. Many small-town dwellers saw the loss of the local high school as tantamount to economic decline. High-school functions attracted family members for sporting, musical, and dramatic events. The town with the high school thus served as a social center for local families, which usually translated into business for small-town merchants. Regardless of impassioned pleas, however, the trend toward consolidation continued throughout the 1950s and into the decades beyond.

Viewed in a wider context, the merging of school districts into larger units provided yet another example of the decline of rural interests in the fifties. If urban interests represented the wave of the future, and an increasing number of Iowans believed they did, through consolidation, small-town schools were being recast in the likeness of urban educational institutions. For many small-town residents the loss of the high school, the busing of local children to a nearby community, and the further decline of local businesses seemed the dominant issues rather than more modern educational facilities and broader curricula.

Of all issues facing Iowans in the 1950s, however, reapportionment was the major one reflecting Iowa's transition from a rural to an urban state. The issue also focused greater attention on the power struggle between rural and urban interests. According to the Iowa Constitution, the General Assembly must reapportion itself after every federal census. Rural legislators who controlled the General Assembly had long refused to deal with the issue, and as a result, reapportionment haunted lawmakers in every legislative session in the decade. Veteran legislative observer Frank T. Nye of the *Cedar Rapids Gazette* wrote in his assessment of the Fifty-Sixth legislature that as a result of the legislature's refusal to deal with the issue, the situation "promised to become one of the hottest issues" confronting the next session. Nye believed the situation in Iowa was not unlike that in many other states "where legislatures have steadfastly refused to act on reapportionment which in each instance, would effect rural-urban representation to the very obvious disadvantage of farm communities."[50] Although Nye said nothing about reapportionment in his summary of the Fifty-Seventh General Assembly two years later, he reported that the legislature had introduced five resolutions dealing with the issue; however, they all failed to become law.[51]

By 1959 both large and small newspapers around the state were calling for action on reapportionment. The *Dubuque Telegraph-Herald* called
the inaction a "deplorable failure." Small community newspapers supported action as well; the *Williamsburg Journal-Tribune and Shopper* declared: "We feel that those who opposed any reapportionment 'missed the
boat' because reapportionment in some form is going to come as sure as
'death and taxes'."[52] But even with governors, urban legislators, and
newspapers editors calling for action, the reapportionment issue would remain unresolved throughout the fifties.

Although urban population increased in the fifties, this change should
not be allowed to overshadow the continued importance of Iowa's smaller
communities. Like open-country residents, small-town citizens believed
their children were exposed to proper moral values, a good work ethic,
personal responsibility, and self-sufficiency. For all its physical change,
Iowa remained strongly influenced by the values and perceptions of small-
town residents. Moreover, the hundreds of communities under twenty-five
hundred still accounted for the image that Iowa projected to the world—
that of America's heartland, where people still found the most basic values as well as social stability. The view of the heartland, with its enduring
qualities of honesty, self-reliance, and hard work, emanated from the open
country and the small towns, not from the emerging industrial centers such
as Des Moines or Waterloo. The moral values of most Iowans, regardless
of residence, were perceived to be those espoused by small-town citizens.

The years between 1945 and 1960 brought major change. Iowans
readjusted to a peacetime economy when prosperity on the farm—and,
consequently, in the towns—seemed an enduring way of life. In 1953,
however, that prosperity vanished when farming experienced a downturn,
a highly significant event for a state heavily dependent on agriculture. Perhaps of greatest importance between 1945 and 1960 was the transition toward a more urban orientation; this trend rested on several major changes,
particularly a population shift toward the cities and a major increase in industrial operations. The state's experience in World War II helped foster
positive social attitudes toward industrial expansion, and that positive outlook blossomed during the fifties as economic development became the
watchword heard throughout the state.

By 1960 Iowa was entering a new era. For the first time agriculture and industry were fairly balanced in terms of economic importance; urban areas were growing and, in turn, residents were becoming more vocal about inadequate representation in the state legislature. Reapportionment and other urban-favored issues, such as liquor-by-the-drink, would become realities in the next two decades as Iowans witnessed a growing equality between the Republican and Democrat parties. The 1950s represented the last of the old order, during which rural life had clearly dominated. The decade, therefore, served as a major transition to a new, more urban-directed future.

16

Iowa in the Sixties and Seventies

I n the 1960s and 1970s Iowans would leave behind the difficult days
of the fifties and move into an era with a greatly improved economy.
Agriculture would recover early in the sixties, and by the next
decade many farm families were experiencing robust times. Because agriculture was (and is) the engine that propels other sectors of the
economy, including manufacturing and retail trade, those areas also enjoyed prosperity. Some concerns of the fifties carried over, however.
Rural-urban tensions did not go away as urban populations continued to
grow at the expense of rural areas, and Iowa legislators struggled to respond to urban needs and concerns. Reapportionment remained the dominant issue facing the state legislature, an issue that received serious at-

*Iowa's varied landscape is illustrated in this view of the
Loess Hills in western Iowa. Photo courtesy of the State
Historical Society, Iowa City.*

tention in the 1960s and was finally resolved in the early seventies. Liquor-by-the-drink, another issue strongly favored by urban interests, finally became law. Politically, the Democratic party made major gains in winning state offices as well as improving their statewide party organization. Iowa remained a fairly balanced state politically, with both parties boasting popular governors. In general, during the sixties and seventies, most Iowans enjoyed some prosperity and witnessed a society influenced more heavily than before by urban constituents.

Reapportionment, the issue that would not go away throughout the 1950s and 1960s, finally reached closure in 1972. During the 1950s, as urban population increased, rural legislators refused to take action that would diminish their power. In the 1960s legislators struggled with the difficult issue in each session of the legislature, facing special sessions and court challenges. They finally agreed on a plan in the late sixties, but it proved temporary: In 1971 the supreme court ruled the plan unconstitutional and imposed a court reapportionment plan. As a result, by 1972 Iowa had the most equitably apportioned state legislature in the nation.[1]

The struggle for an equitable reapportionment plan would involve not only population shifts but also roadblocks imposed by earlier political action. In 1904 and 1928 amendments were added to the state constitution that made it "virtually impossible" to reapportion the General Assembly on the basis of population. The first amendment provided for a 108-member House "with one representative from each county, except for the nine most populous counties which were granted two representatives." The second amendment stipulated that no county, regardless of population, could have more than one senator in the 50-member Senate. Given the reluctance of rural legislators to give up power and the presence of the 1904 and 1928 amendments, Iowa had not been reapportioned to compensate for urban growth since 1886.[2]

After World War II, conservative forces made up of Iowa's rural legislators and represented most visibly by the Iowa Farm Bureau Federation and the Iowa Manufacturers Association, resisted change by adopting several strategies. At first they argued there was no need for reapportionment, as they were properly looking after the interests of all Iowans. Around 1955, however, they changed to a position favoring reapportionment, but with the condition that "adequate safeguards be provided to assure area representation to one chamber of the legislature." This latter position led to a proposed constitutional amendment eventually known as the Shaff Plan. The amendment carried the name of its proposer, David Shaff—a senator from Clinton. The proposed change called for the Senate to be apportioned on a population basis and the House on an area basis, but with the guarantee that there would be one representative from each county. As Charles Wiggins has pointed out, the rural forces had proposed a plan that would guarantee them "a future veto power in one chamber."[3]

Supporters of reapportionment reacted with some negativism. Although they were pleased that conservatives finally agreed that change was necessary, they did not agree that the proposed Shaff Plan (sometimes known as the Shaft Plan) was the right approach. For the next five years neither group had sufficient numbers to pass a constitutional plan on reapportionment, but rather succeeded in checkmating each other's moves.[4]

By 1960 supporters of reapportionment had concluded that the best means to obtain their goal was through a constitutional convention. Conservatives responded pessimistically that if held, the convention might result in unwanted change in other issues, such as liquor-by-the-drink and higher taxes; therefore, they opposed holding the convention. In the November election in 1960 Iowans rejected the constitutional convention. According to Charles Wiggins, the split, mainly along urban-rural lines, might have been influenced by voting methods. Voters in rural areas— with separate paper ballots—voted in higher numbers on the constitutional amendment than did urban voters, who used electric machines.[5]

The next step in the reapportionment battle was a vote on the Shaff Plan, but before that could take place, a legal challenge was issued against the reapportionment plan already in effect. The head of the Iowa Federation of Labor filed suit in federal district court in Des Moines asserting that the current plan was unconstitutional. The plaintiff also asked the court to rule on the constitutionality of the proposed Shaff Plan. The court concurred that the then-active reapportionment arrangement was unconstitutional but withheld an opinion on the Shaff Plan because of the upcoming referendum. That vote was taken at a special referendum in December 1963, and with urban voters strongly opposed, the Shaff Plan went down to defeat.[6]

With the prevailing system held to be unconstitutional, the legislature met in special session in February 1964 and passed two reapportionment plans, one temporary and one permanent. The latter provided for a House based on population and a Senate based on area. Soon another legal obstacle appeared, however, when the head of the Iowa Federation of Labor requested a review of the two recently passed reapportionment acts, claiming neither law was in accordance with the recent United States Supreme Court decision, *Reynolds v. Sims* (1964). That decision set down the historic rule that both chambers of a state legislature must be apportioned on a population basis or on the "one man, one vote" principle. The federal district court ruled on the temporary reapportionment plan in February 1965, declaring it unconstitutional since it violated the "one man, one vote" rule in the apportioning of state Senate seats.[7] Further, the court ruled that the deficiency had to be corrected by the 1966 elections. The court did not rule on the permanent plan.

Between 1965 and 1972, when the state supreme court would present its own reapportionment plan, Iowa lawmakers continued to struggle with the issue. State elections would be carried out under both temporary plans, and plans already declared unconstitutional. In 1966 the legislature agreed to establish a bipartisan committee to draw up a new plan, a move possible, no doubt, only because the legislature was under divided control: Republicans controlled the House, and Democrats the Senate. At another point the legislature offered two reapportionment amendments at the same time, one permanent plan deemed to be unacceptable and another correcting the deficiencies of the first permanent plan. In 1968 voters overwhelmingly approved the permanent reapportionment amendment, which called for a House with one hundred members and a Senate with fifty. The plan, eventually implemented by the legislature, also called for reapportionment of both chambers on a population basis, with "the territory of districts being as compact and contiguous as possible."[8]

As with several previous reapportionment plans, a challenge quickly followed. In 1969 Democratic state chairman Clark Rasmussen brought suit, charging the new plan was unconstitutional because "it provided for too much population deviation among districts and for districts that were not as compact in territory as they could be." The following year the state supreme court concurred. Because there was no time to draw up a new temporary plan, elections in 1970 were carried out under a plan already declared unconstitutional.[9]

The reapportionment quagmire that began in 1950 would finally near resolution twenty-one years later when the state supreme court assumed responsibility for a permanent plan. In 1971 the legislature had drawn up yet another plan that was immediately challenged by a "liberal coalition" made up of five groups—the Iowa Civil Liberties Union, the League of Women Voters, the United Auto Workers, the Iowa Federation of Labor, and the Democratic party. These organizations filed three separate suits challenging the legality of the new plan. The state supreme court ruled on January 14, 1972, that the plan was unconstitutional, declaring that it "involved 'invidious discrimination' against voters in more populous districts, and this arrangement constituted violation of 'equal protection' under the federal constitution and the 'apportionment according to population' provision in the state constitution." The state supreme court then proceeded to draw up its own plan, completed in 1972. The court plan contained population deviations of less than one-tenth of 1 percent. After some twenty-two years of frustration, procrastination, and interparty feuding, Iowa had the most equitably districted legislature in the nation.[10]

Reapportionment battles would span the years that brought considerable change to Iowa's political leadership, both in the legislature and in the governor's office. The major change came with the growing vitality of the Democratic party, reflected clearly in the several challenges to Republican reapportionment plans and in the election of Governor Harold Hughes in 1962. Two years later Iowans reelected Hughes as well as a Democratic majority in both houses of the General Assembly; moreover, Iowans elected six Democrats (out of seven) to the U.S. House of Representatives. The Democratic sweep in Iowa corresponded with—and was undoubtedly influenced by—the Democratic landslide at the national level. For the Iowa Democrats it was a landslide of almost unbelievable proportions. At the top of the party stood Harold Hughes. Handsome, charismatic, and a spellbinder in front of an audience, Hughes perhaps best symbolized the Iowa Democratic party in the sixties, as well as the public persona of the decade. Hughes gave definition to the Democratic ideals and proved to be the party's most popular leader in many decades. And, though Democrats had started a comeback in the mid-1950s, Hughes played a major role (some would say *the* role) in ushering in the true renaissance of the party in the sixties.

The election of Harold Hughes seemed somewhat improbable in 1962. Norman Erbe, a popular two-term Iowa attorney general in the fifties, had been elected governor in 1960; Erbe was the Republican gubernatorial candidate again in 1962. Although Iowa was well on its way to becoming balanced in regard to political parties, the election of Hughes—

a reformed alcoholic, a former truck driver, and a man with minor political experience—seemed unlikely. Moreover, Hughes campaigned on the issue of liquor-by-the-drink, a seemingly illogical move by a reformed drinker, as well as an unlikely move in a socially conservative state like Iowa.[11] Hughes would win the governorship in 1962 and again in 1964 and 1966.

Once in office, Hughes began pushing an agenda of social and economic reform. The first campaign pledge realized was liquor-by-the-drink. Hughes believed that the state liquor statutes could not be enforced, because a majority of Iowans did not support them. Further, liquor was sold illegally in many parts of the state, which Hughes believed created an "atmosphere of hypocrisy." The issue, which had been pushed by urban interests throughout the fifties, commanded a great deal of attention in the 1962 campaign. Hughes later commented that "Liquor by the drink was probably the least important thing I did, even if it is the most remembered." As James Larew has observed, however, "repeal was important because it symbolized a new political attitude in the state."[12]

During his three terms as governor, Hughes would successfully promote numerous economic and social changes, many of which passed during the 1965 Democratic-controlled General Assembly. Included were a tax-withholding system, establishment of a state law-enforcement academy, creation of Iowa's first alcoholic-treatment facility, increased workers'-compensation benefits, creation of a human-rights commission, abolition of capital punishment, and creation of a statewide system of community colleges.[13] In his history of the Iowa Democratic party, James Larew writes:

> Hughes promoted "Great Society" attitudes toward taxes and social services. Whereas earlier governors had often denied the need for increased tax rates or had proposed to increase regressive sales taxes, Hughes supported new and primarily progressive taxes that would finance the broadened social service legislation. With the governor's prodding, legislators increased the state income tax rate levied on high income brackets and boosted taxes on cigarettes, on gasoline, and on inheritances.[14]

Hughes would also become involved in an emotional school controversy in the sixties that involved Iowa's Old Order Amish. In 1965, because of local antagonisms stemming from a recent school-consolidation referendum in Buchanan County, a longtime arrangement that allowed the

Amish to maintain two rural schools was terminated. Amish families who did not send their children to the public school were then fined. The situation soon became highly volatile when local school officials tried to transport Amish children forcibly into Oelwein to attend classes.[15]

Governor Hughes moved to cool passions and to seek a solution fair to both the Amish and the public-school authorities. After his reelection in 1966, Hughes borrowed the idea of his Republican opponent, William Murray, and established an advisory committee to examine the problem. The committee recommended that the Amish be allowed to run their own schools and to hire uncertified teachers, but their children would be tested periodically by officials from the State Department of Public Instruction. If Amish children performed satisfactorily on the tests, the school arrangement would continue. As James Larew has observed, the Amish controversy symbolized Iowa's transition from a rural to an urban society, highlighting the sometimes painful transitions along the way. At the same time, the incident showed that Governor Hughes was not afraid to immerse himself in potentially controversial situations when he believed larger issues were involved, such as preserving "inconvenient rural customs" in the "midst of Iowa's collective rush to the city."[16]

During his second term Hughes emphasized that Iowa's economy was on the move again. The state's general fund had a surplus of about $30 million, and for the first time the state's industrial production had "topped" $8 billion.[17] Certainly good times had returned to Iowa's most important industry, agriculture. Not only had farming become profitable again, but other important changes were taking place on the farm. For some time Iowa's farmers had been moving toward greater specialization and a stronger business orientation. These changes had produced, in the view of some, a new farmer, as Cooperative Extension director Floyd Andre noted in 1960: "[Keen observers] describe [Iowa's new farmer] as a professionally oriented man who sees his farm as a business, rather than solely as a 'way of life,' and who sees himself as a manager. He operates a highly capitalized business; he is increasingly in the cash market buying production items; his income is from sales on the market; and his family buys rather than produces goods used in family living."[18]

A similar view of agricultural change was described by a midwestern business leader, William A. Hewitt, chairman of Deere and Company: "We have all seen how the mechanical revolution changed American agriculture. Now a NEW revolution is unfolding in the United States, forged by a new kind of farmer—the businessman farmer. The key word of this new revolution is MANAGEMENT—it might well be called a farm management revolution."[19] Although all Iowans might not agree with these views, there was little doubt that Iowa farms had changed dramatically in terms of size, production, and labor roles since World War II.

The changes described by Andre and Hewitt reflected the trends that had been developing in agriculture since World War II. Farmers had started relying more heavily on mechanization even in the latter 1930s, and that trend accelerated during the war. In the last half of the forties and beyond, farmers moved rapidly toward greater use of commercial fertilizers and chemicals to control weeds and insects. At the same time, average acreages increased and the number of farms declined. Changes in the countryside then set off a chain reaction as small towns, always the service-and-retail centers for open-country residents, began to lose population and businesses. In turn, public-school populations declined and school consolidations became more common.

For the dwindling number of farm residents themselves, however, life on the farm had finally become synonymous with life in town. Historically, farm residents had long considered themselves second-class citizens because of social isolation and lack of modern conveniences. By the 1950s life on the farm could be as physically comfortable as elsewhere. With the advent of television, farm residents also had equal access to educational and entertainment programs. These changes resulted in many retired farm couples remaining on the farm rather than moving to town. The increasing number of females working off the farm was another experience shared with town women who worked outside the home.

By the 1960s yet another trend had appeared in rural Iowa. Historically, public officials had tended to look at rural areas as integrated units of society. In other words, farms and small towns were two parts of the same whole, with agriculture determining either prosperity or hard times. According to this long-held view, if agriculture was ailing, small towns were ailing; therefore, providing relief to farmers would in turn bring relief to small-town economies.

By the sixties state officials—particularly the Cooperative Extension Service—began looking at nonfarm rural entities in their own right. Although agriculture was generally doing well, some other rural areas remained depressed. The extension service, founded primarily to dispense new technological and scientific information to farm families, began reaching out to new rural constituencies including low-income families and senior citizens. Extension economists also provided assistance to small-town business leaders hoping to attract new industries to their communities.[20]

Adams County provides a case in point. In 1964 county extension director David May wrote in his annual report that his office had "reached out" to low-income residents in Adams County for the first time when he presented information on commodity foods. When it became evident that some low-income homemakers were interested in a makeover clothing project, May's office responded. May enlisted the aid of other extension personnel and local farm women belonging to the Iowa Farm Bureau Federation to assist with the project. The Singer Sewing Machine Company at Creston lent portable machines for the project. Twenty-two women then took part in six lessons during which they primarily remodeled used clothing into children's clothing. At the end of the project the participants held a potluck dinner and a style review in which their children modeled the clothing. May believed the project had been highly successful and that it clearly spoke to the needs of an income group that the extension had not served before.[21]

The extension service also responded to rural areas in other ways. In 1961 residents of ten counties in southern Iowa (Appanoose, Davis, Keokuk, Lucas, Mahaska, Marion, Monroe, Van Buren, Wapello, and Wayne) met to find ways to alleviate the areas' economic distress. In the previous decade the ten-county area had experienced dramatic declines in local businesses: Agricultural employment had declined by 35 percent, coal mining by 50 percent, and repair services by 33 percent. The group anticipated that public-school enrollment would drop by over four thousand in the 1960s. The ten-county effort, eventually named TENCO, cooperated with the ISU Extension Service to study economic problems on a regional basis.[22]

In the sixties attention also focused on low-income families residing in urban centers. No doubt the major impetus for this recognition was President Lyndon Johnson's War on Poverty, which made substantial federal funds available to eliminate poverty through programs in education, community development, and Volunteers in Service to America (VISTA), among others. In 1968 the USDA received $10 million from Congress to initiate the Expanded Food and Nutrition Education Program (EFNEP) to develop nutritional programs for low-income Americans. The Cooperative Extension Service administered the program in Iowa, selecting twelve sites including both urban and rural communities. In Des Moines the extension service hired paraprofessionals to present twelve lessons prepared by ISU home economists for young low-income homemakers.[23] The EFNEP continued operating through the 1980s.

Public education had long been a concern of Iowa lawmakers, and in the 1960s that concern manifested itself in the creation of a new type of educational institution. In keeping with the trend away from agricultural rural-based institutions to urban industrial facilities, the General Assembly—with the urging of Governor Hughes—provided for a system of community colleges.

A major impetus behind the founding of the new vocational schools stemmed naturally out of Iowa's increased industrialism, particularly evident in World War II. Earlier, with the passage of the Smith-Hughes Act in 1916, schools had provided for vocational training in agriculture and home economics; many high schools also taught secretarial courses. But during World War II and continuing into the fifties, an impressive number of new industrial firms began operation in Iowa, creating a greater demand for skilled workers. At the same time, given the many changes in production, such as industrial automation and electronics, a constant need existed for reeducating the workforce. By the 1950s and early 1960s it was apparent that changes in technology had created the need for expansion of programs, particularly in the areas of trade, industry, business, and service.[24]

A study of higher education initiated by the legislature also supported the need for additional education. The Gibson report, published in October 1960, predicted that during the next decade Iowa's colleges would experience a 70 percent increase in undergraduate college enrollment. The report recommended the creation of community colleges in different parts of the state that would teach two years of a general college curriculum and also "offer post high school vocational training in trades, industries, and other services." The General Assembly soon passed four related pieces of legislation, which, among other changes, increased state funding for vocational education.[25]

In 1961 the legislature directed the State Department of Public Instruction to develop a plan for community colleges offering two years of general college courses, and "to study the possibility and need for offering vocational-technical courses." The department's plan called for the creation of sixteen area districts "with enough population and taxable property in each district to support a public community college." Legislation allowed for public junior colleges (sixteen at the time) to be integrated into the area schools. By 1966, the initial year of operation for the community colleges, 10,165 students were attending sixteen area schools that provided two years of liberal-arts education, vocational and technical training, worker retraining, community services, and adult education courses. The area community colleges and centers have continued to grow both in student enrollments and in course offerings. By the mid-1980s fifteen area schools operated in Iowa, thirteen organized as community colleges and two as area vocational schools; nine have developed as multicampus institutions.[26]

One proposed educational institution that did not materialize was a four-year state college in western Iowa. Although capital funds had been allocated to the board of regents for purchase of a site near Atlantic, the idea was abandoned in the 1970s, no doubt at least partially because of the rapid expansion of community college campuses in Sheldon, Sioux City, Council Bluffs, Clarinda, and Creston.

In the same decade that community colleges opened, another longtime project would realize success: In 1965 the General Assembly created a state-funded Iowa Civil Rights Commission. Legislative reapportionment had increased the representation of urban areas in the General Assembly, a crucial prerequisite to the establishment of the commission. The struggle to create such an organization reached back to the days following World War II and included many hearings that clearly documented widespread economic discrimination against African Americans.

The first civil-rights bill to appear after World War II was introduced in 1947. In that year Des Moines legislator Ted Sloan sponsored legislation calling for the creation of a state "commission against discrimination." Although the bill died in committee, between 1947 and 1955 Iowa legislators introduced eight fair-employment-practices bills, all of which proposed prohibiting discrimination in employment based on race, creed, and color. None of these bills reached the floor of the legislature for a vote. As Benjamin Stone points out in his study of the commission, "It would appear that most if not all of the legislative sponsors of these eight bills were giving the appearance of fighting for legislation against employment discrimination while actually doing very little to see that their bills would become law."[27]

In 1955 Governor Leo A. Hoegh appointed a state commission to study both racial and religious discrimination in Iowa. The commission held hearings in Burlington, Waterloo, Davenport, Council Bluffs, Cedar Rapids, Ottumwa, and Sioux City that revealed widespread employment discrimination against African Americans. In Keokuk, with approximately fifteen hundred blacks in 1950, an informant testified that of the twenty factories there, only three employed blacks. In Davenport the city's local industries employed no skilled black workers. The city itself employed only four black workers: two garbage collectors and two janitors. Other testimony revealed that neither Cedar Rapids nor Ottumwa had black teachers in their public schools.[28] In 1957 the Hoegh Commission to Study Discrimination in Employment presented its report, which read in part:

> Negroes in Iowa are generally excluded from or given only limited op-
> portunities for employment in professions, office and clerical work, re-
> tail trade, transportation, teaching, municipal employment, skilled crafts
> and trades, and in restaurants. ... Negroes in Iowa, in the main, have
> found employment in factories or in service or custodial. However, in
> many cases, specific factories have discriminated against Negroes.[29]

The Iowa Civil Rights Commission created in 1965 had the power to hold hearings, subpoena witnesses, and issue cease-and-desist orders. For the first time a formal, legal structure existed in Iowa empowered to hear cases of discrimination in employment. However, the commission did not have coercive power to force compliance with directives.[30]

At the same time the Civil Rights Commission was created, Des Moines voters elected the first African American to the state legislature: In 1965 Willie S. Glanton of Des Moines was elected to serve in the Iowa House of Representatives; the following year James H. Jackson was elected to the House from Black Hawk County. Two years later Cecil Reed from Linn County and A. June Franklin from Des Moines also joined the General Assembly.[31]

By the end of the 1960s Iowans again witnessed a major shift in po-
litical leadership. In 1968 the Republicans took over the executive branch with Robert D. Ray's election as governor. Born and raised in Des Moines,

trained as a lawyer, and formerly state chairman for the Republican party, Ray represented a new breed of politician. Perhaps more than any other development since liquor-by-the-drink, Ray's election dramatically symbolized that Iowans were moving away from their rural roots. Whereas Iowa's two previously elected governors had been from Boone and Ida Grove, Ray's urban political base seemed to correspond well with Iowa's coming of age as a state with balanced rural and urban interests. At the same time, some things had changed little: Ray, the Republican, and Hughes, the Democrat, would both be regarded as popular leaders, strong executives, and progressives in their social thinking.[32]

In his study of Iowa Democrats, James Larew describes Robert Ray as combining "youthful good looks with an iron will and an unusually even-keeled personality." During Ray's first race for governor in 1968, those latter two qualities served him well when he narrowly escaped death in a plane crash near Mason City. Larew believes that episode characterized the way Iowans perceived Ray's temperament. According to the pilot, just before Ray lost consciousness, he said: "I hate to be a back-seat driver, but I just saw some telephone poles go past the window."[33]

The man who would serve for fourteen years as Iowa's chief executive would be in office at a fortuitous time. Though the sixties included some good years in the Hawkeye State, the 1970s were prosperous times indeed. In an oral biography of Robert Ray, author Jon Bowermaster quotes countless Iowans on the state of the economy (and the surprisingly large state surpluses) in the 1970s. The comments of former Republican legislator Jim West seem typical when he noted that although Ray had some tough times early in his governorship, "that all changed in the mid-1970s, when those good agricultural years just stuffed the treasury."[34]

As West implied, agriculture—always the key barometer of the state's economic condition—was doing extremely well. By 1972 Iowa's farm families were experiencing highly favorable conditions. As Gilbert Fite has written, "Prices began to rise sharply in the fall of 1972, exports shot up, and by early 1973, the American grain cupboard was almost bare." With agricultural surpluses declining, the USDA urged farmers to grow more, thus producing even higher profits. As Fite observes: "For hundreds of thousands of productive commercial farmers, 1973 and 1974 were a bonanza." That bonanza, in turn, provided the state with higher than anticipated revenues for several years.[35]

Also in the seventies important changes would occur in the state leg-

islative and executive branches. The first change came when annual sessions of the legislature were initiated for the first time in January 1970;
five years later Ray started serving his first four-year term, marking the
change from a two-year to a four-year term for state officials.[36] The place
of residence for Iowa's first family also changed. In 1971 the Hubbell family of Des Moines donated Terrace Hill, the Hubbell family home since
1884, to the state. The Ray family moved into the Victorian mansion in
1976.

The size of state government, including budget and revenues, would
greatly expand in the seventies. Funds coming into the state treasury from
state revenues, federal aid, and tax receipts all tripled, which led to a major increase in the total budget. During Ray's first term the budget totaled
$350 million; during his last year in office it had escalated to just under $2
billion. The number of people employed by state government increased
almost 19 percent during Ray's tenure.[37] One area did not increase, however: Early in the seventies the legislature redefined Iowa's congressional
districts to accommodate the state's loss of one U.S. representative, leaving six congressional districts.

Property taxes, an important issue in the 1960s, would carry over into
the seventies. Given a downturn in the state's economy in 1969 and 1970,
state officials faced growing protest over property tax rates. Farmers especially were becoming more and more irate over their taxes, demanding
that some of the burden be shifted to other sources. In fact, during the
1970 session "taxpayer revolt groups" had been organized in western and
north central Iowa. At the same time, other groups of Iowans, particularly
public-school officials and the board of regents, were calling for higher
appropriations to provide educational institutions with more assistance.
Taxes were raised in 1971: Individual income-tax rates were increased almost one-third in the middle- and upper-income brackets; the cigarette tax
was increased from ten to thirteen cents a pack; and the beer tax increased
from twelve to fourteen cents a gallon. Funding for public education,
which through the seventies averaged about 55 percent of the total state
budget, lay at the heart of the issue.[38]

In 1971 the Iowa legislature passed the Iowa school foundation plan
intended to reduce reliance on property taxes as well as lessen inequities
among school districts. In the early seventies "more than half of school
operating expenses in Iowa came from property taxes." The school plan

called for a reduction of reliance on property tax for public education, instead transferring some educational costs to other sources of taxation. Governor Ray decided that the major alternate source of funding would be income tax. Over twenty years later, according to the *Des Moines Register,* the Iowa school-aid plan "has been looked to as a model for some other states." The editorial stated that in 1994 there was about a 5 percent variation in what school districts spend on a per-pupil basis, whereas in the early seventies "there was a big difference."[39]

The early 1970s would include another type of unrest, this time on the nation's college and university campuses as students staged anti–Vietnam War protests. Some student protests would take place at Iowa State University, but the major antiwar protests in the state would be at the University of Iowa. In the spring of 1970 students at Iowa City attempted to block Interstate 80. The highway patrol responded by turning the students back; the governor then kept the National Guard on alert, but did not station Guard members on campus as university officials did in some states.[40] University of Iowa officials dismissed classes early in May, thus avoiding further confrontations involving antiwar demonstrations.

A legacy of Ray's administration, apart from accomplishments within state government, lay in the humanitarian realm: In 1975 the governor invited some thirteen thousand refugees from Southeast Asia to resettle here. Because of political activity in their homelands, it had been determined that these people would be persecuted if they returned home; therefore, they were granted refugee status. Since 1975 several thousand have left the state to resettle elsewhere, but the great majority have remained, going to work in a variety of occupations and locating in various parts of Iowa. By the mid-1980s most Southeast Asians lived in Des Moines and in cities with meat-packing operations, such as Dubuque and Sioux City.

The refugees began to arrive in Iowa only after many years of resettlement in various Southeast Asian countries. One group, the Tai Dam, had fled communist-governed China in 1952 for Vietnam. Two years later, when Vietnam was divided into two countries, they fled again, resettling in Laos; there they remained for twenty years. One Tai Dam, Houng Baccam, explained: "We had been on the move for over twenty years. Three times we left our homes and possessions to escape communism. [Once in Laos,] we really thought we had found a safe haven." But as American troops left South Vietnam, and Saigon fell, many Tai Dam believed that political stability in Laos was threatened and that they must move again. This time 1,228 Tai Dam crossed the Mekong and sought asylum in Thailand, where they resided in the Nong Khai refugee camp.[41]

The Tai Dam's hope for resettlement would soon materialize. Arthur Crisfield, a United States government employee who had had previous contact with the Tai Dam in Laos, visited the Nong Khai camp. Among other efforts to help the group, Crisfield wrote to thirty American governors, asking for assistance. Crisfield pointed out that the Tai Dam at the camp "are the last group of Tai Dam still able to preserve their songs, their dress, and their traditions within the mainstream of the free world."[42]

Robert Ray was one of the governors to receive Crisfield's letter, along with a similar request from President Gerald Ford. Ray went to work creating the Governor's Task Force for Indochinese Resettlement and appointed Colleen Shearer to head the agency. The Tai Dam soon began to arrive, and later other refugees from Southeast Asia. In total, five major groups from Southeast Asia resettled in Iowa. In 1978 officials renamed the task force, the Iowa Refugee Service Center. The group served as a center for refugees arriving in 1975 as well as for those groups sponsored by churches.[43]

Once in Iowa the Tai Dam, along with the other refugees, would go to work in a variety of settings, including meat-packing plants, manufacturing firms, and as custodial workers. The majority would be employed in the former category. A much smaller number would find professional positions, including physicians, engineers, and social workers. Some would start grocery stores specializing in ethnic foods. The children would go to the public schools, where many distinguished themselves academically.[44]

A major characteristic of much of Robert D. Ray's administration was economic prosperity. Because Iowa's economic fortunes were on the rise by 1973, state officials, as well as Iowans everywhere, could rest more easily. It seemed that the governor (starting his third term) had been fortunate, indeed, that the state's economy, particularly agriculture, had turned around. With higher revenues, and undoubtedly a more expansive frame of mind among legislators, many of Ray's earlier proposals became a reality. These included the creation of the Department of Transportation (replacing the State Highway Commission), assistance for Iowa's elderly and disabled, creation of the office of state ombudsman, the easing of the property-tax burden, appropriating more money for higher education, and the passage of a controversial bottle bill. The latter required a nickel deposit on cans and bottles and was bitterly opposed by a coalition of grocers, beer and soft-drink distributors, and bottlers. At the time of the bottle bill's passage in 1978, only three states had similar legislation.[45]

Iowa's prosperous times would last almost into the next decade but then would begin to wane, forcing major adjustments in state budgets and programs. According to former legislators and other state officials, the downturn in 1980 came as a surprise. Interviewed for an oral biography on Robert Ray, official after official commented on the surprising rapidity of change in 1980. It seemed that the "congenital optimism" of farmers had pervaded the entire state in the seventies, as almost everyone, Democrats and Republicans alike, believed prosperity would go on forever. Lowell Norland, Democratic majority leader of the House in the mid-1980s, stated, "I look back and I think we were very cocky in those years. As a state we thought things were going to go like that forever." Don Avenson, longtime Democratic speaker of the House, agreed: "Everybody thought Iowa was recession-proof. This food-processing industry and this implement industry is recession-proof because the world is hungry. It's hard to go against the grain, and none of us tried; everybody was fooled."[46]

Some state officials, such as former Iowa Development Commission director Del Van Horn, spoke of the state's decreased emphasis on industrial development in the seventies. Although the legislature did appropriate money to create Iowa offices in Japan and in Germany (for contact with the European Common Market), in general, legislative reviews and the print media reflected a reduction in the promotion of industry, particularly in contrast to the 1950s.[47]

It is perhaps not surprising that, given the excellent state of Iowa's economy during much of the seventies, officials gave increasingly less thought to furthering industrial growth. For several decades the pattern had been clear: When agriculture was doing well, Iowans promoted greater production and succumbed to the belief that good times would go on forever. If agriculture was doing poorly, as in the fifties, Iowans concentrated on ways to develop a diversified economy through the development of more industry. Whether Iowans might be regarded as cocky, short-sighted, or merely steadfast in the belief that the economy was recession proof, their actions in the seventies seemed in step with earlier thinking: During good times agriculture could and would do it all.

Ironically, throughout much of the seventies, as the state responded more frequently to urban needs and demands and clearly moved toward a balance between rural and urban interests, rural Iowa did indeed provide most of the economic buoyancy. When that buoyancy began to disappear, as it did in the late seventies, rural and urban Iowans alike would pay a heavy price for some time to come.

17

Iowa: The 1980s and 1990s

B y the mid-1990s Iowans could reflect on dramatic changes
within their state during the previous decade and a half. Beginning in the early eighties, the state would experience a devastating farm crisis that would speed along the trend toward
fewer and fewer farms, as well as the further decline of many medium-
and small-town economies. By the 1990s, partly as a result of previous
agricultural distress, attention often focused on the economic future of
Iowa's smaller communities. Various public and private officials predicted
that small towns would find it increasingly difficult to survive.

Other significant changes also took place in the eighties and early
nineties. During these two decades many Iowans began to concentrate on

*Open-country Iowa showing conservation measures where
plowing follows the contour of the land. Photo courtesy of
the State Historical Society of Iowa, Iowa City.*

environmental concerns in agriculture, with the result that more and more farm families began using sustainable farming practices. Iowa's social climate also underwent change as Iowans zealously moved to embrace various forms of gambling. In the 1980s and early 1990s—in a state where bingo had been illegal until 1970—Iowans would initiate a state lottery, followed by the construction of numerous gambling casinos. In general, however, Iowa continued to move toward a more balanced economy, whereby rural and urban issues were mutually visible and equitably represented in state government. Although Iowa was still viewed as a rural state by outsiders, for Iowans the designation "rural" had become questionable.

The decade of the eighties in Iowa can be characterized in two words: farm crisis. While state officials began to experience reduced revenues in 1980, most Iowans seemed slow to realize that the farm sector was heading toward real trouble. During the 1970s the value of farmland had increased dramatically. Between 1970 and 1981, an acre of farmland in the United States, on average, had increased from three hundred to seventeen hundred dollars. During the prosperous days of the seventies, farmers often expanded their land base, purchased new machinery, and generally spent more money. These actions led to debt that could be maintained only if farm prices remained high.[1] By 1981, however, agricultural prices began to decline and land prices fell precipitously.

During the worst days of the farm crisis, the *Des Moines Register* ran a series entitled *Riches to Rags: Iowa's Economic Upheaval.* Pocahontas County was selected as the focus for the series. As the *Register* explained, one big problem in the eighties was the contrast with the prosperity of the previous decade: "During the 1970s, landowners [in Pocahontas County] saw their holdings increase by more than $500 million to a collective value of more than $1 billion. An acre of land ... sold for $3,500 and more." Jim Hudson, a Pocahontas lawyer, also commented on the good times of the seventies: "You wouldn't believe the way money was tossed around here. ... If a farmer wanted something, he'd just grab a blank check and write it out. A college education? Write a check. A new combine? Write a check."[2]

By the mid-1980s, however, all that had changed, not only in Pocahontas County but throughout the state. Underscoring that change, on December 21, 1984, a *Register* headline proclaimed: "Iowa Farmland Values Plummet." The article reported that the value of Iowa farmland had fallen by almost 20 percent in the previous year. According to an ISU land survey, that decline marked the biggest single-year drop in farmland value since the Great Depression. By the mid-1980s the crisis had affected a large number of farmers, particularly those thirty-five years old and younger, threatening many with loss of their farms.[3] Later studies would show that approximately 40 percent of the state's farm families had been seriously affected by the depression.

The first line of support for vulnerable farm families was provided by groups such as the Iowa Farm Unity Coalition, formed in January 1982, and PrairieFire. The latter group provided advocacy work with Iowa farmers. In his study of the farm crisis, Mark Friedberger perceives the Iowa Farm Unity Coalition as being "alone in its monitoring of the condition of farm families at a personal level" between 1982 and 1984.[4]

By 1984 the Iowa Cooperative Extension Service had started responding to the depressed farm situation with a variety of programs. In that year the extension service began to administer the ASSIST Program, which provided computerized financial management assistance for farm families; assistance in locating community resources to deal with the physical and emotional hardships created by the crisis; and agricultural short courses for agricultural lenders, professional farm managers, and others who worked with stressed farm families. The extension service, in cooperation with the Iowa Department of Human Services and the United Way of Central Iowa, set up the Iowa Rural Concern Hotline, a toll-free telephone hot line. Eventually a wide range of extension personnel became involved in programs related to the farm crisis.[5]

County extension directors also worked directly with stressed family members. The late Dan Merrick stated that as extension director in Cass County, he frequently talked with farmers about financial matters, including such fundamental concerns as one's ability to feed livestock. Merrick recalled a farmer who confided that when cultivating his corn, he "thought three or four times about killing myself. But then I also knew that I would be leaving that burden on my wife and children." As Merrick's experience indicates, the farm crisis created immense, sometimes unbearable, burdens on farm families caught in a situation of high fixed costs and falling income and land values.[6]

Throughout most of the 1980s the farm crisis dominated the media, particularly television and the front page of the state's most widely circulated newspaper, the *Des Moines Register*. Farm-support organizations began erecting crosses to call attention to the increasing number of families losing their farms. Movies like *Country,* documenting the financial difficulties of an Iowa farm couple (and filmed in Iowa), called national attention to the farm disaster. The *Register* carried numerous series on changes in agriculture and in rural Iowa brought on by the depression. The farm crisis dominated the thinking of people everywhere in the state.

When the crisis began to ease by 1987, it was clear that the state had been altered in numerous ways. In addressing the 1987 General Assembly, House Speaker Don Avenson compared economic conditions in Iowa in that year with conditions fourteen years earlier, when Avenson had begun serving in the state legislature. The comparisons were startling: In 1973, for example, Iowa had 22,000 more farms than in 1987 and 160,000 more students in public schools. Avenson believed "the 'Iowa of the '80s and '90s can never be the Iowa of the '60s and '70s' and 'we must realize that going back is no longer possible. We have not seen a mere deviation in course—we have witnessed fundamental change.'"[7]

A part of the change evident in the latter 1980s was the decline of industrial activity, particularly in the area of farm machinery. Farm-implement dealers and manufacturers had suffered badly during the eighties. This development had major implications for Iowa, as Deere and Company, the largest farm-machinery producer in the country, had five plants located here. The *Des Moines Register* reported a decline by 1987 in manufacturing jobs "from 23 percent of Iowa's work force in 1979 to 18.3 percent in 1987." Given the growth of lower-paying service-sector jobs at the expense of manufacturing jobs, "Iowa lost 84,000 jobs in the $20,000-a-year range and gained instead 37,000 service jobs paying $11,500 a year or less."[8]

In the midst of the farm crisis state leaders decided to initiate a new method of raising funds—a lottery to support state government. Since August of 1985 lottery officials have introduced a variety of games, some handled through weekly drawings and some through scratch-off tickets, thus enabling purchasers to know immediately if they are winners. In 1988 Iowa joined five other states and the District of Columbia to initiate Lotto America. Adoption of lottery games would come about in the face of initial opposition from Governor Terry Branstad and strong, sustained opposition from other Iowans, particularly the United Methodist Church.[9]

Even though some Iowans opposed the lottery, this form of gambling had a long history, going back to colonial America. In fact, the first permanent settlement in North America—Jamestown, Virginia—was partially financed by lottery money from England. Some 160 years later the American Revolution was financed in part by a lottery established by the Continental Congress. During much of the nineteenth century lottery activity waxed and waned as some states outlawed the practice because of mismanagement and fraud; in 1895 a scandal resulting from the Louisiana lottery led the federal government to prohibit lotteries from engaging in interstate commerce. Almost seventy years passed before lotteries legally reappeared, this time in New Hampshire; in 1967 New York State initiated a monthly sweepstakes game. Neither New Hampshire nor New York raised the projected revenue, however. Following the sixties, numerous states would create lotteries, including Iowa in 1985.[10]

Fifteen years earlier, however, Iowa officials had moved to change state gaming laws, specifically to legalize the game of bingo. Iowa attorney general Richard Turner had called attention to the constitutional ban on bingo (actually a ban on lotteries) when his office began strictly enforcing the state's antigambling laws in the early seventies. As a result, "carnival games, cake walks, and bingo became subjects of controversy— and sometimes of prosecution." The climax of Turner's campaign came when state officials raided a Catholic church picnic, "where games of chance were being operated to raise funds." In the process officials arrested a parish priest for keeping "a gambling house." By 1972 the state legislature had twice passed an amendment repealing the prohibition against lotteries; Iowa voters then approved the amendment in the following general election. Originally, legislators intended to change the law only to allow bingo games by specific groups such as churches, but the final version of the law totally repealed the lottery ban.[11]

More than a decade would pass before Iowans moved to establish their own lottery game, a decade during which Iowans apparently developed more positive views toward gambling. As Lee Ann Osbun has noted in her study of the Iowa lottery, public support would increase between 1963, when 25 percent of those polled approved, and 1975, when the approval rating increased to 44 percent. Osbun noted that from the beginning of efforts to create a lottery in 1983, the matter was a partisan one, with Democrats for and Republicans against. Two Republican governors, Robert Ray (who left office in 1983) and his successor, Terry E. Branstad, also took strong stands against the creation of a lottery. Branstad, in fact, twice vetoed lottery legislation. Finally in 1985, after much "uncertainty and indecisiveness" on the part of the legislature, and a change of position by Governor Branstad, the Iowa lottery became reality.[12]

In her study of the Iowa lottery, Osbun concludes that "the lottery seems neither to have met the highest expectations of its promoters nor to have realized the worst fears of the opponents." Regarding the former, proceeds from the lottery have not equaled the earliest predictions; at the same time, fears that lower-income Iowans would spend a disproportionate amount of their income on the lottery also have not been realized. Osbun reported, moreover, that to date (approximately 1988), "there is no evidence that illegal gambling activity in the state has increased." A large share of lottery money has gone to the Department of Economic Development for economic betterment grants.[13]

The legalization of lotteries, however, would be only one step in the proliferation of gambling within the state. Two years before the first lottery, the General Assembly authorized pari-mutuel betting, which allowed for the creation of greyhound races in Dubuque, Council Bluffs, and Waterloo. The state's first horse-racing track, Prairie Meadows, opened in Des Moines in 1989, the same year the legislature authorized riverboat gambling. Two years later Iowa had five riverboat casinos in operation. A major expansion would come the following year when three Native-American groups opened gambling casinos in western and central Iowa. Initially state officials placed limits on casino-boat wagering, but in March 1994, in response to complaints that limits made the Iowa operations uncompetitive with other states, the limits were removed. At the same time, the General Assembly approved placing slot machines at the state's racing tracks. After April 1995 the Council Bluffs, Dubuque, and Des Moines racing tracks all had slot-machine casinos operating.[14]

Even though state government has continued to allow gambling expansion in the state, controversy continues over the pros and cons of the action. Supporters claim that Iowa, buffeted by agricultural distress and the loss of some industrial operations, needs the revenue generated by gambling and that the revenue has created thousands of new jobs. Oppo-

nents argue that the practice is simply wrong, as it sends an inappropriate
message to youngsters, destroys the work ethic, and creates social problems, such as compulsive gambling and family abuse. Regardless of the
arguments, however, one thing seems clear: State officials have unam-
biguously indicated they believe expanded gambling was (and is) good for
the state economically, and that social consequences are of minor importance. For the foreseeable future Iowa appears destined to remain a gambling state.[15]

Although Iowans approved a constitutional change permitting gaming in the 1980s, in the next decade they would not approve a constitutional amendment guaranteeing equal rights for women. When Iowans
went to the polls in November 1992 to elect a president, they had the opportunity to vote yes or no on the following proposed amendment to the
state constitution: "All men and women are, by nature, free and equal, and
have certain inalienable rights—among which are those of enjoying and
defending life and liberty, acquiring, possessing and protecting property,
and pursuing and obtaining safety and happiness. Neither the State nor any
of its political subdivisions shall on the basis of gender, deny or restrict the
equality of rights under the law." The amendment failed as Iowans voted
551,566 for and 595,837 against.

Equal Rights Amendment campaign issues in 1992 paralleled issues
debated in the 1970s, when Americans considered approval of an ERA
amendment to the United States Constitution. In that campaign Iowa's
General Assembly had approved the amendment within a year of its passage by Congress. By 1980, however, ERA supporters still needed three
more states to approve the national amendment; two years later the
amendment was declared dead. While supporters of Iowa's ERA argued
that passage of the amendment was needed to safeguard women's rights
(regardless of laws already in effect), ERA opponents—like opponents of
the earlier national ERA amendment—created linkages between the ERA
and unpopular or controversial issues. One piece of literature widely distributed by Iowa anti-ERA forces suggested that passage might lead to
abortions paid for by tax dollars, inclusion of homosexual rights in the
state constitution, higher insurance rates for women, and the forcing of religious schools to forfeit their tax exemption.[16] Assessments of the failure
of the national ERA amendment conclude that opponents succeeded in
raising sufficient doubts about ERA to cause people to oppose it. It ap-

pears that the same tactic worked in Iowa. Two additional factors that affected the outcome of the vote may have been a long ballot, which confused some voters, and unclear wording of the amendment.[17]

If one was to observe the changes in Iowa's recent past from the vantage point of the early 1990s, one's first observation might be that although the state has changed in major ways, most basic institutions have remained remarkably stable during the past thirty to forty years. The next decade or two, however, may well serve as a watershed for greater economic and social change, which, in turn, may alter both the physical and cultural landscape of the state.

Although agriculture remains Iowa's single most important industry, that activity has undergone significant change in the past forty years. Given the trend toward increased farm size and greater specialization, and the agricultural distress of the eighties, the number of farms has greatly declined; during the 1980s alone more than 140,000 people moved off Iowa farms. By 1992, according to the latest farm census, the number of Iowa farms had dropped to 96,543.[18] Moreover, Iowa's farmers are aging: The 1992 farm census showed that the average age of an Iowa farmer was fifty, while the number of farmers younger than 34 years had declined by more than 20 percent between 1987 and 1992. For men and women who remained on the farm, there was yet another trend: More of them needed to work off the farm in order to keep the farm going.[19]

The disappearance of more than 100,000 farms in the past forty-five years has not only altered the appearance of the countryside, but, in turn, has had a dramatic effect on small towns that have long served as retail-and-service centers for the surrounding countryside. One demographic expert predicted in 1994 that "Iowa's smallest communities, which have remained resilient despite several decades of population decreases on the state's farms, will likely begin disappearing over the next decade." The disappearance of small towns will, no doubt, be selective, as those close to larger communities will have continued economic vitality. According to an ISU demographer, many small communities "are assuming roles as satellites to roughly 50 regional shopping centers emerging across the state." Ames and western Story County serve as an example. Small-town civic leaders in communities such as Kelley and Huxley, both located some ten to twelve miles from Ames, believe that "any development in Ames is bound to send ripples of growth their way."[20]

The disappearance of some small towns will bring about major demographic—and in turn, cultural—change as Iowa's small towns are most closely identified with what Iowans perceive to be the state's social and political values. Similar values certainly exist in urban areas, but they are more strongly articulated in smaller towns. Iowa is presently a state that seems to maintain a comfortable balance between rural small-town society and the ever-expanding urban industrial sector, but that rural presence will undoubtedly diminish in the years ahead. Great stretches of the countryside will indeed appear abandoned and isolated—but the greatest change may be cultural, with the loss of stability and continuity traditionally inherent in small-town society.

In the industrial sector Iowans have also experienced change. The industry of meat packing has undergone major change in the past thirty-some years. In 1960 the Iowa Beef Packers (today known as IBP) opened its first plant in Denison and greatly altered the industry there through specializing in one type of meat production; today IBP has pork-processing plants in four Iowa communities. Iowa's traditional industries, such as Maytag, have expanded to take on new lines, and at the same time, farm-related industries such as John Deere and Quaker Oats are still highly visible. Major new industries have also developed. In the 1960s, reflective of Americans' prosperity, leisure-time interests, and the development of a national interstate highway system, Winnebago Industries started building recreational vehicles in Forest City. Although the industry has experienced many adverse trends, it has always rebounded. A major change affecting all Iowa industries is an increase in the number of working women. By 1990, 57.8 percent of Iowa women aged sixteen or older were in the labor force. This meant that eighty-five women were employed for every one hundred men.[21]

At the same time, particularly because of the dark days of the eighties, state leaders have recognized that Iowa needs a more balanced economy to offset the inevitable periodic downturns in agriculture. This recognition has led to major efforts—apparent in communities of all sizes—to attract new industries. Efforts to do so, however, have often brought disagreement between legislators and the governor as to the amount of financial assistance needed to secure additional industries. Disagreements also have persisted over the value of attracting industries that sometimes pay little more than minimum wage. There is no question, however, that by the mid-1990s the race was on to attract more industrial firms to the state, regardless of the fact that greater and greater financial incentives were needed to lure new companies.

A look at Iowa's landscape would also indicate additional cultural changes after 1950. In that decade Iowans would begin to build centers, such as Hancher Auditorium at the University of Iowa and Stephens Auditorium at Iowa State University, that would bring world-renowned performers and symphonies to the state, thereby making such attractions available to thousands of Iowans living in nearby communities. Furthermore, citizens in communities such as Dubuque would refurnish nineteenth-century opera houses, thus creating facilities for the performing arts. Des Moines citizens would construct their Civic Center in the 1970s. Some three decades earlier the *New Yorker* magazine had questioned whether such events would appeal to "the little old lady in Dubuque," but by the 1980s, given the development of several performing centers, Iowa's image was no longer that of a parochial population.

In a different cultural sense, Iowa has become enriched since the 1950s with a growing number of minorities, including an increased population of African Americans, Hispanics, and Southeast Asians. Iowa's Native-American population, particularly the Meskwaki, have experienced major success with their gambling casino at the Meskwaki Settlement, leading to improved physical and social conditions there.

At the same time, some values, traditions, and institutions have not changed since the 1950s. Iowans still value public education and provide strong economic and social support for that system. Politically, Iowa has remained a two-party state, with most state offices considered up for grabs at election time. Demographically, the state has grown increasingly more weighted in favor of urban dwellers, but the transition from the farm to the city has been gradual, beginning almost in the early 1900s. Longtime religious and cultural values are still visible, as evidenced by recent protests of Pella community leaders when Wal-Mart announced it would remain open on Sunday afternoon; when Wal-Mart refused to change its policy, local pastors urged their parishioners not to shop on Sunday. Pella has probably retained its Sunday closing laws longer than any other community in the state.

As Iowans near the twenty-first century, they remain somewhat conservative in their politics, usually liberal in their social thinking, and always optimistic about their economic future. Iowans remain in touch with their rural roots but increasingly seem to believe that economic prosperity rests with industrial development. Iowa, unlike midwestern states to the east, has not become predominately industrial and unlike midwestern states to the west, has not remained mostly agricultural. Rather, in politics, in economics, in social values and social actions, Iowa can still be defined as the middle land.

NOTES

PREFACE

1. Laurence Lafore, "In the Sticks," *Harper's*, 1971, 109.
2. Ibid.
3. Leland Sage, *A History of Iowa* (Ames: Iowa State University Press, 1974), xi.

CHAPTER 1

1. See maps of locations of North American Indian tribes in Harold E. Driver, *Indians of North America* (Chicago: University of Chicago Press, 1961), appendix maps #2, #37; and Martha Royce Blaine, *The Ioway Indians* (Norman: University of Oklahoma Press, 1979), 3.
2. Blaine, *Ioway Indians*, 20–25.
3. Ibid., 10, 15; *1700 Iowa Indian Site Manual*. Deposited at Living History Farms, Des Moines (1985).
4. Blaine, *Ioway Indians*, 8, 12.
5. Ibid., 10.
6. F. R. Aumann, "The Ioway," *The Palimpsest*, 50 (1969): 216; *1700 Ioway Indian Site Manual*, 3, 5; Blaine, *Ioway Indians*, 27, 37. LeSeur also noted the defense alliance between the Dakota and the Ioway—Blaine, *Ioway Indians*, 27.
7. *1700 Ioway Indian Site Manual*, 4, 5.
8. Edgar R. Harlan, *A Narrative History of the People of Iowa*, vol. 1 (Chicago: The American Historical Society, 1931), 59; *1700 Iowa Indian Site Manual*, 8. In 1824 they ceded land in Missouri to the federal government.
9. William T. Hagan, *The Sac and Fox Indians* (Norman: University of Oklahoma Press, 1958), 30–31.
10. Ibid., 29; Harlan, *Narrative History*, 63.
11. Hagan, *Sac And Fox Indians*, 30.
12. Ibid., 31–34.
13. John E. Hallwas, "Black Hawk: A Reassessment," *The Annals of Iowa* 45 (1981): 602–3; Hagan, *Sac and Fox Indians*, 32.
14. Donald Jackson, ed., *Black Hawk: An Autobiography* (Urbana: University of Illinois Press, 1964), 3, n. 2; Hallwas, "Black Hawk," 610.
15. A. R. Fulton, *Red Men of Iowa* (Des Moines: Mills & Co., 1882), 57.
16. T. A. Richard, *A History of American Mining* (New York: McGraw Hill, 1932), 147–50.
17. Sage, *History of Iowa*, 39–40.

18. Donald Jackson, "Old Fort Madison—1808–1813," *The Palimpsest,* 47(1966): 12–13.

19. Ibid., 17–19.

20. Ibid., 60–61.

21. Hallwas, "Black Hawk," 604–13; Sage, *History of Iowa,* 40; Harlan, *Narrative History,* vol. 1, 62.

22. Joseph F. Wall, *Iowa: A Bicentennial History* (New York: W. W. Norton, 1978), 11.

23. Jackson, *Black Hawk,* 7–8, 56. At this time Black Hawk had his portrait painted by Charles Bird King. See Jackson, 18 n. 5.

24. Harlan, *Narrative History,* vol. 1, 70; Jackson, *Black Hawk,* 155; Sage, *History of Iowa,* 45. Sage includes a map on p. 45 that shows the area.

25. Jackson, *Black Hawk,* 155; Sage, *History of Iowa,* 45 (includes a map of Indian cessions in Iowa).

26. "Sac and Fox Indian Council of 1841," *The Annals of Iowa* 12 (1920): 323.

27. Ibid., 329.

28. Ibid., 330–31.

29. Robert A. Trennert, Jr., *Indian Traders on the Middle Border: The House of Ewing, 1827–54* (Lincoln: University of Nebraska Press, 1981), 95–98, 111.

30. Ibid., 95–98.

31. Ibid.

32. "Sac and Fox Indian Council of 1842," *The Annals of Iowa* 12 (1920): 338–40.

33. Michael D. Green, "'We Dance in Opposite Directions': Mesquakie (Fox) Separatism from the Sac and Fox Tribe," *Ethnohistory* 30 (1983): 135.

34. Ibid., 136.

35. Wall, *Iowa,* 61.

36. Ibid., 61–62; Sage, *History of Iowa,* 109.

37. Harlan, *Narrative History,* vol. 1, 70–71.

CHAPTER 2

1. William J. Petersen, "The Joliet-Marquette Expedition," *The Palimpsest* 49 (1968): 430.

2. Sage, *History of Iowa,* 34; see William J. Petersen, "Spanish Land Grants in Iowa," *The Palimpsest* 46 (1966): 97–144, for full treatment of the three grants.

3. Petersen, "Spanish Land Grants," 107, 112–13.

4. Ibid., 108. Although Dubuque had permission from the Meskwaki to operate in the area, he felt it necessary to solidify his claim in the eyes of the Spanish government. In 1796 he requested and apparently received from the Spanish governor of Louisiana a deed to his holdings which he named "the Mines of Spain." See Wall, *Iowa,* 20.

5. William J. Petersen, *Story of Iowa* (New York: Lewis Historical Publishing Co., Inc., 1952), vol. 1, 208–9.

6. Paul S. Boyer et al., *The Enduring Vision: A History of the American People,* vol. 1 (Lexington, Mass.: D. C. Heath and Company, 1990), 250.

7. Sage, *History of Iowa,* 37–38; Wall, *Iowa,* 18; and Petersen, *Story of Iowa,* vol. 1, 230.

8. Quoted in Wall, *Iowa,* 18.

9. Petersen, *Story of Iowa,* vol. 1, 234–36; Sage, *History of Iowa,* 38.

10. Sage, *History of Iowa,* 39.

11. Quoted in Wall, *Iowa,* 22.

12. Ibid.

13. Petersen, *Story of Iowa,* vol. 1, 296–97; Wall, *Iowa,* 23.

14. Petersen, *Story of Iowa,* vol. 1, 307.

15. Ibid.; Robert V. Wells, *Revolutions in Americans' Lives: A Demographic Perspective on*

the History of America, Their Families and Their Society (Westport, Conn.: Greenwood Press, 1982), 92.

16. Sage, *History of Iowa,* 310; Richard, Lord Acton, "Rainy July 4, 1838: Iowa Territory's Birth," *Des Moines Sunday Register,* 4 July, 1993.

17. See W. J. Rorabaugh, *The Alcoholic Republic: An American Tradition* (New York: Oxford University Press, 1979) for an excellent discussion of Americans' drinking habits in the nineteenth century. Quoted in Harlan, *Narrative History,* vol. 1, 119.

18. Harlan, *Narrative History,* vol. 1, 112, 115, 155; Anne Beiser Allen, "Friendly's Frontier: Images from the Life of Friendly Lucas, Iowa's First 'First Lady,'" *The Palimpsest* 73 (Spring 1992): 23–24.

19. Wall, *Iowa,* 36.

20. Sage, *History of Iowa,* 64–65; Wall, *Iowa,* 35. See Sage for a good discussion of the dispute, a part of which is known as the Honey War.

21. Allen, "Friendly's Frontier," 19, 20.

22. Ibid., 24, 25, 27, 31. Iowa also had two additional territorial governors, John Chambers and James Clarke. See Petersen, *Story of Iowa,* vol. 1, 327–28, for biographical details.

23. Petersen, *Story of Iowa,* vol. 1, 337–38.

24. Ibid., 338.

25. Wall, *Iowa,* 39; Petersen, *Story of Iowa,* vol. 1, 340.

26. Sage, *History of Iowa,* 83–84.

27. Petersen, *Story of Iowa,* vol. 1, 342.

28. Wall, *Iowa,* 42; Sage, *History of Iowa,* 88.

29. Sage, *History of Iowa,* 89, 91.

30. Ibid., 89.

CHAPTER 3

1. Samuel E. Morison and Henry S. Commager, *The Growth of the American Republic,* vol. 1 (New York: Oxford University Press, 1942), 80; John Madson, *Where the Sky Began: Land of the Tallgrass Prairie* (Ames: Iowa State University Press, 1995), 4.

2. Madson, *Where the Sky Began,* 4.

3. Ibid., 8.

4. Quoted in David Kinnett, "Locating in the Garden of the World: The Prairie Factor, 1830–1860." Unpublished paper, 17 April 1973, 5; Diary of Ellen Strang. 1859–1872. State Historical Society of Iowa, Iowa City, 2.

5. Quoted in Kinnett, "Locating in the Garden," 16.

6. Ibid.

7. Herbert Quick, *Vandemark's Folly* (Indianapolis: Bobb-Merrill, 1922), lll–12.

8. Petersen, *Story of Iowa,* vol. 1, 357.

9. Allan Bogue, *From Prairie to Cornbelt: Farming on the Illinois and Iowa Prairies in the Nineteenth Century* (Chicago: Quadrangle Books, 1963), 14, 22–24.

10. Doris Faulkner, ed., "Letters from Algona 1856–1865," *The Palimpsest* 61 (1980): 181, 189, 191.

11. Vesta Robbins, *No Coward Soul* (Ames: Iowa State University Press, 1974), 3–22.

12. Ibid.

13. Ibid., lll–12.

14. Glenda Riley, *Frontierswomen: The Iowa Experience* (Ames: Iowa State University Press, 1981), 45.

15. Jean Zmolek, *Memories ... William McCormick Family* (Ames: privately printed, 1992), 12, 13.

16. Robert Swierenga, ed., "A Dutch Immigrant's View of Frontier Iowa" in *Patterns and Perspectives in Iowa History,* ed. Dorothy Schwieder (Ames: Iowa State University Press, 1973), 64. See Kevin Proescholdt, "The Demography of the New Sweden Settlement in Iowa, 1845–1880," *The Swedish Pioneer Historical Quarterly* (April 1981) for a discussion of Cassel and New Sweden.

17. J. B. Doolittle, *Northern Iowa: Containing Hints and Information of Value to Emigrants* (Dubuque: W. A. Adams, Printer, 1858), 14.

18. Sage, *History of Iowa,* 70.

19. Charles Svobada, interview with author, December 15, 1978; Allan G. Bogue, "Twenty Years of an Iowa Farm Business, 1860–1880," *The Annals of Iowa* 35 (1961): 561; Zmolek, *Memories,* 12.

20. Wallace E. Ogg, "The Ogg Century Farm." Unpublished manuscript, 1980, 1–2.

21. Robert P. Swierenga, *Pioneers and Profits: Land Speculation on the Iowa Frontier* (Ames: Iowa State University Press, 1968), 210; C. J. Niles and Debbie Felton, "He Promised Her a Mansion," *The Iowan* 34 (1985): 53; Sage, *History of Iowa,* 70.

22. Sage, *History of Iowa,* 69–70.

23. Ogg, "Ogg Century Farm," 3; Bogue, *From Prairie to Cornbelt,* 267; Allan G. Bogue, "Pioneer Farmers and Innovation," *Iowa Journal of History* 56 (1958): 4.

24. Riley, *Frontierswomen,* 30–31.

25. Ibid., 43. Also see ibid. for an excellent discussion of all aspects of women and pioneer life.

26. Earle D. Ross, *Iowa Agriculture* (Iowa City: State Historical Society of Iowa, 1951), 20.

27. Madson, "The Running Country," *Audubon Magazine* 74 (January 1972): 8, 17.

28. Bogue, "Twenty Years," 566.

29. Glenda Riley, ed., "The Memoirs of Matilda Peitzke Paul," *The Palimpsest* 57 (1976); Diary of Emily Hawley Gillespie. Papers of Sarah Gillespie Huftalen, State Historical Society of Iowa, Iowa City, August 5 and 26, 1861.

30. Glenda Riley, "Family Life on the Frontier: The Diary of Kitturah Penton Belknap," *The Annals of Iowa* 44 (1977): 43–44.

31. Riley, *Frontierswomen,* 56.

32. Diary of Emily Hawley Gillespie, October 14, November 3, 1862. See also Dorothy Schwieder, "Labor and Economic Roles of Iowa Farm Wives, 1840–80," in *Farmers, Bureaucrats, and Middlemen: Historical Perspectives on American Agriculture,* ed. Trudy Huskamp Peterson (Washington: Howard University Press, 1980).

33. Schwieder, "Labor and Economic Roles," 65.

34. Emily Hawley Gillespie's diary has been published. See Judy Nolte Lensink, *"A Secret to Be Burried:" The Diary and Life of Emily Hawley Gillespie, 1858–1888* (Iowa City: University of Iowa Press, 1989).

35. For contrasts to Iowa's settlement experience, see Walter Prescott Webb, *The Great Plains* (New York: Grosset & Dunlap, 1931) and Richard Lyle Power, *Planting Corn Belt Culture: The Impress of the Upland Southerner and Yankee in the Old Northwest* (Westport, Conn.: Greenwood Press, 1953).

CHAPTER 4

1. Swierenga, "Dutch Immigrant's View," 53. Sipma was referring to the Des Moines Navigation Improvement Company set up in 1846 to improve the Des Moines River for navigation as far north as the present site of Des Moines. A federal land grant was issued, but the project was never completed.

2. Louis C. Hunter, *Steamboats on the Western Rivers: An Economic and Technological History* (New York: Octagon Books, 1969), 420, 422–26, 430–32. Hunter states that the cost from New Orleans to St. Louis or Louisville was as little as $3.00, so the cost from New Orleans to an Iowa river town might have been even lower than $3.50.

3. Ibid., 430–32.

4. Timothy R. Mahoney, *River Towns in the Great West: The Structure of Provincial Urbanization in the American Midwest, 1820–1870* (New York: Cambridge University Press, 1990), 172–73.

5. Ibid.

6. Ibid. Also see William J. Petersen, *Steamboating on the Upper Mississippi* (Iowa City: State Historical Society of Iowa, 1937).

7. Mahoney, *River Towns,* 159, 190–91, 232, 246–54; and Timothy R. Mahoney, "Down in Davenport: A Regional Perspective on Antebellum Town Economic Development," *The Annals of Iowa* 50 (1990): 451.

8. Mahoney, "Down in Davenport," 466.

9. Petersen, *Story of Iowa,* vol. 1, 583.

10. George A. Boeck, "A Decade of Transportation Fever in Burlington, Iowa, 1845–1855," in *Patterns and Perspectives in Iowa History,* ed. Dorothy Schwieder (Ames: Iowa State University Press, 1973), 137.

11. Ibid., 146.

12. Canal building in states like Indiana had led to excessive state debt, and Iowa legislators were determined that situation would not occur here; therefore, they placed the one-hundred-thousand-dollar debt limit on the state; Earle S. Beard, "Local Aid to Railroads in Iowa," *Iowa Journal of History* 50 (1952): 1–2.

13. Beard, "Local Aid," 3–5, ll, and 32.

14. Sage, *History of Iowa,* 109–10; Petersen, *Story of Iowa,* vol. 1, 585–86.

15. Beard, "Local Aid," 18, 22, 30.

16. Ibid., 24, 25. The property-tax legislation was repealed and repassed several times with slight modifications.

17. Frank P. Donovan, Jr., "The Illinois Central in Iowa," *The Palimpsest* 43 (1962): 279–304; "Ft. Dodge, Des Moines and Southern," *The Palimpsest* 35 (1954): 177–85.

18. Donovan, "Ft. Dodge, Des Moines," 177–85; Sage, *History of Iowa,* 115.

19. Petersen, *Story of Iowa,* vol. 1, 587; Beard, "Local Aid," 31.

20. Philip D. Jordan, *Catfish Bend—River Town and County Seat* (Burlington, Iowa: Craftsman Press, Inc., 1975), 111–17.

21. Mahoney, "Down in Davenport," 451–52.

22. Ibid., 471–72.

CHAPTER 5

1. Leola Nelson Bergmann, *The Negro in Iowa* (Iowa City: State Historical Society of Iowa, 1969), 9.

2. Richard, Lord Acton, "To Go Free," *The Palimpsest* 70 (1989): 53–55. Fifty dollars of the $550 was based on what Montgomery would have got had he rented out Ralph's labor for one year. This was not uncommon in Marion County, Missouri. The article now appears in Richard, Lord Acton and Patricia Nassif Acton, *To Go Free: A Treasury of Iowa's Legal Heritage* (Ames: Iowa State University Press, 1995).

3. Joseph F. Wall, *Iowa: A Bicentennial History* (New York: Norton, 1978), 91–92; Acton, "To Go Free," 34–55.

4. Acton, "To Go Free," 58–60; Wall, *Iowa,* 93.

5. Sage, *History of Iowa,* 139–40.

6. John Todd, *Early Settlement and Growth of Western Iowa or Reminiscences* (Des Moines: Historical Department of Iowa, 1906), 9.

7. Ibid., 152–53.

8. Ibid.

9. David S. Sparks, "The Birth of the Republican Party in Iowa, 1854–1856," *Iowa Journal of History* 54 (1956): 31.

10. Wall, *Iowa,* 98–99.

11. Sparks, "Birth of the Republican Party," 9–10, 13; Wall, *Iowa,* 97.

12. Ibid., 25.

13. Sage, *History of Iowa,* 209; Harlan, *Narrative History,* 159.

14. Sage, *History of Iowa,* 153; Stephen Z. Starr, "Hawkeyes on Horseback: The Second Iowa Volunteer Cavalry," *Civil War History* 23 (1977): 212.

15. Sharon Selzer Ham, "The End of Innocence: An Iowa Civil War Experience," (Master's thesis, University of Iowa, 1978), 6.

16. Ibid., 61.

17. Ibid., 10–12; Sage, *History of Iowa,* 153.

18. Ham, "End of Innocence," 25–27.

19. Sage, *History of Iowa,* 154.

20. George Tod, "Source Material of Iowa History," *Iowa Journal of History* 49 (1951): 343–47.

21. Harlan, *Narrative History,* 440–41.

22. Brent Ponsford, "Mayor-General Grenville Dodge's Military Intelligence Operations During the Civil War," (Master's thesis, Iowa State University, 1976), 12–18, 27. After the war Henson returned to the South, where he spent the remainder of his life.

23. Sage, *History of Iowa,* 153–55.

24. Riley, *Frontierswomen,* 112.

25. David L. Lendt, *Demise of the Democracy: The Copperhead Press in Iowa, 1856–1870* (Ames: Iowa State University Press, 1971), 59.

26. Ibid., 38, 80–81; Hubert H. Wubben, *Civil War Iowa* (Ames: Iowa State University Press, 1980), 107.

27. Sage, *History of Iowa,* 159; Lendt, *Demise,* 78.

28. Lendt, *Demise,* 52, 59–60.

29. Wubben, *Civil War Iowa,* 114–16.

30. Lendt, *Demise,* 52, 59–60.

31. Ibid.

32. Quoted in Wubben, *Civil War Iowa,* 185, 187. Davenport was not the only Iowa city with prostitutes. The federal manuscript census of 1860 for Council Bluffs listed the names of five prostitutes and a pimp.

33. Quoted in Wubben, *Civil War Iowa,* 186.

34. Ibid., 182–83.

35. Riley, *Frontierswomen,* 114.

36. Ibid., 131–32.

37. Susan Cheever Cowley, "West Branch, Iowa: Hoover's Boyhood Home," *Americana* 2 (1974): 6–7.

CHAPTER 6

1. In 1870 the Iowa Board of Immigration published *Iowa: The Home for Immigrants Be-*

ing *a Treatise on the Resources of Iowa* (Des Moines: Mills & Co.) in an effort to attract more immigrants to Iowa.

2. Bergmann, *Negro in Iowa,* 34.

3. Ibid., 14.

4. Ibid., 51. After his son became a lawyer, Clark attended the University of Iowa and graduated with a law degree.

5. Robert Dykstra, "Dr. Emerson's Sam: Black Iowans Before the Civil War," *The Palimpsest* 63 (1982): 70–76.

6. Ibid., 73–74.

7. Ibid., 76–78. Dykstra also describes a black settlement in Fayette County where the families were in agriculture.

8. Robert Dykstra, "White Men, Black Laws: Territorial Iowans and Civil Rights, 1838–1843," *The Annals of Iowa* 46 (1982): 403.

9. In 1860 Iowa contained 1,069 blacks, some of whom may have been slaves. See Bergmann, *Negro in Iowa,* 34.

10. Robert Dykstra, "The Issue Squarely Met: Toward an Explanation of Iowans' Racial Attitudes, 1865–1868," *The Annals of Iowa* 47 (1984): 431.

11. Bergmann, *Negro in Iowa,* 15.

12. See Dykstra, "Issue Squarely Met." In this article Dykstra analyzes the composition of the 663-member Republican convention of 1865 and presents statistical evidence based on voting records to support his thesis that Republicans were motivated to take the proper moral action in granting black suffrage.

13. Hubert H. Wubben, "The Uncertain Trumpet: Iowa Republicans and Black Suffrage, 1860–1868," *The Annals of Iowa* 47 (1984): 414, 426, 427. At the same time, the word "white" was removed from the enumeration census and militia clauses. See Wall, *Iowa,* 115.

14. Arnie Cooper, "A Stony Road: Black Education in Iowa, 1838–1860," *The Annals of Iowa* 48 (1986): 119–20.

15. The result of low school attendance by blacks was reflected in literacy figures. The census of 1850 indicated that 31 percent of blacks in Iowa were illiterate. See Cooper, "Stony Road," 122.

16. Ibid., 129; Bergmann, *Negro in Iowa,* 50.

17. Bergmann, *Negro in Iowa,* 50; Wall, *Iowa,* 116.

18. Bergmann, *Negro in Iowa,* 54.

19. Ibid., 40.

20. Dykstra, "Dr. Emerson's Sam," 80–81; Bergmann, *Negro in Iowa,* 35, 36–40.

21. Bergmann, *Negro in Iowa*; Dorothy Schwieder et al., *Buxton: Work and Racial Equality in a Coal Mining Community* (Ames: Iowa State University Press, 1987), 17.

22. Schwieder et al., *Buxton,* 116–17.

23. Bergmann, *Negro in Iowa,* 34–35.

24. Sage, *History of Iowa,* 93.

25. Kjell Nordqvist, "Destination-Iskaloose," *Swedish American Genealogist,* no vol. number (n.d., copyright 1988), 57, 66.

26. Myron S. Anderson, "My Swedish Heritage," *The Palimpsest* 47 (1966): 193.

27. See Hildegard Binder Johnson, "German Forty-Eighters in Davenport," *Iowa Journal of History* 19 (1921) for an excellent account of the Forty-eighters.

28. Maldwyn A. Jones, *Destination America* (New York: Holt, Rinehart and Winston, 1976), 29–34.

29. Anderson, "My Swedish Heritage," 193–96.

30. Ibid., 197.

31. Petersen, *Story of Iowa,* vol. 1, 929.

32. Janice Beran, "The Turners in Iowa, USA: Promotors of Fitness and Shapers of Cul-

ture," in *Turner and Sport: The Cross Cultural Exchange, German and American Studies in Sport,* ed. Roland Naul (New York: Waxmann Munster, 1991), 185–86.

33. Ibid., 94.

34. Ibid., 93–94.

35. Ibid., 98. The Turners would prosper until the early twentieth century; before World War I, however, they began to decline in membership, and after the war the decline accelerated.

36. C. Carnahan Goetsch, "The Immigrant and America: Assimilation of a German Family, Part 2," *The Annals of Iowa* 42 (1973): 116. (Part 1 appeared in *The Annals of Iowa* 42 (Summer 1973).

37. Ibid.

38. Kevin Proescholdt, "The Demography of the New Sweden Settlement in Iowa, 1845–1880," *Swedish Pioneer Historical Quarterly* 32 (April 1981), 147–48.

39. O. M. Nelson, *Swedish Settlements in Iowa: Their Founding and Development and Some Noted Men and Women* (n.p., 1931), 4.

40. Ibid., 10.

41. Ibid., 63–64.

42. Ibid., 64–65.

43. Odd S. Lovoll, *Decorah-Posten: The Story of an Immigrant Newspaper,* Norwegian-American Studies, vol. 27 (Northfield, Minn.: Norwegian-American Historical Association, 1977), 77–80.

44. Ibid., 82, 84.

45. Ibid., 94–95, 100. German-language newspapers were also published in Iowa—Davenport had two.

46. Leigh D. Jordahl, "Stability and Change: Luther College After One Hundred Twenty-five Years," *The Palimpsest* 67 (1986), 111–12.

47. Thomas P. Christensen, *A History of the Danes in Iowa* (Solvang, Calif.: Dansk Folkesamfund, 1952), 67, 69.

48. Ibid., 78, 86.

49. Ibid., 177, 182. See Chapter 14, "The Danish Societies in Iowa" for a more complete discussion of the subject.

50. Peter L. Petersen, "Language and Loyalty: Governor Harding and Iowa's Danish-Americans During World War I," *The Annals of Iowa* 42 (1974): 408.

51. Dorothy Schwieder, *Black Diamonds: Life and Work in Iowa's Coal Mining Communities* (Ames: Iowa State University Press, 1983), 7–9.

52. Rosalie Mullinix, *History of Hiteman, A Mining Town,* (privately published, 1983), p.38.

53. Sage, *History of Iowa,* 93.

54. Jones, *Destination America,* 78–79.

55. Curtis Harnack, *Gentlemen on the Prairie* (Ames: Iowa State University Press, 1985), 9, 85, 194, 195.

56. Ibid., 154–55.

57. *Des Moines Register,* 7 July 1985, 1A, 4A. In 1980 the U.S. census report indicated that 6.5 percent of all Iowans reported having some Dutch ancestry. This is the highest Dutch ancestry of any state.

58. Petersen, *Story of Iowa,* vol. 2, 937–39.

59. Sage, *History of Iowa,* 95. For a detailed study of one Dutch family over several generations, see Brian Beltman, "Ethnic Persistence and Change: The Experience of a Dutch-American Family in Rural Iowa," *The Annals of Iowa* 52 (1993).

60. Petersen, *Story of Iowa,* vol. 2, 942.

61. Ibid.

CHAPTER 7

1. Petersen, *Story of Iowa,* vol. 2, 661.
2. Ibid., 747–49.
3. Ibid., 725, 732.
4. Ibid., 663–64.
5. Thomas Auge, "The Dream of Bishop Loras: A Catholic Iowa," *The Palimpsest* 61 (1980): 171.
6. Ibid., 172, 179.
7. Ibid., 179.
8. Petersen, *Story of Iowa,* vol. 2, 665.
9. Auge, "Dream of Bishop Loras," 176. Bishop Loras would also be responsible for attracting a male religious order, the Trappists, who are still located near Dubuque at New Melleray Abby. A part of the Cistercian Order, the Trappists take a vow of silence, thereafter working and worshiping in near total silence. They live austere lives, arising around three A.M. to begin their daily tasks.
10. Petersen, *Story of Iowa,* vol. 2, 667; "Highlights in 100-Year History of Sisters of Humility," *The Catholic Messenger* (Davenport, Iowa), 25 November 1954, 3. Also see *Centenary Souvenir of the Sisters of the Humility of Mary, 1854–1954* (n.p., n.d.). Deposited at the Ottumwa Public Library.
11. "Highlights," 3. Today, St. Vincent's is the headquarters for the Diocese of Davenport.
12. Ibid.
13. William Sweet, *Rise of Methodism in the West* (Nashville: Smith and Lamar, 1920), 60–67. See Rorabaugh, *Alcoholic Republic* for an excellent discussion of Americans' excessive drinking in the nineteenth century.
14. Petersen, *Story of Iowa,* vol. 2, 668.
15. Ibid., 670.
16. Ibid., 678.
17. See Philip Jordan, *William Salter: Western Torchbearer* (Oxford, Ohio: Mississippi Valley Press, 1939).
18. Ibid., 48, 55, 75.
19. Ruth S. Beitz, "The Iowa Band," *The Iowan* 11 (1963): 12.
20. Jordan, *William Salter,* 69–70.
21. Petersen, *Story of Iowa,* vol. 2, 727–31.
22. Ibid., 748.
23. Michael J. Bell, "True Israelites in America: The Story of Jews of Iowa" (paper, Grinnell College, 1994), 4–5.
24. Ibid., 7; Petersen, *Story of Iowa,* vol. 2, 746.
25. Bell, "True Israelites," 11.
26. Ibid., 13; *Des Moines Register,* 26 May 1985, 1B; Petersen, *Story of Iowa,* vol. 2, 746.
27. Petersen, *Story of Iowa,* vol. 2, 850; Sage, *History of Iowa,* 46.
28. Keach Johnson, "Elementary and Secondary Education in Iowa, 1890–1900: A Time of Awakening, Part 1," *The Annals of Iowa* 45 (1979): 91–93.
29. Petersen, *Story of Iowa,* vol. 2, 370.
30. Sage, *History of Iowa,* 107.
31. Johnson, "Elementary and Secondary Education," 173. Also see Thomas Morain, "The Departure of Males from the Teaching Profession in Nineteenth-Century Iowa," *Civil War History* 26 (1980).
32. Petersen, *Story of Iowa,* vol. 2, 854.
33. Ibid., 860.

34. Ibid., 862.

35. Johnson, "Elementary and Secondary Education," 103–4.

36. Ibid., 96, 108.

37. Ibid., 107.

38. Wayne E. Fuller, *The Old Country School: The Story of Rural Education in the Middle West* (Chicago: University of Chicago Press, 1982), 10.

39. Ibid., 17.

40. Ibid., 7, 10.

41. Johnson, "Elementary and Secondary Education," 195. See also Keach Johnson, "Roots of Modernization: Educational Reform in Iowa at the Turn of the Century," *The Annals of Iowa* 50 (1991); Carroll Engelhardt, "Schools and Character: Educational Reform and Industrial Virtue in Iowa, 1890–1930," *The Annals of Iowa* 47 (1985).

42. Petersen, *Story of Iowa*, vol. 2, 864.

43. Johnson, "Roots of Modernization," 893, 912; Richard Jensen and Mark Friedberger, *Education And Social Structure: A Historical Study of Iowa, 1870–1930* (Chicago: Newberry Library, 1976), 7.4, 7.5.

44. Jensen and Friedberger, *Education and Social Structure*, 7.9.

45. Ibid., 7.2, 7.3, 7.6,

46. Engelhardt, "Schools and Character," 630–31, 636.

47. Petersen, *Story of Iowa*, vol. 2, 875–76; In 1914 Charles City College merged with Morningside. This school had been started in 1868 in Illinois by the Northwest German Conference of the Methodist Episcopal Church.

48. Petersen, *Story of Iowa*, vol. 2, 896.

49. Ibid., 877–82.

50. Ibid., 883; Stow Persons, *The University of Iowa in the Twentieth Century: An Institutional History* (Iowa City: University of Iowa Press, 1990), 3.

51. Petersen, *Story of Iowa*, vol. 2, 896–97.

52. Persons, *University of Iowa*, 3.

53. Ibid., 1–3; Petersen, *Story of Iowa*, vol. 2, 903.

54. Persons, *University of Iowa*, 4, 7, 9; Petersen, *Story of Iowa*, vol. 2, 905.

55. Persons, *The University of Iowa*, 12, 15.

56. Ibid., 16; Sage, *History of Iowa*, 105.

57. Persons, *University of Iowa*, 2; Sage, *History of Iowa*, 106. For several years, the University of Iowa admitted women only into the Normal Department. See Petersen, *Story of Iowa*, vol. 2, 904.

58. Ross, *Iowa Agriculture*, 156–57.

59. Edward A. Goedeken, "An Academic Controversy at Iowa State Agricultural College, 1890–1891," *The Annals of Iowa* 45 (1979): 112–13.

60. Ibid., 120–21.

61. Petersen, *Story of Iowa*, vol. 2, 909.

CHAPTER 8

1. Ross, *Iowa Agriculture*, 72.

2. Ibid., 73–74.

3. Ibid., 77.

4. Donald L. Winters, "The Economics of Midwestern Agriculture, 1865–1900," in *Agriculture and National Development: Views on the Nineteenth Century*, ed. Lou Ferleger (Ames: Iowa State University Press, 1990), 88.

5. Ibid., 86, 89.

6. Sage, *History of Iowa,* 214.

7. Ibid.

8. Myrtle Beinhauer, "Development of the Grange in Iowa, 1868–1930," in *Patterns and Perspectives,* ed. Dorothy Schwieder (Ames: Iowa State University Press, 1973), 226–28.

9. Ross, *Iowa Agriculture,* 98–99. The cooperative aspect also failed before long because of inexperienced management and an inability to extend credit. See Beinhauer, "Development of the Grange," 226–27.

10. Ross, *Iowa Agriculture,* 108–9.

11. Ibid., 113.

12. Ibid., 112, 133.

13. Jeffrey Ostler, *Prairie Populism: The Fate of Agrarian Radicalism in Kansas, Nebraska, and Iowa, 1880–1892* (Manhattan: University Press of Kansas, 1993), 10.

14. Ross, *Iowa Agriculture,* 114.

15. Recent studies that have treated the important role of farm women in Iowa and the Midwest are Deborah Fink, *Open Country Iowa: Rural Women, Tradition and Change* (Albany, New York: SUNY Press, 1986); Deborah Fink, *Agrarian Women: Wives and Mothers in Rural Nebraska, 1880–1940* (Chapel Hill: University of North Carolina Press, 1992); and Katherine Jellison, *Entitled To Power: Farm Women And Technology, 1913–1963* (Chapel Hill: University of North Carolina Press, 1993). Also see Joan M. Jensen, *Promise to the Land: Essays on Rural Women* (Albuquerque: University of New Mexico Press, 1991) for material dealing with rural women in all parts of the country.

16. Some recent studies have stressed mutuality in work roles and decision making between farm men and women. See Nancy Osterud, *Bonds of Community: The Lives of Farm Women in Nineteenth Century New York* (Ithaca, N.Y.: Cornell University Press, 1991).

17. Diary of Margaret Miller, State Historical Society of Iowa, Iowa City, 22 March, 22 April, 22 September, 1858.

18. Clifford Drury, "Growing Up on an Iowa Farm, 1897–1915," *The Annals of Iowa* 42 (1974): 181.

19. See Lensink, "A Secret To Be Burried."

20. James Sanders, ed., "Times Hard but Grit Good: Lydia Moxley's 1877 Diary," *The Annals of Iowa* 47 (1984): 273–75; Ham, "End of Innocence," 94.

21. Fink, *Agrarian Women,* 140.

22. Schwieder, "Labor and Economic Roles," 162; Lensink, "Secret To Be Burried," 184.

23. David Danbom, *The Resisted Revolution: Urban America and the Industrialization of Agriculture, 1900–1930* (Ames: Iowa State University Press, 1979), 4.

24. Thomas J. Morain, *Prairie Grass Roots: An Iowa Small Town in the Early Twentieth Century* (Ames: Iowa State University Press, 1988), 143.

25. Roy Alden Atwood, "Routes of Rural Discontent: Cultural Contradictions of Rural Free Delivery in Southeastern Iowa, 1899–1917," *The Annals of Iowa* 48 (1986): 267–69.

26. Ibid., 268–73.

27. Keith Allan Voss, "Amelia, 1902–1918" (unpublished paper, 25 March 1979), 1–3.

28. Ibid., 2.

29. Ibid., 8.

30. Ibid., 8–9.

31. Ross, *Iowa Agriculture,* 120–21.

32. Ibid., 121–22.

33. Gilbert C. Fite, *American Farmers: The New Minority* (Bloomington: Indiana University Press, 1981), 31.

34. Ross, *Iowa Agriculture,* 125; Rosanne Sizer and William Silag, "P. G. Holden and the Corn Gospel Trains," *The Palimpsest* 62 (1981): 68.

35. Sizer and Silag, "P. G. Holden," 67–69.

36. Ibid., 70.

37. *Annual Narrative Reports of County Agents and Home Demonstration Agents*, Buena Vista County, vol. 4, 1939, 5; *Annual Narrative Reports*, Crawford County, vol. 6, 1939, 6.

38. Ross, *Iowa Agriculture*, 144; Ralph K. Bliss, *History of Cooperative Agriculture and Home Economics Extension in Iowa: The First Fifty Years* (Ames: Iowa State University Press, 1960), 132.

39. Ross, *Iowa Agriculture*, 153; Bliss, *History Of Cooperative Agriculture*, 141–42; Ralph K. Bliss, *Annual Report of Iowa Agricultural and Home Economics Extension Service*, 1 July 1920 to 20 June 1921 (Ames: Iowa State College, 1921), 12–13.

40. Peter Harstad and Bonnie Lindemann, *Gilbert N. Haugen: Norwegian-American Farm Politician* (Iowa City: State Historical Society of Iowa, 1992), 151–67.

41. Leland Sage, "Rural Iowa in the 1920s and 1930s: Roots of the Farm Depression," *The Annals of Iowa* 47 (1983): 97, 99.

42. Harstad and Lindemann, *Gilbert N. Haugen*, 138; and Danbom, *Resisted Revolution*, 127.

43. Dorothy Schwieder, "Rural Iowa in the 1920s: Conflict and Continuity," *The Annals of Iowa* 47 (1983): 110–11; Danbom, *Resisted Revolution*, 128.

44. Fink, *Agrarian Women*, 11; Schwieder, "Rural Iowa," 104–5.

45. Danbom, *Resisted Revolution*, 133.

46. Jellison, *Entitled to Power*.

CHAPTER 9

1. Wall, *Iowa*, 150.

2. Lewis Atherton, *Main Street on the Middle Border* (Quadrangle: New York Times Book Co., 1975), 33.

3. Hamlin Garland, "A Day's Pleasure," in *Main-Travelled Roads* (New York: New American Library, Signet Class, 1962), 179.

4. Christie Dailey, "A Woman's Concern: Millinery in Central Iowa, 1870–1880," *Journal of the West* 21 (1982): 26, 28, 31.

5. Stephanie Carpenter, "Portrait of a Community: Belle Plaine, Iowa" (Master's thesis, Iowa State University, 1992), 22, 23, 29. As Morain has pointed out in *Prairie Grass Roots*, 27, in the latter nineteenth century, small towns increasingly became retail-and-service centers for surrounding farm populations.

6. Atherton, *Main Street*, 222, 227.

7. John B. Harper, "Theaters of Iowa: The Historic & the Unusual," in *Take This Exit: Rediscovering the Iowa Landscape*, ed. Robert F. Sayre (Ames: Iowa State University Press, 1989), 251–55. The terms "theater" and "opera house" were sometimes used interchangeably.

8. Ibid., 251–52.

9. Thomas J. Morain, "Impact on the Automobile," (unpublished paper, Iowa State University, 1980), 4.

10. Atherton, *Main Street*, 247.

11. Ibid., 112–17.

12. Fink, *Open Country Iowa*, 19.

13. Winifred Mayne Van Etten, "Three Worlds," in *Growing Up in Iowa: Reminiscences of Fourteen Iowa Authors*, ed. Clarence A. Andrews (Ames: Iowa State University Press, 1978), 146–47.

14. George Mills, "Iowa Speed Limit Once Was 10 mph," *Des Moines Register*, 10 March 1974, 1A.

15. Quoted in Morain, *Prairie Grass Roots,* 147.

16. Ibid.

17. Ibid., 148.

18. Nancy Ruth Derr, "Iowans During World War I: Study of Change Under Stress." (Ph.D. diss., George Washington University, 1979), 563, 565–66. Also see Chapter 13 for general discussion of these changes.

19. Morain, *Prairie Grass Roots,* 188.

20. Ibid., 203, 188, 202–3.

21. Nancy Derr, "Lowden: A Study of Intolerance in an Iowa Community During the Era of the First World War," *The Annals of Iowa* 50, no. 1 (1989): 22.

22. Morain, *Prairie Grass Roots,* 197–208.

23. Keith Ian Polakoff et al., *Generations of Americans: A History of the United States* (New York: St. Martin's Press, 1976), 598–609.

24. Kay Johnson, "The Ku Klux Klan in Iowa: A Study in Intolerance," (Master's thesis, University of Iowa, 1967), 87.

25. Ibid., 89–91.

26. Ibid., 104; also see Chapter 4, "Greenfield: The Klan in a Rural Setting."

27. Ibid., 98–99.

28. Ibid., 107–12, 186.

29. Morain, *Prairie Grass Roots,* 170–71; Atherton, *Main Street,* 323, 328. The traveling Chautauqua is not to be confused with the Chautauqua institution, which began in Chautauqua, New York, in 1874.

30. Atherton, *Main Street,* 298–99.

31. Morain, *Prairie Grass Roots,* 168, 169; Nancy Woloch, *Women and the American Experience* (New York: Alfred A. Knopf, 1984), 405–6.

32. Woloch, *Women and the American Experience,* 406.

33. Morain, *Prairie Grass Roots,* 160, 165, 171.

34. See Frederick Lewis Allen, *Only Yesterday: An Informal History of the 1920s* (New York: Harper & Brothers, 1931).

35. Stephanie Carpenter, "Portrait of a Community: Belle Plaine, Iowa 1895–1925" (Master's thesis, Iowa State University, 1992), 54–57. Belle Plaine, with eighteen hundred residents, had two theaters in the 1920s.

36. Janice A. Beran, *From Six-on-Six to Full Court Press: A Century of Iowa Girls' Basketball* (Ames: Iowa State University Press, 1993), 181, 183.

37. Carpenter, "Portrait of a Community," 64, 66.

CHAPTER 10

1. U. S. Department of Commerce, Bureau of the Census, *Ninth Census of the United States, 1870: Population,* vol. 1 (Washington, D.C., 1871) 131–42.

2. See Richard Kirkendall, *Uncle Henry: A Documentary Profile of the First Henry Wallace* (Ames: Iowa State University Press, 1993).

3. Earle D. Ross, *A History of the Iowa State College of Agriculture and Mechanic Arts* (Ames: Iowa State College Press, 1942), 43.

4. Lawrence H. Larsen, "Urban Iowa One Hundred Years Ago," *The Annals of Iowa* 49 (1988): 445.

5. Ibid., 447–48.

6. Ibid., 449.

7. Ibid., 453–54.

8. Ibid., 455.

9. Ibid., 458–60; Orin L Dahl, *Des Moines Capital City* (Tulsa: Continental Heritage, 1978), 174.

10. U.S. Department of Commerce, Bureau of the Census, *Twelfth Census of the United States, 1900: Population,* vol. 1 (Washington, D.C.: reprint, 1903), 145–61.

11. John Carlson, "Des Moines Commemorative Section, 150 Years," *Des Moines Register,* 30 May 1993, 6Q, 7Q; Joseph Rosenfield, "A Personal View of Younkers' History," *The Iowan* 16 (1968): 20–21.

12. Dahl, *Des Moines Capital City,* 175; Carlson, "Des Moines," 6Q, 7Q.

13. Ilda M. Hammer, *The Book of Des Moines* (Des Moines: Board of Education, 1947), 76, 78.

14. Dahl, *Des Moines Capital City,* 171.

15. Ibid., 175–78; George Mills, *Looking in Windows: Surprising Stories of Old Des Moines* (Ames: Iowa State University Press, 1991), 160.

16. Dahl, *Des Moines Capital City,* 177; Hammer, *Book of Des Moines,* 100.

17. Dahl, *Des Moines Capital City,* 177; Hammer, *Book of Des Moines,* 102. In the area of government Des Moines would also undergo change, as effective in 1908 the city became recognized nationally for its commission system of city government, known as the Des Moines Plan. See Dahl, *Des Moines Capital City,* 176.

18. Jean B. Kern, "Historical Survey," *The Palimpsest* 30 (1949): 1, 8.

19. Flora Dunlap, "Roadside Settlement of Des Moines," *The Annals of Iowa* 21 (1938): 162–64.

20. Louise Noun, "Roadside Settlement House Remembered," *Des Moines Register,* 11 April 1993, C1; Dunlap, "Roadside Settlement," 165.

21. Dunlap, "Roadside Settlement," 170.

22. Ibid., 170, 173.

23. Ibid., 174–77.

24. Ibid., 183–85.

25. Ibid., 188; Mary Hill, "Willkie House True to Mission," *Des Moines Sunday Register,* 19 December 1993, 2B. In 1945 a new facility was built and renamed Willkie House.

26. Suzanne O'Dea Schenken, "The Immigrants' Advocate: Mary Treglia and the Sioux City Community House, 1921–1959," *The Annals of Iowa* 50 (1989/1990), 190–91; 211–13.

27. Harold F. Ewoldt, *Jane Boyd and Her Times* (Cedar Rapids: Jane Boyd Community House, n.d.), 120.

28. Ibid., 44.

29. Ibid., 46–50.

30. Dunlap, "Roadside Settlement," 167; Ewoldt, *Jane Boyd,* 20.

31. William Hewitt, "Wicked Traffic in Girls: Prostitution and Reform in Sioux City, 1885–1910," *The Annals of Iowa* 51 (1991): 124, 127.

32. Ibid., 148.

33. Mills, *Looking in Windows,* 146.

34. Ibid., 187–91.

CHAPTER 11

1. Steve Wrede, "The Americanization of Scott County," *The Annals of Iowa* 44 (1979), 628–29.

2. Ibid., 630–31.

3. Ibid., 635–36.

4. H. C. Peterson and Gilbert Fite, *Opponents of War, 1917–1918* (Seattle: University of Washington Press), 85.

5. Leola Allen, "Anti-German Sentiment in Iowa During World War I," *The Annals of Iowa* 42 (1974): 420.

6. Myron S. Anderson, "My Swedish Heritage," *The Palimpsest* 48 (1966): 213–14; Schwieder et al., *Buxton,* 162–64.

7. Schwieder et al., *Buxton,* 136–37.

8. Petersen, "Language and Loyalty," 410.

9. See Wilson G. Warren, "The Heyday of the CIO in Iowa: Ottumwa's Meatpacking Workers, 1937–1954," *The Annals of Iowa* 51 (1992) and Roger Horowitz, "'It Wasn't a Time to Compromise:' The Unionization of Sioux City's Packinghouses, 1937–1942," *The Annals of Iowa* 50 (1989/1990). In addition to sources for Italian-American studies cited in this chapter, see Jacqueline Comito, "Porco sei; Porti are: The Autobiography of an American Italian Family in Des Moines" (Master's thesis, Iowa State University, 1995).

10. Cynthia Johnson, "A New Life: The Iowa Coal Mines," *The Palimpsest* 56 (1975): 56–57.

11. Schwieder, *Black Diamonds,* 95–96. Other immigrant women also took in boarders as well as native-born miners' wives.

12. Ibid., 107.

13. Maureen McCoy and William Silag, "The Italian Heritage in Des Moines," *The Palimpsest* 64 (1983): 60–61.

14. Ibid., 62.

15. Ibid.

16. Thomas Shaw, "Oelwein's Italian Neighborhoods: Italian Americans of Oelwein, Iowa, 1901 to the Present," (Master's thesis, University of Northern Iowa, 1978), 2, 148.

17. For population figures, see Sage, *History of Iowa,* 73.

18. See figures for this immigration in Sage, *History of Iowa,* 93.

19. Kathleen Eberdt, *Special People: Ethnic Contributions to the Bettendorf Community* (Bettendorf: Bettendorf Museum, 1981), 77, 81.

20. Ibid., 79–80.

21. Ibid., 80.

22. Ibid., 7. Today Mexican Americans in the Davenport area worship at the Church of Our Lady of Guadalupe, St. Marys, and Sacred Heart Cathedral.

23. "Mexican Festival in WDM Turns into Big Reunion," *Des Moines Register,* 27 June 1993, 1B.

24. Schwieder et al., *Buxton,* 40, 116–17.

25. See Schwieder et al., *Buxton,* Chapter 7, "Buxton and Haydock: The Final Years."

26. Bergmann, *Negro in Iowa,* 34–35.

27. Ibid.

28. Robert Neymeyer, "May Harmony Prevail: The Early History of Black Waterloo," *The Palimpsest* 61 (1980): 85.

29. Ibid., 86–87.

30. Ibid., 86, 87, 90. The number of blacks in Black Hawk County would double by 1920 and reach 1,234 by 1930; it is assumed that all or almost all of these individuals lived in Waterloo.

31. Ibid., 89.

32. Schwieder et al., *Buxton,* 202–3. When interviewed for the Buxton project, Vaeletta Fields still had a clipping from a Waterloo newspaper that reported the hiring of the first African-American teacher in Waterloo.

33. Bergmann, *Negro in Iowa*, 35; William L. Hewitt, "So Few Undesirables: Race, Residence, and Occupation in Sioux City, 1890–1925," *The Annals of Iowa* 50 (1989/1990): 160–62.

34. Hewitt, "So Few Undesirables," 160, 163.

35. Ibid., 174, 176–77.

36. Ibid., 170, 175.

37. Ibid., 175–77.

38. Jack Lufkin, "The Founding and Early Years of the National Association for the Advancement of Colored People in Des Moines, 1915–1930," *The Annals of Iowa* 45 (1980): 442, 455–59. Lufkin also points out that although blacks were one of the largest minority groups in the city, they had little political power. Between 1890 and 1930 only one black was elected to public office: In 1899 Frank Blagburn was elected market master with the responsibility to oversee the city's markethouse operation.

39. Mary Beth Norton et al., *A People and a Nation: A History of the United States,* vol. 2, (Boston: Houghton Mifflin Company, 1986), 651–52.

40. Hal S. Chase, "Struggle for Equality: Fort Des Moines Training Camp for Colored Officers, 1917," *Phylon* 39 (1979): 297, 385–87. Officials also considered Howard University and Hampston Institute for the camp.

41. Ibid., 297–99, 303, 306–7.

42. Bergmann, *Negro in Iowa*, 57; Chase, "Struggle for Equality," 300, 309.

43. Bergmann, *Negro in Iowa*, 58.

44. Ibid., 59.

45. Lufkin, "Founding and Early Years," 446.

46. Henry G. La Brie III, "James B. Morris, Sr., and the *Iowa Bystander*," *The Annals of Iowa* 42 (1974): 319. La Brie spells the name of one editor Billy "Colson," and Bergmann spells it "Coalson." Morris sold the paper in 1971, and at its peak it had about ten thousand subscribers. Later a newspaper for the African American community was published called *The Communicator.* See "The 'Fighting Press,'" *Des Moines Register,* 8 June 1993, 1T.

47. Lufkin, "Founding and Early Years," 449.

48. Ibid., 460.

49. Diane Barthel, *Amana: From Pietist Sect to American Community* (Lincoln: University of Nebraska Press, 1984), 3, 6, 11, 12. For additional sources on Amana history see Barbara Yambura, *A Change and a Parting* (Ames: Iowa State University Press, 1960); Bertha Shambaugh, *Amana That Was and Amana That Is* (New York: Benjamin Blom, 1971); Jonathan Gary Andelson, "Communalism and Change in the Amana Society, 1855–1932," (Ph.D. diss., University of Michigan, 1974); Charles Nordhoff, *The Communistic Societies of the United States, From Personal Visit and Observation.* Introduction, Mark Holloway (New York: Dover Publications, 1966); and Alfred W. Hinds, *American Communities and Cooperative Colonies,* 2d rev. (Chicago: C. H. Kerr & Co., 1902).

50. Barthel, *Amana*, 33–62.

51. Ibid., 27, 45–47.

52. See Shambaugh, *Amana That Was,* for a good discussion of religious practices.

53. Andelson, "Communalism and Change."

54. Barthel, *Amana*, 100–105.

55. Elmer and Dorothy Schwieder, *A Peculiar People: Iowa's Old Order Amish* (Ames: Iowa State University Press, 1975), 16; also see John Hostetler, *Amish Society,* rev. ed. (Baltimore: John Hopkins Press, 1968).

56. Ibid., 18–19.

57. Ibid., 56–57.

58. Ibid., 23–25.

59. Ibid. See chapters 7 and 8 for a discussion of the school controversy in Iowa.

CHAPTER 12

1. Dan E. Clark, "Recent Liquor Legislation in Iowa," *Iowa Journal of History and Politics* 15 (1917): 42, 43.

2. Clark, "Recent Liquor Legislation," 43, 44; Julie E. Nelson, "Liquor Legislation in Iowa," *The Palimpsest* 62 (1981): 190. The law of 1855 had such a limited impact on the liquor trade that liquor dealers barely protested the measure. See Clark, "Recent Liquor Legislation," 44.

3. Thomas S. Smith, "A Martyr for Prohibition: The Murder of Reverend George C. Haddock," *The Palimpsest* 62 (1981): 186; Clark, "Recent Liquor Legislation," 45.

4. Smith, "Martyr for Prohibition," 189.

5. Ibid., 189, 192.

6. Derr, "Iowans During World War I," 66–67.

7. Ibid., 55–57, 64.

8. Ibid., 52, 57–59. Also see Richard J. Jensen, *The Winning of the Midwest: Social and Political Conflict, 1888–1896* (Chicago: University of Chicago Press, 1971), chap. 4, for a more specific list of pietist and liturgical churches. The brief discussion here does not allow for a full listing.

9. Sage, *History of Iowa*, 210.

10. Clark, "Recent Liquor Legislation," 46; Smith, "Martyr for Prohibition," 190–91.

11. Clark, "Recent Liquor Legislation," 48–50, 56, 58.

12. Herman E. Bateman, "Albert B. Cummins and the Davenport Riots of 1907," *Arizona and the West* 18 (1976). The Anti-Saloon League was also active in Iowa. For a discussion of the League in Sioux City, see Kathleen M. Green, "The Demise of John Barleycorn: The Sioux City Campaign against the Liquor Traffic, 1909–1917" (Master's thesis, University of South Dakota, 1982).

13. Mary Beth Norton et al., *A People and a Nation: A History of the United States,* 2d ed., vol. 2 (Boston: Houghton Mifflin Company, 1986), 588.

14. Sage, *History of Iowa*, 225.

15. Ibid., 220.

16. Ibid., 225. Also see chapters 13 and 14 for a good general discussion of the progressive movement in Iowa, including a discussion of the main participants.

17. Ibid.

18. Ibid., 231.

19. William L. Bowers, "The Fruits of Iowa Progressivism, 1900–1915," *Iowa Journal of History* 57 (1959).

20. Sage, *History Of Iowa*, 231; Bowers, "Fruits," 39.

21. Bowers, "Fruits," 39–42; Sage, *History of Iowa*, 238.

22. Bowers, "Fruits," 41–43; Sage, *History of Iowa*, 238.

23. Sage, *History of Iowa*, 237; Max D. Perdue, "The Progressive Republicans of Iowa: The Development of the Direct Primary Law, 1896–1907" (Master's thesis, Drake University, 1965), 2.

24. Perdue, "Progressive Republicans," 9.

25. Ibid.; Sage, *History of Iowa*, 238.

26. Sage, *History of Iowa*, 243; Bowers, "Fruits," 52–53.

27. Bowers, "Fruits," 60.

28. Sage, *History of Iowa*, 255.

29. Woloch, *Women and the American Experience*, 312–17.

30. Louise Noun, "Annie Savery: A Voice for Women's Rights," *The Annals of Iowa* 44 (1977): 15.

31. Ruth A. Gallaher, *Legal and Political Status of Women in Iowa* (Iowa City: State Historical Society of Iowa, 1918), 195.

32. Ibid., 188–89. The Greenback party, at its state convention in 1881, also supported "equal political rights for men and women."

33. Ibid., 202.

34. Ibid., 215.

35. Derr, "Iowans During World War I," 115.

36. Gallaher, *Legal and Political Status*, 212.

37. Ibid., 219; Steven J. Fuller and Alsatia Mellecker, "Behind the Yellow Banner: Anna B. Lawther and the Winning of Suffrage for Iowa Women," *The Palimpsest* 65 (1984): 107.

38. Green, "Demise," 105.

39. Ibid.; Fuller and Mellecker, "Behind the Yellow Banner," 109.

40. Gallaher, *Legal and Political Status*, 205.

41. Sage, *History of Iowa*, 255. In a one-volume history of the state it is impossible to include all women who played important roles, or to treat the life of Carrie Chapman Catt as fully as she deserves. In 1993 the Carrie Chapman Catt Center for Women in Politics was organized at Iowa State University and a building named for Catt will provide offices for the center.

CHAPTER 13

1. Sage, *History of Iowa*, 310–11.

2. H. H. McCarty and C. W. Thompson, "Meat Packing in Iowa" (Iowa City: State University of Iowa, 1933), 14.

3. Ibid.

4. Luther A. Brewer and Barthinius L. Wick, *History of Linn County, Iowa*, vol. 5 (Chicago: Pioneer Publishing Co., 1911) 339–41; Janette Stevenson Murray and Frederick Gray Murray, *The Story of Cedar Rapids* (New York: Stratford House, 1950), 97; McCarty and Thompson, "Meat Packing," 34, 35; William J. Petersen and George S. May, "Industries of Iowa," *The Palimpsest* 37 (1956): 246.

5. Lawrence Oakley Cheever, *The House of Morrell* (Cedar Rapids: Torch Press, 1948), 72.

6. Ibid.; McCarty and Thompson, "Meat Packing," 29.

7. McCarty and Thompson, "Meat Packing," 32–33; *The WPA Guide to 1930s Iowa* (Ames: Iowa State University Press, 1986), 294.

8. *WPA Guide*, 304; McCarty and Thompson, "Meat Packing," 52; John F. Schmidt, *A Historical Profile of Sioux City* (Sioux City: Sioux City Stationary Co., 1969), 280–81.

9. McCarty and Thompson, "Meat Packing," 54–57, 61; Schmidt, *Historical Profile*, 280.

10. McCarty and Thompson, "Meat Packing," 121–22. As McCarty and Thompson indicated, manufacturing income here referred to "value added by manufacture." It should be noted that through the years many smaller Iowa communities have had meat-packing operations, including Albia, Eddyville, Perry, and Fort Dodge. See McCarty and Thompson, "Meat Packing," 127–36.

11. Ruth L. Hoadley, "Industrial Growth of Iowa," *Iowa Studies in Business*, no. 11, Bureau of Business Research (Iowa City: State University of Iowa, 1928), 13, 19.

12. Murray and Murray, *Story of Cedar Rapids*, 106–7.

13. Harrison John Thornton, *The History of the Quaker Oats Company* (Chicago: University of Chicago Press, 1933), 79. Quaker Oats would prosper through several depressions, and by the 1950s the Cedar Rapids operation ranked as the largest single-unit cereal plant in the world. See Petersen and May, "Industries of Iowa," 37.

14. Hoadley, "Industrial Growth of Iowa," 13–15. These are categories used by the U.S. Census of Manufacturers.

15. Sage, *History of Iowa,* 217.

16. Ibid.; Petersen and May, "Industries of Iowa," 248.

17. A. B. Funk, *Fred L. Maytag: A Biography* (Cedar Rapids: Torch Press, 1936), 33–47.

18. Ibid., 48–52.

19. Ibid., 56–63. The company has developed additional lines, such as dishwashers, which it marketed for the first time in the 1950s.

20. Deborah Fink, "Development and the Threads of Rural Change: Perry from 1910 to 1920" (unpublished paper, 1994), 5, 6.

21. Ibid., 9.

22. Hoadley, "Industrial Growth of Iowa," 9; Howard Bowen, "Iowa Income: 1909–1934," *Iowa Studies in Business,* no. 14 (Iowa City: State University of Iowa, 1935.) Taken from studies by the University of Iowa, these figures vary because of different inclusions.

23. Dorothy Schwieder, *Black Diamonds: Life and Work in Iowa's Coal Mining Communities, 1895–1925* (Ames: Iowa State University, 1987), x; *Biennial Report of the State Mine Inspector* (1951), 35.

24. Schwieder, *Black Diamonds,* 99, 118–19. Census records, which were used for income data, did not indicate which mines the miners worked in. Regardless of whether a mine was shipping or local, there were also other conditions that reduced the number of days worked. Sometimes mines were flooded or had cave-ins, which led to loss of work; strikes also reduced the number of days worked.

25. Ibid., 168.

26. *Biennial Report of the State Mine Inspector,* 35.

27. Ralph Scharnau, "Workers, Unions, and Workplaces in Dubuque, 1830–1990," *The Annals of Iowa* 52 (1993): 55–56.

28. Howard Bowen, "Iowa Income: 1909–1934," in *Iowa Studies in Business,* vol. 14 (Iowa City: State University of Iowa, 1935).

29. Wilson J. Warren, "Heyday of the CIO," 365; Scharnau, "Workers Unions," 50.

30. Sage, *History of Iowa,* 217.

31. The interviews were collected as a part of the Iowa Labor History Project carried out by the Iowa Federation of Labor, AFL-CIO, and are deposited at the State Historical Society in Iowa City.

32. Shelton Stromquist, *Solidarity and Survival: An Oral History of Iowa Labor in the Twentieth Century* (Iowa City: University of Iowa Press, 1993), 58.

33. Ibid., 97–98.

34. Ibid., 82–83.

35. Ibid., 96–97.

36. Horowitz, "It Wasn't a Time," 244–45.

37. Stromquist, *Solidarity and Survival,* 5; Ralph Scharnau, "The Knights of Labor in Iowa," *The Annals of Iowa* 50 (1991): 865.

38. Scharnau, "Knights of Labor," 866, 873, 887.

39. Stromquist, *Solidarity and Survival,* 8.

40. Wilson J. Warren, "The Welfare Capitalism of John Morrell and Company, 1922–1937," *The Annals of Iowa* 47 (1984), 501, 517.

41. Horowitz, "It Wasn't a Time," 241, 256.

42. Sandra Charvat Burke and Willis Goudy, *Women in Iowa: 1980 and a Century of Perspective* (Ames: Iowa State University Press, 1986), 18, 21. As Burke and Goudy point out, however, the procedures followed by the census takers varied, as before 1930 "the age base for information" was ten years and older; after 1930 the age base for information was fourteen years

and older. Also see Alice Kessler-Harris, *Out to Work: A History of Wage Earning Women in the United States* (New York: Oxford University Press, 1982) for a discussion of women's wages in various industries.

43. Burke and Goudy, *Women in Iowa,* 73–74.

44. Rosenfield, "Personal View," 21.

45. Burke and Goudy, *Women in Iowa,* 69–70.

46. *Report of the Bureau of Labor Statistics* (Des Moines: State Printer, 1916), 182.

47. Scharnau, "Workers, Unions," 55; *Report of the Bureau of Labor Statistics,* 206–46. See Kessler-Harris, *Out to Work.*

48. *Report of the Bureau of Labor Statistics,* 203. Also see Gallaher, *Legal and Political Status* for additional information.

CHAPTER 14

1. *The Agricultural Emergency in Iowa* (Ames: Staff of the Department of Economics at Iowa State College, 1933), 1.

2. Ibid., 3.

3. Ibid., 1.

4. Ibid., 5, 6.

5. Theodore Saloutos and John D. Hicks, *Agricultural Discontent in the Middle West, 1900–1939* (Madison: University of Wisconsin Press, 1951), 437.

6. Interview with Czech-American farmer, Clutier, December 1976.

7. Roland A. White, *Milo Reno, Farmers' Union Pioneer: The Story of a Man and a Movement* (New York: Arno Press, 1941), 50.

8. George Mills, "Years of Shame, Days of Madness," *Des Moines Sunday Register,* February 18, 1979, Picture Magazine, 4. Reno had also served as president of the Iowa Farmers Union.

9. Ibid., 4; Saloutos and Hicks, *Agricultural Discontent,* 441.

10. Quoted in Saloutos and Hicks, *Agricultural Discontent,* 439.

11. Sage, *History of Iowa,* 277; Saloutos and Hicks, *Agricultural Discontent,* 442.

12. Sage, *History of Iowa,* 270; and White, *Milo Reno,* 70–71.

13. Saloutos and Hicks, *Agricultural Discontent,* 443.

14. Quoted in Mills, "Years of Shame," 4–5.

15. Wall, *Iowa,* 178.

16. Mills, *Des Moines Sunday Register,* p. 6; John Shover, *Cornbelt Rebellion: The Farmers Holiday Association* (Urbana: University of Illinois Press, 1965), pp. 49–54; and Sage, *History of Iowa,* p. 281.

17. Quoted in Mills, "Years of Shame," 6.

18. Sage, *History of Iowa,* 283.

19. Mills, "Years of Shame," 6, 9.

20. Ibid., 10.

21. Ibid., 10.

22. Ibid., 11, 15; Sage, *History of Iowa,* 297.

23. Mills, "Years of Shame," 15, 16.

24. Ibid. Also see Dorothy Schwieder, *Seventy-Five Years of Service: Cooperative Extension in Iowa* (Ames: Iowa State University Press, 1993) for a full discussion of the Agricultural Adjustment Administration in Iowa.

25. Mildred L. Stenswick, "Certain Home Management Practices of Seventy-three Families in Union County, Iowa," Farm Security Studies 1 (Master's thesis, Iowa State College, 1939), 30–38.

26. Deborah Fink and Dorothy Schwieder, "Iowa Farm Women in the 1930s," *The Annals of Iowa* 49 (1989): 577.

27. Lauren K. Soth, *Agricultural Economics Fact Basebook of Iowa,* Special Report No. 1 (Ames: Iowa State College, 1936), 9.

28. Studs Terkel, *Hard Times: An Oral History of the Great Depression* (New York: Pantheon Books, 1970), 108–9.

29. Scharnau, "Workers, Unions," 63–64; and Jessie A. Bloodworth and Elizabeth J. Greenwood, *The Personal Side,* Works Progress Administration, Division of Research, 1939.

30. Scharnau, "Workers, Unions," 65; Gregg R. Narber and Lea Rosson DeLong, "The New Deal Murals in Iowa," *The Palimpsest* 63 (1982): 986–96.

31. Terkel, *Hard Times,* 25.

32. Ibid., 419–23.

33. Bergmann, *Negro in Iowa,* 73.

34. William J. Maddix, "Blacks and Whites in Manly: An Iowa Town Overcomes Racism," *The Palimpsest* 63 (1982), 134–35.

35. Quoted in Schwieder et al., *Buxton,* 207.

36. "1930s: Battling the Weather," *Des Moines Register,* 8 December 1974, 10C.

37. Ibid.

38. "Scratching out a Living: 1930s," *Des Moines Register,* 15 December 1974, 11C.

39. Ibid.

40. See Caroline Bird, *The Invisible Scar* (New York: David McKay Company, 1966), and Ruth Cavan and Katherine Howland Ranck, *The Family and the Depression: A Study of One Hundred Chicago Families* (Chicago: University of Chicago Press, 1938), chap. 7.

41. Bloodworth and Greenwood, *Personal Side,* 1–2.

42. Ibid., 15.

43. *Iowa State Planning Board: Housing and Health Survey,* Dubuque, Iowa, 1934, 2. The Iowa Emergency Relief Administration would be the state organization involved in the survey work, whereas the Iowa State Planning Board would be the ultimate recipient of the information and would serve as the coordinator for all national, state, and local housing authorities; further, the planning board was to assemble and promote remedial efforts.

44. Also see *Iowa State Planning Board: Report on Housing,* Des Moines, Iowa, 1935.

45. Petersen and May, "Industries of Iowa"; and Nancy Gibbons Zook, "Collins and the Electronic Beanstalk," *The Iowan* 4 (1956): 30–31.

46. George Tindall, *America: A Narrative History* (New York: Norton, 1984), 1072.

47. Fink and Schwieder, "Iowa Farm Women," 580.

48. James Hearst, "Farm Life When the Power Changed," *The Palimpsest* 60 (1979), 145.

49. Fink and Schwieder, "Iowa Farm Women," 585.

CHAPTER 15

1. *Iowa Yearbook of Agriculture,* pt. 9, 1939 (Des Moines: State of Iowa), 347; Ross, *Iowa Agriculture* 179–80.

2. *Iowa Yearbook of Agriculture,* pt. 9, 1940, 378.

3. *Iowa Yearbook of Agriculture,* pt. 9, 1943, p. 3; and *Des Moines Sunday Register,* 14 August 1985, 6A.

4. Schwieder, *Seventy-five Years,* 107–8; and "$1,000,000 Camp Contract Let," *Kossuth County Advance,* 21 September 1943, In total 1,509 Jamaicans and 2,645 Mexicans were involved; they worked in many different parts of the state, including Emmet and Muscatine counties.

5. "Nazis Do Good Job on Iowa Farms," *Des Moines Register,* 10 October 1944, 1A.

6. Schwieder, *Seventy-five Years,* 109; *Annual Narrative Reports,* Fremont County, vol. 4, 1945, 2. Branch camps were established in Pocahontas, Emmet, Dickinson, Floyd, Hardin, Fayette, and Fremont counties, among others.

7. "Trainloads Arrive Here on Milwaukee," *Kossuth County Advocate,* 20 July 1944; and "Kids and Old Men Make up Bunch of Prisoners of War," *Kossuth County Advance,* no date, clipping in World War II file, State Historical Society of Iowa, Des Moines. It is not clear how many men might have tried to escape from the Iowa work camps, but one account tells of an unsuccessful attempt at Clarinda. See Arnold Kramer, *Nazi Prisoners of War in America* (New York: Stein and Day, 1947), 144.

8. *Des Moines Sunday Register,* 11 August 1985, 4A; 14 August 1985, 6A.

9. "War Ended 40 Years Ago, and Iowa Hasn't Been the Same Since," *Des Moines Sunday Register,* 11 August 1985, 1; Sage, *History of Iowa,* 317; "Lists 19,948 on Disability," *Des Moines Tribune,* no date, clipping file on World War II in State Historical Society of Iowa, Des Moines; and *Des Moines Sunday Register,* 11 August 1985, 4A.

10. *Des Moines Register,* 8 November 1992, 2B. Several accounts say that Joseph survived the torpedoing, but did not live until the group was rescued.

11. "The Coast Guard and The Women's Reserve in World War II," *Commandant's Bulletin,* October 1992, U.S. Coast Guard Public Affairs (G-CP-1), Washington, Issue 10-92, 8.

12. Ibid., 9.

13. "Waves Invasion Recalled," *Des Moines Register,* 4 January 1993, 11A.

14. Charity Adams Earley, *One Woman's Army: A Black Officer Remembers the WAC* (College Station, Texas: Texas A & M University Press, 1989), 17, 19, 22, 43.

15. Donna Marie Sciancalepore, "The Contribution of Working Women of Waterloo During World War II" (Master's thesis, University of Northern Iowa, 1990), 22–24.

16. *Des Moines Sunday Register,* 11 August 1985, 1A.

17. Sage, *History of Iowa,* 317; *Des Moines Sunday Register,* 11 August 1985, 1A.

18. *Kossuth County Advance,* 26 January 1943, no page, clipping file, State Historical Society of Iowa, Des Moines.

19. *Des Moines Register,* 14 August 1985, 1A, 4A.

20. *Kossuth County Advance,* 26 January 1943.

21. In most communities companies typically preferred male workers, but when they were no longer available, employers began to hire women.

22. *Clinton Herald,* 18 May 1943, 3.

23. Bergmann, *Negro in Iowa,* 94.

24. Glenda Riley, *Inventing the American Woman: A Perspective on Women's History, 1865 to the Present,* vol. 2 (Arlington Heights, Ill.: Harland Davidson, 1986), 113.

25. "Watch 'Battle' Opening Bond Drive," *Des Moines Register,* no date, clipping file on World War II, State Historical Society of Iowa, Des Moines.

26. *Annual Narrative Reports,* Johnson County, vol. 5, 1944, 3, 15; *Annual Narrative Reports* Kossuth County, vol. 5, 1944, 16.

27. *Des Moines Sunday Register,* 13 September 1992, B1; *Des Moines Register,* 14 August 1985, 6A.

28. Norton et al., *A People and a Nation,* vol. 2, p. 866.

29. Quoted in Schwieder, *Seventy-five Years,* 153.

30. "Report on Iowa—1956: The Working World," *The Iowan* 5 (1957): 42.

31. George S. May, "Iowa in 1955," *The Palimpsest* 37 (1955): 363.

32. "Report on Iowa," 42.

33. Robert Hogan, "Oleo's Case Against Butter," *The Iowan* 1 (1953): 9, 10, 42; George Mills, "Showdown over Oleo: The 1950s Battle," *Des Moines Sunday Register,* 9 January 1994, C1; Frank Nye, "The 55th General Assembly of Iowa," *The Palimpsest* 35 (1954): 29; James C.

Larew, *A Party Reborn: The Democrats of Iowa 1950–1974* (Iowa City: Iowa State Historical Department, 1980), 48.

34. Hogan, "Oleo's Case," 9, 10, 42; Mills, "Showdown," C1. When housewives purchased oleo in Iowa, the product was white and came with a bean containing coloring; the bean then had to be broken and the margarine massaged to spread the coloring throughout the product. Housewives complained of the inconvenience of coloring the margarine and about the tax-inflated price.

35. Mills, "Showdown," C1.

36. Sage, *History of Iowa*, 314.

37. Willis J. Goudy and Sandra Charvat Burke, "Iowa's Changing Population," in *Issues in Iowa Politics* (Ames: Iowa State University Press, 1990), 40, 41.

38. Quoted in Larew, *Party Reborn*, 23, 25.

39. George S. May, "Recent Industrial Development," *The Palimpsest* 37 (1956): 231.

40. Frank T. Nye, "The 57th General Assembly of Iowa," *The Palimpsest* 38 (1957): 470.

41. "Waterloo," *The Iowan* 2 (1954): 14.

42. Larew, *A Party Reborn*, 2.

43. Ibid, 52-59; May, "Iowa in 1955," 370.

44. Wall, *Iowa*, 186–87.

45. Ibid., 188. In 1945 the General Assembly appropriated $2 million for transportation costs and also passed the Agriculture Land Tax Credit Act, which resulted in shifting some educational costs from farmers (through property taxes) to the state's general fund.

46. Nye, "55th General," 30; Wall, *Iowa*, 188; Sage, *History of Iowa*, 331. Iowa had 4,558 school districts in 1953 and 452 in 1972. See Sage, *History of Iowa*, 330.

47. May, "Iowa in 1955," 380–81.

48. Nye, "57th General Assembly," 470.

49. Kent H. King, "The Case for Small High Schools," *The Iowan* 2 (1954): 8.

50. Frank T. Nye, "The 56th General Assembly of Iowa," *The Palimpsest* 36 (1955): 325.

51. Ibid., 325; Nye, "57th General Assembly," *The Palimpsest* 38 (1957), 491.

52. Frank T. Nye, "The 58th General Assembly in Iowa," *The Palimpsest* 40 (1959): 517.

CHAPTER 16

1. Charles W. Wiggins, "The Post World War II Legislative Reapportionment Battle in Iowa Politics," in *Patterns and Perspectives in Iowa History*, ed. Dorothy Schwieder (Ames: Iowa State University Press, 1973), 430. Because of its long tenure and the fact that it involved so many different governors and legislative sessions, I have chosen to treat reapportionment as a separate topical issue rather than in a chronological manner as it related to individual governorships. I believe the topical treatment allows for a better understanding of a complicated issue. Also, I have relied heavily on Wiggins's account of the subject.

2. Ibid., 407.

3. Ibid., 408.

4. Ibid., 408–9.

5. Ibid., 417.

6. Ibid., 418.

7. Ibid., 428.

8. Ibid., 424.

9. Ibid., 424–26.

10. Ibid., 428, 430.

11. See Larew, *Party Reborn*, chap. 4, for a discussion of Hughes and the election of 1962.

12. Ibid., 76, 86.

13. Ibid., 95, 119.

14. Ibid., 95.

15. See Elmer Schwieder and Dorothy Schwieder, *A Peculiar People: Iowa's Old Order Amish* (Ames: Iowa State University Press, 1975), chap. 7.

16. Larew, *Party Reborn,* 99–109. An additional highly sensitive issue was the matter of Iowa's right-to-work laws. See Larew, chap. 4.

17. Frank T. Nye, "The 61st General Assembly of Iowa," *The Palimpsest* 46 (1965): 449.

18. *Iowa Yearbook of Agriculture,* pt. 10, Fifth Biennial Report of Iowa Agriculture and Home Economics Extension Service, 1960–61, 286.

19. "The Changing Economy of Rural Iowa," *The Iowan* 15 (1966): 2.

20. Schwieder, *Seventy-five Years of Service,* chap. 7.

21. Ibid., 160–61.

22. Ibid., 164–65.

23. Iowa also carried out its own research on poverty and welfare in the mid-1960s. The late Wallace Ogg, formerly an extension agricultural economist who helped develop and carry out the study, believed that Iowa was the only state that "tried to research poverty and welfare in depth and teach what was learned." See Wallace Ogg, "My Career as a Public Affairs Specialist," 1989, included in unpublished memoirs of Wallace E. Ogg, "In retrospect," which describes twenty years of Ogg's professional work. Copy deposited at Special Collections, Parks Library, Iowa State University, Ames, 10.

24. I. W. Arthur, "A New Challenge for Our Educators," *The Iowan* 11 (1963): 3.

25. Ibid., 2, 3, 5. In 1963 Iowa had twenty-one junior colleges and twenty-one private four-year colleges.

26. Ibid., 5; *Iowa Official Register,* (Des Moines: State of Iowa, 1985–86) vol. 61, 291–92.

27. Benjamin Stone, "The Legislative Struggle for Civil Rights in Iowa: 1947–1965" (Master's thesis, Iowa State University, 1990), 32, 33, 35.

28. Ibid., 42–43. The Des Moines hearing was canceled because local officials felt there was not sufficient time to prepare a report properly.

29. Ibid., 47.

30. Ibid., 1. In 1963 the General Assembly had passed a "weak fair employment's practices act." As Ben Stone has pointed out, civil-rights bills between 1945 and 1965 were generally concerned with employment discrimination and more commonly referred to as fair employment practices bill. In 1970 the commission's mandate was expanded to cover cases involving sex discrimination. See Edward S. Allen, *Freedom in Iowa: The Role of the Iowa Civil Liberties Union* (Ames: Iowa State University Press, 1977), 103.

31. Bergmann, *Negro in Iowa,* 91, 92.

32. Certainly Hughes had a stronger record as a progressive, but "moderate progressive" was a term frequently used to describe Ray.

33. Quoted in Larew, *Party Reborn,* 124. Ray suffered a broken leg in the crash.

34. Jon Bowermaster, *Governor: An Oral Biography of Robert D. Ray* (Ames: Iowa State University Press, 1987), 232.

35. Fite, *American Farmers,* 202.

36. Except for the secretary of agriculture, because that office was established by statute rather than by the state constitution.

37. Bowermaster, *Governor,* 253–54.

38. Frank T. Nye, "The 63rd General Assembly of Iowa (Second Session)," *The Palimpsest* 51 (1970): 291, 300; "The 64th General Assembly of Iowa," *The Palimpsest* 52 (1971): 477–78. In Ray's first term, "education at all levels" was 54 percent of the total budget. See Nye, "The 63rd General Assembly of Iowa," *The Palimpsest* 50 (1969): 588.

39. "School Finances—Iowa's a Leader," *Des Moines Register,* 18 March 1994, 14A. Prop-

erty tax is still an issue that will not go away. In March 1994 Democratic candidate for governor Bill Reichardt advocated cutting Iowa's property-tax bills in half by "eliminating the use of the property tax to finance public schools." See *Des Moines Register,* 22 March 1994, Ml.

40. Bowermaster, *Governor,* 85. Another highly emotional issue in Ray's early years as governor (1969, 1970) was that of liberalizing Iowa's abortion laws. Ray proposed this in both 1969 and 1970, but the legislature did not pass such legislation. See Nye, "63rd General Assembly" (1969), 594; in 1969 Frank T. Nye wrote that "In the most dramatic and emotional debate of the 1969 session the Senate defeated a bill liberalizing the abortion law." Ray requested a liberalized abortion law again in 1970. See Nye, "63rd General Assembly (Second Session), 310. By 1973, with *Roe v. Wade,* which declared abortions legal, state action seemed to be unnecessary. For an excellent overview of Iowa's abortion laws and attitudes toward abortion, see James C. Mohr, "Iowa's Abortion Battles of the Late 1960s and Early 1970s: Long-term Perspectives and Short-term Analyses," *The Annals of Iowa* 50 (1989).

41. Mary Hutchison Tone, "On the Road to Ioway," *The Iowan* 29 (1980): 37–43.

42. Ibid., 41.

43. Ibid., 42.

44. "Refugees Seizing Iowa Opportunity," *Des Moines Register,* 9 October 1988, 1A; "One of Iowa's Finest Hours," *Des Moines Register,* 9 January 1994, B1.

45. See Bowermaster, *Governor*, who devotes a chapter to "The Bottle Bill." Ray has stated that of all legislation passed during his years as governor, he was most proud of the bottle-bill legislation. Also during Ray's tenure, the voting age was reduced to eighteen. For a full discussion of Ray's years from 1968 to 1974, see yearly reviews of the legislature in *The Palimpsest,* vols. 50–55.

46. Quoted in Bowermaster, *Governor*, 233, 236.

47. Ibid., 256; Frank T. Nye, "The Sixty-Fifth General Assembly of Iowa (First Session)," *The Palimpsest* 54 (1973): 10.

CHAPTER 17

1. Mark Friedberger, *Farm Families and Change* (Lexington: University Press of Kentucky, 1988), 7; and Fite, *American Farmers,* 208.

2. *Des Moines Sunday Register,* 16 June 1985, 1A.

3. "Harl: Farm Debt Concentrated in Younger Hands," *Des Moines Sunday Register,* 21 December 1984, 4B.

4. Friedberger, *Farm Families,* 196.

5. Schwieder, *Seventy-five Years,* 202–4.

6. Ibid., 206.

7. Quoted in Steffen W. Schmidt, "Challenges for the Future," in *Issues in Iowa Politics* (Ames: Iowa State University Press, 1990), 232–33.

8. *Des Moines Register,* 19 February 1988, 12A. Quoted in Schmidt, "Challenges."

9. Lee Ann Osbun, "Of Chance and Finance: Passage and Performance of the Iowa Lottery," *Issues in Iowa Politics* (Ames: Iowa State University Press, 1990), 214–15.

10. Ibid., 215–16. Three years later New Jersey created a highly successful state lottery, and by 1975 ten more states had followed suit. By 1985 eight more states (including Iowa) and the District of Columbia had been authorized to initiate lotteries.

11. Ibid., 217–18; Nye, "63rd General Assembly (Second Session)," 306.

12. Osbun, "Of Chance and Finance," 218, 219, 221. The approval rate would increase to 62 percent in 1984. Part of the problem lay in the fact that legislators had tied together the issue of the World Trade Center and the lottery. See Osbun, "Of Chance and Finance," 220–21 and

James Strohman, "The Iowa World Trade Center," in *Issues in Iowa Politics* (Ames: Iowa State University Press, 1990).

13. Osbun, "Of Chance and Finance," 223–24.

14. *Des Moines Register,* 1 September 1994, 4. As of November 1994, five more Iowa cities have proposed floating casinos. See *Des Moines Register,* 19 November 1994, 11.

15. In 1991 Prairie Meadows filed for bankruptcy protection. See *Des Moines Sunday Register,* 14 November 1993, 2A, for a listing of gambling facilities in Iowa and in the Midwest.

16. *Vote No on ERA* (West Des Moines: Iowa Committee to Stop ERA, n. d.). Pamphlet distributed door to door shortly before the election in November 1992.

17. As of yet, no comprehensive assessment has been made of the 1992 ERA campaign in Iowa. Typically, an amendment to the U.S. Constitution has seven years to be approved. With the ERA, Congress extended the deadline until 1982, a move that might have been declared unconstitutional if the amendment had been approved.

18. By comparison, in 1950 Iowa's farms totaled just over 203,000 and the average farm size was 169 acres; by 1970 there were 135,000 farms and the average farm size was 249 acres. See Sage, *History of Iowa,* 315.

19. In 1994, the average size of an Iowa farm was 325 acres, the average farmer was fifty years old, and the number of farms in the state was 96,543. Individual- or family-proprietorship farms still accounted for 84 percent of the farms in Iowa. See "Number of Young Farmers Shrinking," *Des Moines Register,* 3 March 1994, 1A.

20. "Bleak Outlook for Small Towns." *Des Moines Register,* 24 March 1994, 10S; and *Ames Tribune,* 19 March 1994, A5.

21. "Supply a Factor in IBP Closing?" *Des Moines Register,* 1 February 1994, 1A.

A Note on Sources

IN THE 150 YEARS since statehood, a variety of studies have been published on Iowa history. In the nineteenth century, county histories predominated; in the first half of the current century, multivolume histories appeared; and during the post–World War II era, Iowa historians began to publish an increasing number of monographs covering many topics. Fortunately for interested lay persons and for professional historians, each year the number of publications on state history increases.

The four multivolume histories of Iowa are: Benjamin F. Gue, *History of Iowa*, 4 vols., 1903; Johnson Brigham, *Iowa—Its History and Its Foremost Citizens*, 3 vols., 1915; Edgar R. Harlan, *A Narrative History of the People of Iowa*, 5 vols., 1931; and William J. Petersen, *The Story of Iowa*, 4 vols., 1952. All four series emphasized political history and nineteenth-century events. Petersen's volumes provide the most information on nonpolitical topics such as business and industry, religion, and education.

Several single-volume state histories have also been published. A handful published before 1950, included Cyrenus Cole, *A History of the People in Iowa*, 1921. The two major works in this category are Leland Sage, *A History of Iowa*, 1974, and Joseph F. Wall, *Iowa: A History*, 1978. Sage's work concentrates primarily on political history with good coverage of the first half of the twentieth century, while Wall's book—published as one volume in the 1976 national bicentennial series—is primarily an interpretive essay.

In the past forty-some years, a myriad of monographs on various aspects of Iowa history provide excellent secondary material for anyone interested in the history of the state. While earlier works emphasized political events and personalities, after 1950 studies increasingly dealt with social, cultural, or economic topics. The following discussion of monographs provides only a partial listing of published titles according to topics, and includes some studies dealing primarily although not exclusively with Iowa history.

Important economic studies include Earle D. Ross, *Iowa Agriculture: An Historical Survey*, 1951; Allan G. Bogue, *From Prairie to Cornbelt: Farming on the Illinois and Iowa Prairies in the Nineteenth Century*, 1963; and H. Roger Grant and L. Edward Purcell, eds., *Years of Struggle: The Farm Diary of Elmer G. Powers, 1931–1936*, 1976. Two recent economic studies are Timothy T. Mahoney, *River Towns in the Great West: Structure of Provincial Urbanization in the American Midwest, 1820–1870*,

1990*; and Shelton Stromquist, *Solidarity and Survival: An Oral History of Iowa Labor in the Twentieth Century,* 1993.

Books dealing with social and cultural topics that should be consulted include Lewis Atherton, *Main Street on the Middle Border,* 1954; Carl Hamilton, *In No Time at All,* 1974; Elmer and Dorothy Schwieder, *A Peculiar People: Iowa's Old Order Amish,* 1975; Diane L. Barthel, *Amana: From Pietist Sect to American Community,* 1984; Dorothy Schwieder, Joseph Hraba, and Elmer Schwieder, *Buxton: Work and Racial Equality in a Coal Mining Community,* 1987*; Thomas J. Morain, *Prairie Grass Roots: An Iowa Small Town in the Early Twentieth Century,* 1988*; and Hamilton Cravens, *Before Headstart: The Iowa Station and America's Children,* 1993.

Women's history has received considerable attention in recent decades. Important Iowa titles include Louise R. Noun, *Strong-Minded Women: The Emergence of the Woman-Suffrage Movement in Iowa,* 1969; Glenda Riley, *Frontierswomen: The Iowa Experience,* 1980; Deborah Fink, *Open Country, Iowa: Rural Women, Tradition and Change,* 1986; Katherine Jellison, *Entitled to Power: Farm Women and Technology, 1913 1963,* 1993; and Suzanne O'Dea Schenken, *Iowa's Women Lawmakers,* 1995.

While studies on political history have declined in number, the topic remains popular. Several works in this category appeared in the 1980s and 1990s, including James C. Larew, *A Party Reborn: The Democrats of Iowa, 1950–1974,* 1980; Robert Cook, *Baptism of Fire: The Republican Party in Iowa, 1838–1878,* 1994*; Jeffrey Ostler, *Prairie Populism: The Fate of Agrarian Radicalism in Kansas, Nebraska, and Iowa, 1880–1892,* 1993; and George William McDaniel, *Smith Wildman Brookhart: Iowa's Renegade Republican,* 1995.

Richard, Lord Acton and Patricia Nassif Acton look at the state's legal history in *To Go Free: A Treasury of Iowa's Legal Heritage,* 1995.

Other significant works include those on the Civil War era, particularly Hubert H. Wubben, *Civil War Iowa and the Copperhead Movement,* 1980; and Robert R. Dykstra, *Bright Radical Star: Black Freedom and White Supremacy on the Hawkeye Frontier,* 1993*.

Iowa's three major history journals should be consulted on any topic. *The Iowa Journal of History* ceased publication in 1961 but remains an extremely valuable source on state history, particularly political and economic topics. *The Annals of Iowa* presents scholarly research and book reviews and *The Palimpsest* is devoted to popular history. An additional state publication, *The Goldfinch,* is published for youthful readers.

Two bibliographies that should greatly aid any researcher are William J. Petersen, ed., *Iowa History Reference Guide,* 1952; and the far more comprehensive *Iowa History and Culture: A Bibliography of Materials Published Between 1952 and 1986,* compiled by Patricia Dawson and David Hudson, 1989. *The Annals of Iowa* has published a supplemental bibliography of Iowa topics from 1987 to 1993 in three issues: Vol. 52, Spring, Summer, and Fall.

While the number of publications in Iowa history has expanded in the past two decades, there are still neglected areas. There is presently no comprehensive study of

---

*Winners of the Benjamin Shambaugh Award for the best book on Iowa history.

Iowa manufacturing and industry nor is there any history of urban development. No studies have been done that focus on important events such as the Depression of the 1930s, World War I, or World War II. Nor is there any monographic treatment of Prohibition—an extremely important issue throughout most of the state's history. Also awaiting researchers is a general study of immigration to Iowa—both in the nineteenth and twentieth centuries—and an in-depth study of African Americans.

INDEX

Bock, Art, 262
Boeck, George, 60
Bogue, Allan, 39, 45
Bohemian immigrants, 91, 105-106
Bohemian Savings and Loan Association,
    106
Boies, Horace, 72, 216, 218
Bolshevik Revolution, 164
Booge, James E., 234
Boone County
    African Americans in, 90
    railroads in, 63
    Swedish coal miners in, 98, 188
Bosch, John, 260
Bowermaster, Jon, 309
Boyd, Jane, 181-182
Bradley, Judge, 263, 264
Branstad, Terry, 319, 320
Briar Cliff College, 126
Briggs, Ansel, 34
British. *See also* English Americans;
    Irish Americans; Scottish Ameri-
    cans; Welsh Americans
    Chief Black Hawk and, 14
    in French and Indian War, 23
Broadlawns Hospital, 177
Brown, Joe S. and Sue M., 200, 201
Brown, John, 71
Brown, Marjorie, 194, 268
Buchanan, James, 72
Buchanan County, 208, 302-303
Bucknell, 195
Buena Vista College, 126
Buena Vista County, 149
Burlington
    African Americans in, 90
    city life in, 172, 173, 174
    Congregationalist Church in, 115
    early settlement of, 57
    German immigrants in, 93, 94
    Great Depression in, 267
    Hawk-Eye newspaper of, 79
    immigrants in, 55, 93, 94
    plank roads in, 59-60
    railroads in, 59-60, 61, 64
    steamboats and, 64
    as territorial capital, 29
    WWII in, 281, 283

Burlington Northern Railroad, 44, 58, 61,
    62, 98
Butterworth, Alexander, 69
Buxton
    African Americans in, 194-195
    Buxton Iowa Club in, 203
    coal mining in, 240-241
    Swedish Americans in, 188

Camp Dodge, 177, 200
Camp Franklin, 72
Canal transportation, 60
Cantwell, Henry, 264
Carpenter, Cyrus, 76
Carroll County, 96
Cartwright, John, 73, 75
Carver, George Washington, 126
Carver, Roy, 281
Cascade, 116
Cass County, 98, 101, 317
Cassel, Peter, 42, 97
Catfish Creek, 23-24
Catholic Church. *See* Roman Catholic
    Church
Catt, Carrie Chapman, 226, 227, 228
Cedar County
    farm protests in, 259
    Quakers in, 116
    rural teachers in, 124
    tuberculin testing program in, 258
Cedar Falls
    first woman voter in, 228
    Iowa State Normal School in, 120
    Iowa State Teachers College in, 128,
        130-131
    WWII training centers in, 279-280
Cedar Rapids
    African Americans in, 195, 268
    city life in, 171, 173, 175, 178,
        181-183
    Coe College at, 126
    community centers in, 181-182
    Czech immigrants in, 105-106
    Czech and Slovak National Museum
        and Library in, 203
    Danish immigrants in, 101
    employment discrimination in, 308

Sinclair Company, 232-233
Siouan Indian language family, 5
Sioux City
    African Americans in, 84, 89-90, 195,
        197-198, 267
    Briar Cliff College in, 126
    city life in, 172, 175, 178
    communist agitators in, 261-262
    community centers in, 181
    community college in, 307
    corn production in, 135
    crime in, 183
    farm strike and, 260-261
    Jewish organizations in, 118
    Ku Klux Klan in, 198
    meatpacking industry in, 146, 175,
        189, 197-198, 234, 244, 248, 267,
        289
    Morningside College in, 126
    Prohibition and, 213-214
    railroads at, 62
    Roman Catholic Diocese of, 112
    settlement houses in, 179
    South Bottoms area of, 182
    Southeast Asian refugees in, 311
    unions in, 246, 248
    women's suffrage in, 227
    WWII training centers in, 279
Sioux Indians, 15, 17
Sipma, Sjoerd, 41-42, 54
Sisters of Mercy, 177
Sisters of the Holy Humility of Mary,
    112-113
Skunk River, 97
Skunk River War, 78
Slavery, slaves
    Fugitive Slave Act and, 69
    "In the matter of Ralph on Habeas
        Corpus" opinion and, 68-69, 85
    Kansas-Nebraska Act and, 70-71
    popular sovereignty and, 71
    pre-Civil War status, 68-73
    Underground Railroad activity, 69-70
Sloan, Ted, 307
Smith-Hughes Act, 306
Smith-Lever Act, 148
Social development. *See* Progressive Era;

Prohibition; Women's suffrage
Society Scandia, 99
Sokol (gymnastics organization), 106
Soldiers' Relief Society, 51
*Solidarity and Survival: An Oral History
    of Iowa Labor in the Twentieth Cen-
    tury* (Stromquist), 245
South English, 78
Spain, 22, 23, 24-25
Spedding, Frank, 285
Spillville, 105
Spirit Lake, 7
Spring Grove, 73, 142
Springarn, Joe E., 199
Springdale, 69, 78, 116
Springville, 116
Stanton, 98
Stanton, Elizabeth Cady, 222
State Agricultural Society, 134
Statehood process
    boundary issue and, 33
    under Chambers, John, 31
    under Clarke, James, 34
    under Lucas, Robert, 31
    Northwest Ordinance and, 28-29
    ratification of, 34
State Railroad Commission, 219-220
Steamboats, steamships
    agricultural products and, 54, 55, 65
    cabin passage on, 56
    deck passage on, 55-56
    fur products and, 54-55
    immigrant passengers on, 55-56, 93
    lead mining products and, 55
    steamboatmen and, 56-57
Stemma D'Italia, 192
Still College of Osteopathy, 177
Stone, Benjamin, 307
Storm Lake, 62, 126
Story County
    1990s economic development in, 322
    Great Depression in, 256-257
    Iowa State Agricultural College and
        Model Farm in, 129-130
    Norwegian immigrants in, 99
Strang, Orpah and Ryal, 38
Streetcars, 176